Planning, Scheduling, Monitoring and Control

Planning, Scheduling, Monitoring and Control

The Practical Project Management of Time, Cost and Risk

Association for Project Management

Association for Project Management
Ibis House, Regent Park
Summerleys Road, Princes Risborough
Buckinghamshire
HP27 9LE

© Association for Project Management 2015

All rights reserved. No part of this publication may be reproduced, stored in a retrieval system, or transmitted, in any form or by any means, without the express permission in writing of the Association for Project Management. Within the UK exceptions are allowed in respect of any fair dealing for the purposes of research or private study, or criticism or review, as permitted under the Copyright, Designs and Patents Act, 1988, or in the case of reprographic reproduction in accordance with the terms of the licences issued by the Copyright Licensing Agency. Enquiries concerning reproduction outside these terms and in other countries should be sent to the Rights Department, Association for Project Management at the address above.

British Library Cataloguing in Publication Data is available.
Paperback ISBN: 978-1-903494-44-8
eISBN: 978-1-903494-48-6

Illustrations by Gary Holmes
Cover design by Fountainhead Creative Consultants
Typeset by RefineCatch Limited, Bungay, Suffolk
in 11/14pt Foundry Sans

Contents

List of figures and tables	xviii
Foreword	xxiv
Preface	xxvi
Acknowledgements	xxviii
Peer review	xxx
Purpose	xxxi
The PSMC process map	xxxii

1 Overview — 1
   1.1 Part One: Definition — 1
   1.2 Part Two: Planning — 2
   1.3 Part Three: Scheduling — 3
   1.4 Part Four: Monitoring and control — 4
   1.5 Part Five: Record keeping and learning — 6
   1.6 A note on the Contents, Index and Glossary — 7
   1.7 Management issues — 7
      1.7.1 Behaviour and resources — 7
      1.7.2 Processes and tools (scheduling software) — 8
      1.7.3 Common sense — 8

Part One: Definition — 9

2 Business case — 11
   2.1 Definition of the business case — 11
   2.2 Purpose of a business case — 11
   2.3 Contents of the business case — 12
      2.3.1 Structure of the business case — 12
      2.3.2 Planning information — 15
      2.3.3 Funding requirements — 16
      2.3.4 Resource requirements — 16
   2.4 Acceptance criteria in the business case — 16
   2.5 Benefits realisation in the business case — 17
   2.6 Procurement strategy — 17
   2.7 Project review and assurance process of the business case — 19

Contents

3 Scope management — 21
- 3.1 Definition of scope management — 21
- 3.2 Purpose of scope management — 21
- 3.3 The scope management process — 22
    - 3.3.1 Defining the scope — 22
    - 3.3.2 Describing the scope — 22

4 Requirements management — 25
- 4.1 Definition of requirements management — 25
- 4.2 Purpose of requirements management — 25
- 4.3 Process of defining requirements — 25
    - 4.3.1 Requirement description — 26
    - 4.3.2 Factors to consider when defining requirements — 26
    - 4.3.3 Inputs into requirements management — 27
- 4.4 The requirements management process — 27
    - 4.4.1 Capture and define requirements from all stakeholders — 27
    - 4.4.2 Link requirements to the product breakdown structures and work breakdown structures where appropriate — 27
    - 4.4.3 Decompose requirements — 28
- 4.5 Works information (WI) — 29
- 4.6 Statement of work (SOW) — 30

5 Stakeholder management — 31
- 5.1 Definition of stakeholder management — 31
- 5.2 Purpose of stakeholder management — 31
- 5.3 Managing stakeholders through the project — 31

6 Project familiarisation — 33

Part Two: Planning — 35

7 Introduction to planning — 37
- 7.1 Definition of planning — 37
    - 7.1.1 Definition of the planning role — 37
- 7.2 Purpose of planning — 38
    - 7.2.1 Benefits of planning — 39
    - 7.2.2 Success in planning — 40
- 7.3 The difference between planning and scheduling — 41

7.4		Principal scheduling components	42
	7.4.1	Process step schedules	42
	7.4.2	Time-based schedules	42
	7.4.3	Schedule narrative	43
7.5		Approaches to planning	43
	7.5.1	Top-down planning	43
	7.5.2	Bottom-up planning	44
	7.5.3	Agile planning in the software industry	47
7.6		Planning strategies	49
7.7		Allowing for risk	51

8 Breakdown structures — 53

8.1		Definition of breakdown structures	53
8.2		Purpose of breakdown structures	53
8.3		Creating breakdown structures	53
	8.3.1	Level 1	53
	8.3.2	Level 2	53
	8.3.3	Level 3 and beyond	55
8.4		Product breakdown structure (PBS)	57
	8.4.1	What is a 'product' in planning terms?	57
	8.4.2	Definition of a PBS	57
	8.4.3	Purpose of a PBS	57
	8.4.4	Constructing a PBS	57
8.5		Work breakdown structure (WBS)	59
	8.5.1	Definition of a WBS	59
	8.5.2	Purpose of a WBS	59
	8.5.3	Constructing a WBS	60
	8.5.4	Principles of designing a WBS	60
	8.5.5	WBS dictionaries	61
8.6		Organisational breakdown structure (OBS)	64
	8.6.1	Definition of an OBS	64
	8.6.2	Purpose of an OBS	64
	8.6.3	Constructing an OBS	65
8.7		Responsibility assignment matrix (RAM)	65
	8.7.1	Definition of a RAM	65
	8.7.2	Purpose of a RAM	65
	8.7.3	Constructing a RAM	66
	8.7.4	The step-by-step approach to constructing a RAM	67

Contents

8.8	RACI matrix	68
	8.8.1 Definition of a RACI matrix	68
	8.8.2 Purpose of a RACI matrix	68
	8.8.3 Constructing a RACI matrix	68
8.9	Cost breakdown structure (CBS)	69
	8.9.1 Definition of a CBS	69
	8.9.2 Purpose of a CBS	69
8.10	Resources breakdown structure (RBS)	70
	8.10.1 Definition of a RBS	70
	8.10.2 Purpose of a RBS	71

9 Dependency management   73
9.1	Definition of dependency management	73
9.2	Purpose of dependency management	73
9.3	Interface scope	74
9.4	Schedule impact	74

10 Health, safety and environmental   75
10.1	HSE issues at strategic level (planning)	75
10.2	HSE issues at tactical level (scheduling and method statements)	76

11 Cost estimating   77
11.1	Definition of cost estimating	77
11.2	Purpose of a cost estimate	77
11.3	Cost estimating and the project life cycle	77
11.4	Estimate types	78
	11.4.1 Scope development estimates	78
	11.4.2 Other types of estimate	79
11.5	Contents of an estimate	80
11.6	Estimating methodologies	80
	11.6.1 Approximate estimating methods	80
	11.6.2 Definitive estimating methods	82

12 Budgeting   83
12.1	Definition of budgeting	83
12.2	Purpose of budgeting	83
12.3	Funding and budgets	83
12.4	Producing a cost budget	84
	12.4.1 Cost breakdown structure	84
	12.4.2 Cash-flow statements	84
12.5	Budget transfers	87

Contents

Part Three: Scheduling — 89

13 Introduction to scheduling — 91
- 13.1 Definition of scheduling — 91
- 13.2 Purpose of scheduling — 91
- 13.3 The scheduling process — 92
  - 13.3.1 Steps in establishing the schedule — 92
  - 13.3.2 Once the schedule is created — 93
- 13.4 Schedule structure — 94
  - 13.4.1 Schedule density — 94
  - 13.4.2 Detail density: considerations — 98
  - 13.4.3 Network templates (fragnets) — 99

14 Types of schedule — 101
- 14.1 Schedule types: time-based — 101
  - 14.1.1 Development or strategic schedule — 101
  - 14.1.2 Tender schedule (or 'bid schedule') — 102
  - 14.1.3 Contract schedule — 102
  - 14.1.4 Baseline schedule — 103
  - 14.1.5 Summary schedule — 103
  - 14.1.6 Working schedule or 'forecast schedule' — 103
  - 14.1.7 Target schedule — 104
  - 14.1.8 Short- and medium-term schedules — 104
  - 14.1.9 As-built schedule — 105
  - 14.1.10 Post-build schedule — 106
  - 14.1.11 'What ifs' (scenario planning) — 107
- 14.2 Schedule types: tracker schedules — 107
  - 14.2.1 Procurement schedules — 107
  - 14.2.2 Design deliverables tracker — 109
  - 14.2.3 Other tracker schedules — 109

15 Schedule design — 113
- 15.1 Definition of schedule design — 113
- 15.2 Purpose of schedule design — 113
- 15.3 Elements of schedule design — 113
  - 15.3.1 Activity identity numbers (IDs) — 113
  - 15.3.2 Activity descriptions — 114
  - 15.3.3 Different activity types — 115
  - 15.3.4 Activity steps — 116
  - 15.3.5 Time units — 118

Contents

15.3.6	Calendars	118
15.3.7	Project, activity and resource coding	120

16 Building the schedule   **121**

16.1 Creating a critical path network   121
     16.1.1 Definition of critical path method   121
     16.1.2 Purpose of critical path network   121
     16.1.3 Methods of constructing a critical path   122
     16.1.4 Inputs into a critical path analysis   123
     16.1.5 Introduction to creating a network analysis   124
     16.1.6 Step 1: Create a logical network   125
     16.1.7 Step 2: Forward pass   125
     16.1.8 Step 3: Backward pass   126
     16.1.9 Step 4: Calculation of total float   127
     16.1.10 Step 5: Identification of critical path   128
     16.1.11 Training in network analysis: a note   130
     16.1.12 Float   130
     16.1.13 Types of logic linking   132
     16.1.14 Lags and leads   135
     16.1.15 Use of constraints   136
     16.1.16 Types of constraints   138
     16.1.17 Displaying networks on bar charts   147

16.2 Estimation of durations   147
     16.2.1 Three-point estimates   148
     16.2.2 PERT (programme evaluation review technique)   148
     16.2.3 Comparative   149
     16.2.4 Benchmarked data   149
     16.2.5 Resource-dependent   150
     16.2.6 Expert opinion   150
     16.2.7 Personal experience   150
     16.2.8 Social media   151

16.3 Resourcing the schedule   151
     16.3.1 Definition of resources   152
     16.3.2 Purpose of resourcing the schedule   152
     16.3.3 Process of resourcing the schedule   153
     16.3.4 Resource smoothing   154

16.4 Horizontal and vertical integration of schedules   156
     16.4.1 Horizontal integration   156
     16.4.2 Vertical integration   157

16.5	Scheduling interfaces and dependencies		157
	16.5.1	Identification	157
	16.5.2	Coding	158
	16.5.3	Integration and impact analysis	159
	16.5.4	Impact resolution	163
16.6	Time contingencies		164
	16.6.1	Definition of buffers	164
	16.6.2	Use of buffers	164

17 Communicating the schedule — 167

17.1	Bar charts		167
	17.1.1	Presentation considerations	167
	17.1.2	An alternative to bar chart reporting	170
17.2	Line of balance		172
	17.2.1	Creating a line of balance chart	172
	17.2.2	Advantages of line of balance	173
	17.2.3	Limitations of line of balance	174
17.3	Time chainage		174
	17.3.1	Definition of time chainage charts	174
	17.3.2	Explanation of the time chainage technique	175
	17.3.3	Advantages of time chainage	177
	17.3.4	Limitations of time chainage	177
17.4	Schedule narrative		177
	17.4.1	Scope	179
	17.4.2	Health, safety and environmental considerations	179
	17.4.3	Risks, opportunities and contingencies	179
	17.4.4	Breakdown structures	179
	17.4.5	Project phasing	179
	17.4.6	Stakeholders	179
	17.4.7	Resources	179
	17.4.8	Critical path(s)	180
	17.4.9	Assumptions	180
	17.4.10	Calendars	180
	17.4.11	Activity codes	180
	17.4.12	Details of any possessions, shut-downs or other special working conditions	181
	17.4.13	Consents required	181
	17.4.14	Permits and licences	181

Contents

18 Schedule review — 183
- 18.1 Definition of schedule review — 183
- 18.2 Purpose of schedule review — 183
- 18.3 Checking the schedule — 183
  - 18.3.1 Understanding the project schedule — 184
  - 18.3.2 Components of the schedule display — 184
  - 18.3.3 Critical matters not included in the display — 187
- 18.4 Planning checks — 188
  - 18.4.1 Administration — 188
  - 18.4.2 Management issues — 188
  - 18.4.3 Contract requirements — 188
  - 18.4.4 Scope — 189
  - 18.4.5 Associated documents — 189
  - 18.4.6 Planning issues — 189
  - 18.4.7 Progress update — 190
  - 18.4.8 Communication of the schedule — 190
- 18.5 Scheduling checks — 190
  - 18.5.1 Activity checks — 191
  - 18.5.2 Logic checks — 193
  - 18.5.3 Float and critical path checks — 196
  - 18.5.4 Resources checks — 198
  - 18.5.5 Review of schedule risk — 198

19 BIM (Building information modelling) — 199
- 19.1 Definition of BIM — 199
- 19.2 Purpose of BIM — 200
- 19.3 BIM technology — 201
- 19.4 The BIM culture — 201

20 Agile — 203
- 20.1 Definition of agile — 203
- 20.2 Purpose of agile — 203
- 20.3 Methods — 204
  - 20.3.1 Advantages — 205
  - 20.3.2 Limitations — 206

Part Four: Monitoring and control — 207

21 Baseline — 209
- 21.1 Definition of the project baseline — 209

21.2	Purpose of a project baseline	211
21.3	Principles of project baselining	211
21.4	When to set the baseline	212
21.5	Establishing the baseline schedule	212
21.6	Definition and purpose of baseline maintenance	213
	21.6.1 Definition of baseline maintenance	213
	21.6.2 Purpose of baseline maintenance	213
	21.6.3 Baseline maintenance as a result of schedule changes	213
	21.6.4 Illustration of the principle of baseline maintenance	214
21.7	Re-baselining: re-planning	216
	21.7.1 When to consider re-planning	217
21.8	Re-baselining: re-programming	218
	21.8.1 When to consider re-programming	218
21.9	Notes and rules for schedule maintenance, re-planning and re-baselining	220
21.10	The link between change management and the project baseline	220

22 Performance reporting — 221

22.1	Definition of performance reporting	221
22.2	Purpose of performance reporting	222
22.3	Evaluating and recording progress	223
	22.3.1 Progress assessment	223
	22.3.2 What needs to be recorded in the schedule?	223
	22.3.3 What else needs to be recorded in a report?	224
	22.3.4 How often is progress recorded?	224
22.4	Variance analysis methods of progress monitoring	224
	22.4.1 Drop line method	224
	22.4.2 Activity weeks method	226
	22.4.3 Milestone monitoring	228
	22.4.4 Progress on a line of balance chart	229
	22.4.5 Cash-flow monitoring	230
	22.4.6 Resource monitoring	230
	22.4.7 Cost value analysis	231
	22.4.8 Quantity tracking	231
22.5	Performance analysis methods of progress monitoring	234
	22.5.1 Network analysis and measurement of float usage	234
	22.5.2 Earned value analysis	235

Contents

23 Cost control — 251
    23.1 Definition of cost control — 251
    23.2 Purpose of cost control — 251
    23.3 The cost control process — 252
        23.3.1 Performance measurement baseline (PMB) — 252
        23.3.2 The link between cost control and change control — 252
        23.3.3 Performance measurement — 253
    23.4 Learning lessons from cost control — 253

24 Short-term planning — 255
    24.1 Definition of short-term planning — 255
    24.2 Purpose of short-term planning — 255
    24.3 The short-term planning process — 255
        24.3.1 Make ready needs — 257
        24.3.2 Coordination meeting — 257
        24.3.3 Performance reporting — 257

25 Change management — 259
    25.1 Definition of change management — 259
    25.2 Purpose of change management — 259
    25.3 Principles of change management — 260
    25.4 Change control — 260
        25.4.1 Why change control is needed — 260
        25.4.2 Change control considerations — 261
    25.5 Project-level change: process overview — 261
    25.6 Raising a change request — 263
        25.6.1 Drafting a change request — 263
    25.7 The change log — 263
    25.8 Initial evaluation of the change request — 264
    25.9 Estimating impact of change — 264
    25.10 Detailed evaluation of change request — 264
        25.10.1 Rejected request — 265
        25.10.2 Deferred request — 265
    25.11 Approved request — 266
        25.11.1 Change orders — 266
        25.11.2 Scope transfers — 267
        25.11.3 Schedule revisions — 267
        25.11.4 Corporate governance — 267
    25.12 Implementing the change — 267
        25.12.1 Adjusting schedule in line with change — 268

  25.13 Communicating the change 269
  25.14 Monthly change reporting requirements 269
     25.14.1 Managing the schedule change process 271

26 Risk management 273
  26.1 Definition of risk management 273
  26.2 Purpose of risk management 273
  26.3 Risk management plan 274
  26.4 The risk management process 274
    26.4.1 Planning 274
    26.4.2 Risk identification 276
    26.4.3 Risk assessment 277
    26.4.4 Risk response 280
    26.4.5 Risk review 280
    26.4.6 Risk reporting 281
  26.5 Risk draw down 281
    26.5.1 When risks are mitigated 283
    26.5.2 When risks are realised 283
    26.5.3 When risks are closed 283
    26.5.4 When opportunities are realised 283
    26.5.5 Documenting changes in the risk budget 284
  26.6 Quantitative schedule risk analysis (QSRA) 284
    26.6.1 Definition of QSRA 284
    26.6.2 Purpose of QSRA 285
    26.6.3 Key requirements for a QSRA 286
    26.6.4 The stages of schedule risk analysis 286
    26.6.5 Distribution types 288
    26.6.6 Application of risks to schedule activities 291
    26.6.7 QSRA output 292
    26.6.8 Reporting 294
  26.7 Quantitative cost risk analysis (QCRA) 296
    26.7.1 Definition of QCRA 296
    26.7.2 Purpose of QCRA 296
    26.7.3 The QCRA process 297

27 Forensic analysis 303
  27.1 Definition of forensic analysis 303
  27.2 Purpose of forensic analysis 303
  27.3 Methods of forensic analysis 303
    27.3.1 As-planned versus as-built method (AP v AB) 304

Contents

27.3.2	Impacted as-planned method (IAP)	305
27.3.3	Collapsed as-built method or as-built but for (CAB)	306
27.3.4	Time impact analysis method (TIA)	307
27.3.5	Windows analysis	309
27.3.6	Other considerations	309

Part Five: Record keeping and learning — 311

28 Record keeping — 313
- 28.1 Definition of record keeping — 313
- 28.2 Purpose of record keeping — 313
- 28.3 How to record — 313
- 28.4 What to record — 314
- 28.5 Methods of keeping records — 315

29 Document management — 317
- 29.1 Definition of document management — 317
- 29.2 Purpose of document management — 317
- 29.3 Document control systems — 318
- 29.4 Version control — 318
- 29.5 Handover of documentation — 318

30 Handover and closeout — 319
- 30.1 Handover — 319
  - 30.1.1 Definition of handover — 319
  - 30.1.2 Purpose of the handover process — 319
  - 30.1.3 Planning handover — 320
  - 30.1.4 Issues in the management of handover — 321
- 30.2 Project closeout — 322
  - 30.2.1 Definition of project closeout — 322
  - 30.2.2 Purpose of project closeout — 322
  - 30.2.3 The project closeout process — 322

31 Lessons learned — 325
- 31.1 Definition of lessons learned — 325
- 31.2 Purpose of lessons learned — 325
- 31.3 Productivity data — 325
- 31.4 Qualitative lessons learned — 326
  - 31.4.1 Stakeholders involved in a lessons learned review — 326
  - 31.4.2 Considerations — 327

The final word	**329**
Glossary	**331**
Acronyms	**343**
Index	**345**

Figures and tables

Figures

1.1	The importance of planning and control in project management	2
3.1	Types and relationships of breakdown structures	23
4.1	Design and development V model	28
7.1	Top-down vs. bottom-up planning	44
7.2	Rolling wave planning	46
7.3	Agile planning	47
7.4	Setting early and late curves	50
7.5	Interpreting 'S' curves	51
8.1	Creating a breakdown structure level 1	54
8.2	Creating a breakdown structure level 2	54
8.3	Creating a breakdown structure level 3	55
8.4	Types and relationships of breakdown structures repeated	56
8.5	Sample product breakdown structure	58
8.6	Work breakdown structure	59
8.7	Work breakdown structure dictionary (defence)	62
8.8	Work package content sheet (construction)	63
8.9	Organisation breakdown structure	64
8.10	Responsibility assignment matrix	66
8.11	Example of a RACI	69
8.12	Cost breakdown structure	70
11.1	Cost estimating process	78
12.1	Time measured in financial periods	85
12.2	Generating a cost forecast using a banana curve	86
13.1	The scheduling process in the context of planning, monitoring and control	94
13.2	Relationship of different densities in schedules	97
13.3	A hierarchy of plans and planning documents	98
14.1	Distorting the time/cost/quality triangle	105
14.2	Types of time-phased schedules and their relationship	106
14.3	A sample procurement schedule	108
14.4	Time-phased procurement schedule	110

Figures and tables

14.5	Design deliverables tracker	111
15.1	Establishing steps/objective criteria	117
15.2	Suitability for steps/objective criteria	117
16.1	Example of the precedence diagram method (PDM)	122
16.2	Example of the arrow diagram method (ADM)	123
16.3	Typical time analysis coding	124
16.4	Step 1: Create a logical network	125
16.5	Step 2: The forward pass calculation	126
16.6	Step 3: The backward pass	127
16.7	Step 4: Calculation of total float	128
16.8	Step 5: Identification of critical path	129
16.9	Longest path calculations	129
16.10	The alternative method of calculation in a network	130
16.11	Float types	131
16.12	Finish to start relationship	133
16.13	Start to start relationship	133
16.14	Finish to finish relationship	134
16.15	Start to finish relationship	135
16.16	Summary of types of logic and lags	136
16.17	'As late as possible' constraint	138
16.18	'Finish on' constraint	139
16.19	'Finish on or after' constraint	140
16.20	'Finish on or before' constraint	141
16.21	'Mandatory finish' constraint	142
16.22	'Mandatory start' constraint	143
16.23	'Start on' constraint	144
16.24	'Start on or after' constraint	145
16.25	'Start on or before' constraint	146
16.26	Bar chart display	147
16.27	Establishing the duration of a task based on resource	153
16.28	First draft resources profile	154
16.29	Resource-smoothed histogram	155
16.30	Resource-levelled chart with resource limit	156
16.31	Internal integration milestones	159
16.32	External integration milestones	160
16.33	Logic-linked dependency schedule	161
16.34	Dependency schedule driving project schedules	162
16.35	Different buffer types	165

Figures and tables

17.1	A simple bar chart	168
17.2	Strategic schedule of a major construction project at low density	169
17.3	Using milestones to give clarity to the schedule	171
17.4	Creating a line of balance chart	172
17.5	Optimising work flow in line of balance	173
17.6	Basic elements of a time chainage chart	174
17.7	Time chainage task 1	175
17.8	Time chainage tasks 2 and 3	176
17.9	Time chainage task 4	176
17.10	Time chainage sequencing	177
17.11	Example of a time chainage diagram for a new railway	178
18.1	Components of a schedule for review	185
18.2	Logic bottleneck	196
19.1	BIM level maturity map	200
20.1	Agile processes	204
20.2	Illustration of an agile methodology using 'scrums' and 'sprints'	205
21.1	Establishment of baseline	210
21.2	Baseline after work starts	210
21.3	Baseline maintenance step 1	214
21.4	Baseline maintenance step 2	215
21.5	Baseline maintenance step 3	216
21.6	Baseline maintenance step 4	217
22.1	Illustration of the drop line method	225
22.2	Simple 'activity weeks' monitoring chart	226
22.3	Cumulative results from the 'activity weeks' chart	227
22.4	Recording actual progress in line of balance	229
22.5	Sample cost value report	232
22.6	Quantity tracking with production curves	233
22.7	Budget allocation to the plan	237
22.8	Planned value curve	240
22.9	Earned value	241
22.10	Actual costs (ACWP) added	241
22.11	Earned value analysis: cost and schedule variance	242
22.12	Cost and schedule variance chart	243
22.13	Earned value analysis with time variance	244
22.14	Bull's eye performance chart	245
22.15	Calculating estimated time to completion	246
22.16	Illustration of various earning techniques and appropriate uses	247

Figures and tables

22.17	Advantages and disadvantages of EVTs	248
24.1	Short-term schedules in context of other plans	256
24.2	Performance analysis on short-term schedule	258
25.1	Process overview: project change control	262
25.2	Example of monthly change reporting	270
25.3	Monthly change report	270
26.1	Risk management life cycle	275
26.2	Risk identification in a typical risk log	277
26.3	Risk assessment matrix: severity ratings score	278
26.4	Opportunity assessment matrix: severity ratings score	278
26.5	Typical risk log continued, showing current impact and response planning	279
26.6	Risk response options	280
26.7	Reporting of basic risk data	281
26.8	Tracking risk performance over time	282
26.9	Normal distribution curve	288
26.10	Log normal distribution curve	289
26.11	Uniform distribution	289
26.12	Triangular distribution: possible options	290
26.13	PERT distribution	291
26.14	Duration uncertainty probability chart	293
26.15	Duration uncertainty tornado chart	294
26.16	QSRA probability distribution chart	295
26.17	Full QSRA tornado chart	296
26.18	QCRA chart	299
26.19	QCRA chart (redraw)	300
30.1	Context of handover and closeout	320
31.1	Example proforma to collect output rates	326

Tables

2.1	Examples of requirements and acceptance criteria	17
6.1	Sources of project information	33
8.1	Explanation of RACI codes	68
12.1	A simple cost budget	84
13.1	Features associated with density of schedules	95
15.1	Example of activity descriptions	114
16.1	Example of three-point estimate	148

Figures and tables

16.2	Example of PERT calculation	148
16.3	Example of comparative estimates	149
16.4	Example of benchmarked data	149
16.5	Example of resource-dependent estimate	150
16.6	Interface impact schedule	163
21.1	Baseline maintenance, re-planning, re-baselining matrix	219
22.1	Measurement of float usage	234
25.1	Example of financial authority	267
26.1	QCRA confidence levels	301
27.1	As-planned vs. as-built method	304
27.2	Impacted as-planned method	305
27.3	Collapsed as-built method or as-built but for	306
27.4	Time impact analysis method	307

Picture credits

The following illustrations have been adapted from originals published by Taylor Woodrow/Vinci Construction: Figure 8.8, Figure 13.2, Figure 13.3, Figure 14.3, Figures 17.4 to 17.10, Figures 21.1 to 21.6, Figure 22.4, Figure 22.14, Figure 24.1, Figure 26.1, Figures 26.7 to 26.8, Figure 31.1

The following illustrations have been adapted from originals published by BAE Systems: Figure 8.7, Figure 17.3

The following illustrations have been adapted from originals published by Turner & Townsend: Table 25.1, Figure 25.2, Figure 25.3

Figure 4.1 courtesy of Neil Curtis

Figure 14.4 courtesy of Balfour Beatty

Illustration on p. 329 courtesy of Simon Taylor/Paul Kidston

All other illustrations are courtesy of the APM PMC SIG

'Planning is an unnatural process; it is much more fun to do something. The nicest thing about not planning is that failure comes as a complete surprise, rather than being preceded by a period of worry and depression.'

Sir John Harvey Jones

Foreword

Planning has been part of my life for so many years now. I trained as a mechanical engineer, and the last assignment of my apprenticeship was within the construction planning department of British Steel's piping division (1974 is a long time ago now, unfortunately!). That experience captured my imagination and I decided to embark on a career as a planning engineer. My many experiences since have taught me how vitally important it is to plan how a project, programme, portfolio or business will be delivered.

Sir John Harvey Jones' quote *'The nicest thing about not planning is that failure comes as a complete surprise, rather than being preceded by a period of worry and depression'* reveals a culture still buried deep within many organisations' and individuals' approach to project or business delivery today. However, when you have been involved in the *'complete surprise'* you realise that if the team involved had opted for the *'worry and depression'* this would have prompted action and led to a more successful outcome.

Fortunately, my involvement in successfully delivered projects or programmes far outweighs my failing project experiences, and, when looking back, success usually comes down to good definition, preparation and planning from inception onwards. The Kuwait reconstruction (1991/1992) and London 2012 Olympic (2008 to 2012) programmes were two big highlights in my career, where the challenge was to achieve delivery within very clearly defined timescales under the highest possible level of public scrutiny.

For these programmes, the creation and maintenance of an integrated suite of plans/schedules allowing project/programme-level decision making to be effective was a key part of the delivery success which both commentators at the time and historians since have recorded.

Now, as a result of the considerable efforts of the APM Planning, Monitoring and Control (PMC) Specific Interest Group (SIG), organisations and programme/project teams will have a guide covering all aspects of planning, from preparing to undertake a project to executing that project, controlling its safe delivery to budget, time and quality.

Foreword

I believe that this publication has captured the best practices for planning and will become the reference document of note for organisations and their teams during future project deliveries.

David Birch
Head of capital delivery project controls – National Grid
Formerly head of programme controls – ODA delivery partner CLM
(2008–2012)

12 June 2014

Preface

Sir John Harvey Jones said that *'Planning is an unnatural process...'* and we all love this quote, as it says something that we recognise about human nature. In this guide we contend that planning is partly a process, a 'science' if you like. But there is also an art to planning, one which requires good ideas, experience, deep thought and creative thinking, particularly around business planning, consideration of options and choosing methodologies. This book discusses the art of planning, but places an emphasis on the scientific side of planning – the processes of scheduling, risk analysis, management of change (and so on) – in what we hope is a practical manner.

The guide was conceived after the formation of the Planning, Monitoring and Control (PMC) Specific Interest Group (SIG) in late 2010 to fill a gap in published APM knowledge. It was intended to cover all planning aspects of preparing to undertake a project, executing a project, controlling its delivery to budget, time and quality, and delivering it safely. The guide was to be about planning in the widest sense of the word. Just as with the formation of the PMC SIG, its aim has been to bring together different project specialisms, rather than focus on a particular area of specialist knowledge.

After much discussion and debate, a basic structure for the guide was agreed upon, and content started to be written. By late 2013 a large amount of material had been gathered but momentum had flagged, so a sub-committee of the SIG was formed to pull together all the material and fill the gaps that inevitably still existed at that point. An intense period of writing and re-writing, as individuals and as a group, followed.

Reading this book

We have covered a lot of material in this book and realise that it may look a daunting read – but it has been written as a reference guide to dip into, so we have provided a comprehensive contents and index that will, we hope, assist in navigation through the book.

We have tried to write this guide in plain English as far as we possibly could, adopting the 'Emily test' to challenge ourselves whenever we slipped into 'management speak' or other pretentious or pompous language. No doubt we have not always passed the test, but we have done our best! (Emily is Simon Taylor's 10-year-old daughter, who challenged such language when being subjected to the drafts of this guide for bed-time reading!)

This book has been written entirely by volunteers, giving their own and their employers' time freely and willingly for the purpose of advancing and disseminating knowledge. The effort and time given by the group were well beyond the call of duty, and I cannot express my gratitude for the amount of time that already busy individuals were prepared to put into writing and illustrating the guide.

This book may not be perfect – there surely remains work to be done to make it so – but we have reached the point where this group has done its best, and we look to the project management community to provide the feedback and expertise to strengthen the guide in what we hope will be future editions in years to come.

Paul Kidston
Lead author
June 2014

Acknowledgements

This guide was discussed, debated and drafted over a number of years, but written and finalised by a small team who formed a sub-committee of the Association for Project Management's Specific Interest Group 'Planning, Monitoring and Control', consisting of:

Lead author: Paul Kidston	(Head of project control, Taylor Woodrow Civil Engineering)
Co-author: Keith Haward	(Associate director, Turner & Townsend)
Jenn Browne	(Programme manager, Ministry of Defence)
Carolyn Limbert	(Principal planner, Harmonic Ltd)
Simon Taylor	(Head of planning, Transport for London)

In addition, significant contributions were made by the following members of the PMC SIG:

Mike Prescott	(Head of project control management, Cavendish Nuclear)
Stephen Jones	(Sellafield Ltd, chairman of the APM PMC SIG)
Guy Hindley	(Turner & Townsend, formerly of BAE Systems)
Steve Wake	(SW Projects, chairman of APM)
Alex Davis	(GE Oil and Gas, formerly of MoD)
Ewan Glen	(BMT Hi-Q Sigma)

Significant contributions from outside the SIG were made by:

Franco Pittoni	(Technical director – BIM & Project Controls, Parsons Brinckerhoff)
Ewen MacLean	(Berkeley Research Group, LLC)

Additional material and comments were provided by: Alan Bye (Rolls-Royce); Andrew Chillingsworth (Atkins Rail, formerly of Turner & Townsend); Breda Ryan (Jacobs PMCM UK Infrastructure, formerly of Heathrow Airport Limited); Claire

Acknowledgements

Purser (Capable Consulting, formerly of BMT Hi-Q Sigma); Deborah Perrin (Rhead Group, formerly of Turner & Townsend); Gary Mainwaring (General Dynamics); Ian Williams (Taylor Woodrow); Jim Malkin (Deltek); Jonathan Crone (Foster Wheeler, formerly of Subsea7); Marvin Edwards (Goldheart); Mike Semmons (AgustaWestland); Natalie Evans (BMT Hi-Q Sigma); Rebecca Evans (Turner & Townsend); Roger Joby (1 to 1 to 1); Ros Downs (BAE Systems); Sue Simmonite (BAE Systems); Tina Vadolia (BMT Hi-Q Sigma, formerly of Keval).

BAE Systems, Taylor Woodrow, BAA (Heathrow Airports Ltd) and Turner & Townsend provided much source material, for which we are very grateful.

Venues to meet in, lunches and really strong cups of hot tea were provided by Taylor Woodrow, APM and in particular by TfL and Turner & Townsend, both of whom were particularly generous with their meeting rooms and catering.

Dedication

This book is dedicated to the memory of Rebecca Evans, a much respected SIG member and contributor to this guide.

Peer review

The guide was widely peer reviewed by people with a wide range of experience from outside the SIG, and we are grateful to the following, who provided significant comments and suggestions:

From the Rhead group, Pete Mill, Steve Highfield, John Nixon and Robin Smoult; Ben Whitlock (Babcock International Group); James Manthorpe, Louise Arrowsmith and Sarah Cummins, all of Taylor Woodrow. From the Cross Industry Planning and Project Controls (CIPPC) group, Mark Singleton (Balfour Beatty Construction Services UK), Franco Pittoni (Parsons Brinkerhoff) and Phil Budden (Costain) all provided useful suggestions.

Purpose

The content of this document identifies the scope of planning knowledge as understood by the Association for Project Management (APM) Planning, Monitoring and Control (PMC) Specific Interest Group (SIG). This knowledge was compiled and discussed in a series of working sessions and reviews commencing in October 2010 and concluding, for publication purposes, in July 2014.

It provides reference guidance for practitioners and students along with the study material required for the forthcoming Foundation exam.

This guide covers many topics, but does not attempt to supersede many other notable APM publications; it is hoped that we have achieved a practical guide that sits alongside them, in particular:

Project Risk Analysis and Management Guide
The Earned Value Management APM Guidelines
The Earned Value Management Handbook
The Scheduling Maturity Model
The Earned Value Management Compass

Ultimately, this guide builds on the *Introduction to Project Planning* guide (published by APM in 2008) by the forerunner of the PMC SIG – the Planning SIG, which did what its title suggested and provided an introduction and a manifesto for project planning. Although that book explains the need for planning, this handbook is intended to be the practical guide to best practice in planning.

This guide has been written totally by volunteers. We would welcome any constructive feedback that may be used in improving future editions of this guide, which we hope will follow and build on this starting point.

Note

Within this guide, text highlighted in blue means that the term thus highlighted is referred to in the glossary.

The PSMC Process Map

The illustration gives a graphical representation of the stages a project will go through. This guide follows this structure and uses the icons to introduce each section. This shows how each of the control stages relates to the others.

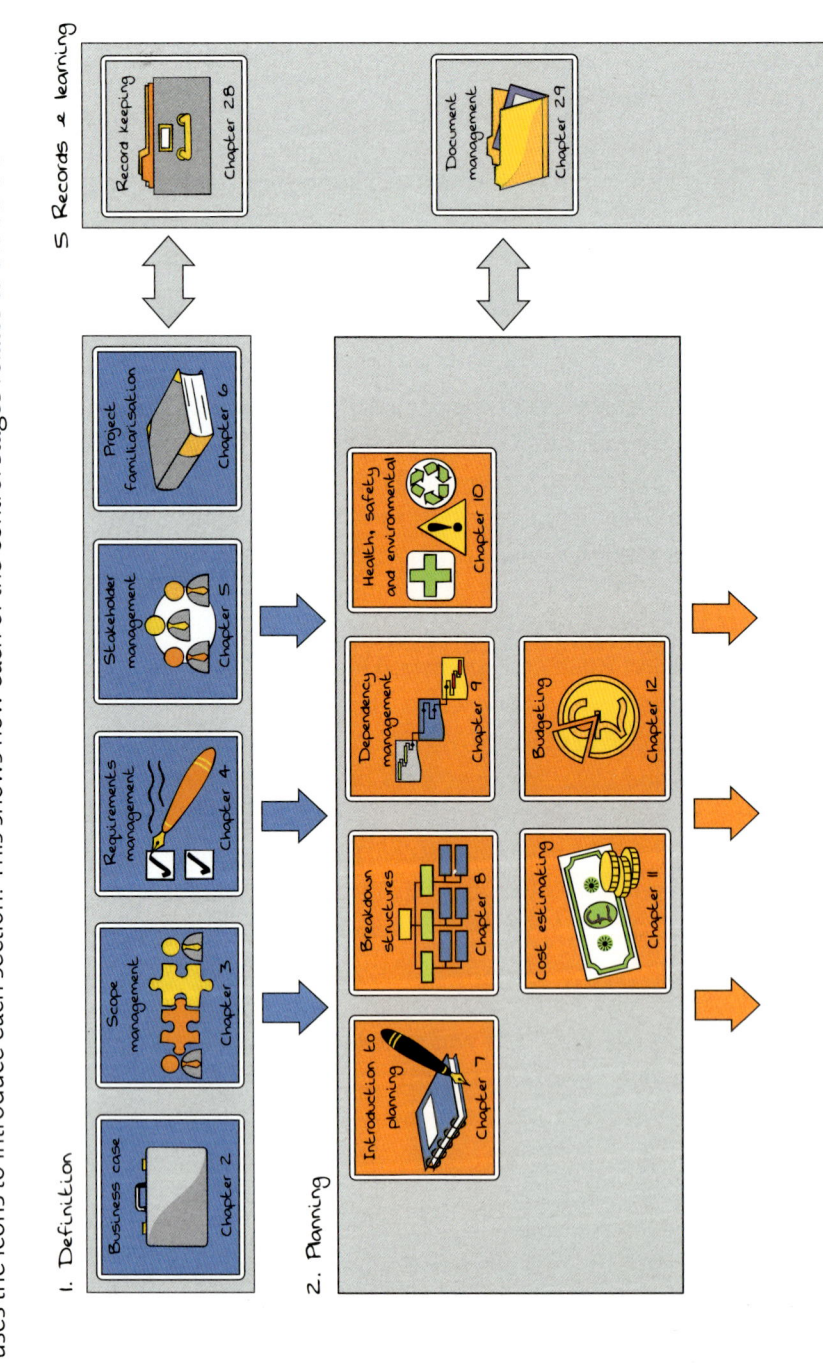

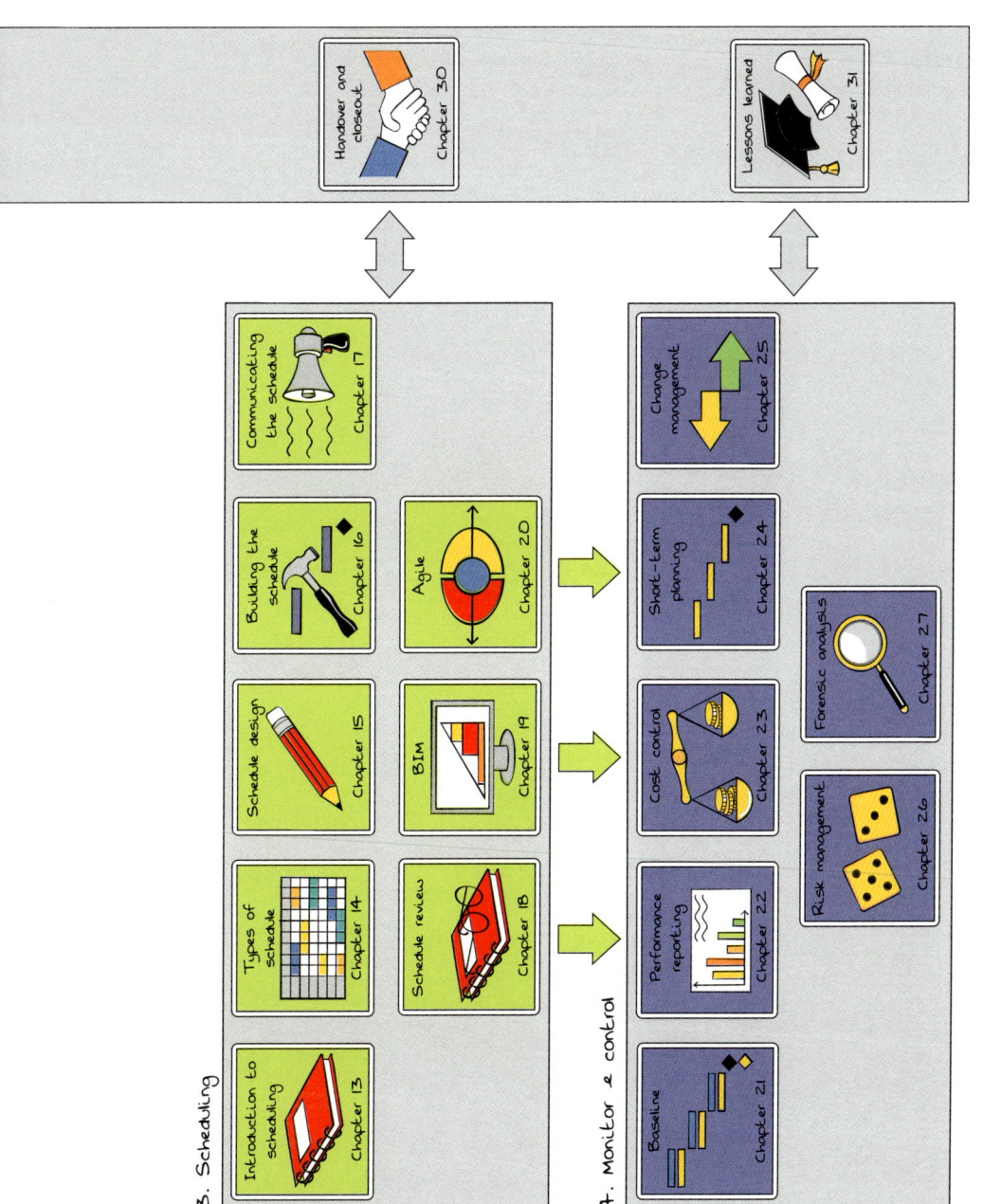

1

Overview

Effective project management requires effective planning and control. Effective planning and control requires:

- the clear definition of the project;
- a robust approach to planning the project;
- selection and use of the appropriate scheduling techniques;
- rigorous monitoring that enables proactive control of the project;
- a sound basis for this is good record keeping, which also facilitates the virtuous feedback and learning cycle.

This book offers tried and tested techniques and principles covering these aspects of project management. It introduces some lesser-known and emerging practices, some of which will move into mainstream project management in the years to come.

The book is structured into five main sections reflecting these requirements, and a brief introduction to each section and chapter follows.

1.1 Part One: Definition

At a strategic level, there are a number of fundamental questions that need addressing:

- Why is the project required?
- What does the customer want the project to deliver?
- How will the success of the project be measured?
- How will the project be procured?
- What is the attitude of its customers (or its funders) to risk?
- Similarly, what is their attitude to quality (including scope)?
- When does the client want the capability delivered by?

Part One of this guide describes the principal processes that define the project, and answers these questions.

Planning, Scheduling, Monitoring and Control

The first topic dealt with is the creation of the business case (Chapter 2). This is the starting point in the life of any project, and it is a vital step in ensuring that the project is viable, affordable and desirable. It sets the scene for all that follows – the planning, scheduling, monitoring and control, and, not least, the delivery of the project.

Assuming the business case is approved, the scope of the project must be defined and agreed with all stakeholders (Chapter 3). Defining the scope will begin the process of making key decisions about the project, defining and selecting from various options until a preferred solution is agreed and approved.

Once the scope has been agreed, the details of the requirements are determined. See Chapter 4 (*Requirements management*).

Stakeholder management (Chapter 5) is dealt with briefly, as the responsibility for this falls mainly on the project manager (see Soft Issues – Project Management Time in Figure 1.1).

Chapter 6, the final chapter in Part One (*Project familiarisation*), is a checklist of the project documentation that has been created during the definition stage. These are the key documents that must be read and understood to enable the planning – and subsequent processes detailed in the guide – to be carried out in an informed way.

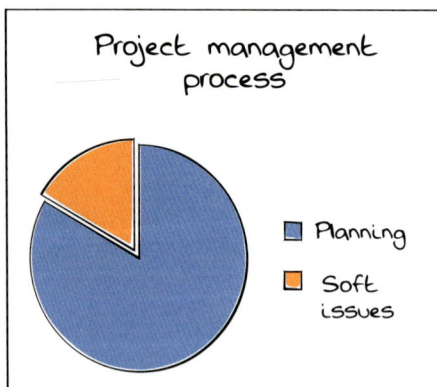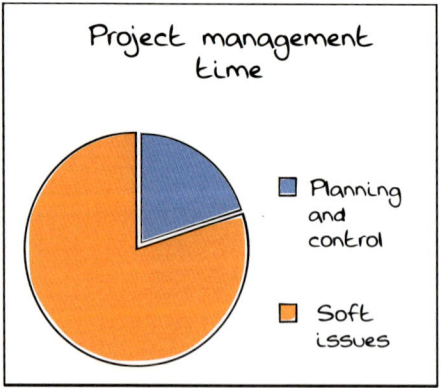

Figure 1.1 The importance of planning and control in project management

1.2 Part Two: Planning

The planning phase of the project needs to answer some fundamental questions, such as:

- How much will the project cost?
- How long should the project take?
- Are there benefits to finishing early, and what are they?
- What are the costs of an earlier completion, and do they outweigh the benefits?
- On the other hand, how is funding released, and are there any limits on this?
- How will the performance of the project be measured, through all its phases?
- Can the project be delivered safely?

Chapter 7 introduces planning – the team approach to working out how to deliver the project. After discussing and defining the difference between planning and scheduling (a point worth making to help define the two terms) – these terms are often used interchangeably, but they are two very different processes and require different skill sets – the opening chapter of this section goes on to discuss the principal components that will make up the overall project plan – the various schedules and narratives. It is important to understand these at the planning stage, and, whilst they are introduced here, they will be covered in further detail in Part Four.

Chapter 8 defines and discusses the purpose of the various breakdown structures that are used in project management. We also propose a method of creating these structures. Chapter 9 introduces the concept of dependency management. This theme is returned to in Part Four, when the specifics of schedule dependencies are defined in greater detail.

A critical concern of all project management must be the highest standards of health, safety and environmental management (Chapter 10). We cannot do justice to this topic in a book aimed across all industries, but it is a very important aspect when planning any project. It will have a fundamental influence on the project – how it is planned, designed/engineered and constructed.

Finally, in Chapters 11 and 12, we discuss the cost-estimating process and the budgeting process that follows it. The former is an essential step in the definition and planning (and, indeed, scheduling) of the project. The latter is essential in the creation of targets and baselines that will form the basis of monitoring and control.

1.3 Part Three: Scheduling

A fundamental question is: who owns the schedule? The answer is, of course, that it is the project manager, with the support of the whole project team. The schedule is created by collating the thoughts of many people; the specialist planner's role is to form these thoughts into a coherent schedule, and then to communicate it effectively. This will include:

- developing logistical plans;
- setting up the schedule in planning software;
- deciding how the plan is to be presented and communicated.

Part Three commences with a chapter (13) setting the scene; it discusses the purposes of scheduling and some of the basic philosophies and structures. Chapter 14 describes the various types and purposes of schedules that might be used on a project.

Chapter 15, entitled *Schedule design*, details the various elements of a schedule that need to be considered prior to commencement of any scheduling: for example, what type of activity should be used, or what coding and other structures should be applied.

Chapter 16 addresses the construction of the schedule. It is this guide's contention that all scheduling starts with the creation of a logic-linked network. On simple projects a bar (or Gantt) chart may suffice, but we have chosen to describe these as outputs, or communication tools, rather than scheduling tools in their own right. We believe this is consistent with current practice. Within this chapter we discuss not only networks but also how durations may be calculated, the importance of considering and scheduling resources, and how schedules are interfaced with other stakeholders.

Chapter 17 follows with a number of suggestions about how the schedule is communicated – from the aforementioned bar charts through to line of balance and time chainage charts that are useful in particular circumstances. One very important and sometimes overlooked document is the schedule narrative. This document serves to explain and clarify the planning and scheduling effort that has resulted in the (suite of) schedule(s) that have been created. Without this, the project cannot be clearly understood. We suggest appropriate contents for this narrative.

The final part of the generic process is schedule review (Chapter 18), describing the basic and detailed checks that should be made on the plans and schedules.

Turning once again to the question of who owns the programme, the final two chapters of this part (Chapters 19 and 20) deal with two emerging practices that have an important part to play in sharing the planning and the schedule with the project team: the agile approach, used mainly in software development, and the building information modelling (BIM) approach for use in asset design, construction and management. The latter is mandated for use in all government procurement activity from 2016, so it is very likely to grow in significance over the coming years.

1.4 Part Four: Monitoring and control

Once the project is in its delivery phase, there are four fundamental questions that project stakeholders will ask of the project manager:

- Where are we?
- What has it cost to get here?
- Where are we going?
- How can we correct any problems?

The first question (Where are we?) may be decomposed into further questions such as: Are we on schedule? If not, where have the delays occurred? What caused the delay? Who is responsible, and what effect will it have on the project? Finally, what can be done to recover?

The second question (What has it cost to get here?) may also be broken down into similar questions: Where and why did any over or under spend occur? Who is responsible and how will we recover?

The question 'Where are we going?' may be considered in terms of time (When are we going to finish?), cost (What is it going to finally cost?) and quality (Will the finished product do what we intended?). The analysis of current trends will enable forecasting and/or challenge on these matters.

The fourth and final question (How can we correct any problems?) also requires project-specific experience and very often innovative thinking, topics that this guide does not, indeed cannot, cover. The monitoring and control process provides the basis for asking the right questions, and perhaps the basis for answering them.

The chapter on baselines (Chapter 21) could be a section in its own right, as it is the pivot between the planning and scheduling effort and the processes of monitoring and control. It is, however, a useful introduction to performance management, and touches on issues of change and other forms of control that are dealt with later in this part of the book.

Performance reporting (Chapter 22) covers the collection of progress and cost information and how this is turned into useful management data. Various reporting techniques are discussed: first, variance reports that simply measure differences, exposing them (hopefully) to potential management action; second, a category that we have called 'performance analysis methods' that includes potentially the most valuable reporting of all, earned value analysis. As stated in the earlier purpose section of this guide, this book does not supersede the APM's own *Earned Value Handbook*, and readers with a further interest in this subject should refer to that guide. However, this guide does cover the basic principles of earned value.

Cost control is given its own chapter (Chapter 23), and, although it is covered with some brevity, the fundamental principles are discussed.

After the project has started, the project needs to react to progress made and re-plan as necessary. This is often the driver of short-term planning (although breaking plans into greater levels of detail (or 'densities') is also a function of this). In Chapter 24, we outline this process.

Chapters 25 and 26 discuss two processes that will actually be active throughout the whole life of the project. The former discusses change management, and the latter gives an overview of risk management. This chapter provides details of the QSRA and QCRA processes, which are the quantitative analyses of schedule and cost, respectively (hence the acronyms). These are tools that check the initial and ongoing robustness of the project plans.

The last chapter in Part Four (Chapter 27) discusses forensic analysis and delay and disruption analysis.

1.5 Part Five: Record keeping and learning

Record keeping (Chapter 28) is vital to provide a comprehensive history of the project. It forms both the basis of updating the schedules and plans for performance reporting, and to enable forensic analysis should it be necessary. It provides the basis of much of the learning from the project that can be used to improve future projects. Document management (Chapter 29) ensures that this and all other relevant project information is available to those who need it.

The closely allied (but separate) processes of handover and closeout of the project are dealt with in Chapter 30. The handover process ensures that the project and its obligations are complete and signed off; closeout essentially closes down all the support structures and commercial settlement of the project.

The final chapter of the book deals with another process that exists throughout the life of the project: lessons learned (Chapter 31). This includes both hard and soft data. An example of the former would be productivity outputs achieved; an example of the latter might be an analysis of why the outputs were at the levels achieved.

1.6 A note on the Contents, Index and Glossary

We have included comprehensive contents and index to facilitate easy referencing throughout the book. This is in keeping with the belief that this is a guide to dip into rather than read cover to cover (although the reader is welcome to try!). Cross referencing in the book is kept to a minimum, and as a result there is a small amount of repetition, but in general a familiarity with the structure of the book will aid navigation through it. As stated in the preface, we have tried to only use plain English in this guide. However, when writing about technical subjects, there are always going to be words used that the reader is not familiar with. In these instances we have highlighted the word in blue, and added a definition in the glossary.

1.7 Management issues

There are many other factors that an organisation needs to consider that cannot be covered by this guide, but are fundamental to successful delivery of projects; these include:

1.7.1 Behaviour and resources

The behaviours within the organisation must allow proper recognition, time and resource to allow the planning and control processes to happen. Making sure that there is a development route for project teams such that the organisation/project has suitably qualified and experienced people is similarly important.

1.7.2 Processes and tools (scheduling software)

Each organisation must set down its own planning and scheduling processes. As with all processes, making sure that planning and control processes are audited to check for appropriate implementation is important. Processes must be robust enough to deliver the project efficiently, but scaled to suit the size and complexity of the project as appropriate.

Some research and effort are required to ensure that the tools used and their configuration are suitable for the organisation or project and the team who will be using them. In some industry sectors a big consideration will be client expectations, and this cannot be ignored.

1.7.3 Common sense

The most important piece of advice of all is to make sure that the guidance in this book is interpreted with common sense. Any action or process that is established must be appropriate and must show a benefit that outweighs the cost of its implementation. This cost is not just in financial terms, but also in the use of the available time of the team. Projects of differing complexity will require different implementations: the highly complex and risky project will require something close to everything in this guide! A simple project will only need to apply the principles, often in a very informal way. It is up to the skill and judgement of the organisation's senior management to determine what is relevant.

Part One

Definition

Business case	Scope management	Requirements management	Stakeholder management	Project familiarisation
Chapter 2	Chapter 3	Chapter 4	Chapter 5	Chapter 6

'The beginning of wisdom is the definition of terms.'

Socrates

2.1 Definition of the business case

The business case provides the justification for undertaking a project, in terms of evaluating the benefit, cost and risk of alternative options and rationale for the preferred solution. Its purpose is to obtain management commitment and approval for investment in the project.

The business case summarises the 'why' of the project and should be reviewed at the start of each project life cycle stage in order to confirm that the project is achieving its objectives. This is to test the ongoing viability of a project before proceeding into the next phase of work. It should be read alongside the project brief (to understand 'what' is being delivered), and the project execution plan (PEP) (to understand 'how' the project will be delivered). Alternatively, the business case may determine that the project is not viable and should not proceed. The business case is owned by the project sponsor.

2.2 Purpose of a business case

The purpose of generating a business case is to make the case for a particular project to proceed, and to define and validate, in broad terms, the constraints within which it may be delivered. In some cases the outcome of the business case may be that the proposed project does not proceed. A key part of the business case is the communication of the resources, commercial strategy and capital investment necessary to realise the business benefits that the project is due to deliver.

Planning, Scheduling, Monitoring and Control

2.3 Contents of the business case

2.3.1 Structure of the business case

2.3.1.1 Executive summary

This brief introduction to the business case will contain at least the following sections:

- description of project scope;
- key reasons for proceeding with the project;
- conclusions of cost/benefit study;
- recommended option (assuming a number of options are available);
- outputs: list of key deliverables.

2.3.1.2 Strategic case

This key section describes to the sponsors/stakeholders why the project is required. It covers the details of the issues to be addressed, or the opportunity that has arisen.

2.3:1.3 Economic options

There are generally three financial aspects to be addressed when considering a new project:

- business as usual: no project to invest in;
- mission critical: deliver absolute minimum of benefits to solve the problem;
- comprehensive change: a decision that will lead to a fully scoped project (or projects in the case of a change programme).

Each of the economic options must be appraised in terms of costs, benefits, risks and opportunities. Having considered the options, this section should then clearly present the recommended option to the sponsors/stakeholders.

2.3.1.4 Benefits: advantages of undertaking the project

The benefits of undertaking the project must be made clear. These may include:

Business case

- return on investment;
- improved productivity;
- lower maintenance costs;
- safer operations;
- providing essential services;
- training for increased productivity;
- enhanced customer experience.

Making the benefits SMART (specific, measurable, achievable, relevant, time-bound) will facilitate decision making and, in time, assist with the benefits realisation analysis.

2.3.1.5 Compromises: disadvantages of undertaking the project

The compromises that will be required whilst undertaking the project must be made clear. These may include:

- disruption to the organisation or other stakeholders whilst the project is undertaken;
- drop in productivity;
- capital expenditure required and/or financing costs.

Dis-benefits should be analysed as part of the investment appraisal to ensure that they do not outweigh the expected benefits of the project.

As with the benefits, the compromises that the organisation will have to make will need to be translated into SMART objectives to aid the decision-making process.

2.3.1.6 Timescale

Different parts of the business case are emphasised at different life cycle stages:

- initiation stage: consider the different options and include a summary of each option;
- planning stage: the case must be made for the preferred option, with detailed costs and benefits for each to clearly show why the preferred option is recommended;

Planning, Scheduling, Monitoring and Control

- execution stage: the project progress is compared with the business case to ensure that the project continues to deliver the expected benefits, and for an acceptable cost;
- closeout/handover: comparison between the project outcome and that defined in the business case. Have the defined benefits of the project been achieved, or are they going to be achieved?

However, the two key stages are the time over which the project will be run and the period over which the benefits will be realised. The former is required to understand cash-flow forecasting, periods of disruption etc., and the latter to facilitate the cost/benefit analysis.

2.3.1.7 Cost and performance analysis

This section contains a comparison of the benefits and dis-benefits compared with the risks and costs of the project, along with any ongoing operational or maintenance costs.

Financial commitment across the whole project life cycle needs to be analysed. This includes:

- project cost, including cash-flow forecasts;
- ongoing operations and maintenance costs;
- life cycle revenue;
- one-off and ongoing cost savings;
- value of benefits.

Anything that delivers more savings than it costs will produce a positive net financial effect, and this should be quoted with the relevant back-up data.

2.3.1.8 Resources

Ideally, projects should be possible to carry out using existing resources. Where there are insufficient internal resources to deliver the project, proposals must be made to either recruit additional, or acquire external, resources to complete the work. This aspect can clearly have a major impact on the viability of a project.

Business case

2.3.1.9 Risks and opportunities

Although this is not the main location for communicating or managing risk and opportunity, it should summarise the impact on value for money and decision making. It should include:

- a summary of major risks identified with the project and their likely impact, including any mitigation plans;
- the financial provision for risk, including the method for its evaluation;
- the financial benefits of realising opportunities, including the method for their evaluation.

Risks and opportunities considered in this section should include risks to cost, time, health and safety, the environment, reputational damage, the effects on third parties and so on, as is relevant to the particular sector or organisation.

If the project is considered too risky, then the project sponsor may decide to not proceed.

2.3.2 Planning information

Planning information is fundamental in informing and validating the business case, in particular:

2.3.2.1 Strategic fit within the business

The plan should demonstrate how the project aligns with the business strategy. This will highlight potential relationships with other projects, programmes or portfolios within the business or externally.

Visibility of the bigger picture could identify constraints or issues associated with resource availability, materials or funds. Just as large national projects like the building of new nuclear power stations, or upgrading the UK rail network, can generate shortages within the resource market, the same can happen with the company's internal resources.

2.3.2.2 Time assumptions

Time assumptions may be based on benchmark data from similar projects, or learning from experience. There may be time constraints around funding

Planning, Scheduling, Monitoring and Control

availability that may factor into the business case, such as the ability to expend money, or other constraints, such as the availability of key resources.

In addition, information for inclusion in the business case, such as resource histograms or high-level schedules, should be provided.

2.3.3 Funding requirements

The business case may need to stipulate when further funding needs to be approved – possibly at a key milestone or gateway during the project life cycle.

The spend profile of the capital costs may need to be generated from the strategic schedule. This would enable the project cash-flow to be determined in line with the key phases or milestones of the project. In most organisations, annual spend profiles are important for managing the business. This will be used as part of the financial planning of the organisation.

The business case should be reviewed regularly until such time as the project is 'brought into use'.

2.3.4 Resource requirements

The quantity of resources required and the availability of these resources is a key factor in determining the viability of undertaking the project. The capacity to undertake the project internally or the procurement of external resources must be determined and appropriate options highlighted in the business case.

2.4 Acceptance criteria in the business case

Acceptance criteria define how the requirements will be demonstrated to the customer to determine whether the project is complete. All project outputs must be delivered fit for purpose, to the standards and specification outlined in the requirements.

Examples of acceptance criteria:

Table 2.1 *Examples of requirements and acceptance criteria*

Requirement	Acceptance criteria
Higher productivity	30% increase in manufacturing output within 3 months
Reduced maintenance	Planned preventative maintenance systems available within 1 month
Increased operational resilience	Back-up systems online

The business case may contain a summary list of key project milestones relevant to stakeholders (acceptance events).

2.5 Benefits realisation in the business case

Project success is partially the achievement of requirements and is measured by meeting the acceptance criteria as identified and agreed in the business case. However, it is possible to have a successfully delivered project that fails to deliver expected benefits, or a project that delivers significant benefits but is considered a failure.

Achievement of project requirements and end-user benefits needs to be considered together, because it is the creation and use of deliverables that produces benefits. For this reason, benefit realisation measures should be identified and baseline data should be collected before implementation begins. This should be presented alongside the project outcomes.

Business case benefits are very theoretical, which is why 'easy to measure' statistics should be collected for benefit realisation purposes that indicate whether the theoretical benefits have been delivered. The post-implementation survey is simple and proves whether the benefits predicted by the model have been realised. If not, there may be various reasons for this, and these need to be analysed and interpreted in a benefit realisation review.

2.6 Procurement strategy

Specifying the procurement strategy at the business case stage allows the project manager to define the most effective procurement scenario, so establishing a clear way forward.

The procurement strategy should consider the following, but these will differ from organisation to organisation:

- Funding processes: how will funding be obtained for the project, and what type of approvals will be required and when?
- Contract procurement framework: will the project require new procurement (because of the size, complexity or specialist nature of the project), or will an existing framework of suppliers be used?
- Contracting strategy: what type of contracts will be used?
- Financing constraints: are there any constraints on the financing of the project? If so, cash-flow forecasting may be required, as will the introduction of spending caps.
- Risk and contingency processes: how will the project obtain and draw down (allocate) risk and contingency monies?
- Security issues: sensitivity of information and security concerns will influence the procurement strategy. Security around intellectual property rights may be a concern.

The business case should define how the scope of the project will be procured. For example, if the business need is for a rapid delivery of the project it may be appropriate to select the shortest procurement route, single source procurement, existing supply chain framework, as opposed to competitive tender.

The commercial project manager or project procurement professional should both have input into the business case and understand it. Much of the activity associated with developing the business case will typically be undertaken as part of the wider project management process. However, if large or key elements of the project are likely to be sourced from outside the customer, the role of procurement is to provide support and information, so that informed early decisions, even if only 'in principle', can be taken.

Project managers must understand the development of the project procurement strategy in terms of how to break a project down into packages of work, and what factors to consider when giving direction on how individual providers will be selected, paid and rewarded, risks allocated, etc. Investing time in developing the strategy both increases the likelihood of the individual packages being successful and, more importantly, allows the business to review how the packages fit together to deliver the overall benefits.

2.7 Project review and assurance process of the business case

The business case may be periodically reviewed to ensure that the project is on track to deliver the business benefits, and that the project is still feasible. These reviews will take place throughout the project life cycle, and additional reviews will take place following handover and closeout to ensure that the benefits are being realised by the organisation.

Scope and requirements definition are the processes that ensure the project includes all the work required to complete it, and then define that work. They define the structures that enable the planning, scheduling and budgeting exercises to be undertaken in a structured manner. This will facilitate the control of the project as it enters its execution phases.

The management of scope should rigorously prevent 'scope creep'. This is the colloquial term given to any scope that is added or undertaken which is not validated and authorised via the project's scope definition or change control process.

These processes control how the project scope is developed and verified. They clearly define who is responsible for managing the project's scope and act as a guide for controlling the scope.

3.1 Definition of scope management

Scope definition is the process of developing the description of the project and its deliverables.

3.2 Purpose of scope management

Scope management should ensure that all work that is specified, and later done, is related to the project objectives. It is also important to clearly establish what is excluded from the project scope. The business plan will define the breadth of the project scope.

Planning, Scheduling, Monitoring and Control

3.3 The scope management process

3.3.1 Defining the scope

The initial part of the process defines the requirements of the project. This will include discussion with a range of stakeholders, such as potential suppliers, to determine what is possible, research and development areas, policy, legal and more. To do this, the following techniques can be used:

- build method;
- brainstorming;
- accurate/agreed requirement setting and capture;
- stakeholder/end-user management (interviews, analysis);
- key assumptions management (creating an assumptions list);
- product analysis;
- options analysis;
- facilitated workshops.

The project manager is responsible for carrying out refinement and agreement of the scope with the project executive, sponsor, programme manager, end-user and other key stakeholders to ensure that the project delivers a relevant and appropriate solution. It is essential that these key individuals sign up to their agreement of scope and that this is recorded in the project management plan.

Once the scope has been agreed it should be put under a formal change control process, as scope creep and uncontrolled change are common causes of project failure.

3.3.2 Describing the scope

When a solution has been identified that meets the stakeholders' criteria and requirements, the scope of work is divided into various hierarchical breakdown structures (see Figure 3.1). These may include:

- Product breakdown structure (PBS): Whilst not all industries and sectors will use a PBS, it can be used as an interim step towards generating a WBS. It is developed at the start of the project when the product or outcomes have been scoped and agreed. The PBS breaks down all necessary outcomes of a project.

Scope management

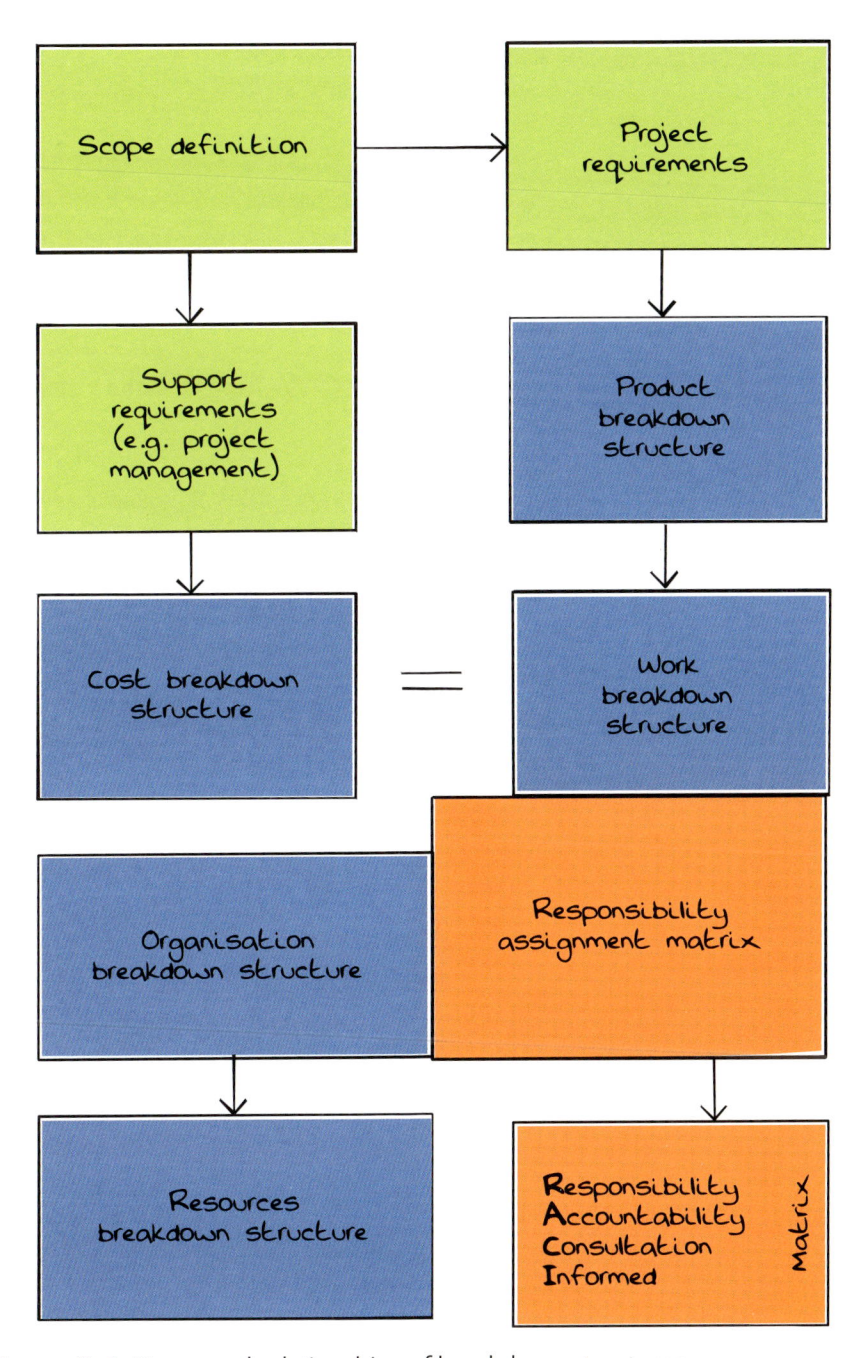

Figure 3.1 Types and relationships of breakdown structures

Planning, Scheduling, Monitoring and Control

- Work breakdown structure (WBS): The WBS breaks down or groups all activities within a project. A WBS can be further broken down into work packages and planning packages.
- Organisation breakdown structure (OBS): This is a hierarchical structure showing organisational accountability for the project and does not need to reflect the organisational structure of the company, just the project accountability. The OBS is defined down to the level of management control required in the WBS. Roles are usually used in the OBS rather than names (e.g. engineering manager).
- Responsibility assignment matrix (RAM): The RAM designates the responsibility of work packages to a team or individual. The RAM is a cross-reference of the WBS and OBS.
- Cost breakdown structure (CBS): The CBS provides a financial view of the project and splits the project scope into its individual cost components. The CBS often highlights any financial coding used for the business accounting system and any booking codes associated with each element of the project.
- Resource breakdown structure (RBS): The RBS organises the project resources in a hierarchical list that is used to plan and control the project. The structure is not usually identical to the CBS, but there will be a relationship between them.

Breakdown structures are dealt with in greater detail in Chapter 8.

To summarise: a PBS tells you what the product is; the WBS tells you about not only the product but the supporting services and how you deliver them; the OBS tells you who has project accountability for elements of the WBS; the RAM shows you the control points for management; the CBS records the costs; and the RBS defines the type of resource and resources on the project.

4.1 Definition of requirements management

Requirements management is the process of capturing, assessing and justifying stakeholders' wants and needs.

It requires the capture of requirements via a structured process. This process should incrementally break down the requirements in a hierarchical manner, considering different conditions and scenarios. The requirements, once defined, must be validated with the project sponsor and/or key stakeholders to ensure the full scope has been captured.

Requirements management is an ongoing process that is maintained throughout the project life cycle.

4.2 Purpose of requirements management

These requirements become the principal project deliverables. Thus, it helps to define the project scope. This allows the project team to understand the exact deliverables of the project and how the work will be structured to meet the requirements and deliver the scope.

4.3 Process of defining requirements

Once the initial identification of requirements has been undertaken, system analysis can then be undertaken, looking at each requirement in turn and

Planning, Scheduling, Monitoring and Control

analysing the risks, assumptions, interfaces, dependencies, opportunities and constraints associated with the requirement. This then allows the design and build phase of the project, which is often the 'implementation' phase of the project life cycle.

Ideally, each phase would be completed prior to the next starting, but in reality this process is often iterative and cyclical, with requirements being continually analysed and evaluated whilst the design is being finalised and build has commenced.

4.3.1 Requirement description

A requirement must be described in such a way that it meets the following criteria:

- It is up to date (e.g. with regard to latest technology or to latest legislation).
- It is relevant to the sponsoring organisations and benefits.
- It does not contradict any other requirement.
- It is concisely, but precisely, described, so that it is not open to different interpretations.
- Its achievement can be demonstrated.
- It can be traced from the operating need of the organisation, through the plan, to what is delivered.
- Its relative importance in relation to other requirements is understood.
- It can be linked to the product breakdown structure/work breakdown structure and activities in the project, for example by using activity coding.

Satisfying all project requirements equates to the completion of the project.

4.3.2 Factors to consider when defining requirements

When defining requirements, it is important to consider what the acceptance criteria will be and how these will be defined. It may be useful to examine requirements and acceptance criteria used for previous projects of a similar nature.

It is important to take standards, legal acts and regulations to be complied with into account when requirements are defined.

Requirements management

4.3.3 Inputs into requirements management

- Mature business case.
- Contractual documentation containing requirements where applicable.
- The current list of project assumptions and constraints.
- Initial risk register.
- Current statement of work.
- Project execution plan.
- Supporting management plans, including benefits, quality and risk.
- Applicable standards.

4.4 The requirements management process

4.4.1 Capture and define requirements from all stakeholders

- Defining requirements requires the identification of all stakeholders, then obtaining and documenting their requirements. The documentation should list all assumptions, exclusions and constraints and the acceptance, handover and closeout criteria. When defining the requirements, it is important to distinguish wants from needs.
- Identify the sources of the requirements. One requirement may have multiple sources, but it is important to identify the owner(s) of each requirement. The owner(s) will need to understand each of the sources' views on assumptions, exclusions and constraints, so that a common understanding of the requirement can be met by means agreed with all stakeholders.
- Capture any dependencies between those requirements within the scope of work and those at the strategic, programme/portfolio level where this applies. Consider horizontal linkage of requirements between projects, plus those requirements/constraints that have an interface/dependency with existing ongoing activities.

4.4.2 Link requirements to the product breakdown structures and work breakdown structures where appropriate

- Identify and define the individual elements of each user/customer requirement that can be linked to individual elements of the supplier's system requirements document (SRD), which in turn link to individual elements of

Planning, Scheduling, Monitoring and Control

the technical specification, which link to individual elements of the work breakdown structure and the associated statement of work.
- Each product described by the WBS should satisfy an element of the requirements.
- The levels of traceability between requirements models must be determined in order to allow for planning the resources and schedule implications for managing requirements.
- The system requirements drive the work to be completed within the system design process and subsequent subsystem and component design, so the link between the system requirement structure and the work breakdown structure must be established.

4.4.3 Decompose requirements

Requirements are decomposed into capabilities, features or attributes of the project's deliverables at a sufficient level of detail to allow verification and validation (see Figure 4.1).

Once requirements are defined, the acceptance criteria for each requirement should be approved by the customer. The method of verification for the criteria

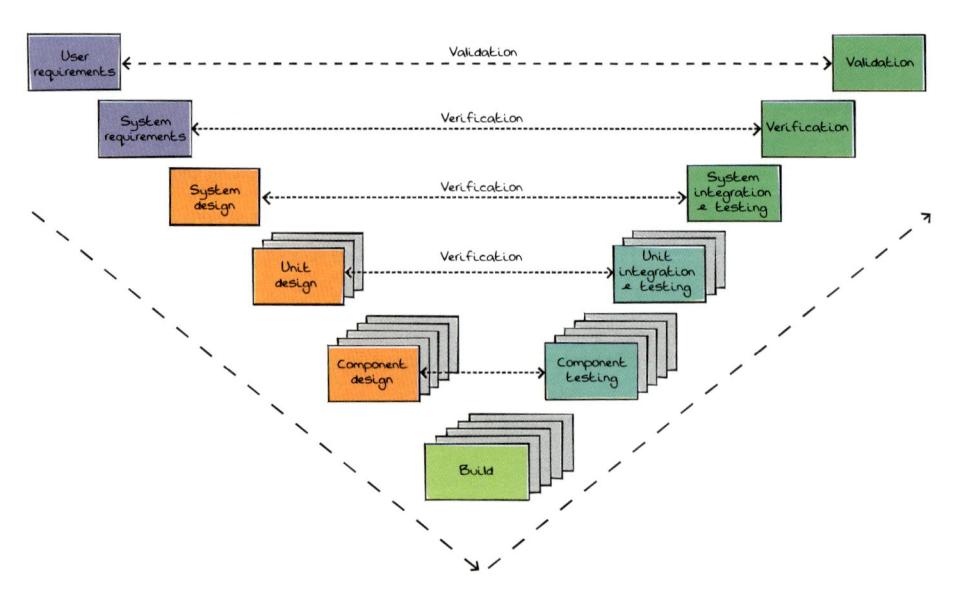

Figure 4.1 Design and development V Model

Requirements management

should also be agreed upon. This could include analysis, inspection, demonstration or test, or simulation. A clearly defined requirement increases the chances of the project sponsor being able to make a clear decision regarding acceptance after completion.

Requirements may be traded where appropriate, to balance time, cost, quality and safety parameters within the scope of work, using an approved change control process.

Once requirements have been clearly defined and agreed, they should be clearly documented, and the strategy for the delivery of the requirements should be detailed within the PEP and the schedule.

The requirements should be baselined before commencing the design and delivery process.

There are a number of design approaches, but for the majority of projects a validation and verification requirements matrix (VVRM) is a useful model to map the user requirements and system design, in order to facilitate the project assurance process; compliance with requirements may be achieved by linking the VVRM to tests, trials, demonstration, analysis and inspections within the relevant plan and then to the project schedule.

Key review points should be identified (for example preliminary design review, critical design review), where certain requirements must be met before the project proceeds further. At these reviews, requirements and acceptance criteria should be validated prior to testing to ensure that they are still appropriate. If not, they can be amended through the relevant change process.

The VVRM should be updated as requirements are met through their acceptance criteria.

Handover and closeout of all requirements and assumptions should be captured in a formal acceptance process

4.5 Works information (WI)

The works information is split into two parts: employers [buyer] and suppliers.

Employers' information specifies the works to be carried out by the supplier, including technical information specifications, system requirements, drawings, and any constraints relating to the supplier, e.g. safety requirements, consents required, etc.

Suppliers will respond with details of how they propose to deliver the works in line with the customers' requirements unless agreed otherwise. In some industries, the suppliers' response is known as the statement of work, as distinct from the works information.

Each works information item must be linked to the formal requirement that generates it. This is to ensure that scope creep is not generated by the creation of the works information (or, indeed, that scope gaps do not appear).

The schedule must contain all the works identified in the works information.

4.6 Statement of work (SOW)

A statement of work (SOW) explains in clear language the customer's needs and requirements, and is therefore often initially drafted at the bid stage of a project by the customer to facilitate the preparation of proposals from multiple potential contractors. It is often developed in line with the business case, and the SOW will then form the basis of contractor selection and contract administration.

The SOW defines all the work that is required to be undertaken in order to develop or produce the outputs of the project, along with work performance requirements for the project (e.g. service levels, minimum down-time, specifications of building safety, structure, size, etc.). It includes qualitative and quantitative design and performance requirements that can be measured to determine project success.

Once a contract has been awarded to a supplier and a project commences, the project team often breaks the top-level SOW into individual or work package SOWs, creating a more detailed and lower-level WBS structure than that which was submitted at bid stage. This facilitates clearer definition of the work packages, as the SOW requirements can be traced throughout the WBS structure, and ownership can be clearly assigned to the work packages.

Relevant parts of the SOWs which are referenced in a WBS dictionary are then considered alongside the constraints, risks, assumptions, interfaces, dependencies and opportunities. This produces the scope baseline for the project team to estimate work schedules and costs. As schedules are worked up, the basis of estimates for duration of activities and cost estimates is recorded for both project audit purposes, and schedule and cost risk assessment activities.

5.1 Definition of stakeholder management

Stakeholders are the organisations or people who have an interest or role in the project, or are impacted by it. Stakeholder management is the formal management of these interests, including the management of the relationships and monitoring the delivery of commitments made to the stakeholders.

5.2 Purpose of stakeholder management

Stakeholders have a key role in setting the criteria used to define the success of the project, and their involvement should not be overlooked. Managing stakeholders can make the difference between success and failure of a project, and as such should feature highly on the list of priorities and be treated with appropriate gravity. Whilst the planner assists with this process, the main responsibility for managing the stakeholders lies with the project manager.

5.3 Managing stakeholders through the project

Setting the scope will include discussion with a range of stakeholders, such as potential suppliers, to determine what is possible, research and development areas, policy, legal and more. The project manager is responsible for carrying out refinement and agreement of the scope with the project sponsor, programme manager, end-user and other key stakeholders to ensure that the project delivers

Planning, Scheduling, Monitoring and Control

a relevant and appropriate solution. It is essential that these key individuals sign up to their agreement of scope and that this is retained for record purposes.

Stakeholders must be identified, their level of interest and power to influence the project analysed, and plans devised for their management. Stakeholder management is an iterative process which starts during project concept.

Stakeholders should be managed to ensure that a positive relationship with the project is built and maintained.

Stakeholder management becomes more complex when stakeholders' views are not consistent throughout the life cycle of the project as changes occur in their opinions, roles and views regarding the project.

The project's communication plan should be employed as a tool for stakeholder management. It may include who the stakeholders are and their communication needs, and who is responsible for their management and planned responses.

Stakeholder management needs to consider interfaces with third parties or outside influences.

Project familiarisation

Chapter 6

When approaching the planning of a project, it is important to gain a wide appreciation of important factors that may influence the project's success, its approach or its complexity. Although a planner will not be expected to know the finite technical detail of the project, planners should have an appreciation of each element of the project. Areas where the project team typically may need to gain a high level of understanding are listed in Table 6.1.

Table 6.1 *Sources of project information*

Document or source	Example of information
Business case	• Key dates for funding approval
The contract, especially identified risks and key deliverables	• Key dates, contract dates, risk ownership, restrictions, limitations on working conditions, and any other requirements
Customers' requirements	• Processes to follow, may include delivery implications and handover or hand-back regimes
Drawings	• Scope, implied methodologies
Specifications	• Standards, methodologies
Previous stage schedules	• Key interfaces with earlier phases
Meetings, workshops	• Insight into the project, in particular the drivers, output rates and methodologies
Stakeholders	• Who are the 'key players' that will impact the success or failure of the project? How does this influence the plans?

(Continued)

Planning, Scheduling, Monitoring and Control

Table 6.1 *Continued*

Document or source	Example of information
Stakeholders (*cont.*)	• Legal agreements with third parties (party wall agreements; intellectual property rights)
External interfaces, i.e. those that will not be covered by the project schedule	• Supply of critical resources, e.g. utilities, power supply
Benchmark data – output or productivity guides	• Refer back to previous similar jobs/projects and use realistic durations in the new schedule
Cost estimates	• Scope verification
	• Identify provisional sums
	• Basis for budget loading of the schedule
Industry specific	• Soil investigation reports, site visits, weather records for construction
	• Planned closures to enable works
	• Capability requirements in defence
Previous projects of a similar nature	• Methods, durations and benchmarking data
Lead-in times	• Investigate any materials that are known to have long procurement times, e.g. lifts or escalators, government-furnished equipment
Available resource	• Check that there are no specialist resources required that may be in short supply, e.g. signalling engineers for rail projects
Gateways and stage approvals	• Critical to a lot of projects. Find out what approval stages are required, e.g. for design or funding
Limitations imposed by relevant legislation	• Safety legislation
	• Security clearances required

Part Two

Planning

- Introduction to planning — Chapter 7
- Breakdown structures — Chapter 8
- Dependency management — Chapter 9
- Health, safety and environmental — Chapter 10
- Cost estimating — Chapter 11
- Budgeting — Chapter 12

'Failing to plan is planning to fail.'

Alan Lakein

7.1 Definition of planning

Planning is the process of identifying the methods, resources and activities necessary to accomplish the project's objectives. It achieves this by drawing on the expertise, experience and knowledge of organisations and individuals (including the lessons that it has learned from previous projects), and on external parties if appropriate, in order to:

- understand the need, problem or opportunity that the project will address and the benefits that it will deliver;
- define what has to be accomplished and delivered, typically stated in terms of scope, time, budgets and quality;
- develop a plan to deliver the project.

Planning is the activity of determining how raw materials and other resources are delivered into a desired outcome. It is also the process that will deliver a competitive edge to organisations competing to win contracts to deliver work.

7.1.1 Definition of the planning role

Planning is an art rather than a science; it is based on experience, industry or sector knowledge and technical skill, and a key ingredient is innovative thinking. Planning is the activity of a team working together to determine the strategy for delivering the project. To achieve this, the project team determines the method or methods that will be used to deliver the project as well as how the project is to be procured.

Planning, Scheduling, Monitoring and Control

The best plans will be created by a team of project managers, engineers, production/design managers and commercial managers working together. Specialist planners may guide and facilitate the process. In principle, planning is an activity that precedes scheduling.

During the planning process, the main interfaces will be identified. It is important that during this process the assumptions made, the risks, opportunities and issues are identified and recorded.

At the planning stage of the project, it is important that the project control and reporting methodologies that will be used are defined so that decisions around the methods of planning effort and toolsets adopted will be adequate.

The outputs of planning are therefore:

- overall strategy for the project;
- overall methodology for the project;
- breakdown structures for managing the project;
- the identification of key dependencies;
- contributions to the project risk and opportunities register and issues log;
- the identification of interfaces.

7.2 Purpose of planning

Planning is used to determine how, when and which project deliverables must be achieved in order to deliver the products (or actions) needed for the project's success. This includes recording any organisational or management approaches and processes that will be used. The planning discipline assesses how and when activities need to take place and defines the acceptable standard required for completion, as well as balancing standards and targets within agreed time, cost and quality parameters. The management approach information will be recorded within the project management plan (PMP) – also known as the project execution plan (PEP) – and the relevant timings for the activities identified will be recorded within a project schedule, included within the PMP/PEP.

Planning enables the project manager and their team to determine what methods and techniques they intend to use to deliver the required outputs, products and activities. Adding the activities to a schedule helps to understand the logical relationships between activities, the impact on resource distribution, the expenditure profile and reporting implications. In a well-planned project,

Introduction to planning

the means of achieving the well-defined outputs, to an agreed standard, have been examined, thought about, optimised and recorded, and are regularly reviewed.

Planning and scheduling are essential to the authorisation of the project delivery stages. Without a robust and realistic PMP and schedule, advancement through the project stages should not be approved. The approval at each stage will look closely at the plan and schedule and consider whether the project is on course to deliver its intended business benefits in accordance with the business case.

Once agreed and authorised, plans and schedules are an essential mechanism for communicating the project strategy and the deployment and tasking of staff, contractors and other resources.

7.2.1 Benefits of planning

- A well-planned project will identify and document the right activities and products to achieve the outputs and will secure the optimum resource level to support this.
- Planning determines what activities and products need to be carried out, when, to what standard and using which resources, including monetary funds. Well-planned projects, where the tasks that need to be undertaken, how and when have been carefully considered, are much more likely to successfully deliver desired outcomes.
- Comprehensive scheduling ensures the optimal allocation and release of resource and the effective control of project activities within time constraints.
- Planning is central to the control of the project and early identification of where the project might be starting to fail.
- Planning is an integral part of problem solving at all stages of the project.
- The project schedule, risk and budget are used to form a baseline against which the position of the project in terms of cost, time and risk, and therefore the performance of the project, can be managed.
- Establishing a baseline enables the project team to check the progress of the project, to measure success, and to identify and assess the impact of deviation from the baseline. Early identification of deviation will allow the maximum time for corrective action and assessment of impact on other planned activities.
- With good planning, it is possible to predict whether the project remains on target to deliver its outputs within the time, cost or performance constraints.

Planning, Scheduling, Monitoring and Control

- Above all, planning is about communicating the sequence, method and time required to complete the project deliverables.

7.2.2 Success in planning

There are a number of key themes that are required for planning to be a success; the key considerations are:

- Ensure that the planning exercise is properly led, and that all input from the project team and other stakeholders is considered, reviewed and included as appropriate. This should assist in achieving buy-in of the project team. Planning should never be an isolated exercise.
- Ensure that the right people are made available to contribute to the planning process in the manner described above.
- Ensure that a structured approach is taken, so that the full scope of the project is planned and that it ties back to all the contractual requirements.
- Ensure that adequate time is allowed to undertake the planning exercise.
- Ensure that there is proper understanding of the scope and all commitments, and that, during the planning exercise, all dependencies are identified and described and all interfaces are understood.
- Ensure all assumptions are defined, documented and taken into account.
- Ensure that adequate scheduling resources such as people and information (e.g. estimating norms), along with an adequate project controls system, are available to convert the planning exercises into understandable schedules, reports and other documentation.
- Planning and control systems will always fail if the human factors are ignored.
- Ensure that the scheduling disciplines discussed in this guide are applied by the scheduler(s) to clearly define, describe and communicate the plan, both in terms of clarity and in terms of appropriate distribution. In practice, no one technique will likely give a definitive answer in terms of both planning and control. Good practices are set up by careful selection of the right tools for the project.
- Ensure that all factors surrounding the project are taken into account. This will include logistics planning, stakeholder management and the availability of suitably trained and numerous resources.
- Ensure all project risks are understood and taken into account, and that any identified risk mitigations are included in the schedule.

7.3 The difference between planning and scheduling

Planning and scheduling are closely related subjects, but they are completely separate processes; however, the terms are often used as if they were interchangeable. To add to the confusion, many schedulers have been given role titles that include the word 'planning'. Planners may have both skill sets, but it is important to be aware of, and for this guide to define, the difference between the two roles.

Whereas planning has to be done well in order to define the best solution to deliver the project, scheduling needs to be done well to determine the project parameters: how long the project will take to complete, for example. Furthermore, it must be done well to communicate the project clearly and precisely. It can then form a sound foundation for project control.

Scheduling is more of a science compared with the art of planning; it usually involves the input of planning information into scheduling software. Scheduling uses the WBS as the framework on which to build all the project activities. It calculates the dates from the activity/task durations and determines the resources required. It also defines the logical sequence of activities and calculates the critical path (the path or chain of activities which, if delayed, will cause a corresponding delay to the overall project completion date). In this process it computes the start and finish dates and identifies the float on all the activities. The final outcome of this process is to determine the feasibility of delivering the project to the required completion dates.

At the outset of a project, planning is the art of deciding the best strategy for designing a project, implementing a project and bringing a project into use. The key to good planning is effective communication of the strategy and method(s) that are decided upon as the most efficient way to deliver the project. Thus, it is about:

- defining requirements, scope, purpose and objectives;
- defining methodology;
- definition of deliverables;
- clarity of organisation and organisational responsibility;
- the identification and management of risk – both threats and opportunities;
- supporting the business case to gain funding;
- getting agreement of all stakeholders in the project;

Planning, Scheduling, Monitoring and Control

- defining constraints;
- establishing priorities;
- defining and documenting assumptions.

A key part of planning is creating the project schedule. (This is often referred to as the programme, but, in order to avoid confusion with programmes of work and other uses of the word 'programme', it is common to use the term 'schedule', and this guide uses this convention.)

7.4 Principal scheduling components

7.4.1 Process step schedules

The schedule will usually be presented in a graphical format. The schedule should have enough information in it to manage the project and accurately model the impact of change and progress. Information that can be held in a separate tracker should not be included in the schedule. Examples of separate trackers include:

- design deliverable schedules;
- method statement schedules;
- consents trackers;
- handover or hand-back trackers (also known as interfaces);
- approval chains (managed by specialist resource – the details of testing and commissioning, for example).

Collectively, these documents do all form part of the schedule, and links between these documents and the master/working schedule must be actively managed and updated.

It is not useful to manage all this in the specialist scheduling software, because it increases the size of the schedule to less manageable proportions (it is likely to be a high-density level of detail). It would also make it harder for the project manager to access the data, thus detracting from the main purpose of the schedule.

7.4.2 Time-based schedules

It is almost certain that, for any project of complexity, the schedule will be contained in specialist scheduling software. This may include Gantt charts, time

Introduction to planning

chainage charts, line of balance graphs, etc. – these are dynamic, logic-linked, usually critical path views of the schedule for the physical and deliverable works.

7.4.3 Schedule narrative

e.g. WBS dictionary

A schedule narrative (sometimes known as the planning method statement) will be required to accompany a schedule of medium to high complexity, to explain, illuminate and communicate methodology, timing, and the risks and constraints on the schedule. It should give a clear understanding to both project and non-project team members of the way the work has been planned and scheduled, with associated assumptions.

7.5 Approaches to planning

7.5.1 Top-down planning

Top-down planning describes an approach that starts with strategic planning of a project and is worked into greater detail (and certainty) in parallel with the commencement of the project. Top-down planning is 'events' focused. It defines a period of time/work leading up to a key event that occurs at the culmination of a number of project activities – for example, a preliminary design review, which is an 'event' that has much activity leading up to it, and effectively validates that work, thus making it an important 'event'.

Typically, this top-down approach will define the overall project life cycle along with key events that will need to happen in order to achieve each gate review. As the top-down plan is more requirements driven and needs driven, it tends not to be date focused, and works instead on establishing the essential logic flows and sequences required for the successful completion of the project.

Bottom-up planning then complements this approach by validating the effort and duration required to deliver the requirements on the project, and should result in a resource-driven schedule showing the project dates by which key events can be met. Often, there is then a rationalisation period whereby the bottom-up and the top-down plans are aligned and trades in time, cost or quality are made to ensure that the project can be delivered to the timescales, cost or quality standards outlined by the customer.

See Figure 7.1 for a comparison of top-down and bottom-up planning.

Planning, Scheduling, Monitoring and Control

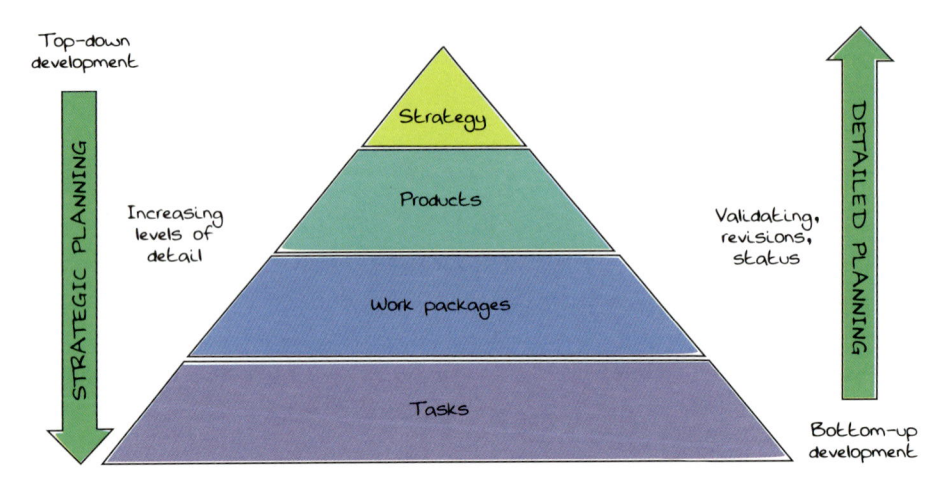

Figure 7.1 Top-down vs. bottom-up planning

7.5.2 Bottom-up planning

Where full details of the scope of work are known, a detailed schedule can be produced, starting at the lowest level and usually measured in days. This is typically a high-density schedule, and would be one of the more detailed planning outputs. Fully logic-linked and usually held in a scheduling software tool, this approach can be effectively utilised through collaborative planning techniques.

7.5.2.1 Collaborative planning

'Collaborative planning' is a technique that ensures that all key stakeholders are actively involved in the bottom-up planning of a project, and promotes team 'buy-in' to the schedule and planning strategy. It is usually undertaken via a facilitated workshop, whereby the facilitator will help to guide the team to create a bottom-up schedule of activities required to successfully reach an agreed end-point. There are multiple ways of facilitating planning workshops – one effective approach is for all of the team to create task names on sticky notes, which are then categorised and reviewed. Logic, durations, resources and any constraints are then discussed and agreed until a fully logic-linked schedule has been created. This approach takes a number of iterations; however, it should foster a collaborative approach and help to ensure that all team members are fully engaged in the planning process.

Introduction to planning

7.5.2.2 Summarising the output

Once this higher-density schedule has been created, the detail is then summarised into larger sections such as design, procurement and construction. These items cover weeks or months. This provides a view of the project useful for briefing new team members, senior management, executives and/or the customer.

7.5.2.3 Rolling wave planning

If the plan, and hence the schedule, is created once all the design is complete, after all contractors and sub-contractors are appointed, and after all methodologies have been agreed, then the creation of a fully detailed, budgeted and resourced schedule will be achievable at the outset of a project. If, however, some or all of these are not in place, some form of rolling wave planning is required. A rolling wave approach can also be adopted for highly complex projects, where there is a high risk of change, and/or a project spans multiple years (e.g. a defence build project), or where there is a reasonable degree of uncertainty in the project.

Rolling wave planning describes the scheduling density that is achieved at different moments in time. Figure 7.2 shows a typical schedule in terms of its current state of development. The project is broken down into 'waves', which are typically anchored to key gate reviews or significant events in the project. The project then uses the top-down plan and systematically plans each wave to an increasing level of granularity, starting with a high-density schedule upfront in the first wave, and gradually reducing the level of density and hence the requirement to fully define details which may not be fully available to the project until a later date.

In large-scale, long-duration projects, it may not be feasible to structure the rolling waves according to gate reviews, as these may be many years apart. Where this is the case, the project may choose interim milestones or deliverables by which the rolling waves should be completed, or, alternatively, may choose a set number of periods of time (e.g. months) which should have a detailed plan (typically 3–6 months). Where such an approach is taken, tasks and work packages should always be fully planned out to their natural conclusion, irrespective of the 'cut-off' of the rolling wave.

As the project moves nearer to the end of the first phase, the second phase will be planned to a higher level of density and detail, as the project team will have more information available than at project inception.

Planning, Scheduling, Monitoring and Control

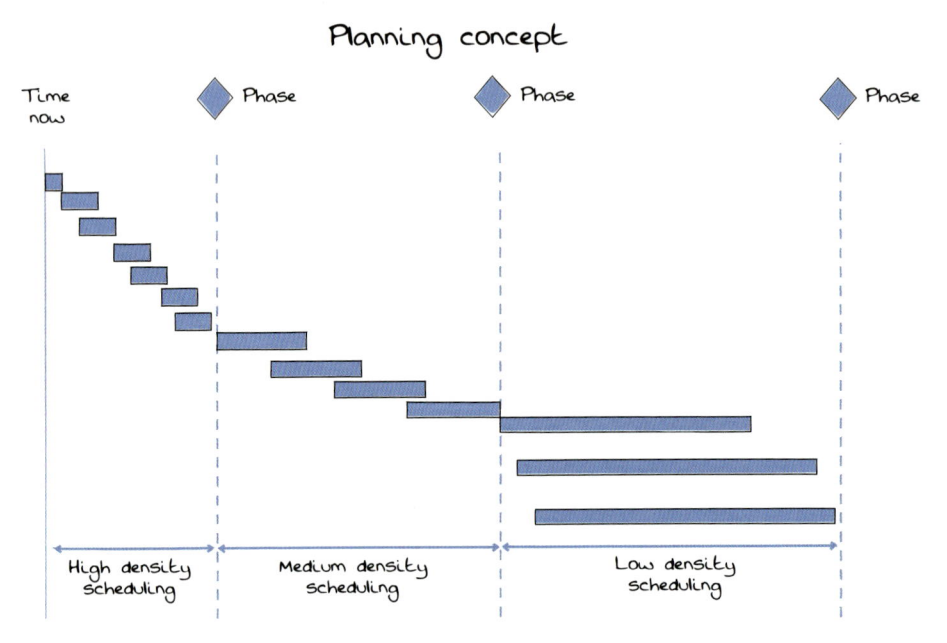

Figure 7.2 Rolling wave planning

It should be noted that each wave end-point is a guide, and, when scheduling out work, each work package should be planned to its natural conclusion, rather than cut at a specific point in time to meet the wave end date. The waves may relate to phases of the project as shown in the illustration above.

7.5.2.3.1 Advantages of rolling wave planning

- It allows an incremental approach to planning high-density detail, to allow project 'unknowns' to be resolved over time rather than at project inception.
- It reduces the level of upfront planning effort required.
- It is suitable for projects with changing or emerging scope, as scope can be added or removed from future waves in a controlled way.
- It allows management of an uncertain schedule.

7.5.2.3.2 Limitations of rolling wave planning

- Effort to plan next rolling wave may divert critical resources from schedule delivery tasks if not planned correctly and incorporated into the original estimates.

Introduction to planning

- There is the possibility that, in future rolling waves, the granularity can be manipulated to display an intended critical path, rather than the actual critical path for the project.
- Lack of detail in future phases may hinder adequate risk analysis.
- Critical path activities are unclear until detail is fully understood in future waves.
- Thus, there is a high probability that the project end date may be affected after each wave of detail is added.

7.5.3 Agile planning in the software industry

7.5.3.1 Definition and purpose of agile planning

Agile planning is a means of adapting rapidly to changes in a business environment. An agile approach integrates planning with execution almost concurrently, allowing early and continuous delivery. For a full definition and purpose statement, see Chapter 20.

7.5.3.2 The agile planning process

Agile planning is similar to rolling wave scheduling. Work is planned as time-boxed iterations called 'sprints'. These are typically 2 to 4 weeks in duration. The sprints can be grouped into versions or 'releases' (see Figure 7.3). Releases that are planned in the near term are shown in more detail than later ones. For example, on a bar chart earlier releases would contain each sprint, but releases

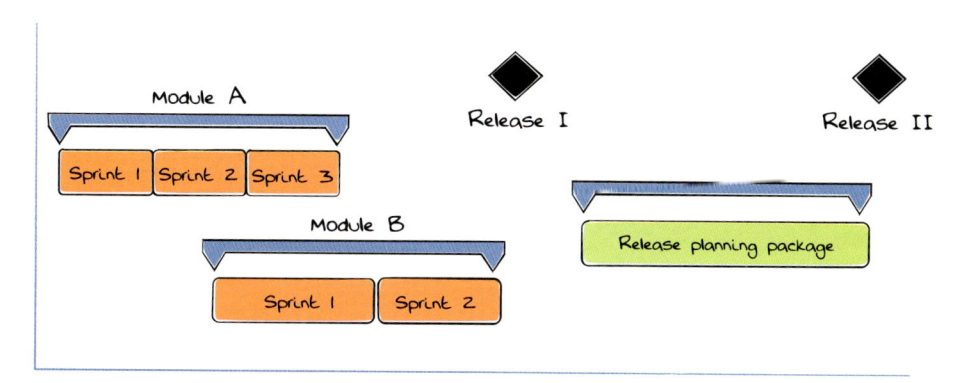

Figure 7.3 Agile planning

Planning, Scheduling, Monitoring and Control

scheduled later in the future might be shown as single releases, using a longer duration.

Not all activities are constrained to sprints; for example, procurement activities or activities involving external stakeholders.

There is a common misconception that is it not possible to reliably develop and use a baseline for an agile project, but this is not the case. Welcoming change does not mean undisciplined or ad hoc delivery. The project still has a vision, a timescale in which the vision needs to be achieved, and a budget. The planning of the sprints is guided by the project vision.

A baseline provides the basis for specifying expected outcomes of each iteration. As a result, customers have the ability to hold the team accountable to the project vision at the end of each iteration and version release.

Being agile means that there is less resistance to changing the schedule; the highest priority is to satisfy the customer by early and continuous delivery of valuable software. Delivery can be prioritised, using the MoSCoW technique, to ensure the prioritisation of critical aspects of the solution:

- Must have: These are the requirements that are completely non-negotiable. Without them, the project will not provide a solution to the customer's problem. Wherever possible, these are the requirements that are developed first, to gain customer trust and confidence in the system, providing early functionality.
- Should have: These are the requirements that are still important, but, with some pain, could in the worst case be taken out; however, there would need to be 'work-arounds' and stakeholder management and buy-in to remove these requirements from the scope of the project.
- Could have: These are the 'nice to have' requirements. Without them, the project solution will still deliver; however, there is value to adding these requirements for a more complete system. These are the requirements which, if time or cost becomes tight, are the first to be cut out of the scope.
- Won't have (this time): These are the requirements that have been agreed by the customer and project team to be non-essential, and are therefore being left out of the scope of the project deliberately. This is not to say, however, that if the project is awarded an extension, or if there is a delay elsewhere, some of these non-essential requirements cannot be added in at a later date if they do not detract from the main project priorities.

Introduction to planning

7.5.3.3 Planning requirements for adopting an agile approach

An agile approach requires the strategy of setting up the project to include:

- development of self-organising teams;
- engagement of business resource throughout the project;
- collaborative approach – paying attention to behaviours is crucial;
- delegated authority suited to agile change needs to be established.

7.6 Planning strategies

As part of the business strategy, it will need to be decided how best to deliver the project. Some of the factors that may influence an adopted strategy would be:

- best commercial solution based on earliest completion;
- most economical solution based on availability of funds;
- the rate at which funds can be committed (sometimes referred to as 'cash-flow');
- availability of resources (labour and material);
- the rate at which the project can be mobilised;
- external factors such as a relationship with other projects.

Once the strategy has been decided upon, it will direct the rest of the planning, estimating and scheduling efforts of the project, potentially imposing constraints and other limitations on the schedule and methods to be adopted.

Different strategies can be described with differing planned value curves. The basic possibilities are based on the critical path method (CPM), which calculates two sets of dates based on the same schedule logic (an early completion and a late completion for each activity). The combination of these forms an envelope in which the works can logically be completed without delaying the desired project completion date (see Figure 7.4).

Relying purely on CPM, the curves produced would not make achievable plans:

- The early curve, though logically possible, relies on every aspect going perfectly to plan, the absence of risk realisation and the availability of unlimited resource. This never happens. This curve is often referred to as the P0 plan, P0 referring to *zero* percent probability of achievement.

Planning, Scheduling, Monitoring and Control

- Working to the late curve may be logically achievable, but will allow no deviation from plan, as all float has been eliminated. If a delay to an activity were to occur, delivery on time or to budget with the existing logic and assumptions would be impossible. Attempting to work to this curve would be to assume that no risk will be realised.

It is not, therefore, appropriate to rely on these sorts of planned values without further refinement, and the use of resource-levelled schedules is therefore recommended in this guide (Chapter 16).

Figure 7.5 shows the effect of applying a resource-levelling exercise to the schedule. It is part of the planning strategy to decide what resources can be applied and what limitations on them are sensible to account for in the project schedule.

Figure 7.5 also shows a line denoted the 'economic best fit'. This is based on constraints around the availability of funds – caps on spending at particular points, for example. A commercial benefit can be achieved from reducing financing costs, but if delivery on time is a priority it will have the effect of adding risk into the project, as it will be harder to recover from unforeseen delays.

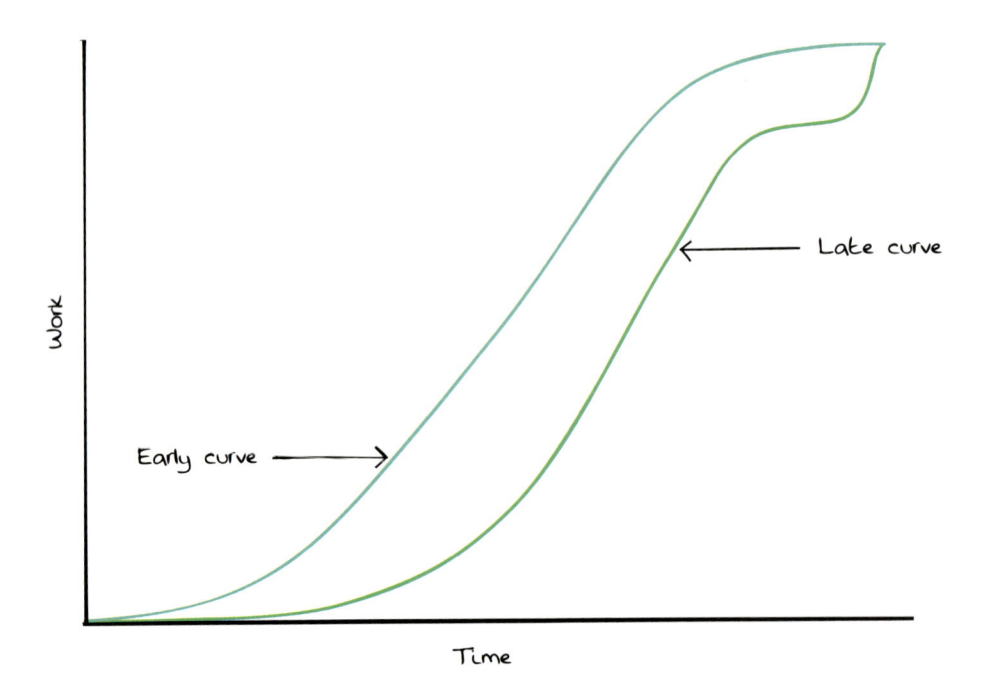

Figure 7.4 Setting early and late curves

Introduction to planning

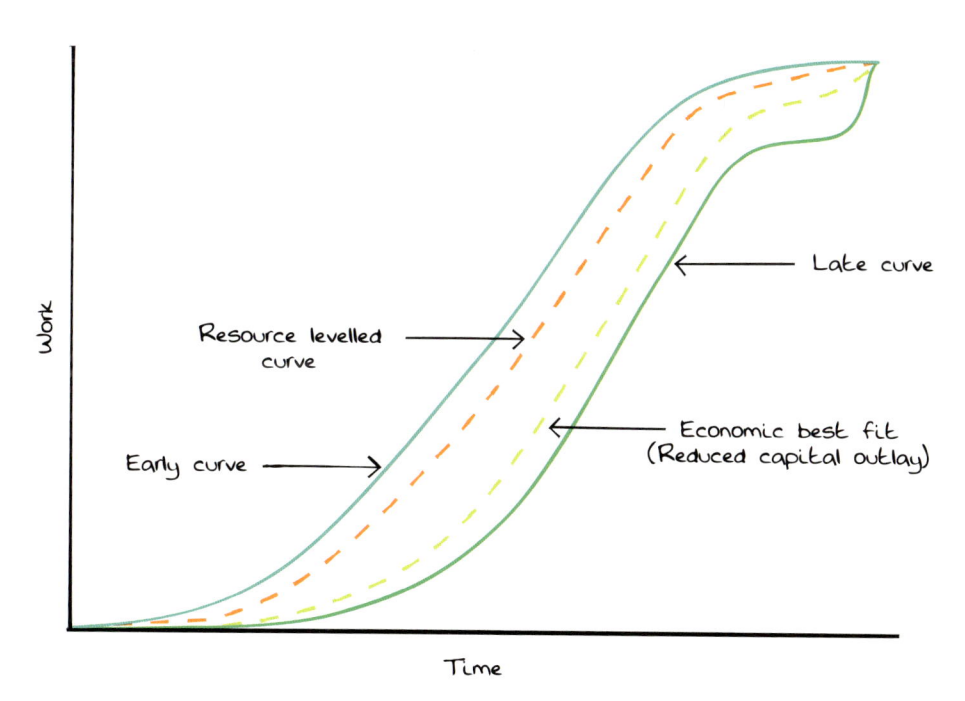

Figure 7.5 Interpreting 'S' curves

7.7 Allowing for risk

The future is unwritten, that is to say uncertain. It is necessary to allow for the unknown when planning for the future. Depending on the stage of the project, it is advisable to allow a 10%–20% time contingency. The former will be applicable at later stages of the project life cycle, such as at the point of going into contract. Chapter 26 will discuss the assessment and management of risk in general, and specifically in relation to time, under the process of quantitative schedule risk analysis (QSRA).

8.1 Definition of breakdown structures

Breakdown structures are tools used to break down the project into smaller elements to facilitate the delegation of responsibility.

8.2 Purpose of breakdown structures

Breakdown structures are used to create discrete packages of work to define responsibility for delivery and to facilitate project control (see Figures 8.1–8.3).

8.3 Creating breakdown structures

8.3.1 Level 1

Level 1 of a breakdown structure is based on the ultimate project output (WBS), the top of an organisation structure (OBS), the highest project-level cost control package (CBS), the highest-level product (PBS), etc

8.3.2 Level 2

The next step is to break out the structure into more manageable levels to make the planning process easier. In the example, the product is now broken down into phases.

Planning, Scheduling, Monitoring and Control

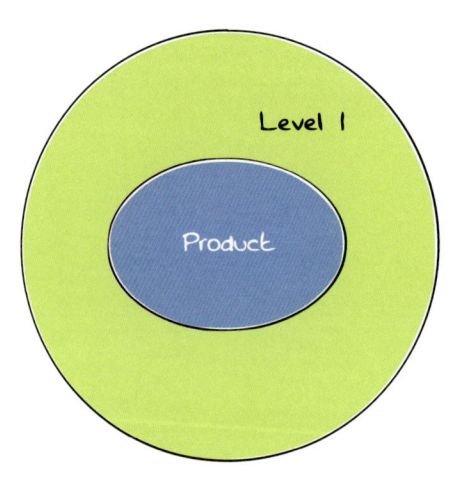

Figure 8.1 Creating a breakdown structure level 1

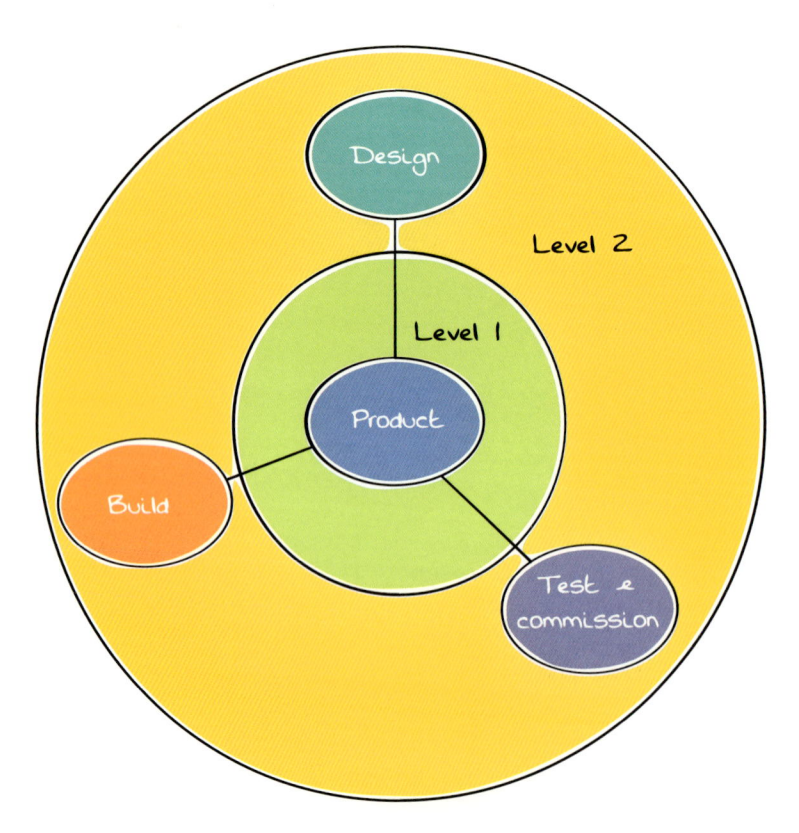

Figure 8.2 Creating a breakdown structure level 2

Breakdown structures

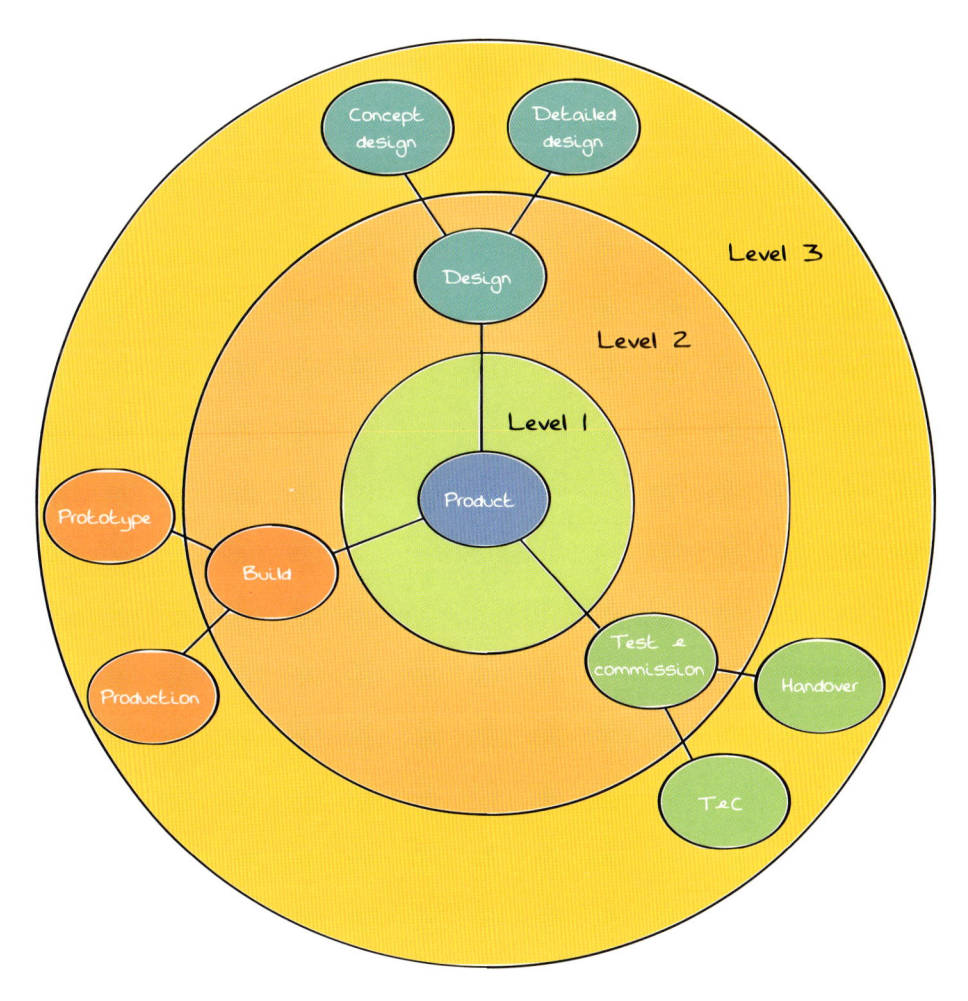

Figure 8.3 Creating a breakdown structure level 3

8.3.3 Level 3 and beyond

This exercise continues until the project team feel that they will be able to define tasks and logical dependencies which deliver the lowest level of a structure (node). At this point there is no need to break out the structure any further.

There are a number of different breakdown structures that a project may employ (Figure 8.4).

Planning, Scheduling, Monitoring and Control

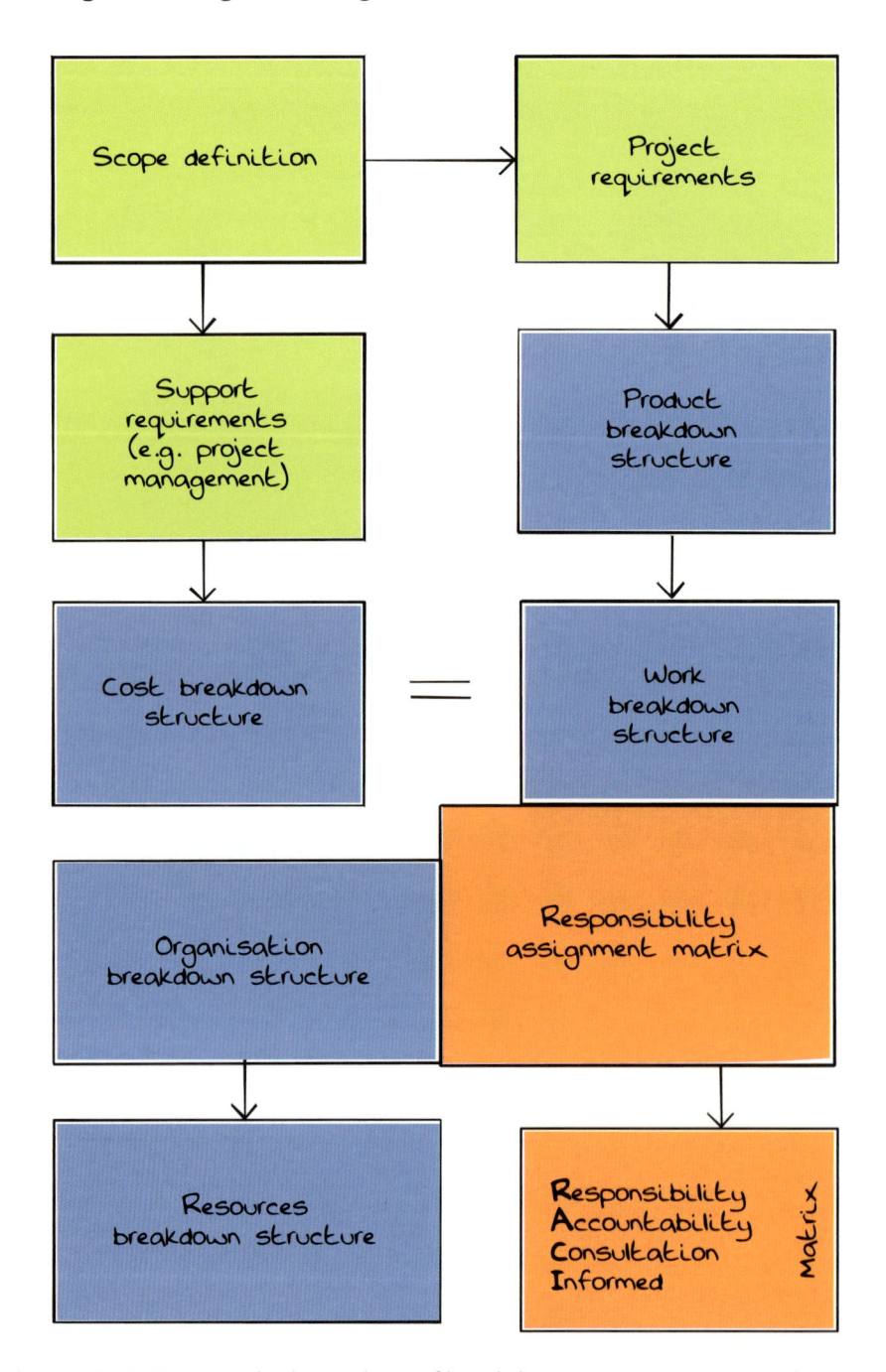

Figure 8.4 Types and relationships of breakdown structures repeated

8.4 Product breakdown structure (PBS)

8.4.1 What is a 'product' in planning terms?

A product is an output which meets the scope or requirement, sometimes referred to as (a) deliverable(s).

8.4.2 Definition of a PBS

A product breakdown structure (PBS) is a key step in a product-based planning approach. It provides a hierarchical tree representation of the relationship between the products and sub-products such as assemblies, sub-assemblies and parts, which contribute to delivering the scope and objectives of a project or programme. It provides the outline framework for planning, contracting, budgeting and reporting. An example is shown in Figure 8.5.

Some examples of products required to manage the project are reports, test documentation, requirement specifications and safety certifications.

8.4.3 Purpose of a PBS

A PBS provides a top-down hierarchical view of all of the products (outputs) within a project. This makes it easier to ensure that all the outputs have been identified before going into the detail of identifying the work packages or activities within a work breakdown structure (WBS). Additionally, the PBS helps create a common understanding of the deliverables in a project, and aids objective progress capture by defining a physical output.

8.4.4 Constructing a PBS

A PBS is developed at the start of a project, once the required scope or requirements have been agreed. The PBS provides a breakdown of all the necessary products (outputs) of a project, whereas a WBS provides a breakdown of the all work packages or areas of the project.

The PBS should be included as part of the project plan and stage plans, with progressively more detail at each level.

To construct a PBS, first identify those products that meet the client/customer's scope or requirements, such as specialist products. (A useful approach is to gather stakeholders together to brainstorm the products needed.)

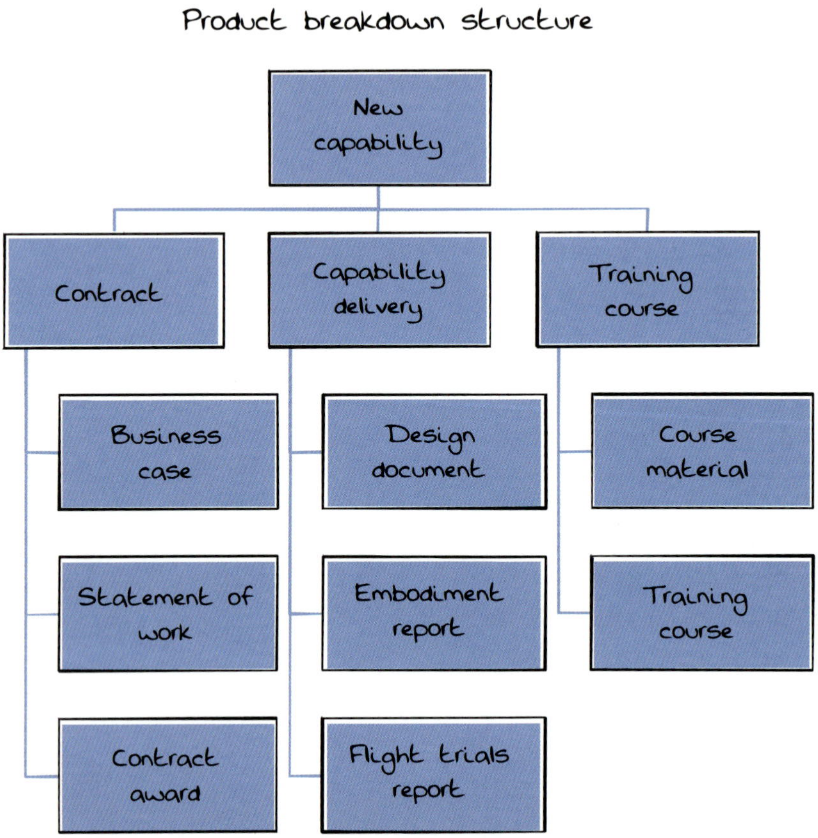

Planning, Scheduling, Monitoring and Control

Product breakdown structure

Figure 8.5 Sample product breakdown structure

The next step is to identify the plans and reports needed to manage products in the project.

A PBS is drawn in a hierarchical structure from the top down. The first box summarises the overall product, with the subsequent branches showing intermediate products such as assemblies, sub-assemblies and components or parts.

It may be useful to break down products into specialist products, which are those products required to meet the scope or requirement, and management products, such as reports and plans.

8.5 Work breakdown structure (WBS)

8.5.1 Definition of a WBS

A work breakdown structure (WBS) is a hierarchical breakdown of the scope or requirement of the project into a series of manageable work packages or areas that can be estimated, planned and assigned to the appropriate person or department for completion. It can be based on design systems, construction/installation zones or individually commissionable systems. An example is shown in Figure 8.6.

8.5.2 Purpose of a WBS

A major benefit of the WBS is that it breaks down the work required within a project into work packages or areas, which can be assigned to a responsible party. Once a project has been broken into small packages of work, there is a better chance of understanding what needs to be done.

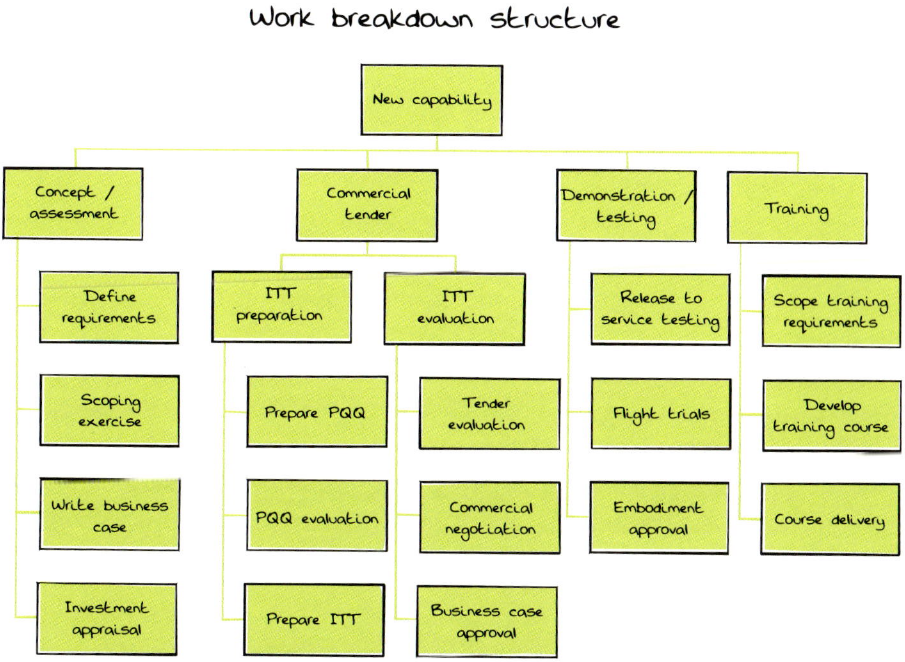

Figure 8.6 Work breakdown structure

Planning, Scheduling, Monitoring and Control

The WBS provides a common framework for the development of the planning and control of a project. It divides work into definable work packages from which a statement of work can be developed and technical, schedule, cost and resource reporting can be established. Individual work packages or areas of the WBS may be broken down further to give better schedule segregation.

A WBS code must be applied in order to identify the work packages within the project in a logical manner. This then forms the basis for accurate reporting and mapping of time, cost and resources.

Each section of the WBS or work package can then be assessed to:

- describe what the work is;
- estimate how long it will take;
- estimate the resources and costs;
- identify who needs to be involved;
- work out the potential threats and opportunities.

A WBS can be combined with an organisational breakdown structure (OBS) to produce a responsibility assignment matrix (RAM) showing the responsibility for each work package.

8.5.3 Constructing a WBS

A WBS is initially developed at the start of the project and is reviewed iteratively at the beginning of each stage as a minimum.

It is good practice to use a WBS when developing any project schedule.

If a product breakdown structure has already been produced, this provides a good breakdown of all necessary products and outputs of a project, and can form the primary input to the WBS.

Note: in the construction sector the WBS is more usually used to identify geographical areas where work will be carried out. However, the hierarchy principle still applies.

The individual work packages may themselves be further sub-divided down to individual activities. The key thing about the WBS is the ability to break down the project into work packages that can be assigned to a resource.

8.5.4 Principles of designing a WBS

There are three principles that should be applied when designing a WBS:

Breakdown structures

8.5.4.1 The 100% rule

The WBS should define the total scope of the project and capture all deliverables, both internal and external, including project management:

- The sum of the work at the 'child' level must equal 100% of the work represented by the 'parent'.
- The WBS should not include any work that falls outside the actual scope of the project, i.e. it cannot include more than 100% of the work.

8.5.4.2 'Parent/child' relationship

There should be no overlap in scope definition between any two elements in a WBS. Each 'child' element of work should only be associated with one 'parent'. If not, then you run the risk of duplicating work in the project execution, and would therefore exceed the 100% rule!

8.5.4.3 Use common sense

- Remember the aim is to define the work of the project so that it can be planned, managed and controlled.
- Therefore, there needs to be a sufficient level of detail in the WBS, but:
- Do not decompose the WBS to a level beyond that necessary to achieve these aims.

8.5.5 WBS dictionaries

A work breakdown structure dictionary is sometimes used on more complex projects.

8.5.5.1 Definition of a WBS dictionary

A WBS dictionary is a tool that helps to clearly define the work content of each WBS node. This helps to ensure a consistent and coherent approach to the project and clearly defines the key deliverables for each WBS node.

In construction, the WBS dictionary is often called the work package scope sheet, and is a key document in defining scope and the key interfaces with other

Planning, Scheduling, Monitoring and Control

works. In other words, it is a tool to identify scope gaps or overlaps and assist in their elimination.

8.5.5.2 Purpose of a WBS dictionary

WBS dictionaries can be used with the customer to ensure that the scope of work to be undertaken is agreed by all contracting parties. When a project is up and running, change control of the WBS and associated dictionaries should be applied. An example of a WBS dictionary is shown in Figure 8.7.

In addition to the fields illustrated, additional information may be contained in a WBS dictionary, such as clarification to suppliers or sub-contractors of services or free issue materials to be provided (or not) to the supplier by the contractor or client. See Figure 8.8 for an example.

WBS number:	1.1.1.2
Work breakdown element title:	Design sensor system

Work breakdown element description:
- Produce the design, documentation and design evidence of the sensor system
- Documentation and evidence completion of the Preliminary Design Review (PDR)
- Documentation and evidence completion of the Critical Design Review (CDR)
- Drawings to be produced at a standard for the production of prototype sensor system

Dependencies:	• Physical space dimensions available • Electrical power availability to the sensor defined • Availability of cooling supply
Key deliverables:	• Certificates of completion of PDR & CDR • Drawings at production standard
Assumptions:	• Sub system supplier details available • Uses standard industry connectors
Responsible manager:	G. N. Hindley

Issue:	Date:	Authorised:
02	12/12/12	A. Dent

Figure 8.7 Work breakdown structure dictionary (defence)

Breakdown structures

PROJECT TITLE:	Station upgrade project		
DOC NO.	H2-G2-DA-1001	CBS REF.	DLA42
WBS NO.	DL-42	WP TITLE	Partitions & dry lining
ISSUE DATE	12-Oct-79	REVISION	B

WORK PACKAGE CONTENT:

- All partitions and dry lining detailed on the listed drawings
- Studwork, plasterboard and insulation infill, where specified
- Includes taping and jointing to allow decoration by others
- Provide and fit Pattresses as specified to receive fixtures and fittings by others. Setting out by others
- Provide cut outs for fittings supplied and installed by others. Setting out of these by others
- Allow for 3 visits to each partition: First fix studwork and one side boarding; second fix second side boarding; Third Fix Taping and jointing
- Trim details as shown on drawings H2-G2-DA-DRG 1060 to 1075

WORK PACKAGE DESIGN SCOPE

- Record drawings and O & M manuals
- H & S file

DRAWINGS & INFORMATION ISSUED WITH TENDER

ATTENDANCES		TENDERERS/CONTRACTOR
Shared welfare facilities	YES/NO	
Shared first aid facilities	YES/NO	
Temporary water supply	YES/NO	
Temporary power supply	YES/NO	
Common user plant:		

KEY DATES

DESIGN STAGE x		START ON SITE	
DESIGN STAGE x		Key date 1	
OUT TO TENDER		Key date 2	
CONTRACT AWARD		COMPLETION	

Figure 8.8 Work package content sheet (construction)

Planning, Scheduling, Monitoring and Control

8.6 Organisational breakdown structure (OBS)

8.6.1 Definition of an OBS

Within product-based planning, the organisational breakdown structure (OBS) is a top-down hierarchical representation of the management structure and people within a project. It is used to convey the communication routes and reporting lines within the project. A project's OBS may differ from that of the organisation. See Figure 8.9 for an example.

8.6.2 Purpose of an OBS

An OBS is a useful tool – in conjunction with the WBS – for planning projects that interface with complex organisations. It is used to show the project organisation structured in a hierarchical manner. When used in conjunction with the WBS, the OBS helps in producing the responsibility assignment matrix (RAM).

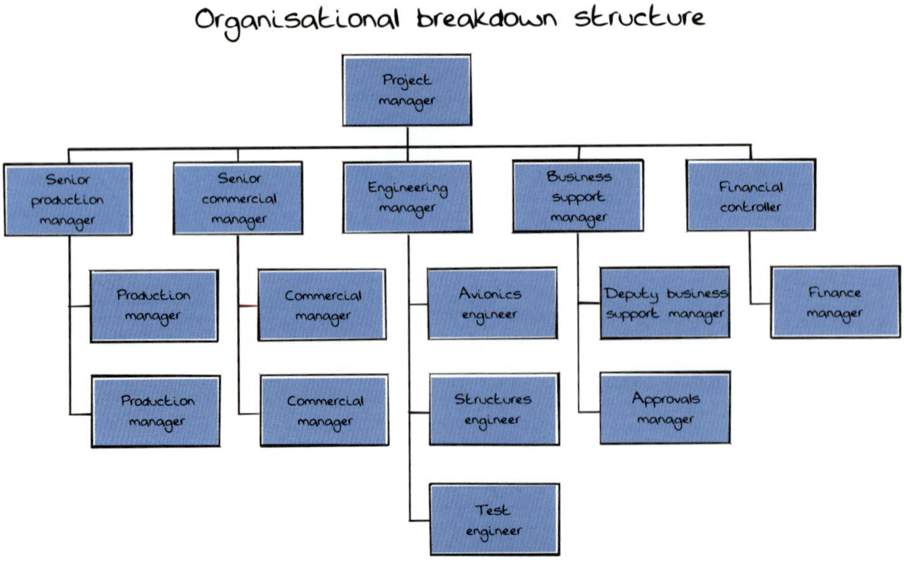

Figure 8.9 Organisation breakdown structure

Breakdown structures

8.6.3 Constructing an OBS

The OBS is initially developed at the start of the project and is reviewed iteratively at the beginning of each stage as a minimum.

An OBS is created by:

- First, identifying the organisational structure for the resources involved in the project.
- This should then be broken out into the areas or departments, sub-areas or sub-departments and down to the role that will be accountable for a WBS element.
- This is then drawn out as a hierarchical organisational tree, showing the reporting lines and communication paths.

8.7 Responsibility assignment matrix (RAM)

8.7.1 Definition of a RAM

A responsibility assignment matrix (RAM) (see Figure 8.10) is a project management tool, often depicted as a table, that shows the project organisational breakdown structure (OBS) in relation to the work breakdown structure (WBS) to ensure that each element of the scope of work is assigned to a responsible team or individual. Larger projects may define RAMs at multiple levels.

A high-level RAM defines which group or organisational unit or team is responsible for each component of the WBS. Lower-level RAMs can be used within teams to assign roles and responsibilities for specific activities to individuals.

(There is an alternative breakdown known as a £ RAM, which is discussed under the heading of Cost breakdown structures, section 8.9.)

8.7.2 Purpose of a RAM

The RAM provides a view of all work packages, or at a lower level, activities. It is used within the project to communicate the required work to stakeholders.

65

Planning, Scheduling, Monitoring and Control

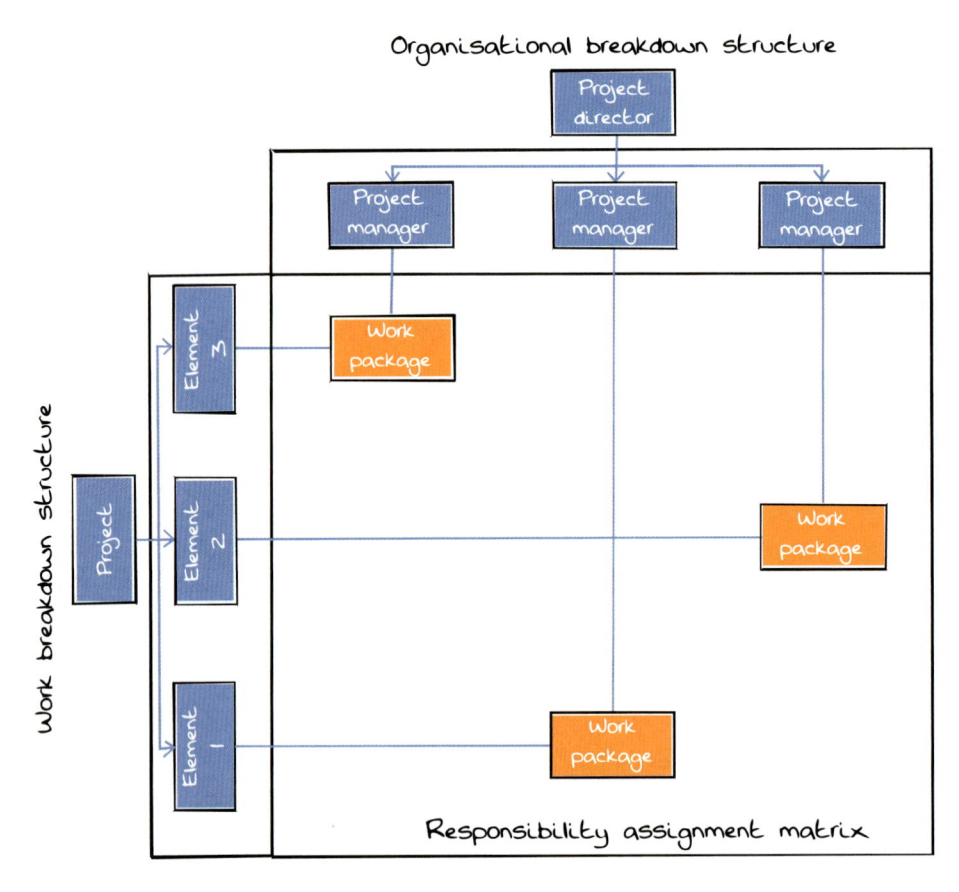

Figure 8.10 Responsibility assignment matrix

It is used to show the accountability for the various work packages or activities within the project team.

The RAM can form the basis for scheduling activities and is a key input when developing the network diagram or Gantt chart.

8.7.3 Constructing a RAM

It is developed at the start of a project where there is a complex division of responsibilities, when the scope has been agreed, the deliverables have been defined and a WBS and OBS have been created.

Breakdown structures

The OBS will be combined with the WBS to create a RAM. Generally, it is shown as a grid with the WBS elements on the left-hand side and the OBS resources across the top, marked at the appropriate intersections to indicate who is doing what. (Sometimes the RAM is drawn the other way around, with the WBS at the top and the OBS at the left.)

8.7.4 The step-by-step approach to constructing a RAM

- **Define your deliverables**. A WBS is a project planning tool used to break a project down into smaller, more manageable pieces of work, called work packages. Work packages can then be broken down further into individual activities and their associated deliverables.
- **Identify the people involved**. An OBS maps the resources available. Create a chart of accountable individuals at departmental or sub-departmental level. For lower-level RAMs, this can cover individuals within the department or sub-department.
- **Create the responsibility assignment matrix**. Draw a matrix. The deliverables form the row headings, and the resources are listed as column titles. Determine responsibilities for each item in the WBS. Note that only one individual should be accountable for any discrete element of work. Lower-level RAMs can record responsibilities for activities within a work package.
- **Assign other roles**. For each section, work package or activity, a RACI analysis (see 8.8) can be used to record who is accountable for that work package or activity, and who should be consulted or informed during its execution. Table 8.1 shows the definition for RACI analysis, though there are other responsibility analysis models.
- **Communicate**. Ensure all groups and roles are informed of their responsibilities.

8.8 RACI matrix

8.8.1 Definition of a RACI matrix

The RACI matrix is a tool used for identifying roles and responsibilities to avoid confusion over those roles and responsibilities during the project. The acronym RACI is explained in Table 8.1.

Table 8.1 *Explanation of RACI codes*

Interest	Definition
R = Responsible	Conducts the actual work/owns the problem
A = Accountable	Approves the completed work and is held fully accountable for it. Usually one accountable role
C = Consulted	Kept fully informed and included in decision making. Primary supportive role
I = Informed	Kept informed of progress and results

8.8.2 Purpose of a RACI matrix

A RACI diagram is a clear and concise summary of tasks or deliverables (or, rather, the specific responsibilities contained within project procedures) and the level of accountability or contribution required from named roles or individuals within the project.

8.8.3 Constructing a RACI matrix

The matrix is developed when the scope has been agreed, the deliverables have been defined and a WBS and OBS have been created.

- **Define your tasks or deliverables**. Identify all the tasks involved in delivering the project. These are listed on the left-hand side of the chart.
- **Identify the people involved**. These are defined in terms of roles, not individuals, and are listed along the top of the chart, as shown in Figure 8.11.
- **Create the RACI matrix**. Complete the chart showing who has responsibility, who has accountability and who will be consulted and informed for each task.
- **Check for accountability**. Ensure that every task has a role responsible and a role accountable for it. No task should have more than one person accountable.
- **Communicate**. Ensure that all groups and roles are informed of their responsibilities. Agree the RACI with project stakeholders before the project starts.

Breakdown structures

Workpackage	Project sponsor	Project board	Project manager	Project support – communications	Project support – procurement	Analysis & design lead	Household collections lead	Industrial collections lead	Wood processing lead	Commercial products lead
Project management	C	C	AR	C	C	C	C	C	C	C
Analysis & design activity	C	C	A	I	I	R	I	I	I	C
Define operational procedures	I	I	A			C	R	R	R	C
Recruitment activities	I	I	AR				I	I	R	I
Training	I	I	AR	I			R	R	R	I
Deliver new facilities	I	I	A	I	C	C	I	I	R	I
Communications	C	C	A	R	I	I	I	I	I	I
Launch new services	C	C	AR	C			C	C	C	C

Figure 8.11 Example of a RACI

8.9 Cost breakdown structure (CBS)

8.9.1 Definition of a CBS

A cost breakdown structure defines the level at which costs will be collected. Unlike the WBS, it has no hierarchy as such (or, at least, no particular need for one), as it comprises a list of cost headings. It is directly related to the WBS, possibly at different levels, as illustrated in Figure 8.12.

8.9.2 Purpose of a CBS

The CBS will be created and structured at a sufficient level of detail to allow budgets to be set, and costs to be collected, recorded, monitored and controlled. Thus, it must be mirrored in the organisation's accounting system as well as the project's reporting system. In some organisations, the CBS will be set as a

Planning, Scheduling, Monitoring and Control

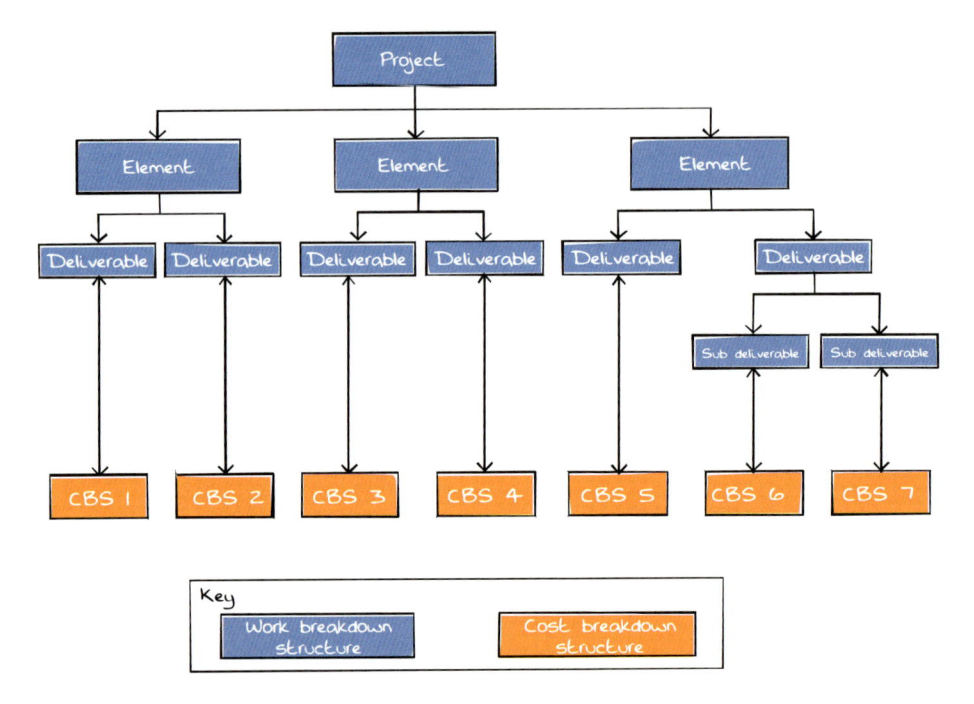

Figure 8.12 Cost breakdown structure

standard and therefore imposed upon the project. In practice, this could influence (or possibly hinder) the project reporting system, so it needs to be taken into account in the establishment of all breakdown structures. Indeed, it may be necessary in these circumstances to put a project specific cost collection system in place, which will require serious design and specification, as well as new business processes and training.

The CBS is sometimes known as the '£ RAM', for example in the defence sector.

8.10 Resources breakdown structure

8.10.1 Definition of a RBS

A resource breakdown structure (RBS) is a hierarchical structure that groups resources that are required to deliver the scope by function, type and grade. Resources may include personnel (defined individually or by discipline), tools, machinery, materials and equipment. Any resource that incurs a cost should be included in the RBS.

8.10.2 Purpose of a RBS

The RBS will be created and structured at a sufficient level of detail to allow the work to be scheduled, monitored and controlled.

9.1 Definition of dependency management

Dependency management is the process of monitoring and controlling the key interfaces on a project.

9.2 Purpose of dependency management

On a typical project there are many interfaces. For the smooth and efficient running of a project, interfaces need to be carefully and regularly monitored and controlled.

At a high level they can be between different organisations:

- suppliers;
- disciplines;
- client;
- third parties;
- sub-contractors;
- other agencies (more typically in Ministry of Defence projects).

Within the project, there can be interfaces for the following:

- approval gateways;
- design reviews;
- client assurance reviews;
- consultation;
- discipline integration/coordination.

9.3 Interface scope

It is important that the scope of the interface between the parties is defined, agreed and, if appropriate, documented. There will be inputs and outputs, and it is important that these are defined and documented to ensure that they align.

Milestones will be introduced into schedules to represent each interface. Whilst the fundamental purpose of the interface milestone is to highlight the passing of a section or piece of work to another party, they may also prove to be a useful way of monitoring progress and performance.

9.4 Schedule impact

Wherever the interface is in the schedule, it can have a significant impact on other activities. For example, an interface may relate to the handover of a piece of work from one team to another. So, if the 'giving' party is late, it could have a detrimental impact on the 'receiving' party, perhaps causing a critical delay to a key milestone. Consequently, there is a need to communicate progress of the interfaces between both parties, for example:

- Is the piece of work likely to be completed early, late or on time?
- Is the piece of work required earlier than originally advised due to changing circumstances?
- Are there any other changes affecting the scope of the interface?

Since the consequences of interfaces can include delays to the 'receiving' party, or acceleration to the 'giving' party, there can be expensive consequences if they are not well managed. The creation of a separate schedule to enable proactive management of dependencies is discussed in Chapter 16.

Health, safety and environment (HSE) is a key area of risk that needs to be planned and managed. Since it is important and strategic in terms of project success, it must be driven from the very top of the organisation and be given at least equal status to other disciplines when planning a project. Considering HSE at the planning level allows all activities required to complete the project to be allowed for, and, perhaps more importantly, safety to be considered when methodologies are derived, such that any unnecessary safety risks are planned out of the project.

It should be recognised that all change must be considered in the light of HSE concerns, as accidents and near misses are frequently caused by last-minute changes of plan, which by their nature may not have received full consideration in the way that long-planned activities have.

From a scheduling point of view, it is important to consider any health, safety and environmental aspects that will need to be incorporated into the schedule. Whilst this guide is not a comprehensive guide to HSE issues, this section touches on some important issues to be considered in the planning and scheduling of a project.

10.1 HSE issues at strategic level (planning)

Health and safety should always be the first priority on any project, but there are some industries where there will be an even greater emphasis: e.g. rail, airports, nuclear and petro-chem. In addition, any project that has an interface with the public will need to make special provisions to ensure the protection of the public. This is likely to involve consultation with various local authorities and emergency services to ensure that the effect on the public and these services is considered and their requirements must be complied with. When designing the schedule, it is important to do so with the relevant level of safety in mind. For example, the aforementioned industries would all require labour to have special training/security clearance prior to being able to work on site.

It is essential that project working areas are established with a clear set of rules and responsibilities:

- Methodology: for example, pre-fabrication off site; sequencing to avoid the need for rework, trades working out of sequence or last-minute changes.
- Time must be allowed in the schedule for obtaining necessary safety permits, which in some industries may take months.

10.2 HSE issues at tactical level (scheduling and method statements)

At tactical level, planning for health and safety is about the sequencing of tasks at a detailed level; some factors to consider include:

- Ensure that safe protection is provided to all workforces, and safety zones are created around dangerous operations.
- Ensure segregation of workforce and public – in particular, safe access and egress of large vehicles and plant from construction sites or assembly plants.
- Segregation within the project environment is also essential where it can be managed – for example, the separation of machines and people.
- Ensure the security of the project.

As part of the planning, method selection and scheduling process, safety items should be considered. Any hazards that are identified must be reported to the relevant authorities or line management.

This guide does not seek to give industry-specific advice, but the principle of considering HSE in the strategic and tactical planning of work is an obligation on all involved in planning.

11.1 Definition of cost estimating

Cost estimating is the process used to quantify the cost of services, materials and resources required to deliver a project.

An estimate should be robust and repeatable. The estimate should contain the source information used to calculate the estimate and associated assumptions.

11.2 Purpose of a cost estimate

The purpose of a cost estimate is to determine the likely cost of the project. It may have a number of uses, for example to create budgets, to draft proposals, to tender for work or to get approval for research studies. Depending on its purpose, the scope and detail of the cost estimate will vary.

11.3 Cost estimating and the project life cycle

Cost estimating has four main stages, as shown in Figure 11.1.

Planning, Scheduling, Monitoring and Control

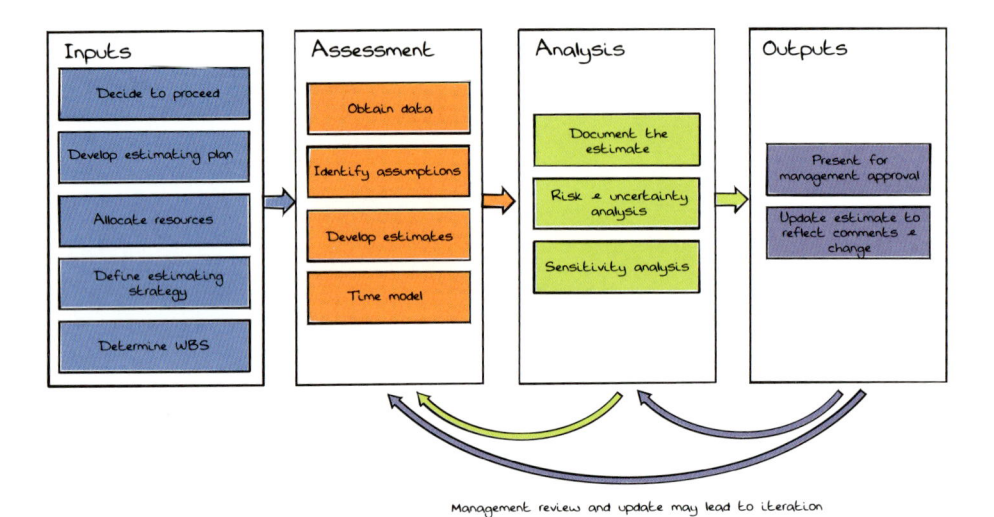

Figure 11.1 Cost estimating process

11.4 Estimate types

Estimates are produced at various stages throughout the project life cycle and for various purposes. The type of estimate to be prepared and the methodology to be employed are dependent on the purpose of the estimate and the level of scope definition.

11.4.1 Scope development estimates

The types of estimate that support the different stages of scope development typically fall into three broad categories:

11.4.1.1 Planning

The planning stage is the earliest stage in scope development. Typically estimates are termed 'conceptual' or 'pre-conceptual' and will rely primarily on approximate methods. Estimates prepared at this stage of the planning process may be termed order of magnitude (OM) or rough order of magnitude (ROM).

Cost estimating

11.4.1.2 Preliminary

The preliminary stage is the next stage in scope definition. Preliminary estimates should use definitive methods for the next stage of scope definition; however, it is acceptable to use approximate methods for those areas of scope remaining undefined.

11.4.1.3 Definitive

The definitive stage is the final stage in scope development. Definitive estimates are prepared using definitive (detailed) estimating methods.

11.4.2 Other types of estimate

Other types of estimate prepared at various points in the project life cycle include:

11.4.2.1 Optioneering

Optioneering estimates are prepared to establish the cost differences between two or more alternative strategies in order to arrive at ranking of alternatives to inform an economic decision. Both approximate and definitive methods are appropriate for these types of estimates, depending on the level of scope definition. These are described later in this section.

11.4.2.2 Fair Price

A fair price estimate is used to determine the reasonableness of competitive or sole source bids received in connection with a proposed sub-contract, and serves as a control in evaluating cost and pricing data in a contract negotiation. These estimates are used in support of change orders or sub-contract compensation event evaluations. The estimate should be produced against an identical scope to that provided to the sub-contractor. Confidentiality of the estimate is essential at all stages of the process.

11.4.2.3 Independent cost estimate

Independent cost estimates are estimates prepared by external or third parties with the express purpose of validating, cross-checking or analysing estimates developed by project teams.

11.5 Contents of an estimate

Estimates should be established after the completion of the project definition phase and in conjunction with other elements of the planning phase. That is:

- They should be based on the defined scope and requirements.
- They should be based on established codes and standards.
- They should be based on the selected procurement planning or contracting strategy.
- They should correlate with the schedule (i.e. allowances for time in the estimate should match those in the schedule).
- They should recognise the available resources.
- They should be based on any known unit rates, with productivity assumptions taken into account.
- They should recognise any stated exclusions.

An estimate should contain both a robust base estimate and a realistic contingency budget.

11.6 Estimating methodologies

The estimating methodology to be employed is directly related to the stage of scope development. These are typically divided into 'approximate' and 'definitive' methods.

Approximate methods should be used for estimating projects in the longer term, with definitive methods being used as the project moves towards and into the near term.

Depending on the estimate purpose and the scope definition, different phases of the project may require different estimating methods. It is, therefore, not uncommon to include both definitive and approximate estimating techniques within the same project estimate.

The main estimating methodologies within these categories are as follows.

11.6.1 Approximate estimating methods

11.6.1.1 Specific analogy estimating

This method of estimating is based upon selecting a costed project that is similar or related to the project costs being estimated. It uses the known cost of

Cost estimating

an item/activity used in the prior project as the basis for the cost of a similar item/activity in the new project. Adjustments are made to account for differences in relative size/complexity of performance, design or operational characteristics. This approach works well for derivative or evolutionary projects but is unsuitable for radical changes or substantially different projects.

11.6.1.2 Parametric estimating (estimating norms)

Parametric estimating uses a methodology that is based on elements of cost extracted or gleaned from historical data acquired from similar systems or subsystems. The data is analysed to find correlations between cost drivers and other system parameters, such as size, design or performance, to derive cost estimating relationships (CERs) that can be scaled and applied to similar systems in different projects to determine likely costs. The derived correlations are expressed as equations or cost estimating relationships, which can be simple cost factor ratios or more complex relational equations. The parametric approach enables costs to be generated quickly from limited data. Care needs to be exercised to ensure that the project being estimated is within the bounds of the CER selected.

The major difference between analogy estimates and parametric estimates is that the parametric estimates use a database of out-turn data from completed projects upon which to base the cost estimate, whereas the analogy estimate may use data from as few as one or two completed projects.

11.6.1.3 Delphi technique

This is a technique based on the principle that estimates from an experienced and structured panel can provide a useful judgement-based output. This approach can be used where analogous or parametric data is not available. Several specialists are consulted in a systematic manner using a series of questionnaires, and answers are then refined based upon feedback from the panel. The range of answers will gradually decrease until a consensus estimate is established. Expert judgement estimates tend to become more accurate as more experts are consulted. It is important to note that responses are kept anonymous to ensure impartial advice is given.

Planning, Scheduling, Monitoring and Control

11.6.2 Definitive estimating methods

11.6.2.1 Detailed

Generally based upon a specification and set of drawings which are used to 'take-off' measured quantities of work required to perform each discrete task to which known or standard unit rates can be applied. Also known as 'bottom-up', 'measured quants', 'full detail' or 'unit cost'. For a design, engineering or services estimate, it should be based on quantified deliverables (drawings, reports, safety cases, etc.) for which established norms are available.

11.6.2.2 'Activity-based cost' (ABC) estimating

ABC estimating is based upon application of a composite all-in rate to a specified team or crew of workers. This method of estimating organises the work into activities that will be accomplished by a specific gang or team of workers. The estimated time taken to complete the work activity is multiplied by the composite hourly rate for the gang, together with additions for materials and equipment. Examples include dismantling and decommissioning redundant nuclear facilities.

11.6.2.3 Task analysis

The activity is broken down into discretely estimated resource types and quantities (labour, materials, equipment, etc.) required to perform the activity, which is then priced at known or standard unit rates. (Also known as 'resource-based estimating'.)

11.6.2.4 Level of effort/business-as-usual/prelims

Used when a minimum level of support is required regardless of the number of tasks to be carried out or in the absence of measurable or quantifiable outputs. This method should be reserved strictly for management and support-type activities that cannot be assigned to a specific work scope or quantifiable deliverables.

12.1 Definition of budgeting

Budgeting is the process of allocating appropriate budgets to different parts of the work breakdown structure. Budgets are often expressed in terms of money, but may equally be described in terms of other resources such as labour, plant or materials.

12.2 Purpose of budgeting

Budgets are set in order to set cost performance targets for the procurement and delivery of the project. The budget will become the basis for a true comparison with actual costs incurred during the life of a project (either in a cost value report, or in earned value analysis). In the former case, the budget will produce the 'value' numbers. In earned value analysis it will form the basis of the planned and earned value.

12.3 Funding and budgets

Funds represent the money available for expenditure in the accomplishment of the effort, and must not be confused with budgets; funds are spent, not budgets.

The estimate at completion provides the project team with visibility of the expected out-turn of costs and therefore the funds that will be required to complete the project. Performance against the budget will be used as an indicator of the rate of spend until completion of the project.

Planning, Scheduling, Monitoring and Control

A business's financial budget is based on identification and management of project budgets in line with available capital expenditure (funds). This is an iterative process usually done on an annual basis.

12.4 Producing a cost budget

12.4.1 Cost breakdown structure

Cost budgets usually start with a procurement strategy, an estimate and the cost breakdown structure. Once contracts are let, the cost information is organised by contract deliverables and mapped to work packages for the purpose of budgeting. Table 12.1 shows an example of a simple cost budget.

When the project's budget is produced, it is important to ensure that there is a direct link between the project's estimated costs and activities within the schedule (CBS and WBS). Most modern planning tools will provide a cost profile based on the time-phased activities and schedule logic. As the project progresses, it is important to maintain an alignment of cost and time so you can forecast as accurately as possible, see Figure 12.1.

12.4.2 Cash-flow statements

Once budgets have been distributed, it has sometimes been traditional practice to create cost or cash-flow forecasts in spreadsheets. Often this is done from a top-down approach, and this is very disjointed from the schedule. It is, therefore, unlikely that meaningful results will be achieved, and certainly it is not easy to adjust and realign these forecasts as the working schedule changes. Thus, it is preferable to use scheduling software to produce forecasts. The budgets are allocated to activities (note: not summary bars) in the project schedule.

Table 12.1 *A simple cost budget*

CBS Id No	Contractor	Work package	Budget
1	Blogs & Son	Concept Design	£1,000
2	Smith Inc.	Detailed Design	£5,000
3	Big Build Co.	Build	£50,000
4	Internal Costs	PM Cost	£2,000

Budgeting

CBS Id No	Contractor	Work package	Budget
1	Blogs & Son	Concept design	£1,000
2	Smith Inc.	Detailed design	£5,000
3	Big Build Co.	Build	£50,000

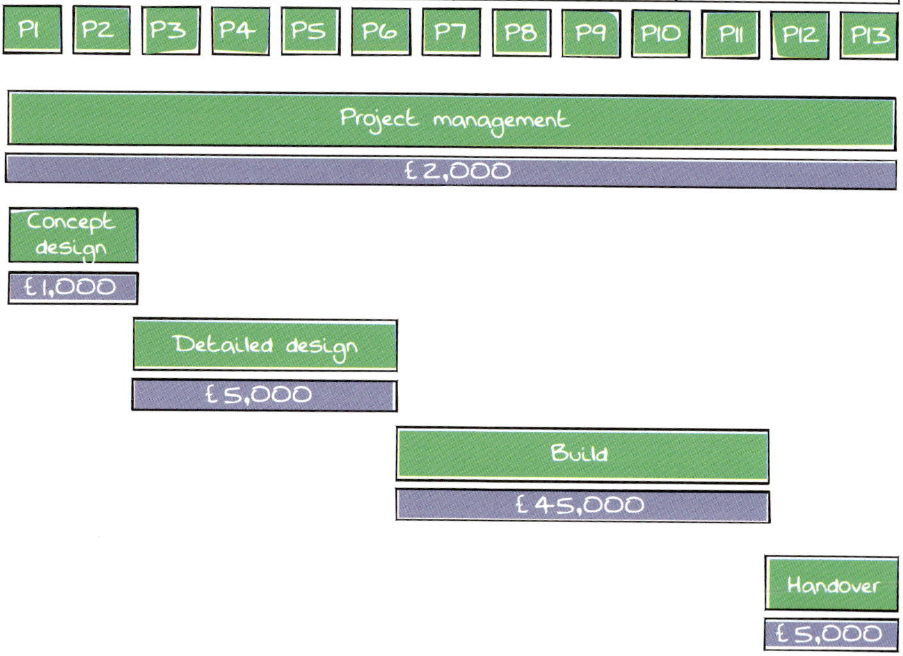

P1 P2 P3 P4 P5 P6 P7 P8 P9 P10 P11 P12 P13

Project management
£2,000

Concept design
£1,000

Detailed design
£5,000

Build
£45,000

Handover
£5,000

Figure 12.1 Time measured in financial periods

Once the budget is allocated in the scheduling software, 'S-curves' can be drawn. These will most likely be based on the early dates, as this is how scheduling software usually defaults. In reality, these activities may have an element of float and are subject to unforeseen change. When attempting to forecast costs, it is important to factor in these variances, otherwise you risk putting an overly aggressive or optimistic financial view to the project manager and business.

Planning, Scheduling, Monitoring and Control

Alternatively, 'S-curves' may be drawn based on late dates. This is equally flawed, as it would be hopelessly pessimistic. No project should assume that late dates are acceptable to work to, as they would make completion on time unachievable – unless the project encounters no risk realisation, no resource limitation and no failure of any other kind. This never happens.

One way to factor in reality is to use a 'mid curve' or 'banana curve' (Figure 12.2). This process uses schedule logic to plot an early and a late curve and calculates the midpoint between the two. This then allows for a portion of project float to be consumed and presents a more realistic cost forecast whilst keeping the schedule aggressive and the project team focused on early completion.

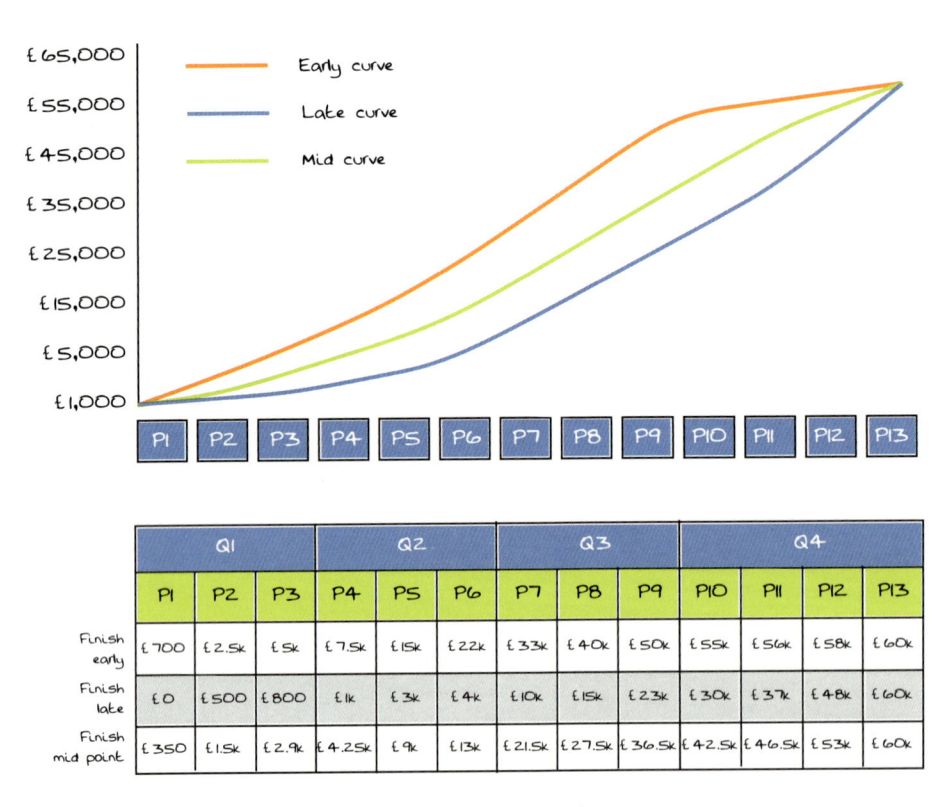

	Q1			Q2			Q3			Q4			
	P1	P2	P3	P4	P5	P6	P7	P8	P9	P10	P11	P12	P13
Finish early	£700	£2.5k	£5k	£7.5k	£15k	£22k	£33k	£40k	£50k	£55k	£56k	£58k	£60k
Finish late	£0	£500	£800	£1k	£3k	£4k	£10k	£15k	£23k	£30k	£37k	£48k	£60k
Finish mid point	£350	£1.5k	£2.9k	£4.25k	£9k	£13k	£21.5k	£27.5k	£36.5k	£42.5k	£46.5k	£53k	£60k

Figure 12.2 Generating a cost forecast using a banana curve

12.5 Budget transfers

Budget transfers are made through a change control process to formalise the movement of scope (budget and schedule) from one part of the project to another, or to move scope into or out of the project.

A secondary reason for budget transfer may be the reallocation of budgets in order to correct data errors, but this must be done through a formal change control process, and it is wise to limit this only to essential major revisions.

Budget transfers must never be made in order to mask or account for cost over- or underspends, either realised or anticipated.

It is good practice to ensure that transfers of budget are communicated and mutually understood by both donor and recipient, and accepted and documented.

Part Three

Scheduling

'The key is not to prioritise what's on your schedule, but to schedule your priorities.'

Stephen Covey

13.1 Definition of scheduling

Scheduling can be seen as a science compared with the art of planning; it usually involves the input of the plan into scheduling software. It involves the calculation of duration and resources required; it defines the logic and sequence and the calculation of critical path, float, and start and finish dates of individual activities, and thus determines the feasibility of delivering the project within the desired completion dates and budget.

Scheduling is:

- integrating different parts of the project;
- identification and management of interdependencies;
- the identification of specific activities, and the resources required to deliver them;
- developing a logical sequence of works based on the planning strategy and methodologies to be adopted;
- establishing expected output rates to be used in the calculation of durations, and hence dates for each of these activities;
- undertaking these calculations;
- identifying the critical path and establishing priorities;
- making due allowances for risks (risk mitigation planning) in the schedule.

13.2 Purpose of scheduling

The purpose of scheduling is to create the following outputs to enable the management of the project:

Planning, Scheduling, Monitoring and Control

- the sequence of project tasks;
- the start and finish dates of all project tasks;
- the critical path (the longest path through the project);
- calculated project float;
- a comprehensive understanding of logical dependencies between tasks;
- the resources required to complete the project;
- a schedule that the project team will use to deliver the work. This may include various schedules dealing with interfaces, key dates etc.;
- diagrams, sequencing drawings etc. to assist in explaining sequences and timing.

Thus, scheduling:

- helps make decisions about strategies and methods considered as part of the planning process;
- focuses management attention on the most important issues and activities;
- considers work calendars;
- considers time contingency;
- starts at strategic level and is decomposed into medium and short-term scheduling;
- defines the sequence of activities with which the project goals can be accomplished;
- quantifies the resources required and cost to be expected as a result of project execution;
- clearly defines the scope of work;
- optimises the use of resources.

13.3 The scheduling process

13.3.1 Steps in establishing the schedule

- Review the business case.
- Review the project requirements and establish key deliverables and risks; define the scope of work.

Introduction to scheduling

- Develop the product breakdown structure and work breakdown structure (PBS/WBS).
- Develop an organisation breakdown structure (OBS) and other project structures.
- Determine and agree the project control requirements with all relevant stakeholders.
- Create the network diagram: sequence the work (referring to the scope documentation), establish technical constraints/logic, estimate durations and identify key milestones.
- Ensure consistency between different levels of schedule (vertical integration) and between schedules at the same level (horizontal integration).
- Develop a schedule that meets the project required dates, using activities and milestones, which should be fully logic-linked and constraint-free.
- Group the activities into work packages and planning packages in accordance with the project structures.
- Assign resources to activities (labour, material, sub-contracts, and other direct costs).
- Assign budgets to activities.
- Run a forward and backward pass and ensure that the critical path runs continuously from the first activity to the last activity; check for other critical paths and the critical path drivers.

See Figure 13.1 for an overview of the scheduling process.

13.3.2 Once the schedule is created

- Perform schedule integrity checks to ensure the robustness of the schedule.
- Undertake the appropriate level of quantitative schedule risk analysis.
- Issue the baseline with the appropriate level of authority and under formal change control.
- Monitor the progress of delivery of the plan, and control divergences from the original plan.

Planning, Scheduling, Monitoring and Control

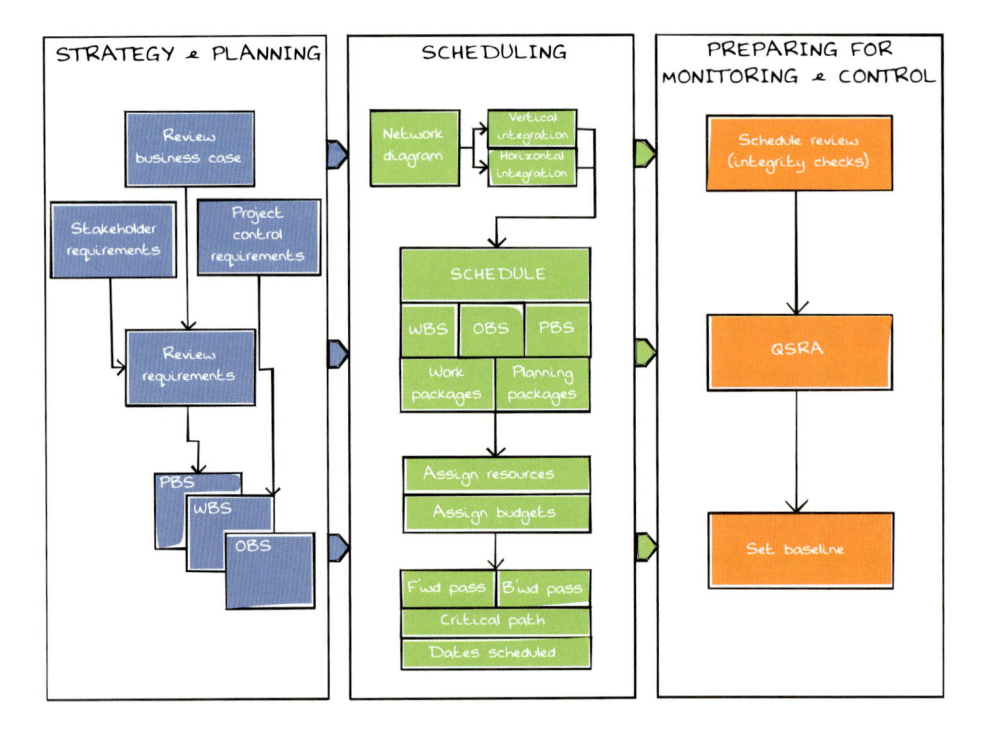

Figure 13.1 The scheduling process in the context of planning, monitoring and control

13.4 Schedule structure

13.4.1 Schedule density

13.4.1.1 Definition of schedule density

Reference is often made to 'levels' of schedules or planning; for example, level 1 may refer to the highest-level strategic schedule, level 3 may be the working schedule and level 5 the short-term, week-by-week schedule. Different organisations have different definitions of these, so to avoid confusion this guide will take the lead of the CIOB's *Guide to Time Management in Complex Projects* and refer to scheduling 'density', where low density means the higher levels or strategic schedules (perhaps simplified schedules for communication), medium density means the working schedule, and high-density means the week-to-week, day-to-day or shut-down scheduling.

Table 13.1 Features associated with density of schedules

Density	Timescale	Activity names	Typical activity duration	Budget/resource loading	Logic (example)	Lags	Calendars	Cost allocation	Contingencies	Comment
Low – the highest level(s) of schedule	+1 year from now	Will tend to be elemental, describing key parts of the project	Per each element	Major budget groups	Logic links of various types will be used to best describe the sequence	May be included for illustrative purposes; negative lags should never be used even at this level	Generic working week with statutory and typical industry holidays included	Major budgetary groups such as designer, contractor, client costs	Since durations will be calculated using empirical data, a high degree of contingency is required. Quantitative schedule risk analysis may be applied to determine	Adequate level of detail for feasibility checks only; in later schedules appropriate level of detail for strategic overview picture only
Medium	3 months – 1 year from now	A further definition into key parts or products of the project	Indicative duration: 4–8 weeks. Durations may be derived from typical outputs	Allocated to activities for first-pass baseline	Mainly finish to start links (FS) will be used	Some lags may exist, though the proportion will be much reduced	Activity-based calendars	Cost coding should be established at this stage	Risk should be reduced with greater clarity. Clear identification of the risk (float) owner at this level	Sufficient detail of allocation to particular contractors or other resources to allow pricing and resource allocation

(Continued)

Table 13.1 Continued

Density	Timescale	Activity names	Typical activity duration	Budget/ resource loading	Logic (example)	Lags	Calendars	Cost allocation	Contingencies	Comment
High – the lowest level(s) of schedule	Next 3 months	Clear, unambiguous and precise with reference to specific location or resource	Indicative duration: 2–4 weeks Durations will be derived from outputs and discussion	Baseline set and not subject to change	Mainly finish to start links (FS) will be used	Rarely acceptable; generally replaced by activities with FS links	Resource-based calendars in place if relevant	All resources must be identified and all relevant activity coded	Clear identification of the risk (float) owner at this level. Design or variation risks should not be required at this level	Adequate for detailed description, creation of day-to-day schedules, and progress reporting. Detailed design is complete and methods defined and agreed

Introduction to scheduling

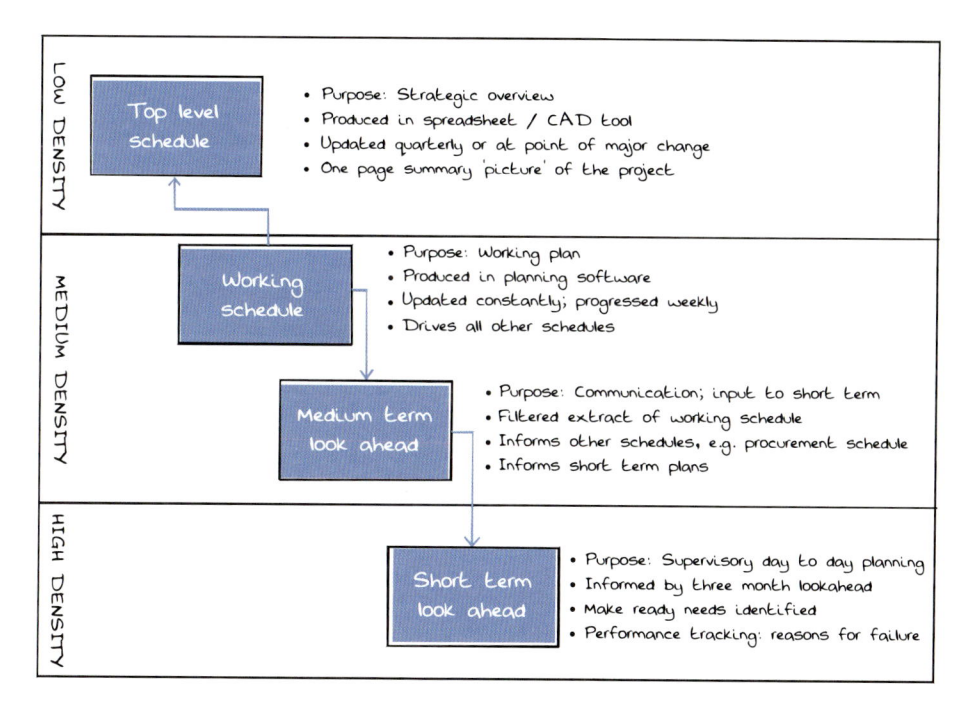

Figure 13.2 Relationship of different densities in schedules

13.4.1.2 Typical features associated with density of schedules

Figure 13.2 shows the relationships between the different levels or density of schedules on a typical project – note the directions of the arrows between the boxes, which relate to the genesis of each revision or update of the schedule. This diagram, therefore, represents the relationship of various schedules in the execution phase.

It is useful to define a hierarchy of schedules that will be used to describe to the project team (and others) the relationship between different schedules that are (to be) produced. A simple diagram of such a description is shown in Figure 13.3, although it will be useful to define which (if any) schedules are contained in the same software database. For example, as shown by the yellow box in the diagram.

Planning, Scheduling, Monitoring and Control

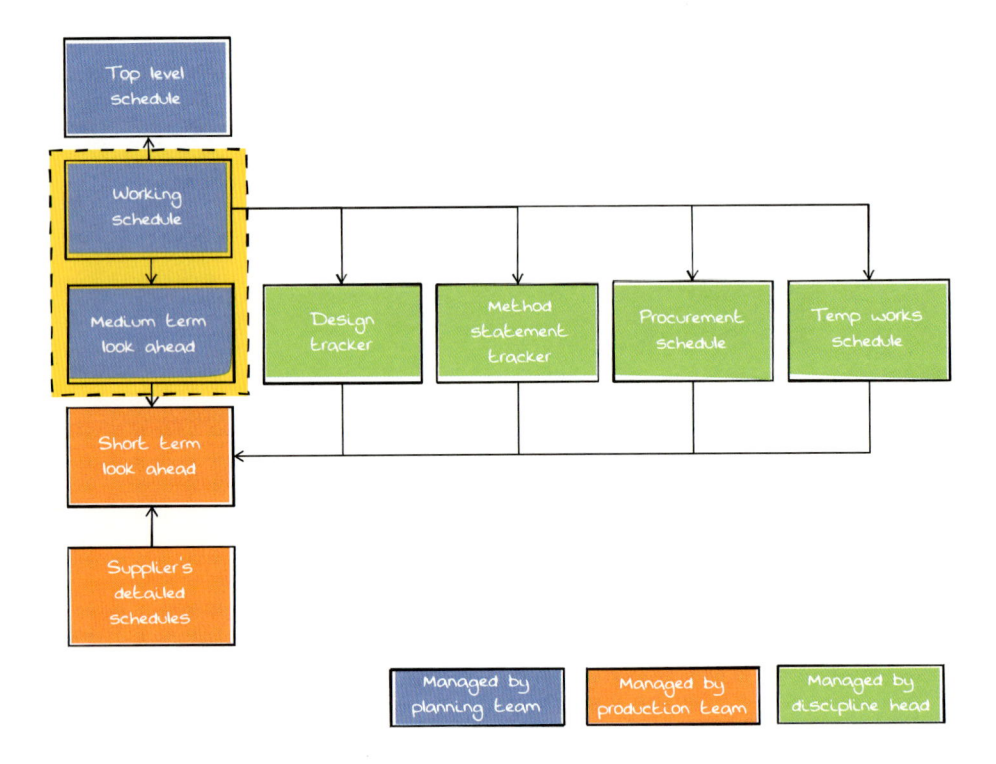

Figure 13.3 A hierarchy of plans and planning documents

13.4.2 Detail density: considerations

Schedules must be produced with the target audience in mind. For example, it is likely that senior management will require low-density schedules that explain blocks of activity and major dependencies and logic links. Management decision making will require medium-density plans, whilst day-to-day supervision of works will require high-density planning and scheduling. Schedules with an inappropriate level of detail may become useless.

13.4.2.1 Schedules with too much detail

Too much detail produces very large schedules. Large schedules with correct logic take a long time to produce. When change comes – for whatever reason – they can be very difficult to revise. A schedule that cannot be easily modified loses its value as a reporting or management/decision-making tool. With greater

Introduction to scheduling

levels of detail comes the risk of errors. Complex logic can hide errors, which will be harder to pick up in a very large schedule.

Also, very large schedules are less likely to be read and/or used. It is important to remember the target audience. The schedule should be in adequate detail for the correct monitoring of the project.

13.4.2.2 Schedules with inadequate detail

Schedules with not enough detail should also be avoided. Too low a density in planning will create schedules that do not fulfil their main purpose – to help coordinate and direct the work. If the activities are too large, then important logic may be missed, and critical tasks overlooked. This could result in a schedule that cannot be used to accurately monitor the progress of the work.

13.4.2.3 Detail density: principles

- At high density, every activity should represent the work of only one resource. This may mean a single trade or even an individual.
- Low density may require a more generic definition of resource, for example 'implementation team' or 'civils work'.
- Probably at medium density, and certainly at high density, there should be sufficient detail to allow only finish to start relationships.
- All activities must be split not only so that they relate to only one resource, as noted above, but so that they relate to only one key or sectional date.

13.4.3 Network templates (fragnets)

Network templates are usually adopted for repetitive sections of schedules, e.g. floors of a multi-storey building. They can be used to quickly build up a schedule made up of many similar phases or sections. They are copied and pasted into a schedule to enable a repetitive schedule to be built up quickly without having to keep typing in the same activities.

14.1 Schedule types: time-based

There are a number of different types of time-phased schedule, created at various stages and by various parties with subtly differing purposes and aims. In order for a project to have clarity, it is important for these to be limited to the key schedules described below.

14.1.1 Development or strategic schedule

This is usually the highest level of logic-driven schedule. This will very likely be created by the customer at the inception of a project. It should incorporate the major elements of the work and include all the key dates. Development schedules are usually low-density schedules.

14.1.1.1 Purpose

- To provide an outline of the project parameters in terms of scope and time.
- To define project gateway stages, including key 'go/no-go' points.
- To illustrate the approvals required for the project to proceed.
- To incorporate key dates over the life of the project.
- To identify a high-level critical path for the project.
- To show the key integration events and acceptance points.

Planning, Scheduling, Monitoring and Control

14.1.1.2 The schedule will include

- Overall completion date.
- Sectional and key dates.
- Details of approval stages throughout the project.
- Third party inputs or outputs.

14.1.2 Tender schedule (or 'bid schedule')

These schedules are created by a contractor/supplier or other delivery organisation when tendering or bidding for work. They can be critical to winning or losing a bid for work. Tender schedules are likely to be medium-density schedules.

14.1.2.1 Purpose

- To assist in the pricing of the tender.
- To identify and communicate the methodologies and timescale for delivering the project.
- To demonstrate good practice to the reviewing authority/customer/client.
- To show the level of resources required to complete the works.
- To define key technologies being proposed and their levels of maturity.
- To define information-required dates.
- To show inputs required from third parties.
- To show all key interfaces.
- To make adequate allowances for risk and schedule uncertainty.
- To define the procurement strategy.
- To clearly show any works by others.
- To include all utilities and statutory undertakings.

14.1.3 Contract schedule

This is the schedule that has been signed up to in the contract. It should be agreed at the start of a contract or programme of works. In a hierarchy of importance, this is probably the most important schedule. It should cover all the scope, whether design, procurement, installation or commissioning. It is the schedule that will form the baseline, and therefore the progress of the works will be

Types of schedule

measured against it. In all contracts there should always be a 'current' contract schedule. There may be changes throughout a project, but, once instructed, these should be included in the contract schedule.

This is the schedule against which the cause and cost of any delays are calculated. It is the schedule that is used as the basis for all monthly or period progress reporting, so it should be at a suitable level of detail. Contract schedules are likely to be medium-density schedules.

14.1.4 Baseline schedule

Generally the first working schedule (or contract schedule) will be copied and set as the baseline schedule. The baseline should be maintained as change is approved. The baseline schedule will reflect the density of scheduling that it relates to, and is thus likely to be a medium-density schedule.

14.1.5 Summary schedule

This is a pictorial, created to explain in very simple terms the schedule and its contents. Whilst it is possible to create such a schedule by rolling up activities in the main schedule software, this is unlikely to produce a clear, logical and well-presented view of the project. It is, therefore, better created in isolation and is often best presented in non-scheduling software. Spreadsheets or presentational tools are particularly good for this type of schedule. Summary schedules will always be low-density schedules.

14.1.6 Working schedule or 'forecast schedule'

It is likely that this will be developed from the tender, or other earlier schedule. It should include all activities relating to the delivery phase, including design activities, procurement activities, installation and commissioning tasks. Working schedules are likely to be medium-density schedules.

14.1.6.1 Purpose

The working schedule directs delivery in the optimum sequence, on time and to cost. Thus, the purpose is to manage the activities that are to be undertaken on an ongoing basis.

Planning, Scheduling, Monitoring and Control

14.1.6.2 The schedule will include

- Design.
- Procurement schedule.
- Approval periods.
- Manufacture.
- Build.
- Temporary works.
- Traffic management (and logistics).
- Labour and plant resources.
- Integration activities.
- Test, commissioning and acceptance activities.
- Handover and closeout process.
- Support activities.

14.1.7 Target schedule

Some projects run with target schedules. These can be set by contractors to challenge the workforce to complete a project earlier than the contracted date. Target schedules will reflect the density of the schedule from which they are created, and are thus likely to be medium-density schedules. However, they may cover the short-term only, and are thus likely to be created at high density.

- Advantages:
    - easy to do and understand;
    - focuses the project team on early delivery.
- Disadvantages:
    - requires rebalancing of the time/cost/scope/ quality triangle (Figure 14.1);
    - requires software;
    - purely tactical, no strategic view;
    - distracts from 'one version of the truth' reporting;
    - dilutes focus, as there is more than one schedule to consider and understand;
    - may engender complacency if it is known that the target schedule is not the definitive schedule.

Types of schedule

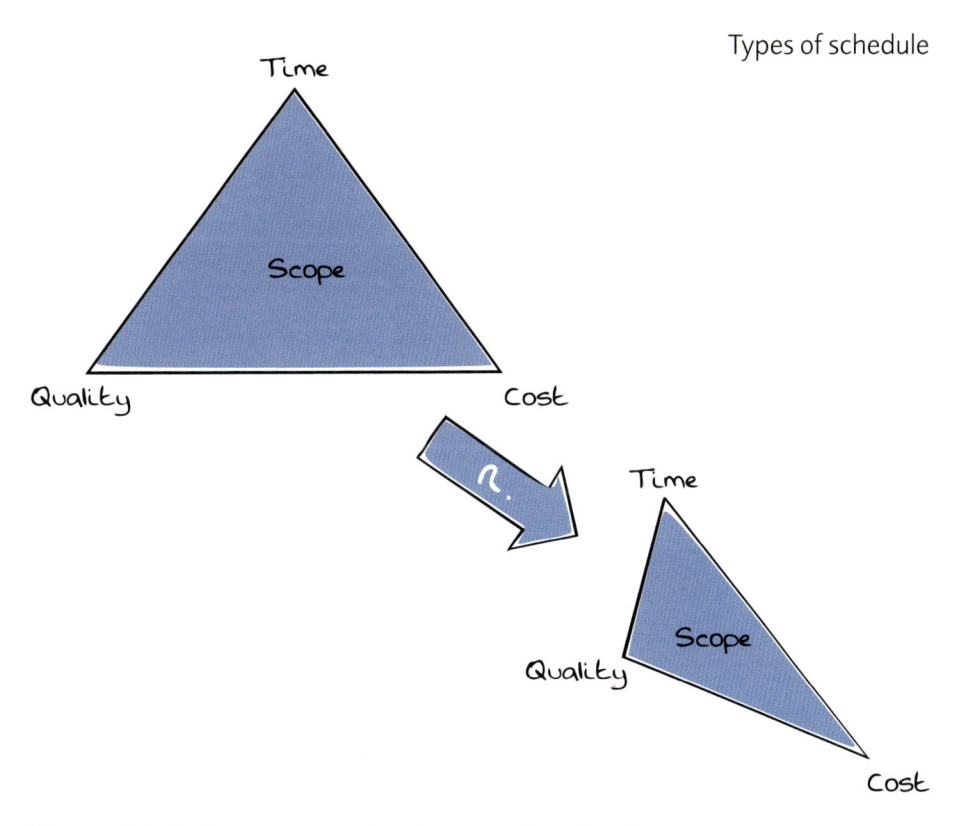

Figure 14.1 Distorting the time/cost/quality triangle

14.1.8 Short- and medium-term schedules

Medium-term schedules will typically be extracts of the working schedule. The extracts are made to facilitate day-to-day planning of the works that will become the short-term schedules. They are typically named to reflect the period of time that they cover. Examples of how they may be named include:

- three-month look ahead (medium-term schedule);
- four-week look ahead (short-term schedule).

It is very likely that these schedules will be high-density schedules, especially if they are weekly 'look aheads'; monthly 'look aheads' may be medium-density.

14.1.9 As-built schedule

This is the schedule that will be developed throughout the life of the project, to provide a record of what actually happened during the course of the project. It will be useful for learning from experience in the lessons learned process, or possibly

Planning, Scheduling, Monitoring and Control

employed in the use of making or rebutting claims on the contract. 'As-built' schedules are likely to be created at medium- or high-density scheduling.

Additional items that this schedule will include:

- baselined or original planned dates;
- actual start and actual finish dates for each activity;
- details of change events;
- details of delay events.

14.1.10 Post-build schedule

The 'as-built' schedule is created as the project proceeds. In its absence it may be necessary to construct a post-build schedule. It is created once the project has finished. It is built from historical records, but shares the aim of the 'as-built' schedule, in that it is created to make or rebut claims. This type of schedule would be created as a last resort, as you would expect an 'as-built' schedule to be in place; when it is not, this approach may be appropriate. Post-build schedules are likely to be created at medium-density scheduling (see Figure 14.2).

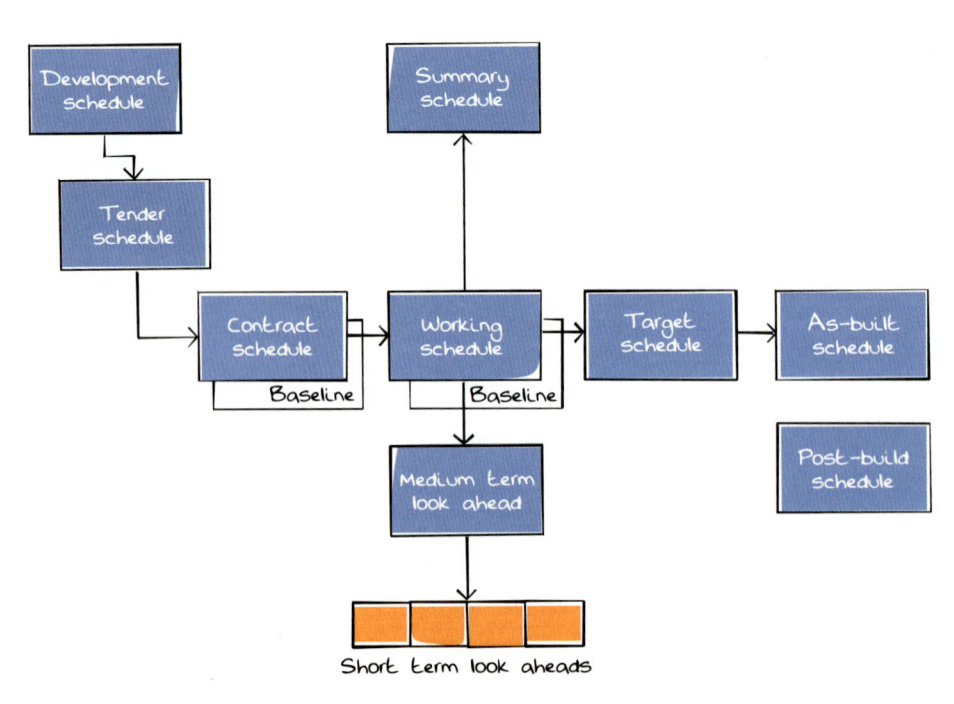

Figure 14.2 Types of time-phased schedules and their relationship

Types of schedule

14.1.11 'What ifs' (scenario planning)

'What ifs' are test schedules that can be produced to see what impact a scope, schedule or methodology change may have on the contract dates – or baseline schedule. 'What ifs' are produced separately from the working schedule. They are only incorporated once all the implications have been examined and the proposed change is agreed.

They may also be used when a critical delay occurs that impacts contractual dates. This 'what if' schedule should show how the works will be re-scheduled to enable the contractual dates to be met. Any additional working hours or resources should be clearly identified. This is sometimes called the recovery schedule.

14.2 Schedule types: tracker schedules

A tracker schedule is one that lists the various steps through a process and details by when each step, or action, should be complete. Typically, it describes steps along a management process, rather than activities that produce a deliverable, such as a design or a product. A typical example, the procurement schedule, is illustrated in the following sections. These are generally and most usefully produced in spreadsheets that can be accessed and updated without specialist software.

It is sometimes suggested that the time-phased schedule should contain every step required to complete a project. The problems that this causes however, include the growth of the schedule into an unfocused and in extreme cases, unmanageable model. Whilst it is true that every step should be represented in the schedule, where there are alternative and better methods of dealing with detail these should be kept separate, and updated by the responsible manager to keep them as a live document. They must be linked to the time-phased schedule, and these links regularly updated. It is usual, and desirable, for tracker schedules to be created and held in widely accessible software, such as a spreadsheet.

14.2.1 Procurement schedules

A procurement schedule is a tracker document that covers all the required steps of the procurement process. It is used to monitor each stage of the process to ensure that it is completed on time. The procurement schedule must be linked to the working schedule or updated on a periodic basis. The project-specific periods will be defined in the project procedures.

Figure 14.3 A sample procurement schedule

Types of schedule

The spreadsheet example shown in Figure 14.3 has the advantage that it can be set up to automatically update some of the data. Also, spreadsheets are generally more accessible to read and update than bar charts, which require scheduling software.

An alternative way of displaying the procurement schedule is to adopt a more traditional time-phased approach, as illustrated in Figure 14.4, which is best displayed in scheduling software.

However, the choice of which method to adopt is a matter of personal preference.

14.2.2 Design deliverables tracker

A design deliverables tracker is a document that covers the full scope of the design in a list of defined deliverables for the purpose of tracking and monitoring. This may be used as a supplement to the design schedule, ensuring that detailed tracking of individual items is possible. The progress claimed against the tracker may be tied to payment. The design deliverables tracker must be linked to the working schedule or updated on a periodic basis. The project-specific periods will be defined in the project procedures.

Figure 14.5 shows a method of monitoring the progress of various design documents until they are complete.

14.2.3 Other tracker schedules

The same principles as outlined above can be applied to many types of activity (usually management effort) that are best kept out of the time-phased schedule to ensure proper focus on that schedule and proper focus on management effort in the deliverable trackers. Examples of other trackers that may be useful to keep detail out of the schedule include:

- method statement trackers;
- quality control inspection trackers;
- consents trackers;
- construction or installation trackers;
- assurance documentation trackers;
- commissioning process trackers;
- handover process trackers;
- progress tracker schedules.

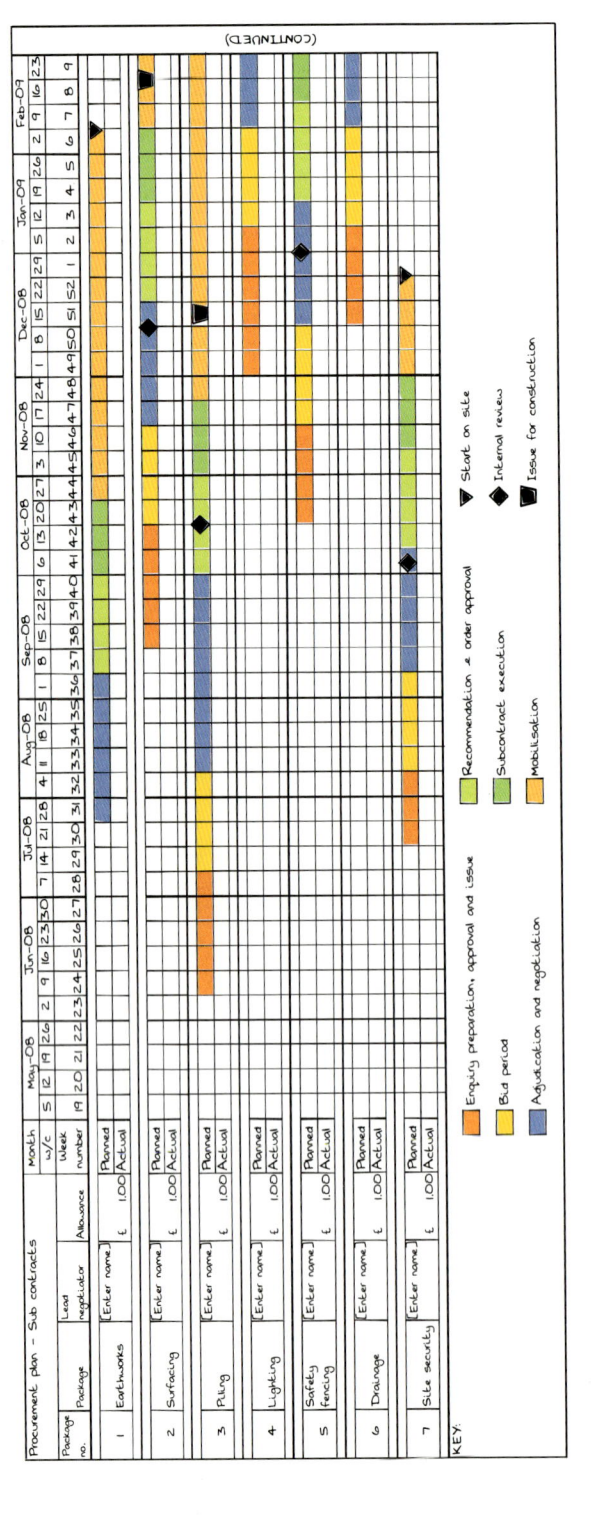

Figure 14.4 Time-phased procurement schedule

							Client submission				Comments					Acceptance				STATUS	
Package	Deliverable name	Lead designer	Approver	Programme ref	Approx no. of deliverables	Purpose of issue	Planned date	Actual date	Status	Document ref	Return date	Status	Document ref	Response date	Document ref	Required date	Actual date	Status	Document ref	RAG	Notes/ comments
1	Piling design	HDB	GH	DESPILI060	20 drawings	Accept	10/03/2010	10/03/2010	On time	MPA-1000 - D 100	07/04/2010	Received	MPA-1000 - D 110	21/04/2010	MPA-1000 - D 114	05/05/2010	05/05/2010	On time	MPA-1000 - D 116		
2	Feasability report on design changes to tunnels	HDB	ST	DESTUNI000	1 report	Inform	30/10/2010	30/10/2010	On time	MPA-1000 - D 101	27/11/2010										
3	Basement redesign	HDB	ST	DESSTRI020	10 drawings	Accept	26/05/2010	26/05/2010	Late	MPA-1000 - D 102	04/07/2010	Over Due									
4	Structural layouts	HDB	CL	DESSTRI021	20 drawings	Accept	18/06/2010	18/06/2010	Early	MPA-1000 - D 103	05/07/2010	Received	MPA-1000 - D 113								
5	Envelope elevations	HDB	JB	DESSTRI022	15 drawings	Accept	19/07/2010			MPA-1000 - D 104											
6	Partitions and dry lining tender package	HDB	SS	DESSTRI023	6 drawings	Accept	06/10/2010			MPA-1000 - D 105											
7	Capping beam drawings	HDB	CL	DESSTRI024	9 drawings	Accept	24/11/2014			MPA-1000 - D 106											
8	Architectural layouts	HDB	KH	DESSTRI025	42 drawings	Accept	06/10/2010			MPA-1000 - D 107											
9	Joinery package	HDB	KH	DESSTRI026	13 drawings	Accept	07/12/2010			MPA-1000 - D 108											
10	Miscellaneous metal work pacakage	HDB	KH	DESSTRI027	5 books	Accept	28/08/2010			MPA-1000 - D 109											

Figure 14.5 Design deliverables tracker

15.1 Definition of schedule design

Schedule design refers to considerations and decisions that are made when setting up the structures for the project. These considerations must be made prior to commencing any scheduling work. The decisions that are made should be detailed in the project-specific procedures.

15.2 Purpose of schedule design

Making and writing down the decisions around these structures should help to ensure that time is not wasted in revisiting schedules to correct defects in settings, structures and other technical aspects of scheduling.

15.3 Elements of schedule design

15.3.1 Activity identity numbers (IDs)

15.3.1.1 Purpose of structured IDs

Activity IDs provide a unique identifier for each activity in the schedule. The ID provides the planner with a quick reference that remains constant throughout the project's duration. It can be auto-generated by the scheduling software, and it is important for forensic analysis of the schedule that the activity IDs, once used, are never changed or re-used.

15.3.1.2 Structure

The structure of an ID may well repeat some or all activity codes, but it can provide a shorthand that the scheduler can use, for example, to trace logic. Care should be taken not to over complicate the structure and the use of letters to abbreviate the names of parts of the project (life cycle stages, geographic areas, etc.).

Structuring activity IDs can often be tailored to the project; therefore, it is recommended to use abbreviations that can be understood, for example life cycle stages such as DE, CN, TC for design, construct, and test and commission. Other structures to consider when generating activity IDs are:

- geographic location;
- section of work;
- who does the work?

To maintain schedule integrity, it is important never to correct errors post formal issue of the schedule, and not to recycle an activity ID (use of redundant activities).

15.3.2 Activity descriptions

Activity descriptions should be clear and unambiguous. Ideally, they should define the work they are describing completely, i.e. not relying on WBS headings to provide context. This is particularly important when filters or alternative views are applied to the schedule so that precision and clarity are maintained. Descriptions should avoid using acronyms and should write out the full description clearly, as far as is possible (see Table 15.1).

If this is not possible, then the schedule should be structured with additional filters, flags or outline codes which provide further detail on the tasks in the schedule.

Table 15.1 *Examples of activity descriptions*

Bad description	Good description
Design	Design – Earthworks
Ground Floor Slab	BUILDING 1 – Formwork, Rebar, Pour Ground Floor Slab Grid 4-7/a-f
RFC to 1st Fl	Reinforced concrete slab to 1st floor

15.3.3 Different activity types

15.3.3.1 Tasks

Activities are usually 'doing' tasks, and therefore should include a verb, e.g. DIG foundations; LAY brickwork; INSTALL steelwork.

15.3.3.2 Level of effort activities

Generally support activities which must be undertaken to support other project activities, level of effort (LOE) activities are typically difficult to forecast, or will not add value to the overall scheduling logic. Examples of level of effort activities include:

- Project manager: It is difficult to predict where the PM's effort will be focused on a daily or weekly basis, as it is generally focused on areas that need support, which often change regularly. Scheduling these activities into a high-density schedule would be very time-consuming and would not add value to the overall logic structure. It is therefore appropriate to assign a LOE activity for the PM spanning the life of the project, as they are helping to facilitate the project's success.
- Planner/Scheduler: Although there may be repetitive work due to the regular reporting cycle which can be predicted and scheduled, it does not add value to the schedule to itemise these activities in a low level of detail; therefore, LOE is appropriate.

Level of effort activities should be used sparingly within scheduling, as they do not provide objective time performance measurement through measurable outputs. Any LOE activities used within the scheduling should be clearly identified and their use fully justified.

15.3.3.3 Hammocks

A hammock is a summary activity that will expand and contract depending on the activities that it is linked to. Hammock tasks are very similar to level of effort (LOE) tasks, differing only in the following:

- A hammock task does not have a calendar assigned to it, whereas a LOE task can have a specific calendar attached (for example, part-time scheduling support).

Planning, Scheduling, Monitoring and Control

- Only a start-start and finish-finish relationship can be assigned to determine the start and end points of the hammock, whereas a LOE activity can have any relationship type as a predecessor and successor.

15.3.3.4 Dummy tasks

Dummy tasks may also be schedule visibility tasks. If an activity is dependent on a lead time, or a customer approval, for example, it may be beneficial to utilise a schedule visibility task (SVT), which is a task entered into the scheduling software with no resource assigned to it, representing the elapsed time of the lead time or the customer approval time. This could also be used in a construction environment, for curing time, as an example.

The main advantage in utilising SVTs rather than leads or lags in the schedule is primarily for visibility. Often, leads and lags are overlooked or hidden in standard scheduling views created by software tools, and can be overlooked by the wider team. Appropriate calendars may also be applied – for example, curing activities would always work on a seven-day calendar, whereas works around them may not. Adding SVTs into the schedule shows clearly the impact of the 'waiting time' and avoids the need to document lead and lag justification in the notes of the schedule, as this can be captured in the SVT title (e.g. 'SVT: six week customer review time for sign-off of Requirements Document').

15.3.3.5 Milestones (start, finish)

A milestone is an event in a schedule with no duration. Examples may include significant start dates, including access dates, the commencement and completion of key phases of the project, and other key or contract dates.

15.3.4 Activity steps

When working on a large-scale project, it is sometimes preferable to manage the quantity of tasks displayed on the schedule. It may be more appropriate to convert a series of sequential tasks into one task which is supported by a number of 'steps' or 'objective criteria'. These steps can have pre-agreed progress weightings to establish progress in an objective way (Figure 15.1).

It should be noted, however, that this approach is only suitable for activities which do not have any external predecessors (Figure 15.2).

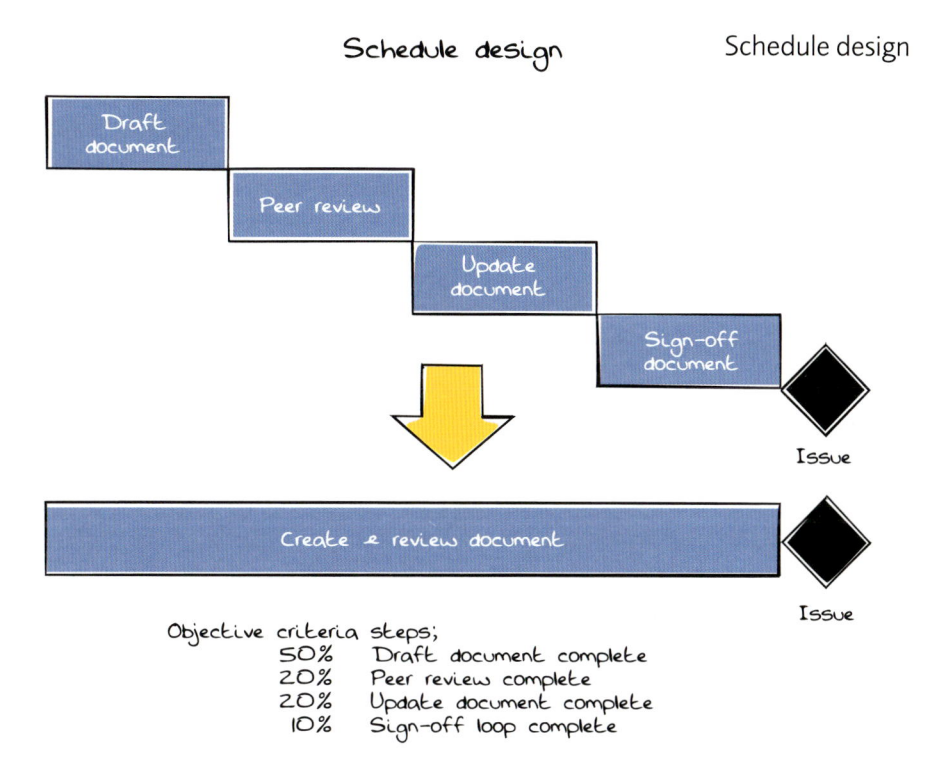

Figure 15.1 Establishing steps/objective criteria

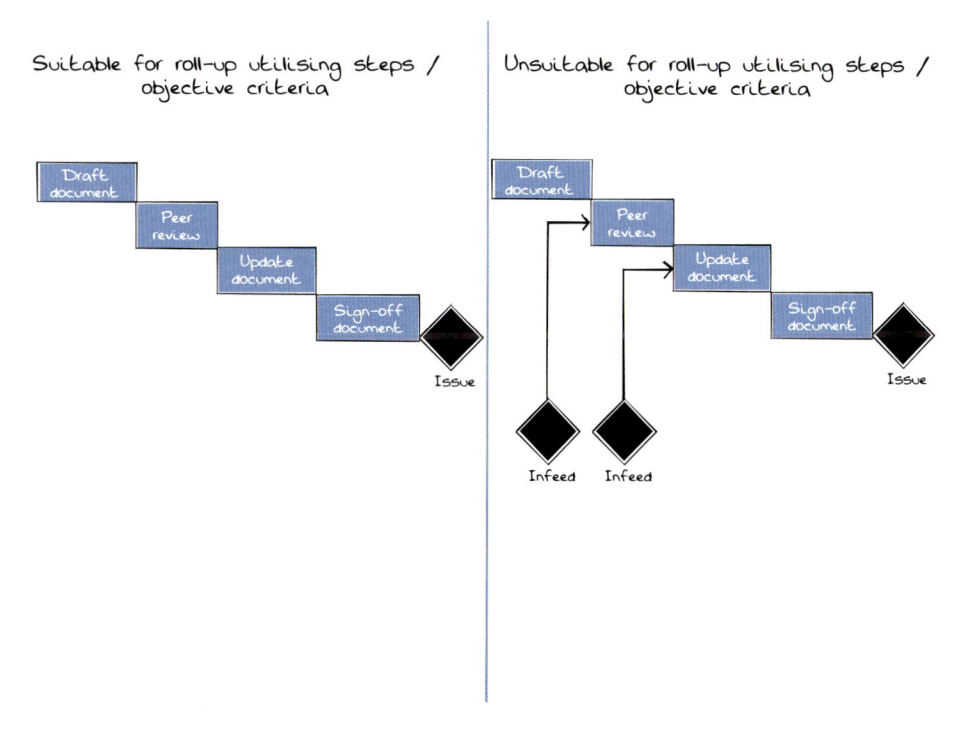

Figure 15.2 Suitability for steps/objective criteria

Planning, Scheduling, Monitoring and Control

If the scheduling software does not have a step function embedded, then it is advised to capture the objective criteria in a notes field held within the tool for transparency and visibility.

15.3.5 Time Units

Time units are a scalable measure of time used to define the duration of activities and the impact of change within the project schedule. Choosing an appropriate time unit depends on the nature of work being undertaken; however, it is important to use only one type when developing the schedule.

The most common types of time unit are days or hours. These units are generally suitable for most projects; however, when planning very long, high-level projects it may be more appropriate to use weeks. In certain circumstances, which are likely to be high-risk and/or relatively short-duration works, it may be appropriate to schedule in minutes. Typical examples would be shut-downs for maintenance of a process plant, or a closure on a live railway.

15.3.6 Calendars

Calendars are used to define the amount of working and non-working time throughout the duration of the project. They are used to determine when the work will be carried out, e.g. night-working or weekends only.

Generally, they show the normal working week, e.g. Monday–Friday, 8.00–5.00 with 1 hour for lunch. This would result in an 8-hour day and 40-hour working week. In the UK, the 8 standard bank holidays would be included. Industry holidays are usually 1 week at Easter and 2 weeks at Christmas.

Consider the level of time unit being used (i.e. an 8-hour day may be used, whatever the real hours are) and decide what is appropriate for the project. In other words, and in general terms only, work is often planned in days regardless of the software that may calculate duration in hours.

15.3.6.1 General considerations

- Permitted working hours, e.g. airports, railways etc.
- Differing shift patterns, e.g. night-shifts or 7-day working.
- Restrictions at particular times or for particular works: for example, some works may be undertaken at any time, while some require particular times,

Schedule design

e.g. booked or planned shut-downs or engineering hours (times when the current is switched off on a railway).
- Planned shut-downs for routine maintenance.
- Resource working hours or availability.
- In addition to the project calendar, additional specific calendars can be set up to cater for individual suppliers, specific customer availabilities, specific resources, specialist facilities, etc.
- Calendars can define reporting cycles – for example, rail industry periods.

15.3.6.2 Holidays and non-working days

Consider the country or religious parties involved:

- Calendars should contain the relevant bank holidays and weekends.
- Where relevant, they should include any known factory/site shut-downs. For example, some Jewish developers/contractors may close their sites on key Jewish holidays.
- Other religious holidays to consider could be not only in the Middle East, but also in Europe, India, the US, etc.
- Be careful when setting up calendars. For example, the national holidays in France: some of the dates stay consistent each year, so that if the date falls on a Saturday or Sunday it is not a national holiday.

15.3.6.3 Applying to schedules

Consider how/whether different calendars are applied to the schedule:

- A schedule can use multiple calendars, for both activities and resources.
- Take care that calendars are correctly assigned, defined and maintained.
- It is important to clearly define which activities take place on which calendar.
- An activity cannot take place on multiple activity calendars; if there is a need to show such working, then the activity needs to be duplicated so that each individual activity occurs solely on one calendar. An example of this could be a situation where a joint team are working on a piece of work shared between two nations, say the UK and Spain. The Spanish take most of August off on holiday, whereas the UK continues to work. Separate calendars, and hence separate activities, would be needed to show this.

Planning, Scheduling, Monitoring and Control

- Leads and lags should not have calendars allocated to them. If a logic link needs to be on a specific calendar, then this should be an activity (dummy task).

15.3.6.4 Ordinal dates

In some cases it will be appropriate to display a number, i.e. Week 1, Week 2 etc. (ordinal dates), rather than calendar dates; for example, when tendering for work with an uncertain start date. It will be important in these cases to be aware of the effect of holiday periods and other working restrictions on the overall duration of each deliverable and the overall project.

15.3.7 Project, activity and resource coding

Project, activity and resource codes are a flexible and powerful aid to optimise presentation of the project schedule. They are generally used to view and analyse the schedule data in multiple ways depending on the specific needs of the audience.

Applying project codes such as location, sponsor, phase, asset group, etc. can also help to view project and group programme or portfolio data in order to manage information efficiently at an enterprise level. They can also be usefully used to identify dependencies and interfaces.

When defining the project WBS, CBS, OBS and RAM, there will be a need to sort data by different groups. By assigning values to activities, it is possible to quickly view and analyse data in the most appropriate way.

Coding can be applied to specific activity resources in order to differentiate between cost accounts, contracts and resource unit information, i.e. concrete, track, pipe, cable, etc. This information can then be extracted for monitoring and control.

It is important to define the level of coding required in the final schedule prior to commencing work on the schedule. This enables easier regular analysis and reporting.

A useful tip is to insist that coding fields are populated against every activity, using a 'N/A' code for those that have no applicable code. This will mean omissions in coding are easily seen and corrected.

Building the Schedule
Chapter 16

There are a number of techniques of scheduling, and these are allied to methods of presentation. Scheduling is undertaken using logic-linked networks and the critical path method of analysis. This is based on either the arrow diagram method or, as is more usual in modern software, the precedence diagram method. The network methods are central to all others in modern planning; the other techniques discussed here may be considered to be alternative means of presentation, albeit they were originally independent techniques.

16.1 Creating a critical path network

A network is essentially a flow chart which describes the logical sequence of activities.

16.1.1 Definition of critical path method

The critical path (longest path) is a series of activities or tasks within a project, none of which can be delayed without affecting the project end date.

It is possible for a network to have more than one critical path if there are multiple key or sectional completion dates. It is also possible for multiple critical paths to exist leading to a single completion date.

16.1.2 Purpose of critical path network

The critical path network must allow you to understand the logical flow of work and how the individual activities relate to each other. As a result of the scheduling process, the network will define:

Planning, Scheduling, Monitoring and Control

- the start and finish dates of activities;
- the completion date of the project;
- total and free float;
- the critical path;
- areas of risk (such as bottlenecks of logic).

16.1.3 Methods of constructing a critical path

Critical paths may be calculated using a number of techniques that may alternatively be known as precedence diagrams, logic diagrams, PERT (program evaluation and review technique), or deterministic network diagram.

16.1.3.1 Precedence diagram method

There are two principal methods; the first method, which will be more familiar to users of contemporary software, is the precedence diagram method (PDM), in which the node designates the activity, and the logical interface is represented by the arrow (Figure 16.1).

This method is sometimes known as AON (Activity on node).

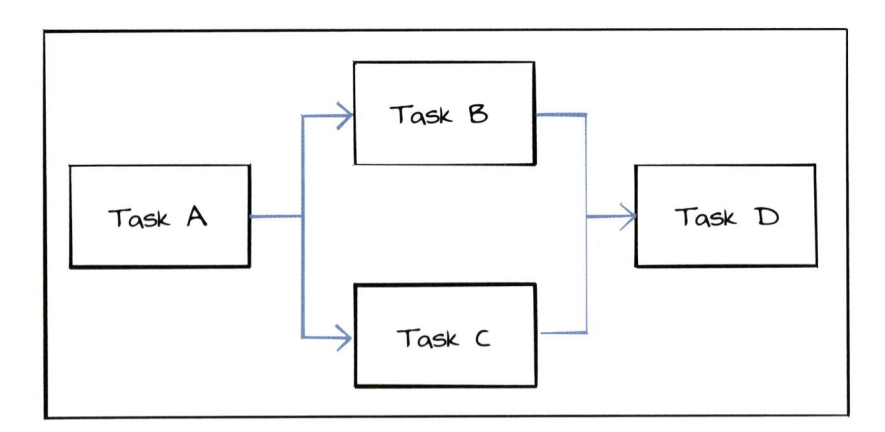

Figure 16.1 Example of the precedence diagram method (PDM)

16.1.3.2 Arrow diagram method

The second method, now superseded, is the arrow diagram method (ADM), in which the activity is shown on the arrow, as illustrated in Figure 16.2.

Building the schedule: network analysis

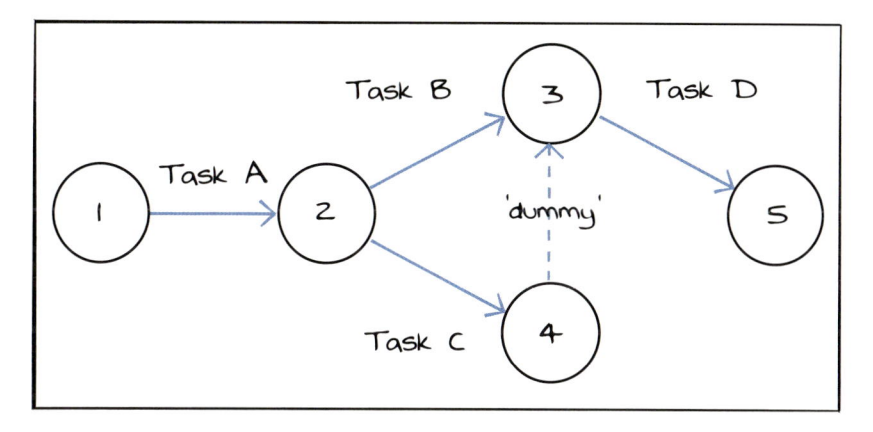

Figure 16.2 Example of the arrow diagram method (ADM)

This approach only allows finish to start relationships.

'Dummy' activities are needed to complete the logic in these diagrams. Task D cannot take place until Tasks B and C have completed; therefore, a dummy task is required to link node 4 to the start of node 3.

This method is sometimes known as AOA (Activity on arrow).

16.1.4 Inputs into a critical path analysis

Prior to undertaking a critical path analysis, the project needs to be broken into its constituent parts and defined in terms of the activities required. The interdependencies between these activities must be defined such that all activities (apart from the starting activity or milestone) have at least one predecessor, and each activity, apart from the final activity or milestone, has at least one successor. The critical path can then be constructed, but, in order to calculate the overall duration, the duration of each activity needs to be calculated or otherwise estimated. It is also worth noting the following:

- Care needs to be taken to correctly define the predecessor activities and ensure that the preceding activities deliver what is required of them.
- Dialogue is required to ensure the logical flow of activities is correctly defined.
- Lags can be introduced between activities to more accurately model the reality of the logic. Lags are to be avoided where possible because they are invisible on the Gantt chart.
- Definition of the project's logic is often an iterative process.

Planning, Scheduling, Monitoring and Control

16.1.4.1 Time analysis

Time analysis is the process that calculates the timeframe in which each activity can take place. It identifies the minimum time in which the network can be completed based on the activity durations and the logical links defined.

The terminology used to describe the timeframe is defined in Figure 16.3.

Time analysis identifies the activities which are critical to the timely completion of the network and the latest dates at which activities can be completed without delaying the end date of the network. It consists of five steps, but before we go through this process it is useful to define the terminology used when undertaking a critical path analysis.

16.1.5 Introduction to creating a network analysis

The following paragraphs describe a step-by-step guide to constructing a network.

- Step 1: Create a logical network.
- Step 2: Forward pass.
- Step 3: Backward pass.
- Step 4: Calculation of total float.
- Step 5: Identification of critical path.

Further detail on types of float, logic and constraints follow.

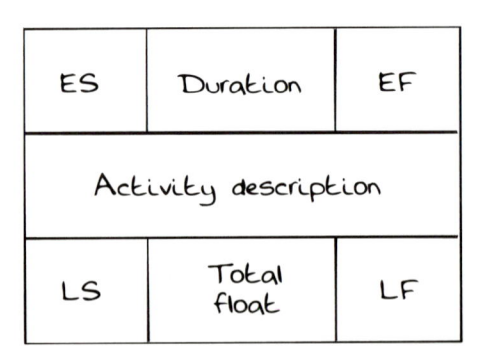

ES	Duration	EF
\multicolumn{3}{c	}{Activity description}
LS	Total float	LF

Figure 16.3 Typical time analysis coding

Note: ES = Early Start; EF = Early Finish; LS = Late Start; LF = Late Finish.

Building the schedule: network analysis

Project management teaching offers two alternative methods of calculating the numbers contained in network analysis. This guide has opted to use the method used by most planning software, starting from day 1 of the project (which planning software usually references as a date rather than an ordinal date).

Note: An alternative method used in teaching begins with the concept of day zero, and after the step-by-step guide an illustration of a completed network is shown for reference purposes, in section 16.1.11.

16.1.6 Step 1: Create a logical network

The first steps in building the network are the identification of the activities required, and the identification of the dependencies, or logic, between them. The duration that each activity will take must be estimated, and it will then be possible to construct a basic network with this information (Figure 16.4).

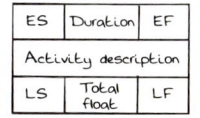

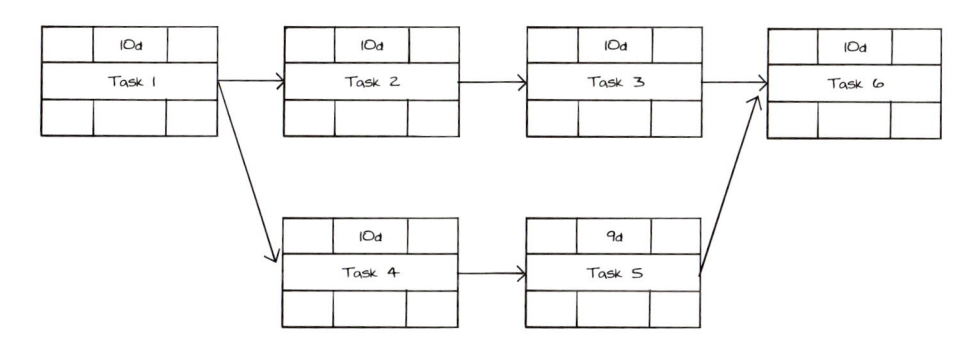

Figure 16.4 Step 1: create a logical network

16.1.7 Step 2: Forward pass

The forward pass calculates the earliest start and finish dates for each activity, based on the activity durations and their logic. For the following example, the diagram below illustrates this base information (Figure 16.5).

Planning, Scheduling, Monitoring and Control

The first activity is given an early start date (Day 1). With the duration, it is then possible to calculate the early finish date (Day 10). Thus, **early start + duration = early finish.**

The second activity can start after the first activity has completed (Day 11). This calculation proceeds forward through the network, eventually calculating the earliest possible finish date for the whole network of activities.

Note that if an activity is dependent on more than one activity, it is important to remember to ensure that the calculations have been completed on all preceding activities. The full forward pass will, therefore, be calculated in Figure 16.5.

- Where two or more dependencies converge at a succeeding activity, there may be a number of different earliest finishes (EF) to use to establish the earliest start (ES).
- The logic states that all preceding activities must be complete for the succeeding activity to start, so the highest preceding EF is used to determine the succeeding ES.

ES	Duration	EF
Activity description		
LS	Total float	LF

1	10d	10		11	10d	20		21	10d	30		31	10d	40
	Task 1				Task 2				Task 3				Task 6	

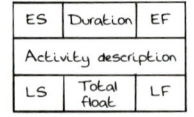

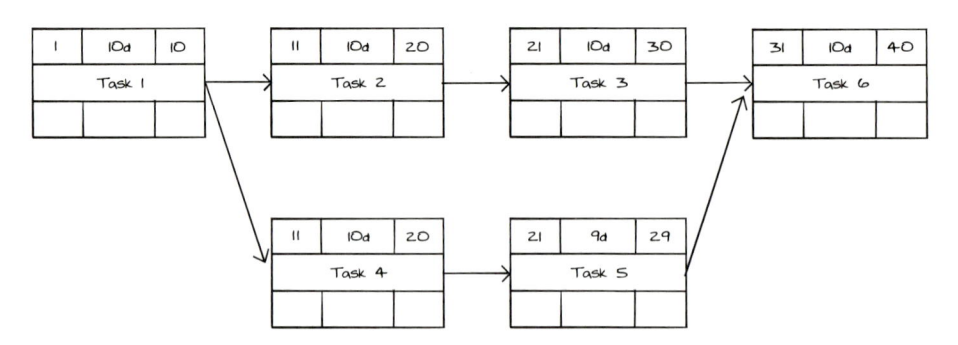

11	10d	20		21	9d	29
	Task 4				Task 5	

Figure 16.5 Step 2: the forward pass calculation

16.1.8 Step 3: Backward pass

The backward pass calculates the latest start and finish dates for each activity, based on the activity durations and their logic. It is essentially the opposite of the forward pass.

Building the schedule: network analysis

Starting from the last activity in the network, the latest finish is set to the same value to determine the early finish. Then from the late finish the duration is subtracted to calculate the late start date. This calculation then proceeds backwards through the network. On completion of the backward pass, the resulting data appears as in Figure 16.6.

- Where two or more dependencies go back to a preceding activity, there may be a number of different latest starts (LS) to use to establish the latest finish (LF).
- The logic states that all succeeding activities must be able to start once the preceding activity is complete, so the lowest succeeding LS is used as the preceding LF.

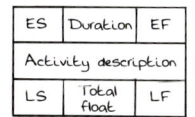

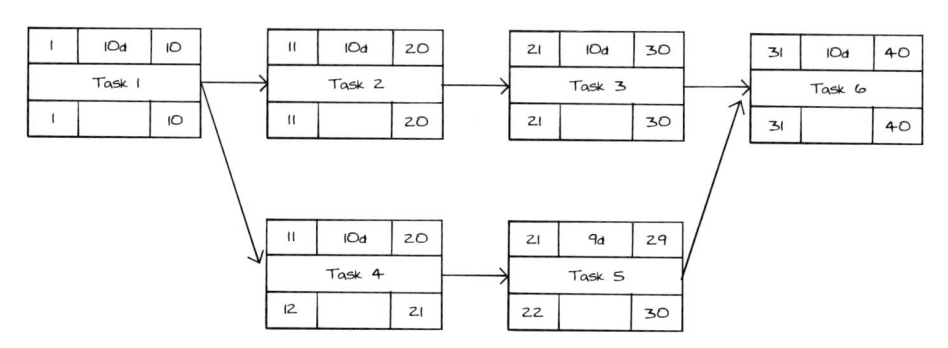

Figure 16.6 Step 3: the backward pass

16.1.9 Step 4: Calculation of total float

Having completed the forward and backward passes, total float can be calculated (Figure 16.7); it is simply the latest finish less the early finish, and is expressed in the relevant time unit (number of days, for example).

Once float is calculated, the critical path also becomes apparent, as the critical path is the chain of activities with zero float, as illustrated in Figure 16.8. Thus, in

Planning, Scheduling, Monitoring and Control

the example the critical path is Task 1–Task 2–Task 3–Task 6. Any delay to any of these activities will delay the completion of the project.

Note also that, in the example below, a delay of 2 days to Task 4 and/or Task 5 will also delay the project, and will also have the effect of changing the critical path to Task 1–Task 4–Task 5–Task 6.

Total float = late finish − early finish (TF = LF − EF)

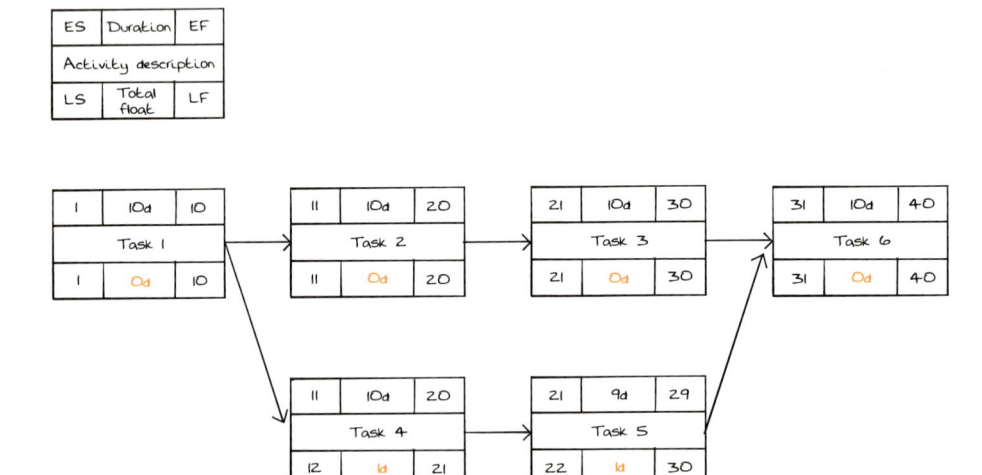

Figure 16.7 Step 4: Calculation of total float

16.1.10 Step 5: Identification of critical path

Once the float has been calculated, the critical path can be identified by tracing the path with zero days' float through the schedule, as shown in Figure 16.8. It is usual to highlight the importance of the critical activities; the critical path activities and critical logic links are shown in red.

There are instances where the critical path may not be defined simply by those activities with zero float. One reason could be that the schedule contains a variety of calendars, which will affect the float calculations. For example, a 7-day calendar for curing of concrete may be included. Therefore, a better definition would be the 'longest path' through the project (Figure 16.9).

Building the schedule: network analysis

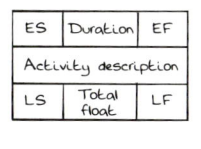

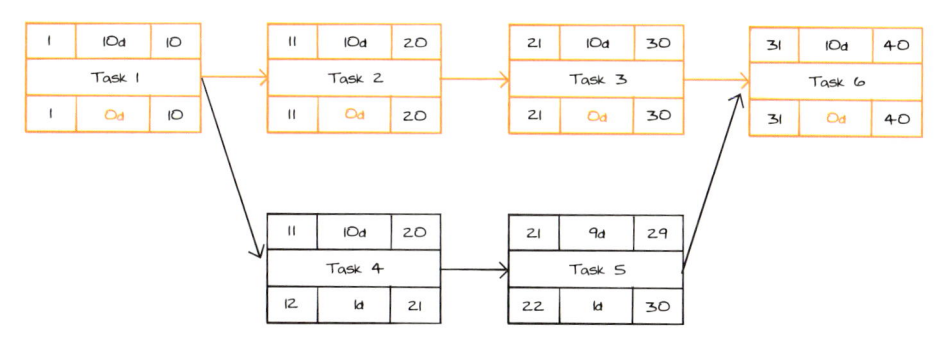

Figure 16.8 Step 5: Identification of critical path

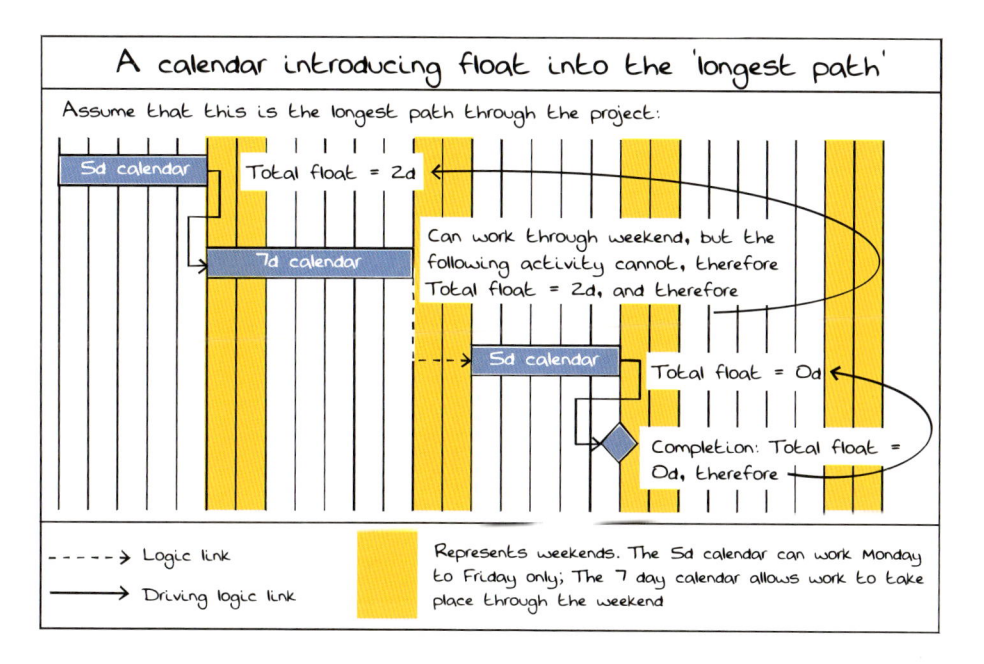

Figure 16.9 Longest path calculations

Planning, Scheduling, Monitoring and Control

16.1.11 Training in network analysis: a note

Training of network analysis takes two distinct forms. First, following the method outlined above, it is taught that early start + duration − 1 = early finish, to enable the project to start on Day 1, not Day 0. (Similarly, late start − duration + 1 = late start.)

The second method adopts a more purely mathematical approach, as follows (Figure 16.10).

The network commences on Day 0 instead of Day 1, which gives different start dates, as illustrated below. The end dates remain the same. However, Day 0 does not exist, so this method does not properly represent reality. Planning software will always work with the Day 1 method.

When transferring the classroom teaching to planning software, the practical calculation should be allowed to occur and the absence of a day zero must be explained.

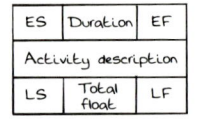

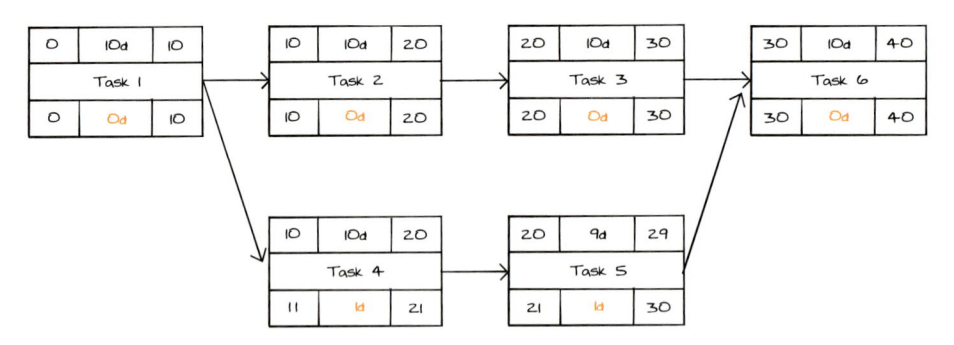

Figure 16.10 The alternative method of calculation in a network

16.1.12 Float

Float is sometimes referred to as 'slack', for example in some scheduling software, but this guide will use the more widely accepted term 'float'. Figure 16.11 illustrates float types.

Building the schedule: network analysis

16.1.12.1 Free float

Free float is spare time at the end of an activity that can be used without delaying its successor activity.

16.1.12.2 Total float

Total float is the amount of time that an activity can be delayed without affecting the network end date. (It is worth noting that total float is the amount of float that typically applies to a sequence of activities on that path, and, if used up on the current activity, will not be available for future activities on the particular path).

16.1.12.3 Negative float

Negative float occurs in a schedule when you do not have enough time to complete the project by the desired (and constrained) completion date. In order

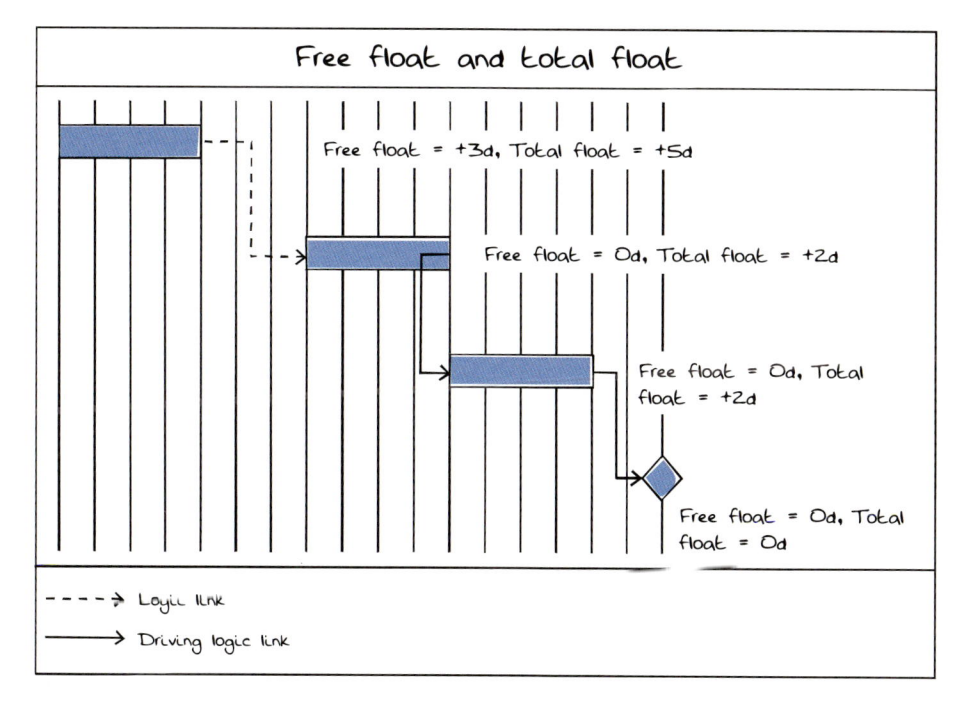

Figure 16.11 Float types

Planning, Scheduling, Monitoring and Control

to achieve the required date, you will need to recover the time in future activities/sequences.

16.1.12.4 Float ownership

On some complex projects, it may be appropriate to share float between teams (e.g. on an international project the float between US and UK elements of the schedule has a share arrangement, with teams obliged to notify each other when they have used up their element). Extreme care should be taken with this approach, and acknowledgement of the ownership of float should be in accordance with the contract conditions.

16.1.12.5 Monitoring of float

Float use should always be monitored so that there is an awareness of the criticality of all works; work that is not critical will become so if it is sufficiently delayed. If this is to be the case, sudden shifts in the critical path should not come as a surprise if the loss of available float has been carefully monitored and brought to the attention of the relevant people.

16.1.13 Types of logic linking

There are many relationship types available for linking activities logically. When developing the schedule, it is possible to use multiple types of logical relationship. It is important to remember that the purpose of scheduling is to forecast accurately, and as such choosing the correct relationship type is critical to building a schedule that is fit for purpose. The most common relationship types are:

16.1.13.1 Finish to start relationships

This is the preferable form of logic: it implies that the schedule has been broken down to an acceptable level of detail, and is the easiest logic to understand and analyse. It creates clear float paths. It is advisable to use this relationship when developing schedule logic, as it provides the simplest schedule and the most robust method of determining project total float.

In Figure 16.12, a finish to start relationship shows that activity 1 has to be 100% complete to allow activity 2 to start. This also means that a delay to activity 1 will have a direct impact on the start date of activity 2.

Building the schedule: network analysis

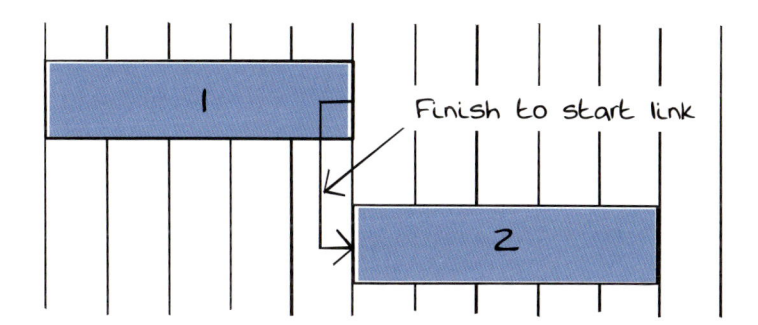

Figure 16.12 Finish to start relationship

16.1.13.2 Start to start relationships

A start to start relationship, as shown in Figure 16.13, shows that once activity 3 has started, activity 4 can also start. This does not necessarily mean that activity 4 must start on the same day – it means that activity 4 can now start at any time in the future.

Note: both activities will also need a successor, and activity 3 will need a predecessor to complete the logic.

This relationship type is used when an activity can only be completed when its predecessor has started; e.g. manufacture may be able to commence once the delivery of necessary components has started, but it is not dependent upon the delivery being completed. Once again, parallel working opportunities must be possible and validated by the project team before being used in the schedule.

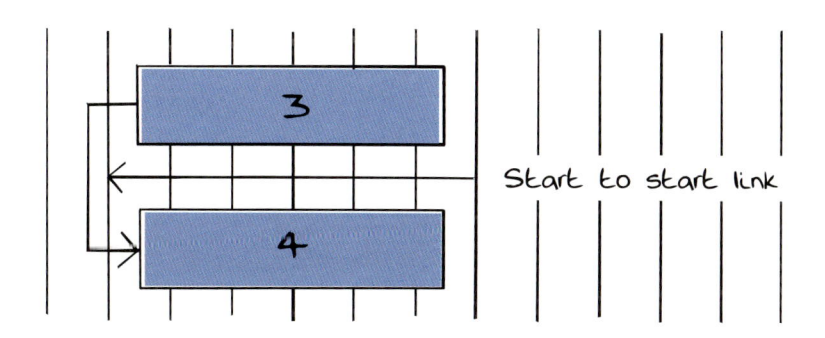

Figure 16.13 Start to start relationship

Planning, Scheduling, Monitoring and Control

Care should be taken when using this type of relationship. It is not as simple as the Finish to Start link. If activity 3 starts, but is stopped or slows down for any reason, can activity 4 really proceed unhindered? Thus these links may often be used with:

16.1.13.3 Finish to finish relationships

A finish to finish relationship, as shown in Figure 16.14, shows that once activity 5 has finished, activity 6 can also finish. This means that these tasks can start independently of each other, but activity 6 cannot finish until activity 5 has completed.

Note: both activities will also need a predecessor, and activity 6 will need a successor to complete the logic.

This relationship type is used when an activity can only be completed when its predecessor has finished. It assumes that activities can proceed without completion of their predecessors and that parallel working is possible; e.g. you can start putting a planning application together whilst site surveys are being undertaken, but you cannot complete the application until you have all the survey information. Parallel working can successfully be used in order to accelerate a project. However, it is important to remember that parallel resources are required as well.

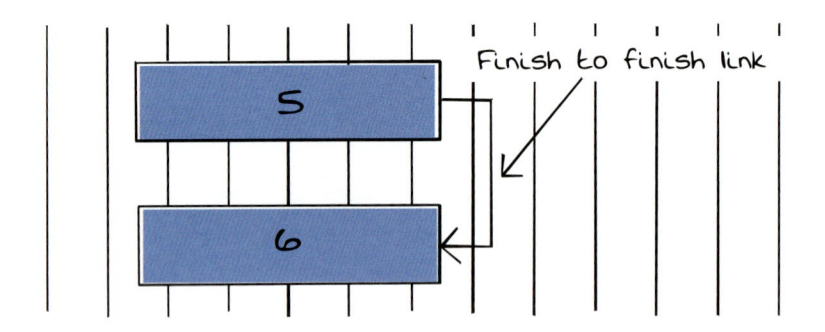

Figure 16.14 Finish to finish relationship

16.1.13.4 Start to finish relationships

This is a very rare link and should be used with extreme caution, if at all. Its use is often an indicator of poor scheduling practice, as it is usually illogical (that activity 8 cannot finish until after activity 7 has started) (Figure 16.15). For this reason, it is normally seen as bad scheduling practice to use this kind of linking.

Building the schedule: network analysis

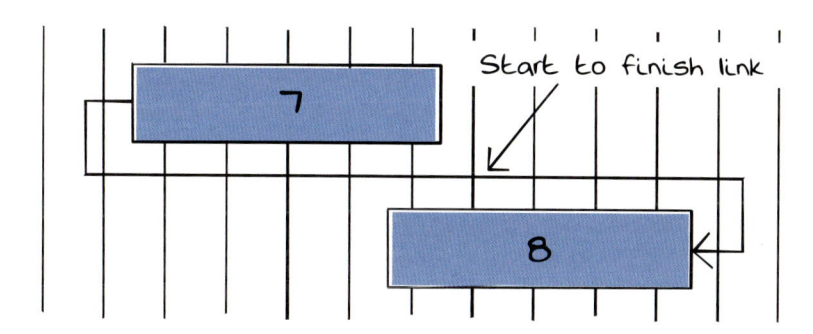

Figure 16.15 Start to finish relationship

It is difficult to give an example of where such a link could be valid. (An example sometimes given is activity 7 in Figure 16.15 being 'mix epoxy resin' and activity 8 being 'apply epoxy resin', but it is hard to imagine planning at this level of detail in most situations.) These types of links are likely to be used as a convenience rather than a true description of logic. For this reason, they should be avoided.

16.1.14 Lags and leads

A lag is the period of time between activities that does not represent any work. It can be used as part of any type of logical link (finish to start, start to start, etc.).

A lead is a negative lag, and by definition illogical, as time only runs forward (so far as we know).

The scheduler also needs to beware of the effect of calendars on lags. An example could be non-activities such as concrete curing (which is one potential use of a lag, as no work is represented). The calendar relating to the lag in this case would show a 24-hour, 7-day a week work pattern. It is unlikely that the preceding (or following) activities will work to the same calendar, and it is worth noting that not all scheduling software can distinguish the calendar being applied to a lag.

Lags and leads are not activities and should not be used as a substitute for an activity. They are generally used in low-density planning, and as detail develops they should be removed.

The use of lags and leads should be avoided as far as possible. Whilst use of lags is common practice within scheduling, excessive reliance on lags, coupled with their inherent lack of visibility, can make them difficult to status and thus undermine the overall accuracy of the schedule. It is therefore preferable to use

Planning, Scheduling, Monitoring and Control

a dummy activity rather than a lag. This will have the added advantage that an appropriate calendar can be applied to the dummy activity.

The use of lags and leads is therefore, in most cases, poor scheduling practice, and they must not be used in high-density scheduling, because as previously stated they are illogical. (Figure 16.16 illustrates that activity 12 cannot start until 2 days before activity 11 completes, but this is an illogical statement – the future is uncertain, but for this to work you have to know 2 days in advance that Activity 11 is going to complete on a particular day.)

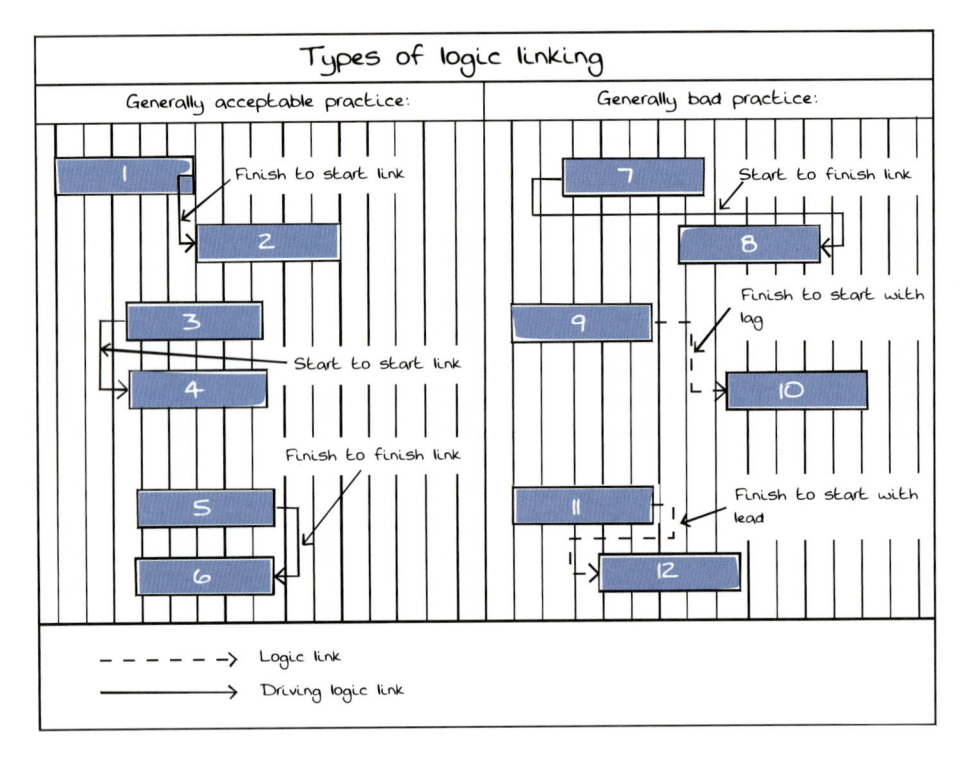

Figure 16.16 Summary of types of logic and lags

16.1.15 Use of constraints

Activity constraints can be used to fix an activity at a particular point in time. All activities should ideally be linked by logic, but in some instances this may not be possible – or desirable; e.g. the start of something where nothing precedes it. 'Start on site' or 'appoint contractor' may be examples. Similarly, finish dates may

Building the schedule: network analysis

need to be fixed without anything following them, e.g. sectional completion dates of various sections of work.

Within scheduling software there is usually a selection of different ways of adding a constraint date, as described below:

- as late as possible;
- mandatory start;
- mandatory finish/deadline;
- (must) start on;
- (must) finish on;
- start on or after/start no earlier than;
- finish on or after/finish no earlier than;
- start on or before/start no later than;
- finish on or before/finish no later than.

Note: The different scheduling software may use slightly different terminology for these constraints; for example, tick-boxes; 'holding pin'; 'start on a new day'. It is important to understand the ways scheduling tools use constraints. This is particularly important where you need to import schedules from different sources into the master schedule.

Care should be taken in the use of multiple constraint dates, as they can give misleading results when the project is scheduled, especially if used in combination. For example, using 'start on or before' and 'start on or after' constraints on the same activity or logical sequence would create a result you might not anticipate or notice if you have not appreciated the combination.

It should be noted that if a constraint date is imposed on an activity then float calculations will use that constraint date to calculate the 'late finish' date for the activity.

If there is not enough time to do the work and to meet the constraint date, then a negative float value will be calculated. Conversely, if there is more than enough time to do the work and meet the constraint date, then a positive float value will be generated. It is worth noting that different toolsets (or scheduling software) can handle this in different ways. Problems may arise when moving data from one software product to another. Different results are very likely except in the case of very simple schedules.

Planning, Scheduling, Monitoring and Control

16.1.16 Types of constraints

In Figures 16.17–16.25, the float calculated assumes we are considering the critical path, or the link into the critical path. This is to simplify the explanation; the principle applies to all float paths.

16.1.16.1 As late as possible constraint: ALAP

ALAP should only be used in circumstances where an activity should be done – as the name suggests – as late as possible. It means that any float on that activity (or milestone) will have been used up and therefore may make the item critical. (Note: schedules should generally be built so that all activities, when scheduled, show the earliest dates they can be carried out – as soon as possible). Scheduling tools typically default to planning tasks as soon as possible unless the user specifies an alternative planning approach or constraint.

This type of constraint may also be known as a 'zero free float' constraint.

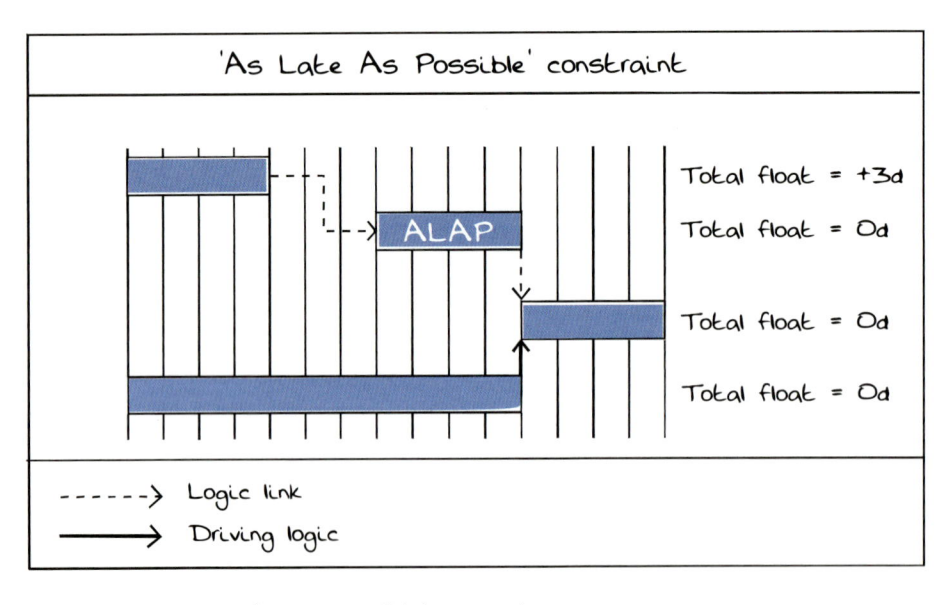

Figure 16.17 'As late as possible' constraint

Building the schedule: network analysis

16.1.16.2 Finish on constraint

Holds an activity at the desired completion date. It will be overridden by preceding logic. Total float will be calculated against the constrained date.

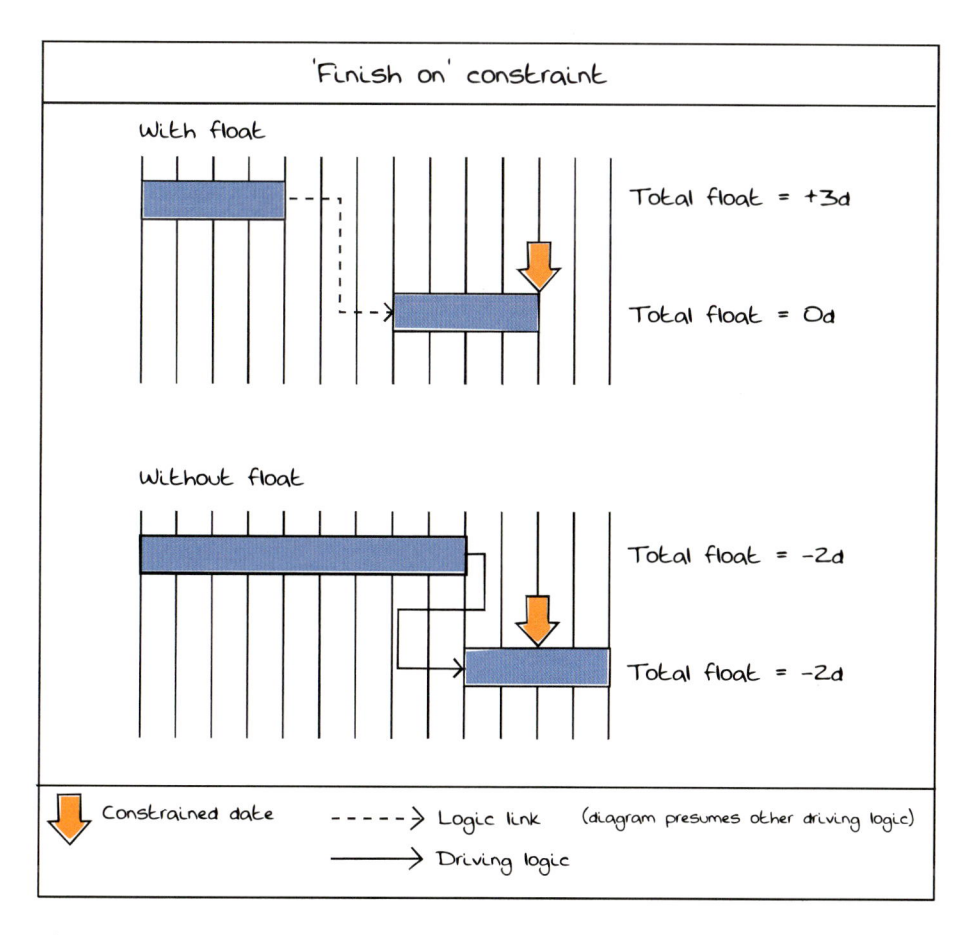

Figure 16.18 'Finish on' constraint

Planning, Scheduling, Monitoring and Control

16.1.16.3 Finish on or after constraint

Allows the activity to finish later than the date entered, so does not create a critical activity. But will not permit the activity to finish earlier – even if the works are completed early. Total float will be calculated against the network completion date.

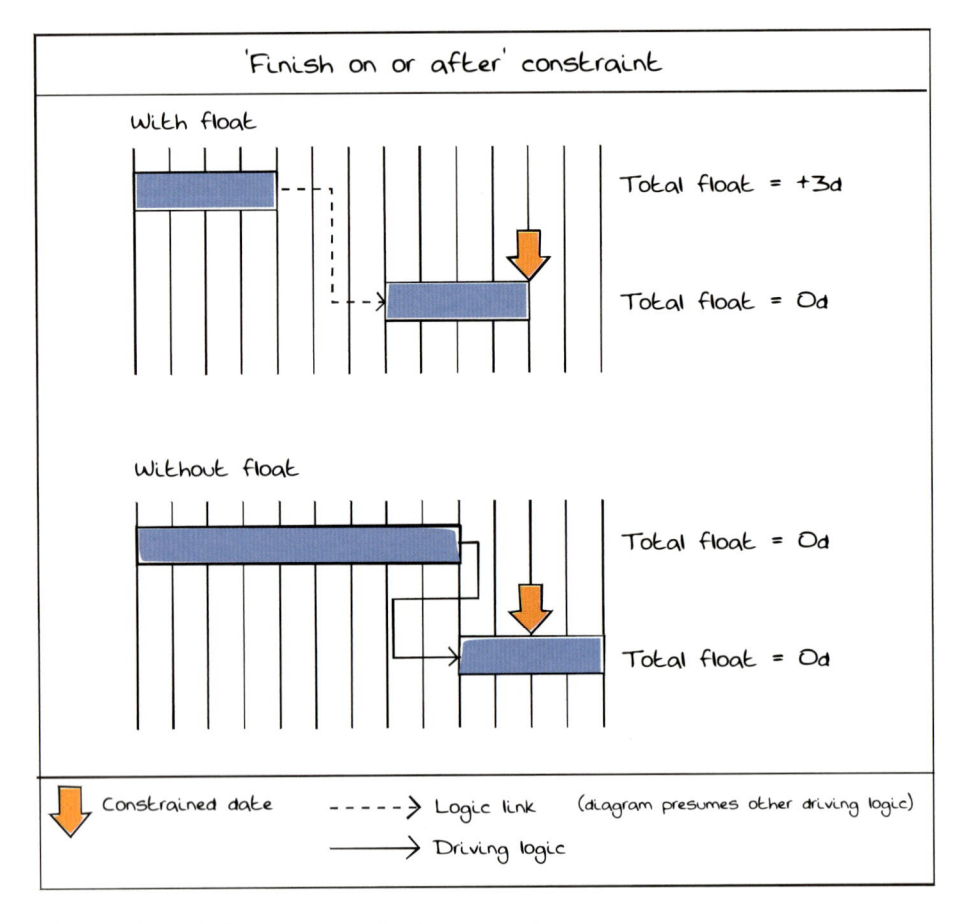

Figure 16.19 'Finish on or after' constraint

Building the schedule: network analysis

16.1.16.4 Finish on or before constraint

Makes the activity critical if it finishes on or after that date. But will allow it to finish early.

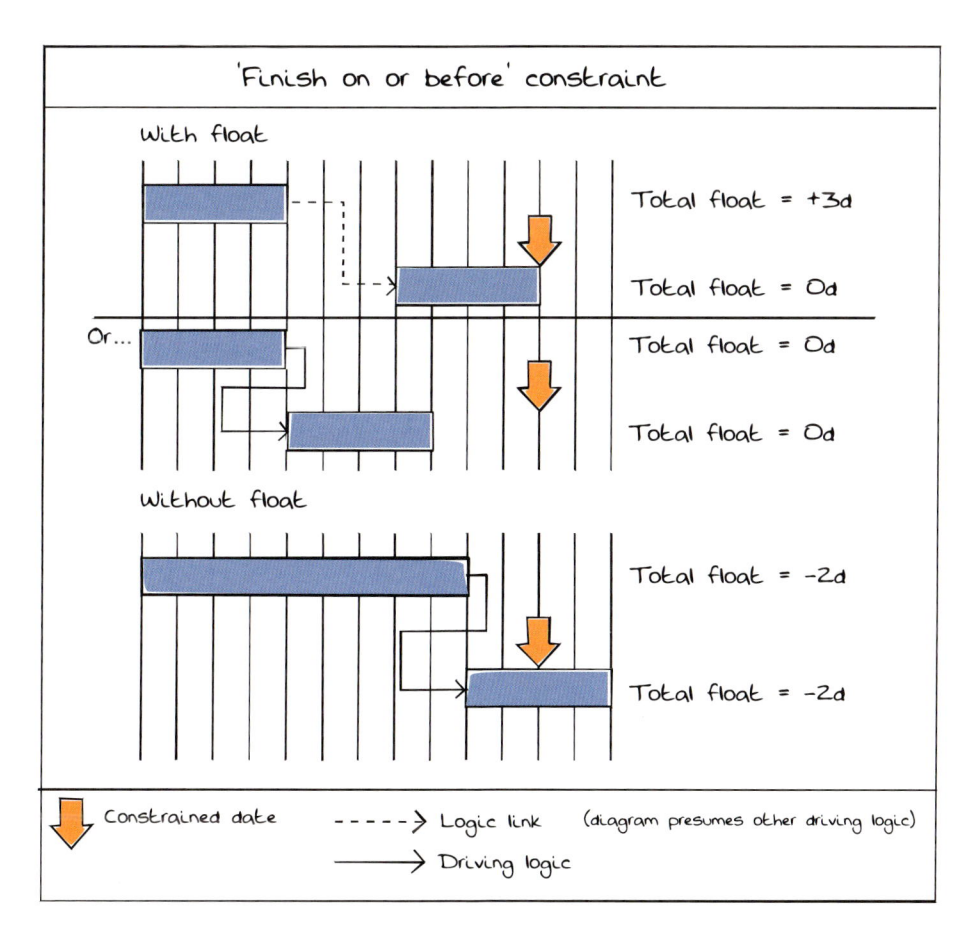

Figure 16.20 'Finish on or before' constraint

Planning, Scheduling, Monitoring and Control

16.1.16.5 Mandatory finish constraint (must finish on)

A rigid constraint that cannot be moved when scheduled. Can be used to create a critical path or to show negative float if works are slipping or in delay. (Note: should not be used casually; it is always better to use 'finish on or after' or 'finish on or before'.) It is often considered to be bad scheduling practice to use this constraint.

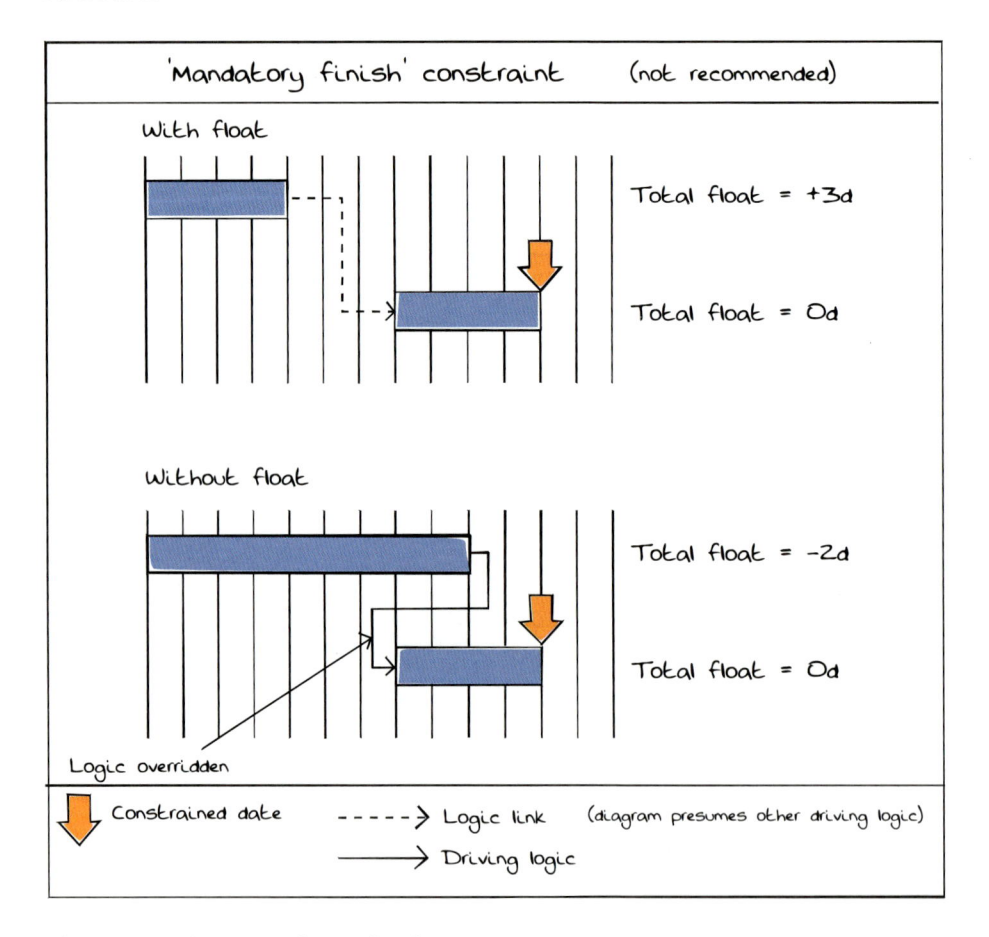

Figure 16.21 'Mandatory finish' constraint

Building the schedule: network analysis

16.1.16.6 Mandatory start constraint

Makes the activity critical, and consequently the predecessor also becomes critical when scheduled. (Note: should not be used casually; it is better to use 'start on or after' or 'start on or before'.)

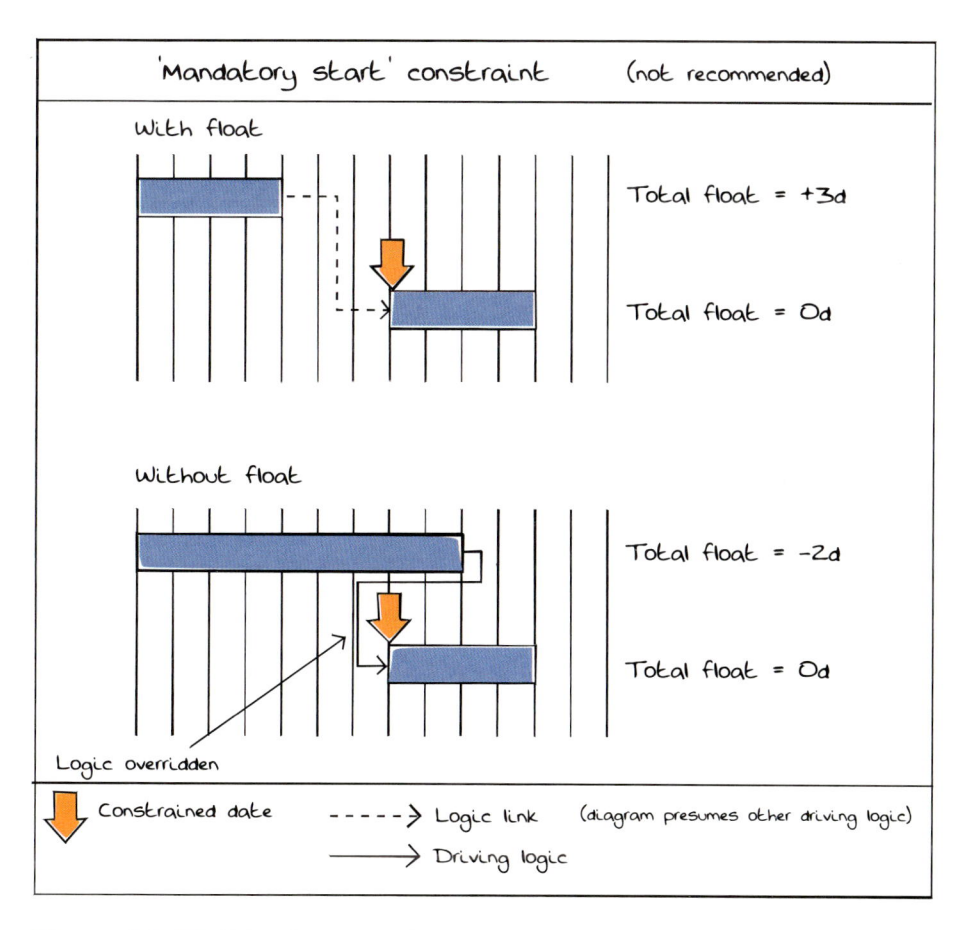

Figure 16.22 'Mandatory start' constraint

Planning, Scheduling, Monitoring and Control

16.1.16.7 Start on constraint

As for 'finish on', it cannot be moved when scheduled, and therefore creates a critical path through the preceding activities. (Note: should not be used casually; it is better to use 'start on or after' or 'start on or before'.)

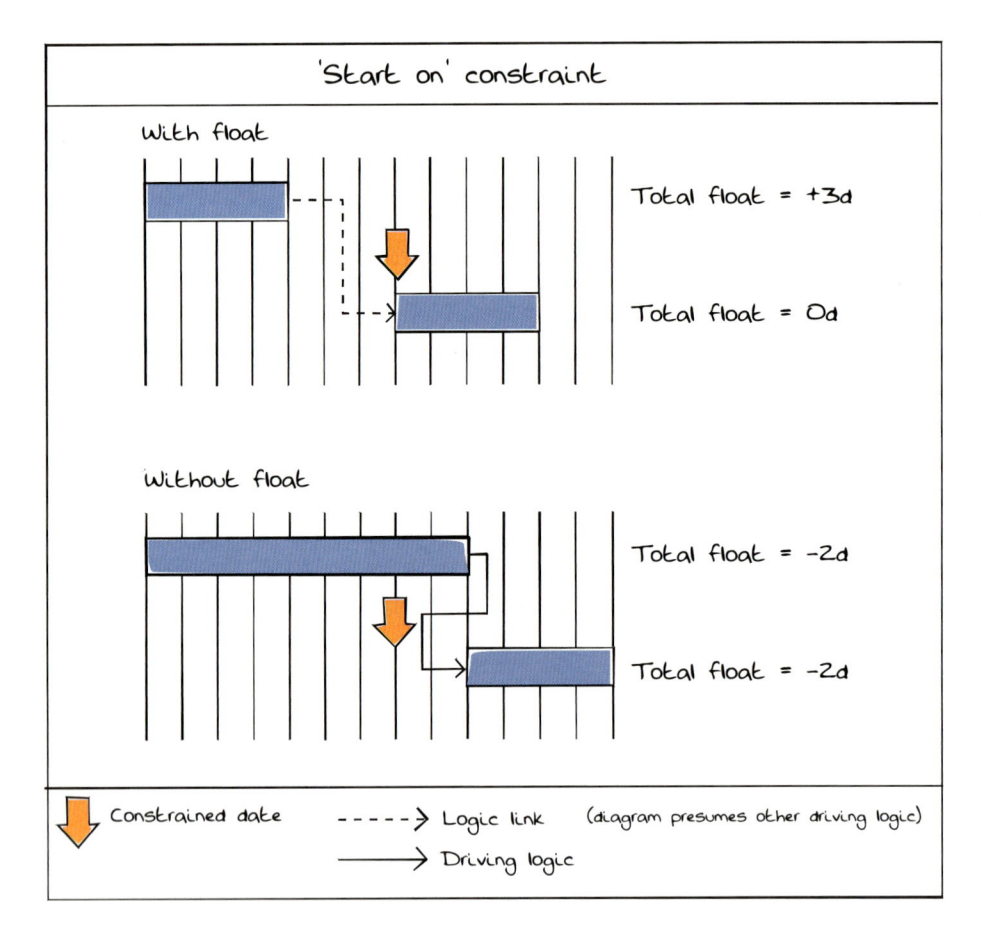

Figure 16.23 'Start on' constraint

Building the schedule: network analysis

16.1.16.8 Start on or after constraint

Allows the activity to start later than the date entered, so does not create a critical activity. But will not permit the activity to start earlier – even if the preceding works are completed early.

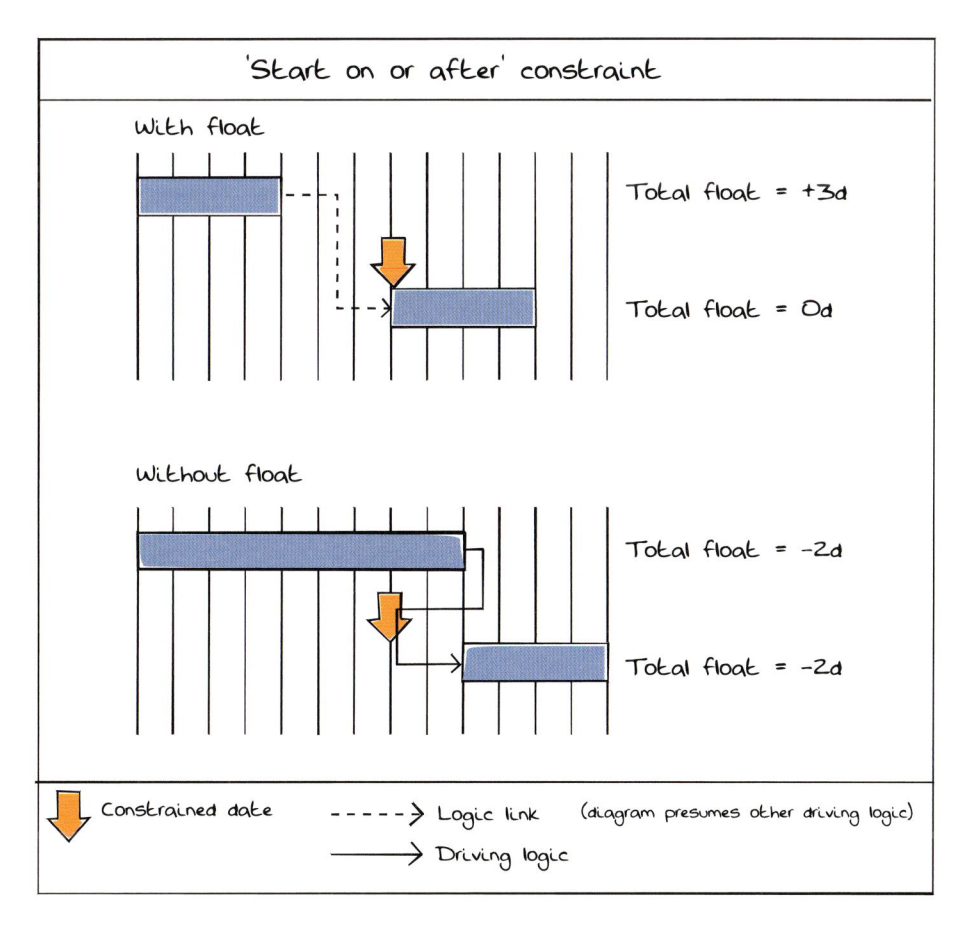

Figure 16.24 'Start on or after' constraint

Planning, Scheduling, Monitoring and Control

16.1.16.9 Start On or Before Constraint

Makes the activity critical if it starts on or after that date. But will allow it to start early.

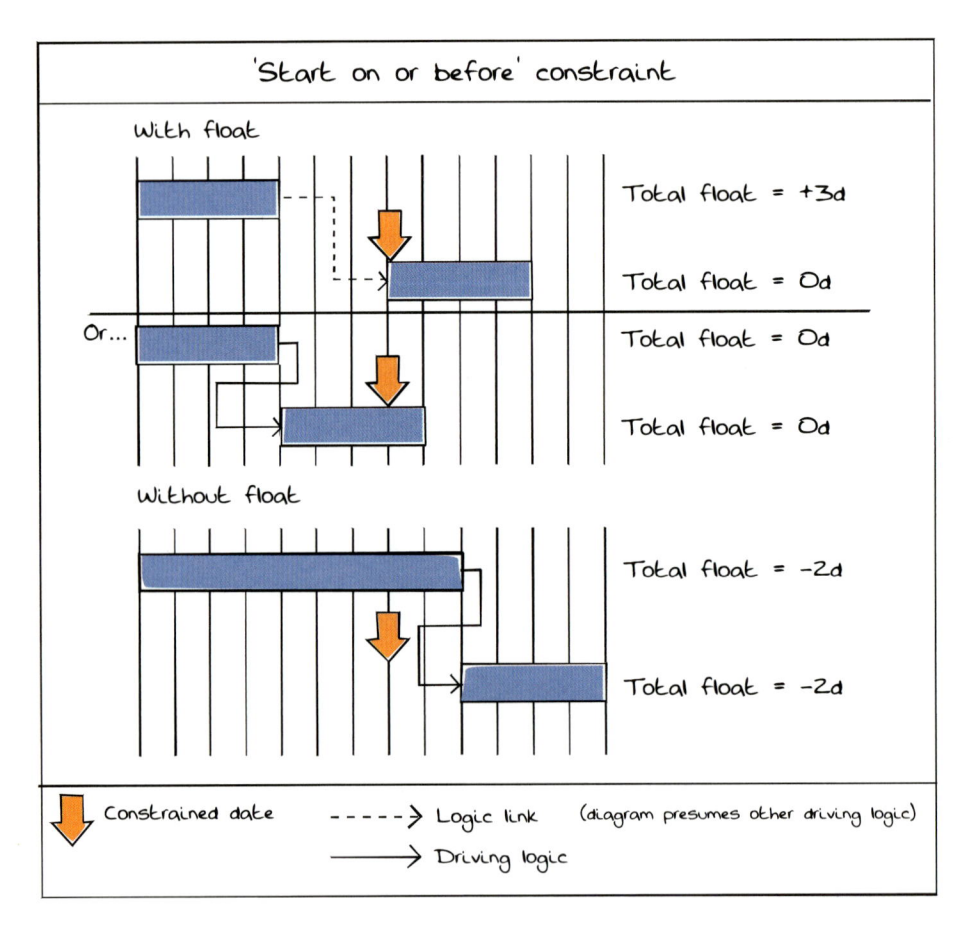

Figure 16.25 'Start on or before' constraint

Building the schedule: network analysis

16.1.17 Displaying networks on bar charts

In scheduling software, the network is created in the way described in the preceding sections, generating the start and finish dates, together with any float values for each activity. It is possible in some scheduling software to display the schedule as a network, and this clearly (if well presented) shows the logical relationships between the individual activities. A more usual representation is in the form of a bar chart (Figure 16.26), which has the advantage of giving a visualisation of where the activities sit in time. Often it is much harder to clearly display the logic in this view. However, most scheduling software packages give the users the ability to show or not to show the logic between the activity bars and milestones.

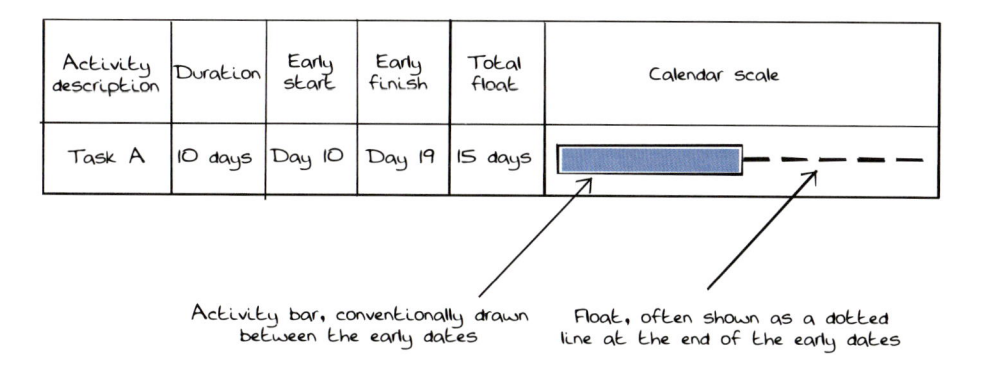

Activity description	Duration	Early start	Early finish	Total float	Calendar scale
Task A	10 days	Day 10	Day 19	15 days	

Activity bar, conventionally drawn between the early dates

Float, often shown as a dotted line at the end of the early dates

Figure 16.26 Bar chart display

16.2 Estimation of durations

The schedule is a model of the future based on the project objectives and outputs. This means that, until such time as the schedule slowly becomes historical fact, the project team estimates how long it will take to achieve these objectives, along with what resources are required and how much it will cost.

To schedule work accurately and effectively, it is important to have a good set of robust scheduling assumptions. As the project moves forward and things change, so must the assumptions. It is this iterative process that ensures that the schedule is designed to deal with the future needs of the project, reducing threats and the range of possible outcomes.

There are many ways of formulating a good set of scheduling assumptions:

Planning, Scheduling, Monitoring and Control

16.2.1 Three-point estimates

Three-point estimates can be used to define minimum, most likely and maximum estimates based on assumptions and previous experience. Actions can arise to address high variances from this work. Monte Carlo analysis can then be used to determine probability of the outcomes.

In this case, the high variance between the most likely and maximum duration is such that the cause of the additional time required should be investigated. In the example, this might be due to unseen services running through the earthworks area. A risk concerning this uncertainty must be registered, and a mitigation developed.

Table 16.1 *Example of three-point estimate*

Activity	A Minimum duration	B Most likely duration	C Maximum duration
Dig Foundations	2 weeks	3 weeks	8 weeks

16.2.2 PERT (programme evaluation review technique)

PERT is a recognised formula to determine activity durations from the three-point estimate, optimistic (O), most likely (M) or pessimistic (P). It produces a weighted average leaning to either the optimistic or the pessimistic, depending on the size of the variance. Once again, significant variances between duration estimates should be explored as potential risks.

Table 16.2 *Example of PERT calculation*

Activity	O Minimum duration	M Most likely duration	P Maximum duration	PERT	
Dig foundations	2 weeks	3 weeks	8 weeks	(O+(4*M)+P)/6	3.7 weeks

Note: the PERT calculation noted above is the most commonly used, although there are alternative calculations, such as the three-point estimate, which is calculated as (P+M+O)/3.

Building the schedule: network analysis

16.2.3 Comparative

Projects of a similar type are used to estimate durations, making appropriate adjustments for scope (i.e. differences in quantities). Other specific differences such as logistical differences, local climate, and local resource availability must be assessed and adjustments made accordingly.

Table 16.3 *Example of comparative estimates*

	Activity	Area	Actual duration
Previous project		2,000 cubic metres	3 weeks
	Dig foundations	Area	Estimated duration
Our project		3,000 cubic metres	4.5 weeks

16.2.4 Benchmarked data

This utilises an existing database of project and activity information regarding timescales and costs for completion. Using this data, average cost and timescales can be applied to a measurable unit and then multiplied by the number of desired units to ascertain an approximate duration. This approach requires a library of reliable data and is best applied to projects where local or project-specific conditions do not provide significant reasons for deviation. Caution needs to be exercised, as differing circumstances will apply to all projects, but it could be used as initial guidance.

Table 16.4 *Example of benchmarked data*

Activity	Project	Volume	Actual duration
	Project A	5,000 cubic metres	6 weeks
	Project B	5,500 cubic metres	7 weeks
Dig foundations	Project C	10,000 cubic metres	10 weeks
	Project D	7,000 cubic metres	8 weeks

Planning, Scheduling, Monitoring and Control

16.2.5 Resource-dependent

Resource-dependent activities, although constraining, are a good way of deriving robust assumptions. Here the limitations are around labour, plant, supply of materials, access to site, etc.

The planner or estimator uses known outputs for the available resource to calculate the estimated duration for an activity (see Table 16.5).

Table 16.5 *Example of resource-dependent estimate*

Activity	Volume	Resource availability	Average gang output	Estimated duration
Dig foundations	2,000 cubic metres	4 gangs + plant	250 cubic metres per week	2 weeks

16.2.6 Expert opinion

One of the best places for assumptions is the project team or people who have expertise in the type of work required. Bringing individuals together in workshops to discuss activity duration, sequence and associated risks can be the best way of producing a realistic schedule.

16.2.7 Personal experience

There is no single right way of developing planning assumptions, but one important element is using as much relevant historical data as you can. When doing so, it is important that you document your assumptions comprehensively. Key project assumptions should be recorded in the risk or assumptions register, as getting them wrong may require working in a different way, which may incur time delay and increased cost.

It is fundamental to the planning process that the project team are involved when developing, iterating and signing off planning assumptions, as, if done in isolation, this can lead to a project schedule that has not gained the buy-in of the project team. This would be worthless as an effective tool to manage the project and forecast outcomes.

The process of planning work as a team, will quickly derive a set of working assumptions against which to base a preliminary schedule, starting with the

WBS. Discreet work packages will be fleshed out against the overall scope of the project. It is important that all elements of work required to deliver the project benefits capability is included within the schedule. Other aspects to be included are, assumptions on tasks, duration, sequence, logical dependencies, interfaces (both internal and external) and costs.

Getting a head start can greatly improve your chance of developing a good schedule; some companies may categorise their projects by discipline or asset type, which makes the process of using existing data much easier.

It is important to realise that assumptions are simply guesses around the future, and therefore can be incorrect. If a specific task is on the critical path, then this may cause delay or increased cost to the project. Key assumptions around activities that can have this effect should be assessed for impact and entered into the risk register. The register should also record the quantified impact in time and cost (along with the corresponding mitigation strategy) which can assist in getting additional funds and/or resources.

16.2.8 Social media

With the increasing prominence and continued evolution of the internet and social media in the workplace, it makes sense to access all planning information available when developing schedules. Caution should be exercised in any resulting information received, particularly with regard to any biases or influences generated by the type of audience.

16.3 Resourcing the schedule

Some organisations have to share resources around the projects they undertake. Consequently the planning of resource usage becomes vital, particularly when resources are limited due to either general scarcity (perhaps because of the wider market) or scarcity of specialist skills. In any project, an assessment of the resources required, and particularly a measure of the quantity of resources required, will be a check on the validity of plans. For example, a schedule created using a network analysis method will consider resources to be unlimited. This is unlikely to be the case in most instances. Introduction of resources to the project should be planned in a realistic manner – sudden increases in resources are not easy to achieve or manage. Similarly, it is not likely that a large mass of resources will suddenly be removed from the project.

16.3.1 Definition of resources

Resources can be one or more of the following:

- labour;
- plant or equipment;
- materials;
- facilities, such as specialist test sites.

In some cases, e.g. high-level budgeting exercises, you may wish to use money as a discrete resource which is not aligned to labour, plant and equipment, or materials. Each of the resources may drive the project pace by constraining the output that can be achieved – for example, a spending cap to a point in time will determine how much work can be completed up to that point. Where resources do constrain the project delivery rate, they are known as 'critical resources'. It is likely that the relative importance of each will vary depending on project type, but also from project to project.

An important consideration may be the relationship between resources and project logistics. Resources generally require space within which to operate, whereas materials need space to be stored.

16.3.2 Purpose of resourcing the schedule

Resourcing of the schedule is a vital stage of the process between creating the network, running a critical path analysis, and issuing the results as the working schedule. It is required in order to:

- determine (low or medium density) or validate (at high density) the duration of each activity;
- promote the consideration of the flow of resources (people, trades or sub-contractors) within the schedule, which will lead to more realistic and achievable outputs;
- lead to an understanding of peak resource requirements, including human resource requirements, funding requirements and peak material supply requirements;
- ascertain the availability of specialist equipment (which may be factored in by use of resource calendars) – this may require advance booking;

Building the schedule: network analysis

- lead to an understanding of logistical requirements: welfare accommodation for the workforce, adequate working space for labour and plant;
- demonstrate the robustness of the schedule to other parties.

16.3.3 Process of resourcing the schedule

16.3.3.1 Estimate the quantity of resources required

Estimates are made using previous projects, experience or standard outputs, as required. These techniques are particularly useful at low or medium-density scheduling. At high-density scheduling, it is more useful to undertake calculations in line with the formulae shown in Figure 16.27. This approach means that the required resources are part of the duration calculation for each activity, and can be allocated to each activity.

$$\frac{\text{Quantity of Work}}{\text{Output}^* \times \text{No of resources}} = \text{Duration}$$

$$^* \text{Output} = \text{standard rate} \times \text{Expected efficiency}$$

Figure 16.27 Establishing the duration of a task based on resource

16.3.3.2 Team sizes

Optimum team sizes for different types of work should be acknowledged when determining resources. This being particularly relevant where crews are made up of front-line production and back-up – bricklayers and their labourers, for example. Particular sets of circumstances may vary the required make-up of such gangs. Specialist advice should be sought in these circumstances.

16.3.3.3 Resource allocation

Resources are allocated to each activity within the schedule, so that when this exercise is complete the sum of all the activities represents the total quantity of resources in the project (in terms of budget, labour, plant).

Planning, Scheduling, Monitoring and Control

16.3.3.4 Resource profiles

Resource demand can now be predicted by looking at histograms – peak requirements can be established:

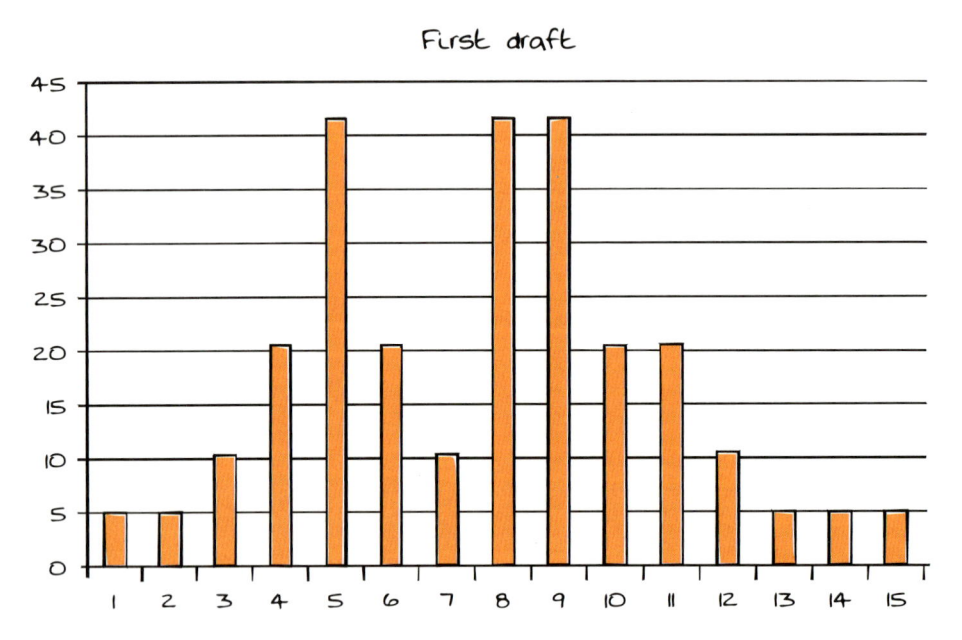

Figure 16.28 First draft resources profile

The diagram above (Figure 16.28) shows resource levels peaking at 42, but the build-up to those peaks does not look realistic in most circumstances; an exercise is required to smooth the build-up and flow of resources.

16.3.4 Resource smoothing

If, as in the example above, the results do not indicate a sensible ramp up and down of resources, it may be necessary to consider resource smoothing. This is the process of smoothing demands so that practical overall levels are achieved, and also that resources are optimised to flow from one piece of work to another.

Resource smoothing needs to be considered on a resource-by-resource basis. When considering human resource, this may mean analysing the requirements for individuals, but it is more usual to analyse by resource type – profession or trade, for example.

Building the schedule: network analysis

The smoothing process should start by initially considering those activities with free float, as moving these will not have an effect on other activities. After the free float has been considered, it may be necessary to consider the use of total float. This exercise will become iterative, as the effects of delaying activities with no free float but some total float will need to be carefully analysed. All smoothing will need to be done within the early and late envelopes for each activity; otherwise the project end date is likely to be compromised.

Figure 16.29 shows the same project as Figure 16.28 above, but this time with optimised resources (resource-levelled chart shown in blue).

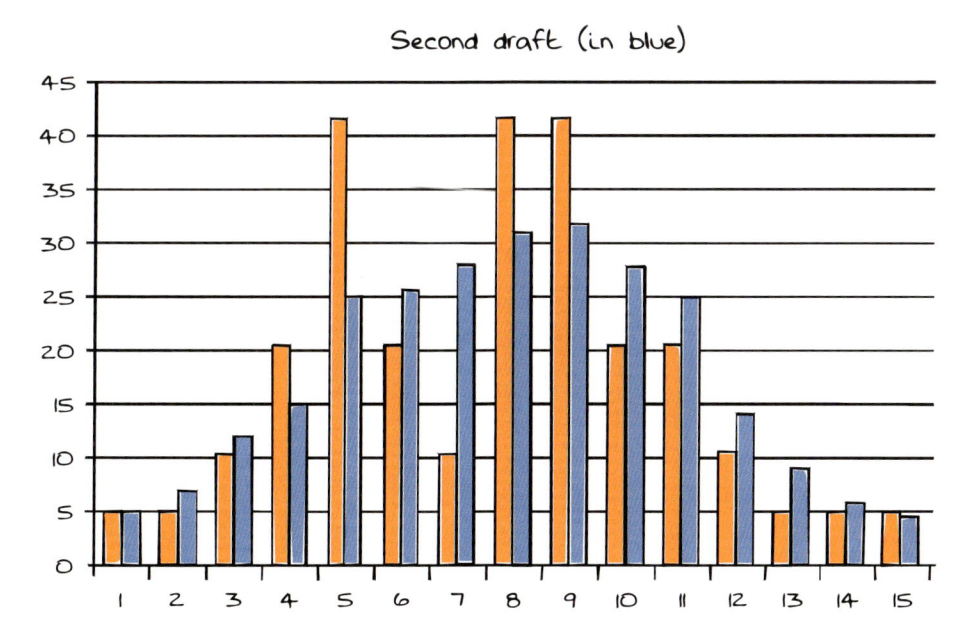

Figure 16.29 Resource-smoothed histogram

Other considerations will be the amount of available resources; where resources are finite, these need to be considered alongside the demand. In Figure 16.30, the orange line indicates the resource limit and shows that, despite the resource-levelling exercise, demand still outstrips availability for a period of time. Management action will be required to solve the shortage.

Resource levelling may be achieved by:

- Redefining the scope of the activities to be undertaken by the particular resource concerned. In simple terms, this might mean giving some of the work to an under-utilised resource.

Planning, Scheduling, Monitoring and Control

- Redefining the specification. This obviously may compromise the quality of the final product.
- Increasing task duration to reduce the overall resource requirements.
- Increasing resources on earlier tasks to bring workload forward, such that peaks in the future are reduced. This will have cost, and possibly quality, implications.
- Delaying non-critical work to reduce demand at peak time – i.e. using free and total float to optimise the schedule.

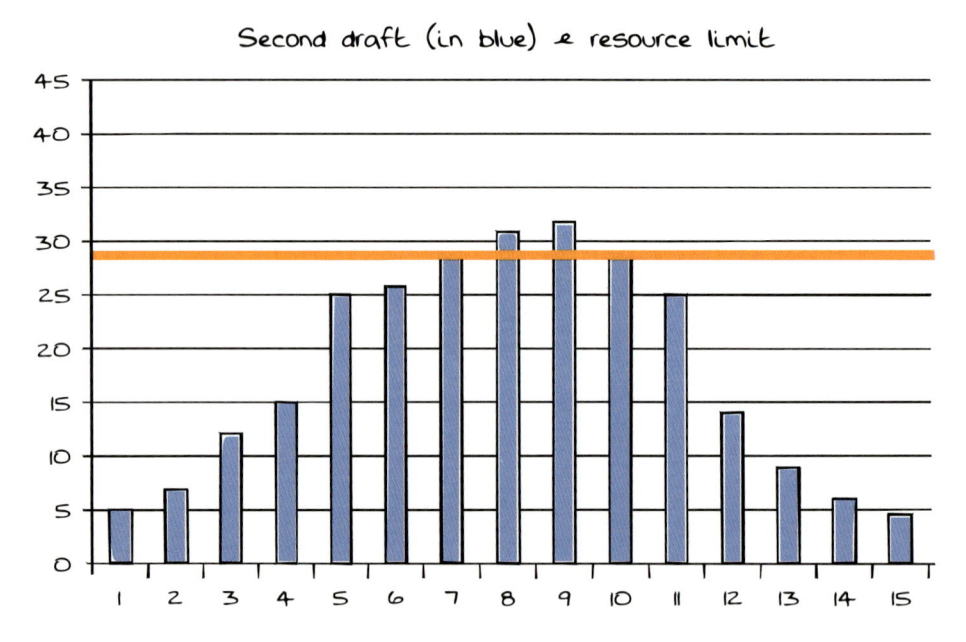

Figure 16.30 Resource-levelled chart with resource limit

16.4 Horizontal and vertical integration of schedules

16.4.1 Horizontal integration

Horizontal integration is the application of logic and the checking of logic through the delivery of products from one part of the process to another. Effectively, it will lead from the start through to the completion of the project. Tracing the schedule horizontally ensures that:

Building the schedule: network analysis

- The schedule is correctly logic-linked.
- The schedule contains all of the scope.
- The schedule identifies the interface milestones between different parties – places where a piece of completed work is passed from one party to another.

16.4.2 Vertical integration

Vertical integration is the process that confirms that the data at different levels of detail is consistent and comprehensive. It should confirm:

- that all schedules cover all the scope (as appropriate to them)
- that all data is consistent between schedules (dates, logic, etc.).

Thus, it allows schedules to be viewed at different levels of detail, as is appropriate for each viewer.

16.5 Scheduling interfaces and dependencies

Managing project interfaces is a fundamental part of successful project management. Whilst it is relatively straightforward to manage a single schedule and its associated dependencies, in most cases there will be deliverables by the project to parties outside the direct control of the project team as well as enabling products or activities required by the project.

It is also possible that you may need to manage many projects that together form an integrated programme or portfolio, and dependency management presents a structured and controlled way of managing change across projects.

It revolves around four key stages:

- identification;
- coding;
- integration and impact analysis;
- impact resolution.

16.5.1 Identification

The project PBS, WBS and RACI will help identify interfaces, as they give a high-level view of work packages, as well as their interfaces with external

Planning, Scheduling, Monitoring and Control

departments or projects. They should also include a list of stakeholders outside the project who may influence the critical path.

Ensuring that all members of the team are consulted during the identification phase is crucial, as it only takes one missed dependency to introduce delay to the project. A group workshop is a good way of generating dialogue, as one person's thought process may stimulate another's.

It is important to note that this process is iterative and should be carried out at the start of each project life cycle as more becomes known about the project and schedule detail is increased.

16.5.2 Coding

Given the size and complexity of modern projects, robust codifying of interfaces is recommended. This could be done with an appropriate activity ID or an activity code. Careful thought must be given to ensuring the coding and naming conventions. It is best to use abbreviations that are readily understood by those reading them (i.e. they relate to the project and work package), thus aiding identification and communication. Given that in a project there will be many hundreds of interfaces, this can greatly increase the chances of slippage due to external influences.

An example dependency code may be:

'INTPROJ0011.1.1001A', where:

- INT=Interface;
- PROJ001=Project ID;
- 1.1.1=Related WBS ID;
- 001=Interface No;
- A='Deliver By' interface.

In the case of interface IDs it is a good idea to use both A and B, which denotes whether it is a 'deliver by' (A) or a 'need by' (B) interface. In the example given, INTPROJ0011.1.1001A would have a corresponding partner, INTPROJ0011.1.1001B.

It is important to note that, even though there are two separate interfaces, they are fundamentally the same thing, and simply represent two separate points of view about when a single event will occur for the purpose of managing variances.

Some interfaces may also include other activity codes, which may denote project life cycle, location and department, but the activity ID will ensure it is visible on a standard layout and is easily picked out from the project schedule.

Building the schedule: network analysis

16.5.3 Integration and impact analysis

Once all interfaces have been identified and the related activities coded, they need to be integrated within the project schedule. There are two primary methods of integration – internal and external.

16.5.3.1 Internal integration

Internal integration is where interfaces are held within the same project schedule, usually within a separate WBS node and/or grouped/filtered by their activity codes. They are logically linked to their corresponding successor or predecessor, and their forecast date is driven by the use of constraints which are determined by the other party (Figure 16.31).

As change happens it is directly represented within the project schedule, and the subsequent impact is modelled throughout the project. When updating dependency forecast dates in this way, it is important to understand the effect of each change, so a step-by-step approach is best. However, it is important to wait until all changes have been made before final analysis, due to the inherent inter-relationships of schedule activities and interfaces.

It is important to take a copy of the schedule before updating, to enable a comparison to be made. This highlights where the project has been impacted and where management time and mitigation efforts should be focused.

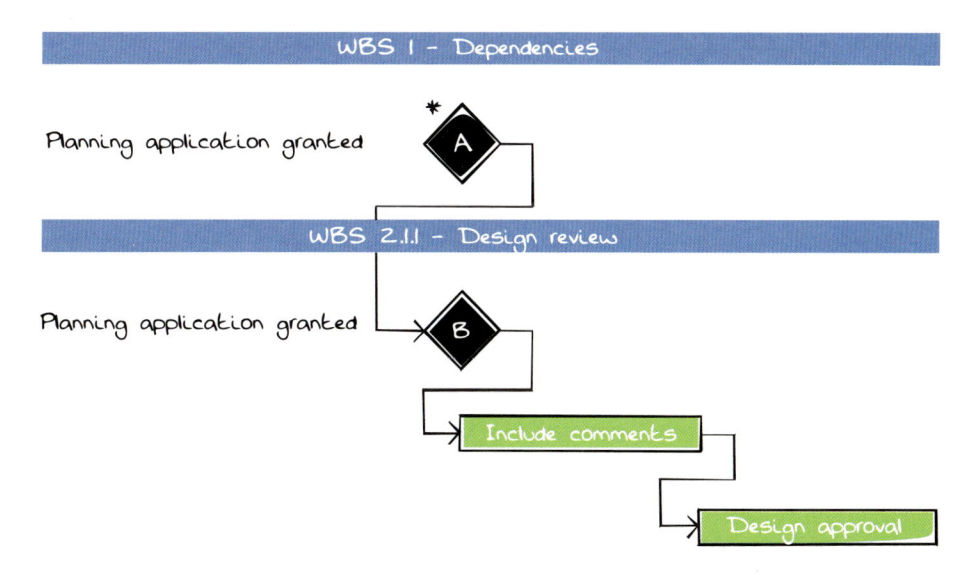

Figure 16.31 Internal integration milestones

Planning, Scheduling, Monitoring and Control

This method is most useful when dealing with a single project.

16.5.3.1.1 Advantages

- Easy to see the context around the dependency, as it is already within its native WBS node
- Ease of visibility within the project schedule focuses the team.

16.5.3.1.2 Limitations

- Impact of changes may be difficult to analyse if the schedule is very large. In these cases, it may be better to consider the use of the external integration method.

16.5.3.2 External integration

External integration is where dependency relationships are held within a separate dependency schedule (Figure 16.32). This method is extremely helpful to the

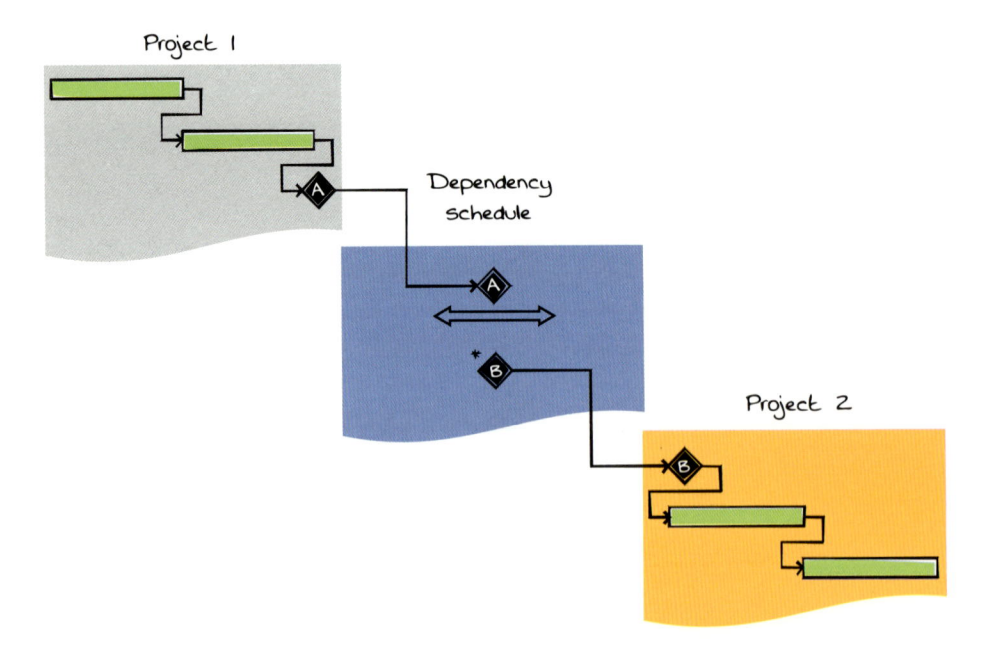

Figure 16.32 External integration milestones

Building the schedule: network analysis

management of interfaces. Not only does it provide a clear picture of all interfaces, but it also allows variance management and impact analysis to happen outside the live scheduling environment. This aids schedule stability.

In this method there are a total of four separate milestones representing the same event. Two are held within each of the project schedules in their corresponding WBS nodes, and two are held within the interface schedule. When movement occurs in interface 'A', the variance can be clearly seen and tracked. Once all the interfaces have been updated, you can then assess the impact by adding logic to the dependency schedule (Figure 16.33).

It is important to ensure that all the dependences are linked to their corresponding partner before the critical path is calculated, as one dependency path can lead through many others. Once the logic linking exercise is complete, you can then schedule the plan (Figure 16.34).

The driving logic from Project 1 will now flow through the dependency schedule and into Project 2 in order to drive the schedule's critical path. (Most enterprise scheduling systems will have the ability to logically link across separate projects, but system capability must be checked, as it is an essential requirement for this method.)

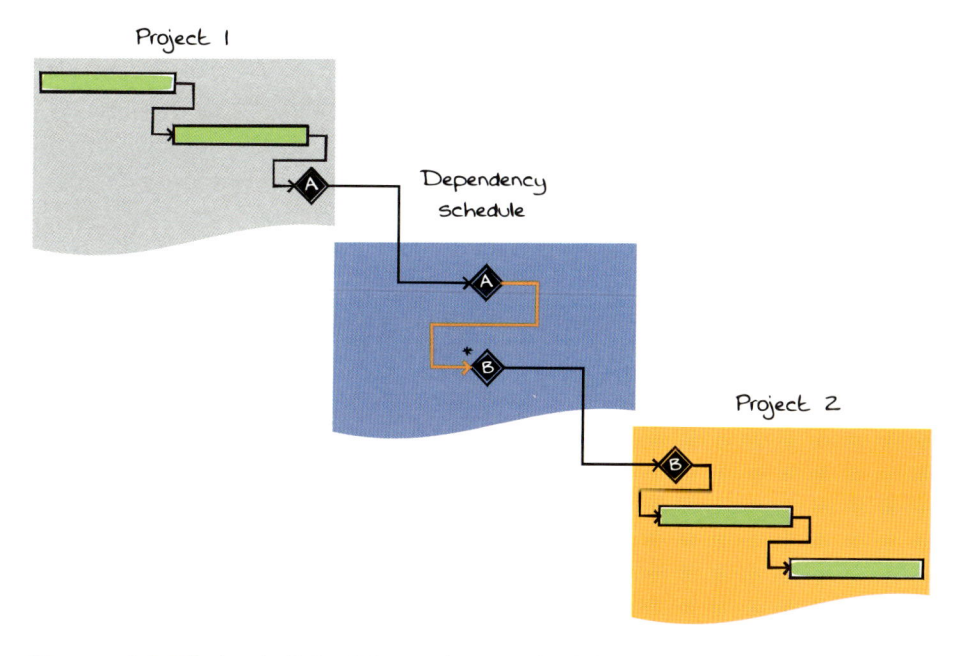

Figure 16.33 Logic-linked dependency schedule

Planning, Scheduling, Monitoring and Control

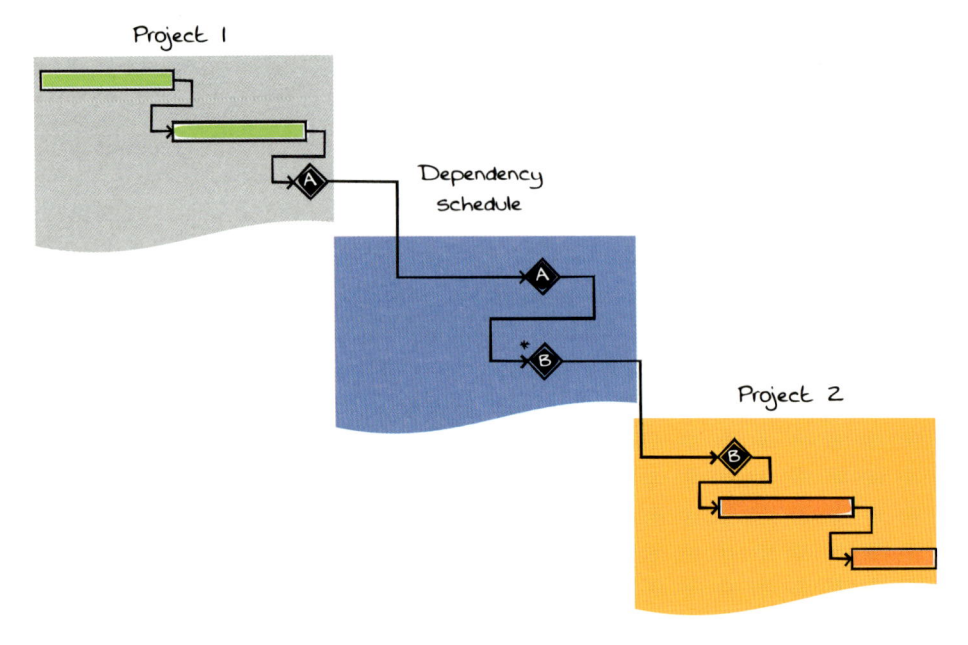

Figure 16.34 Dependency schedule driving project schedules

This method is primarily for use on very large projects, programmes or portfolios where common resources may be shared. The use of interface milestones provides a useful way of controlling the impact of one partner's programme on the rest of the programme. Thus, it is an important way of managing collaborative inputs from different parties on a complex project.

16.5.3.2.1 Advantages

- Manages change in a stable and controlled way that will not disrupt the stability of underlying projects.
- Makes schedule movement and variances easy to identify.
- Clearly defines dependency management as an important part of the schedule.

16.5.3.2.2 Limitations

- Requires robust data quality control measures.
- Requires dedicated resources to execute and manage.

16.5.4 Impact resolution

When dates change, it is important to understand the reason. The first check will be that it has not been caused by an error or misunderstanding.

The schedule data is transferred to a dependency report showing key information for discussion with both project teams to ensure that issues are real and to focus management effort.

The report contains key information about the dependency and is used by the planner, project manager or dependency manager, depending on the scale of management required (Table 16.6).

- Dependency ID: Unique ID that only references either the 'deliver by' or the 'need by' event.
- Dependency name: Standard naming conventions as described in this guide should be adhered to.
- Agreed target date: The date that has been agreed by both projects/parties and is subject to formal change control.
- Current forecast: Schedule logic-driven forecast date representing the most up-to-date position.
- Variance: Difference between target and forecast. This is compared with the dependency threshold and rated with a RAG format (red, amber and green) accordingly, to focus management attention on the most critical issues.
- Threshold: Number of days + or − that a dependency can move without causing an issue with the receiving party (this can, in some cases, only apply to movement one way).
- Reason: Driving issue responsible for the move.
- Mitigation: Action resulting from the dependency management meeting to resolve issue.

Table 16.6 *Interface impact schedule*

Dependency ID	Dependency name	Agreed target date	Current forecast	Variance (days)	Threshold (days)	Reason	Mitigation
INTPROJ001 1.1.1001A	Design released	16-8-18	30-8-18	**−14**	5	Resource	Additional resource being procured

Planning, Scheduling, Monitoring and Control

If the movement is real and the project team is unable to mitigate the slippage, then the receiving project must look to future work to absorb delay by doing things differently or use available project float. Once this has been agreed by both projects, the new dependency date can be changed through the formal change control process.

16.6 Time contingencies

Time contingency is a duration of time assigned to an activity that takes into consideration the impact of uncertainty. During the process of developing planning assumptions, the likely impact of unforeseen events must be taken into consideration. Sometimes a straightforward way of doing so is to assign a percentage of the overall activity duration to the end of the activity, e.g. 10%. A more scientific method might be to use the output of a quantified schedule risk assessment to apportion time risk to activities.

The assessment of risk is heavily influenced by the risk appetite of the organisation undertaking the assessment, and this should be borne in mind. Attitude to risk may also be very subjective, so it is important to consult as widely as possible before attempting to reach a consensus and making due allowances for time contingencies.

16.6.1 Definition of buffers

A buffer is the term used to describe a period of time that is built into a schedule to add greater certainty to the end date (Figure 16.35). There are three types:

- Resource buffer: the additional lead time given to critical resources to forewarn a particular resource that a critical activity is approaching.
- Feeder buffer: the additional time allocated at the end of tasks within a schedule.
- Project buffer: the additional time allocated at the end of a project schedule.

16.6.2 Use of buffers

Buffers may be introduced into the network to provide for time contingency. In some cases these may have contractual significance. In certain types of project,

Building the schedule: network analysis

Buffers introduced into a project network

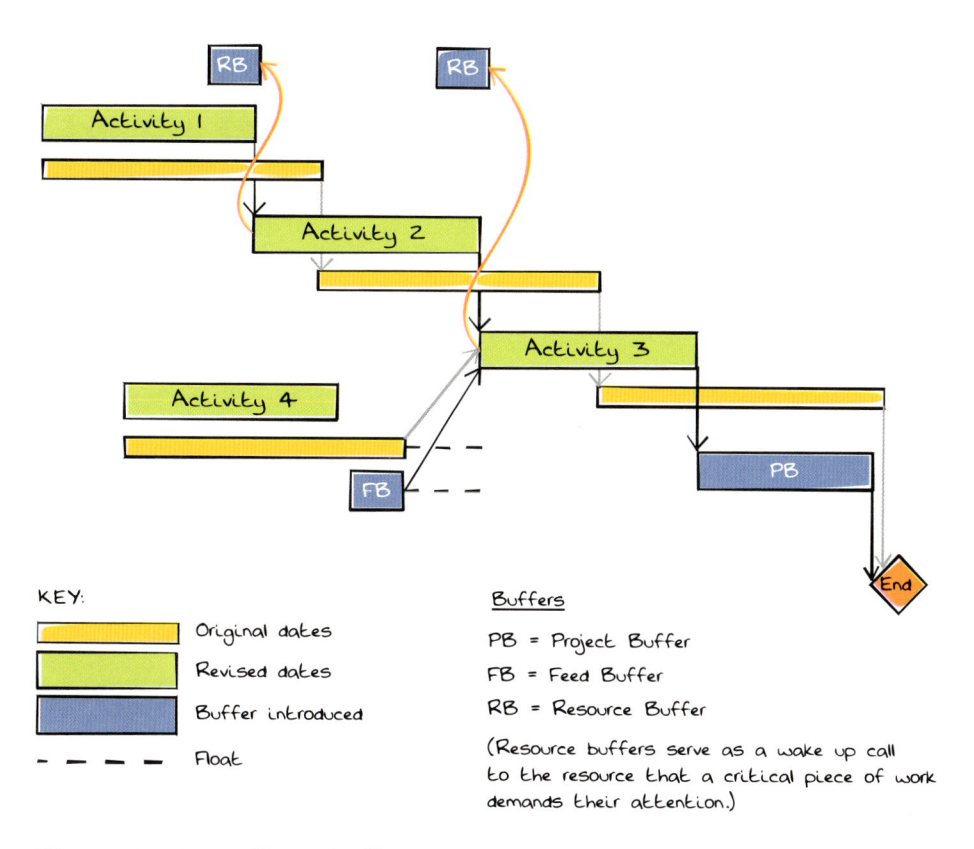

Figure 16.35 Different buffer types

KEY:
- Original dates
- Revised dates
- Buffer introduced
- – – – Float

Buffers
- PB = Project Buffer
- FB = Feed Buffer
- RB = Resource Buffer

(Resource buffers serve as a wake up call to the resource that a critical piece of work demands their attention.)

this may help reduce overall project duration by allowing activities to start earlier. This, in turn, allows the follow-on activities to start earlier.

It is more commonly used on basic or repetitive types of project, but, with appropriate care, may be used on all types. Full buy-in of all parties is, however, essential, and is likely that contract issues will need to be considered. For example, on NEC3 contracts (NEC – New Engineeering Contract) the use of time risk allowance is specifically mentioned in order to bring realism into the contractors' schedule. The use of Buffers as described is less likely to be useful on those projects involving a significant degree of sub-contracting.

165

Planning, Scheduling, Monitoring and Control

16.6.2.1 Advantages of using buffers

- It emphasises doing works as early as possible to promote earlier than planned completion.
- It focuses on the availability of resources and thus produces a more realistic schedule than a pure critical path analysis (presuming that only hard logic has been used in the CPA).
- It promotes emphasis on the critical path.
- It is appropriate for projects with basic or repetitive activities.

16.6.2.2 Limitations of using buffers

- It does not recognise the ways that sub-contracts /specialist resources plan their work. If resources are not on hand, then the advantage of an early start cannot be made.
- Issues around contract and risk ownership need to be identified and resolved.
- There is potential for additional cost due to delay and disruption to follow-on trades.
- There is potential for resources to be unavailable due to workload being repeatedly re-organised to critical activities.
- It may result in a lot of additional activities to the schedule, e.g. feeder and resource buffers, which can add complexity to the logic.
- In addition, there is a lot of extra work required in creating and maintaining the additional activities noted above. Consider reading the existing schedule properly instead!

The results of the scheduling may be presented in a number of ways:

- Bar charts (sometimes known as Gantt charts), which provide a graphical representation and may be used in conjunction with other methods. Originally considered a method of planning, now more usually seen as an output of network analysis.
- Line of balance charts that show the flow of resources, and facilitate the balancing of the same.
- Time chainage charts that introduce a spatial awareness into planning the project.

17.1 Bar charts

Bar charts are sometimes referred to as Gantt charts, and often form the presentation method of the other techniques discussed. Activities are listed with other tabular information, such as dates and durations on the left side with time intervals over the bars on the right-hand side, where the durations are shown in the form of horizontal bars (Figure 17.1).

17.1.1 Presentation considerations

Consideration should be given to the complexity to be displayed and the target audience. For example, the inclusion of logic links detracts from the clarity of the presented chart (as it will on many complex pieces of work). Complex schedules may benefit from high-level, even simplistic explanations (see Figure 17.2 for an example).

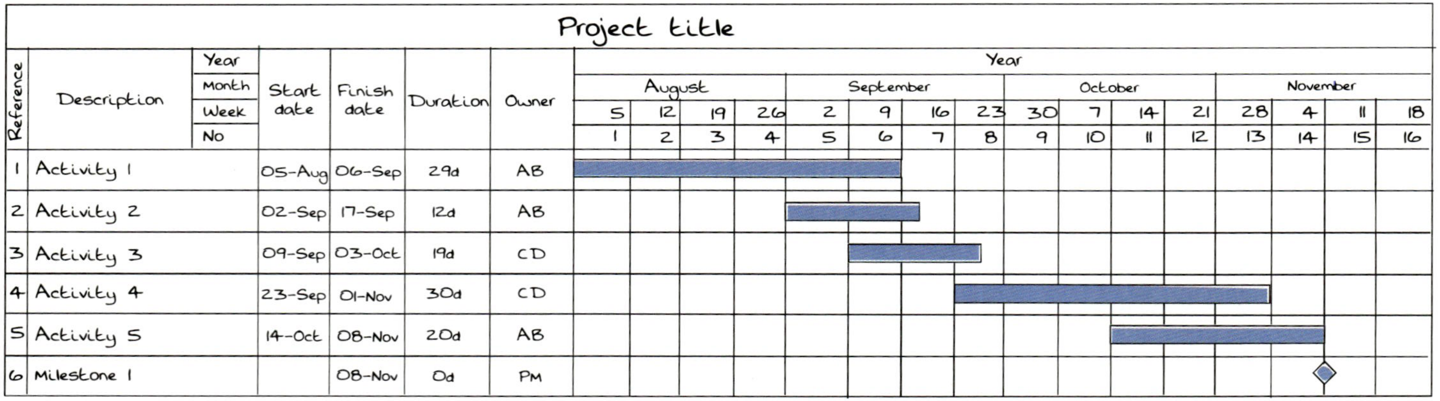

Figure 17.1 A simple bar chart

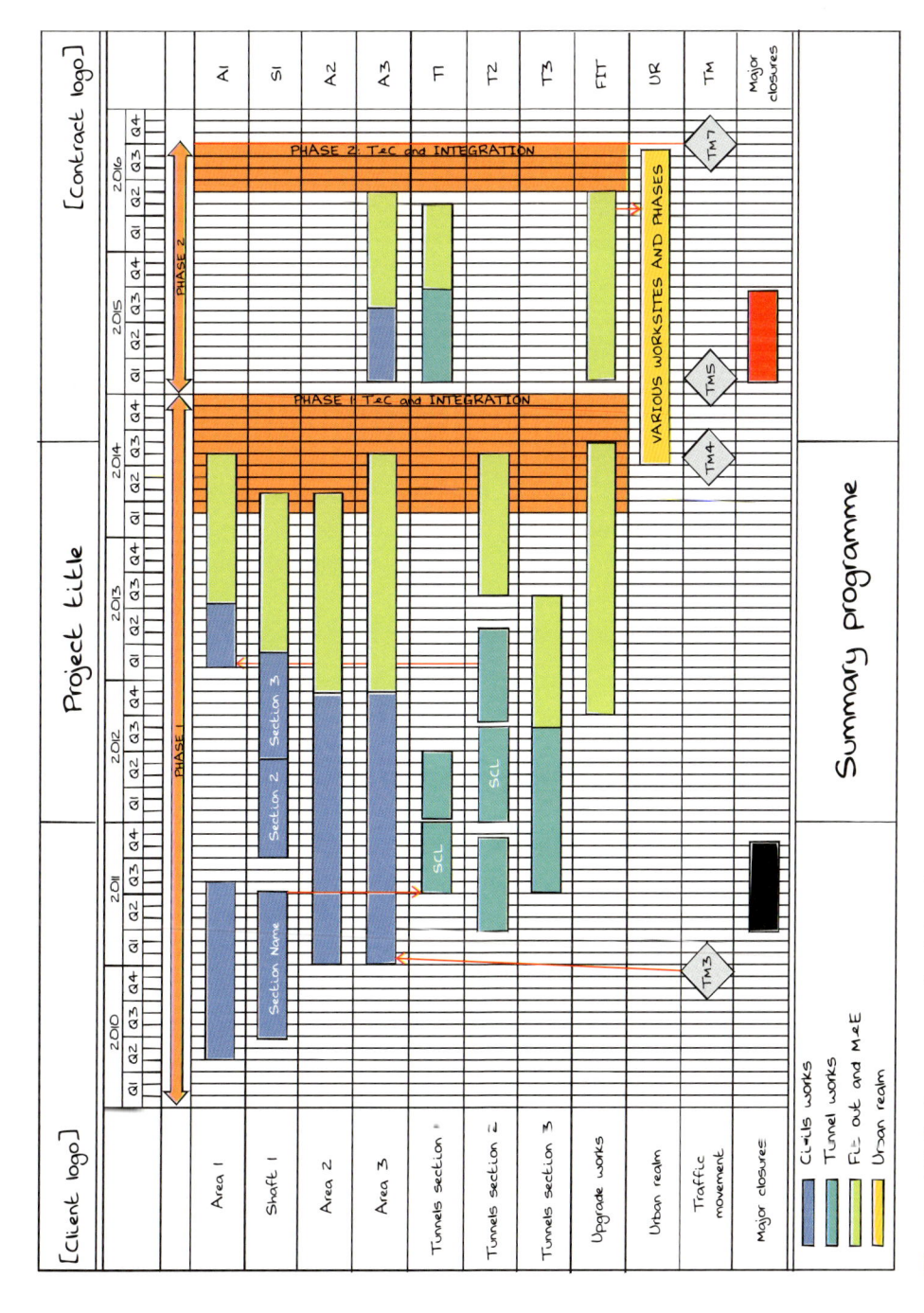

Figure 17.2 Strategic schedule of a major construction project at low density

Planning, Scheduling, Monitoring and Control

Scheduling software may offer seemingly limitless formatting possibilities, but consideration must be given to the viewer. Ideally, schedules should have equal clarity if rendered in 'greyscale' (black and white), if this is how they may be printed.

17.1.1.1 Advantages of bar charts

- Clear, pictorial representation of the plan.
- Generally well understood.
- Relatively simple to create.
- Can be used to show progress.
- Can be used to plan resources.

17.1.1.2 Limitations of bar charts

- On their own, do not show dependencies.
- There is a limit to the size of schedule that can reasonably be read and understood.
- Cannot easily cope with change as a result of progress or scope change.

17.1.2 An Alternative to bar chart reporting

A key part of planning/scheduling is to communicate effectively to a variety of audiences. When reporting to the projects, programmes and portfolio stakeholders, it is always important to consider the audience of those reports. Certain individuals are confident with data presented in a bar chart format, but there may be people who prefer alternative presentations. This is even more important when reporting outside the project.

It is vital to get the 'buy-in' of the key stakeholders, so alternative means of communicating the schedule should be sought. Some people can relate more to a spreadsheet of dates, and some prefer milestones. Choosing the right format could be key to getting a point across or getting an important decision made.

Figure 17.3 shows a format using milestones.

The legend for all the milestones is shown on the chart; but it should be noted that the optimistic, realistic and pessimistic dates are all generated from quantitative schedule risk analysis.

This milestone format can be a clearer way of presenting several dates relating to one activity.

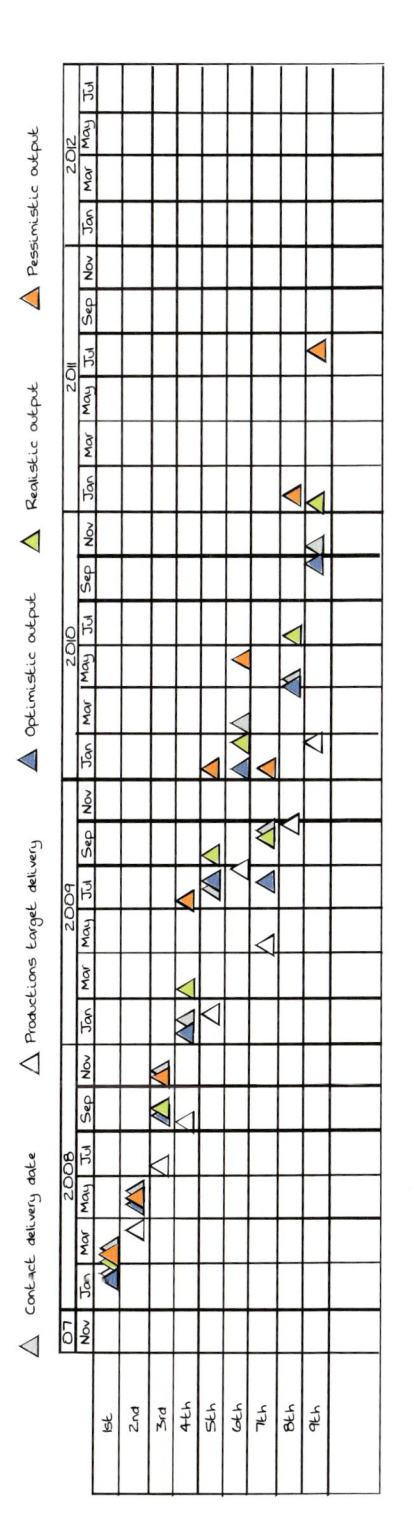

Plus many more options...
Including tabular

Tailor to meet your audience's needs.
Remember you may have multiple audiences.

Figure 17.3 Using milestones to give clarity to the schedule

Planning, Scheduling, Monitoring and Control

17.2 Line of balance

Line of balance is a method most suited to the planning and adjusting of repetitive work. It is particularly used when a series of repetitive units is required, for example in a manufacturing environment. It focuses on resources and outputs to achieve a rate of progress that can be expressed simply and graphically. It is often thought to be most appropriate for residential-type projects, for example, but the technique may equally be applied to repetitive elements of any project. Structural steelwork is a possible example of a trade suited for planning and monitoring in this way.

17.2.1 Creating a line of balance chart

A line of balance chart is created by plotting the output (in no. of units completed, m^2, etc.) on the y axis, and time on the x axis. Thus, a chart can be produced (Figure 17.4).

When the plotting of work is complete, it should then be possible to analyse the trades that are influencing the overall project duration due to their slower rate of progress. In the example below, the mechanical & electrical 1st fix and partitions 2nd fix are progressing at a slower rate. The possibility of optimising the duration,

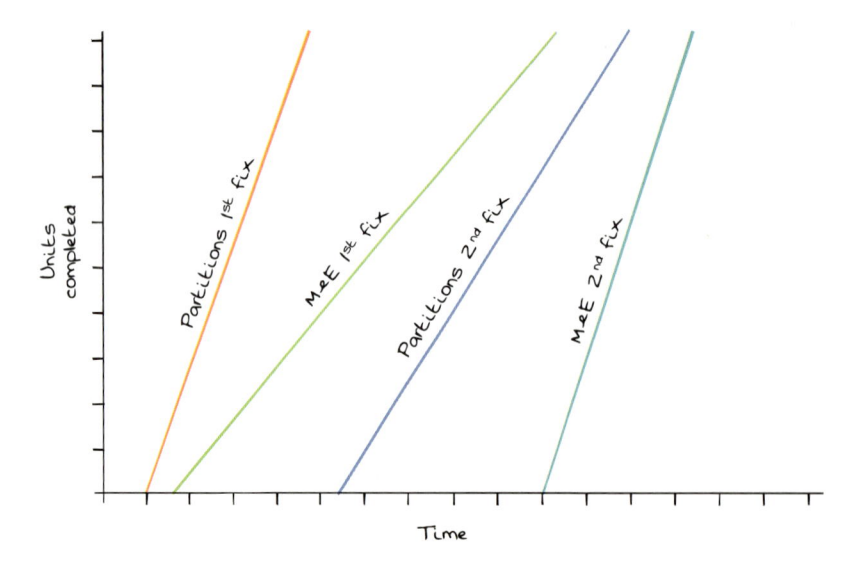

Figure 17.4 Creating a line of balance chart

Communicating the schedule

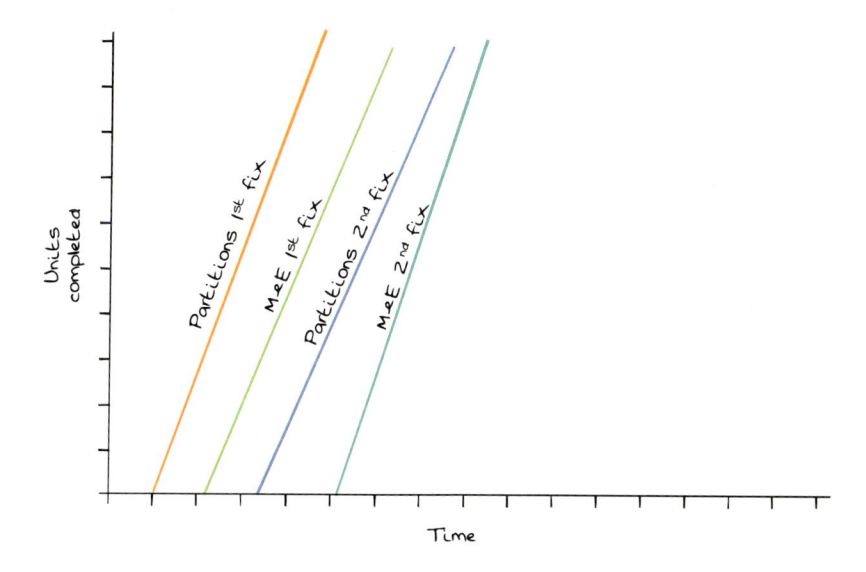

Figure 17.5 Optimising work flow in line of balance

for example by increasing resources on these two tasks, can be examined and put into practice as appropriate (Figure 17.5).

17.2.2 Advantages of line of balance

- Encourages the use of resource levelling, giving the trades continuity of work and a more realistic chance of achieving the plan than a purely logic-driven schedule would.
- Easier to understand than a bar chart.
- More concise form of presentation (fewer pages of schedule).
- Can be used to predict completion by extrapolating the progress to date, or making assumptions about future progress.
- Can be used as a tool that will identify modifications required to the schedule.
- Will clearly highlight ensuing trades that are catching up with their predecessors, and therefore at risk of running out of work.
- This method demands consideration of expected output and will improve the quality of the plan.
- May assist in demonstrating delay and disruption in a claim situation (or rebutting the same).
- Focuses on outputs.

Planning, Scheduling, Monitoring and Control

17.2.3 Limitations of line of balance

- It is purely based on outputs and will not recognise out-of-sequence working.
- Does not show exact or logical relationships.
- Unlikely to be acceptable as a contract schedule.
- Not suitable for all projects or all parts of a project.
- Not supported by standard scheduling software – though special software can be purchased.

17.3 Time chainage

17.3.1 Definition of time chainage charts

Time chainage charts are used to describe projects that are linear in nature (an example being road construction). When well designed and drawn, they are a very useful visualisation tool, often allowing the whole project to be displayed on a single chart (Figure 17.6). They can be highly complex, so their design should take the end-users' requirements into consideration. Software is available that can convert most standard scheduling software into a time chainage chart by using activity coding to define the time and distance parameters.

- The diagram below (Figure 17.6) shows the basic elements of a time chainage chart.

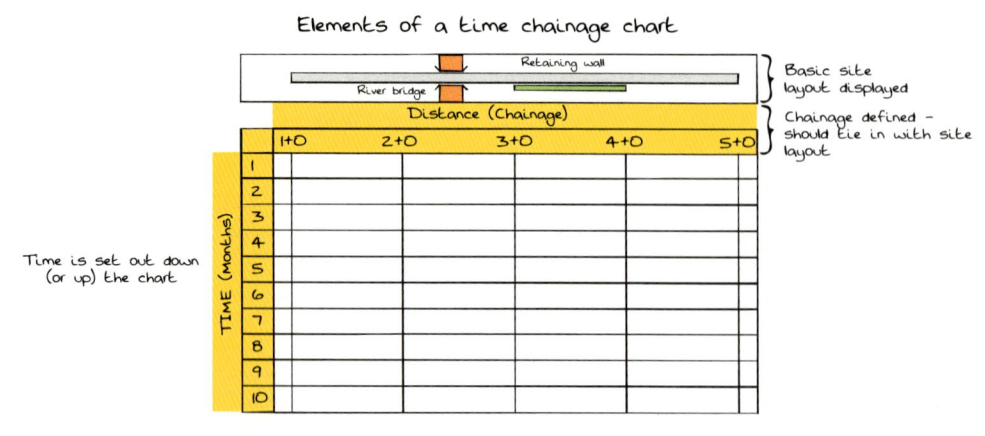

Figure 17.6 Basic elements of a time chainage chart

Communicating the schedule

- Time is defined in appropriate periods down the side of the illustrated chart. The start of the project is usually shown at the top of the chart and the end at the bottom.
- The distance is shown horizontally in the illustrated chart, and may include the chainage (location defined in metres) or named geographic locations, as appropriate.
- At the top of the chart a simple representation or map of the project may be shown to aid visualisation.
- Software is available that allows an automatic update from standard scheduling software.

Below is a simplified explanation of the build-up of a time chainage chart that helps illustrate the technique.

17.3.2 Explanation of the time chainage technique

The project being used to illustrate the technique (Figures 17.7–17.11) is a road project that contains two structures: a retaining wall and a road bridge. In order to construct these structures it is necessary to construct a 'haul road' – a temporary route that allows construction vehicles to traverse the site with heavy loads.

The separate bar section across the top shows the work geographically.

The major section of this project is the bridge, so in order to facilitate its construction; a temporary haul road is required. This is constructed from each end of the site as shown.

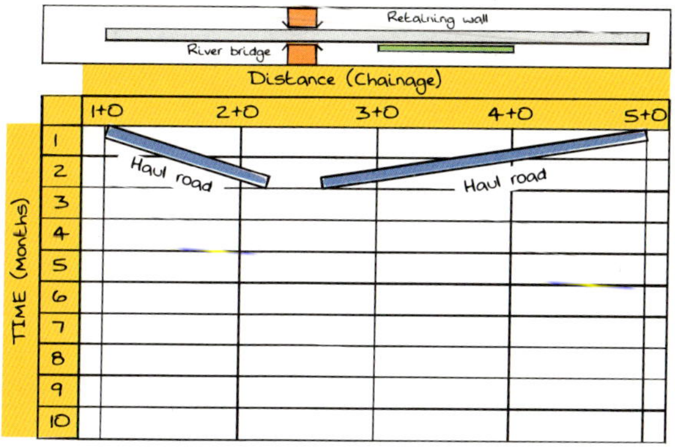

Figure 17.7 Time chainage task 1

Planning, Scheduling, Monitoring and Control

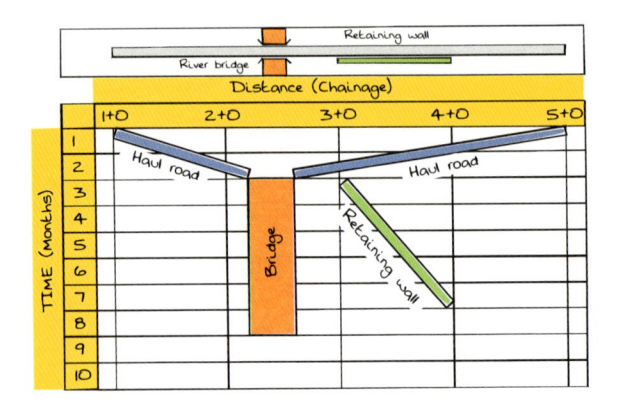

Figure 17.8 Time chainage tasks 2 and 3

The completion of the haul roads allows the construction of both the retaining wall and the bridge:

The road can commence once the bridge is nearing completion; for the purposes of this example, we assume this has to be built in one continuous operation. The first option considers the operation from (say) north to south.

However, by reconsidering this operation and constructing it from south to north, an earlier start can be made and a month saved from the overall duration of the construction schedule.

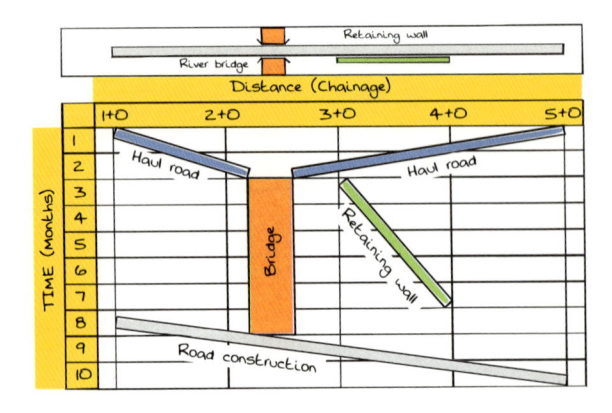

Figure 17.9 Time chainage task 4

Communicating the schedule

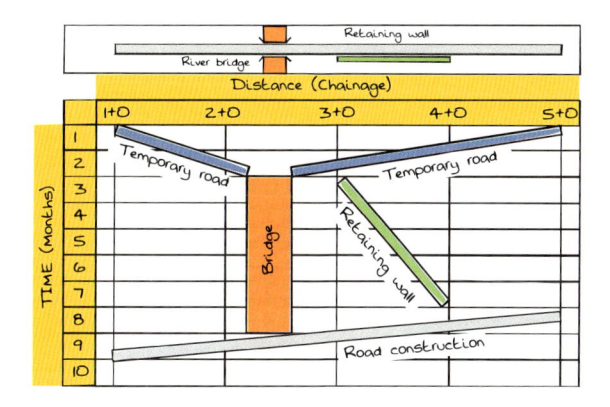

Figure 17.10 Time chainage sequencing

17.3.3 Advantages of time chainage

- It is a very clear way of showing physical build against time.
- It will quickly show if there are spatial clashes in the schedule.
- It shows not only the location of the activity but also the direction of progress and the required progress rate.

17.3.4 Limitations of time chainage

- Only appropriate in certain circumstances – it is particularly useful in geographically spread projects (which would also be 'linear' in character – like a road, a railway or a high-rise building).
- Individual preference for visualising the project (it does not suit everyone).

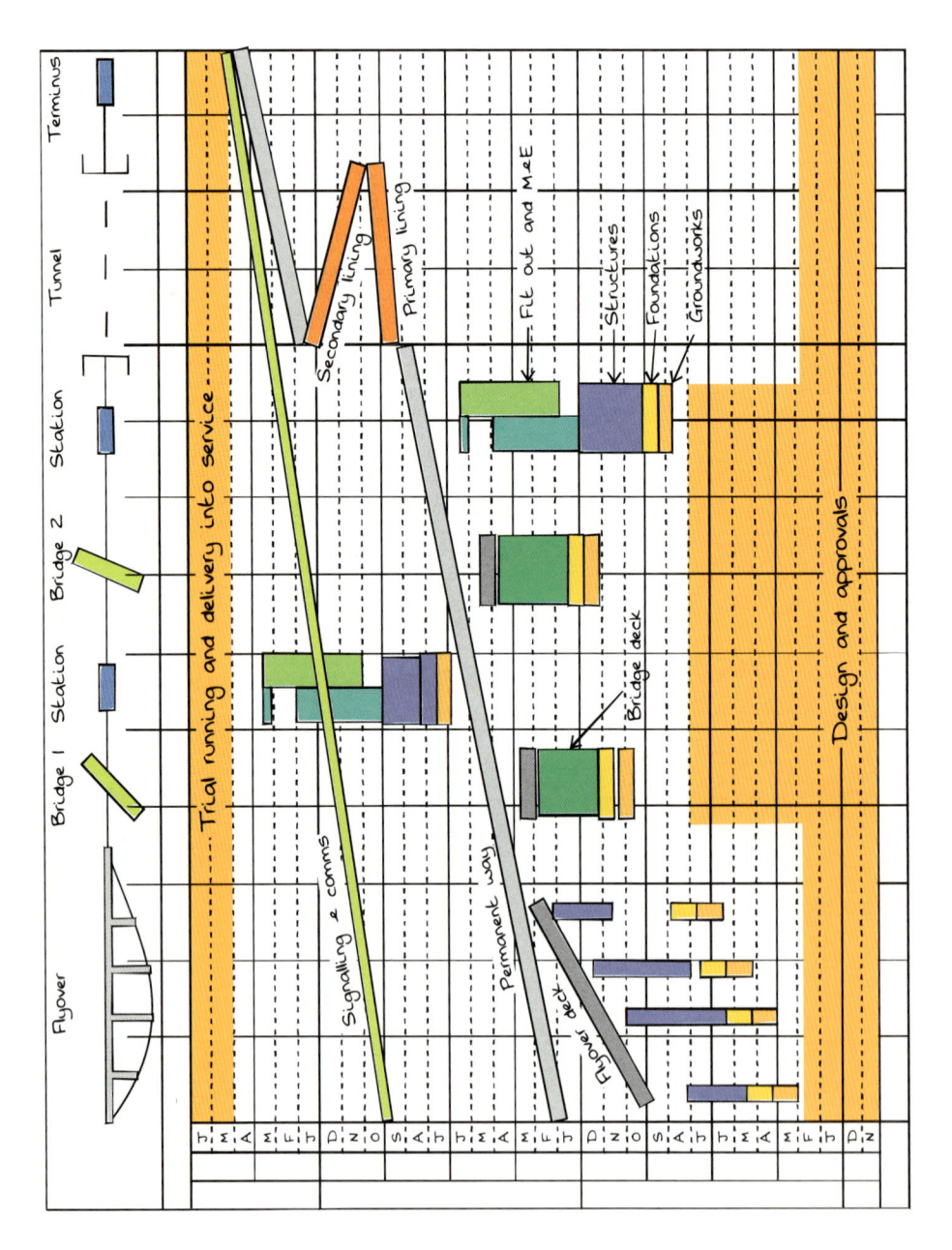

Figure 17.11 Example of a time chainage diagram for a new railway

17.4 Schedule narrative

A schedule narrative is a fundamental part of any complex schedule. It is used to explain, illuminate and communicate. It is used especially when issuing a schedule to a third party, usually for customer approval or acceptance, but is important for clarity in any event. A narrative will typically include some or all of the following:

17.4.1 Scope

A description of the work scope should be included, covering design, procurement, development strategy, implementation phase and testing and commissioning, as appropriate.

17.4.2 Health, safety and environmental considerations

For example, in construction, whether the site is a 'green field', a city centre, a nuclear site, a working railway or an airport, etc., as the HSE requirements will vary considerably.

17.4.3 Risks, opportunities and contingencies

Risks to the time aspects of the project should be identified and discussed. This would include a discussion on the use of any float.

17.4.4 Breakdown structures

There should be adequate explanation in the narrative to describe the hierarchical structures used in creating the schedule, for example geographical or physical work groups.

17.4.5 Project phasing

Project phasing may be driven by other factors, such as financial planning, physical constraints or governance gateways. These should be detailed in the narrative. This is particularly pertinent when these factors are dynamic, for example in construction-site logistics layouts.

17.4.6 Stakeholders

Any stakeholders' interest in the schedule should be identified and described.

17.4.7 Resources

Resources used in execution of the schedule should be described in the schedule; the narrative should note any resource constraints or special resource requirements, in particular highlighting any scarce resources that pose a threat to the delivery of the project if they are unavailable. Any special measures required need to be identified. Resource histograms may be a useful communication tool to indicate the resources to be deployed:

- labour;
- major items of plant or equipment;
- major items of material.

17.4.8 Critical path(s)

A description of the critical path(s) through the project, possibly with simple illustrations to enhance explanation, together with a commentary expanding on any relevant or pertinent issues relating to decisions, progress, strategies, risks or other matters pertaining to the critical works in the project.

17.4.9 Assumptions

A description of the key assumptions that affect the management of time, in order to explain and enhance understanding of the schedule.

17.4.10 Calendars

Calendars which underpin the schedule should be listed and described as part of the narrative. A summary of those used in the schedule should be provided. It should refer to the days/hours to be worked, and describe any exceptional calendars used. For example, there may be separate calendars for:

- normal working hours;
- 7-day working;
- 24-hour working;

Communicating the schedule

- night-shift or weekend working;
- planned closures for special works.

17.4.11 Activity codes

Details of all activity and resource codes in the schedule, and reasons why they are used.

17.4.12 Details of any possessions, shut-downs or other special working conditions

Working railways usually require possessions for track work to be done.

Factories and production facilities require shut-downs. Nuclear sites may require special working conditions.

17.4.13 Consents required

Any consents from third party authorities should be identified either in the schedule or in the narrative, including the required timing for any application or approval periods.

17.4.14 Permits and licences

Any permits and licences required should be identified either in the schedule or in the narrative, including the required timing for any application or approval periods.

It is noted that the above list, though not necessarily exhaustive, represents a considerable effort to create and maintain. Common sense must prevail in determining what is appropriate in different circumstances. It may be appropriate that some of the details listed above form part of the project procedures or other, standalone documents. The central purpose of the narrative – to communicate and explain the schedule – must not be lost in the creation and updating of an exhaustive narrative document.

The narrative is reviewed, revised and re-issued alongside each submission of the schedule and associated documents.

18.1 Definition of schedule review

Schedule review is the process that confirms that the schedule is fit for purpose: i.e. that it can be used to direct and accurately monitor the work. In general, there are two stages:

- initial review of the schedule to confirm its fitness for purpose
- ongoing review of the schedule to ensure that it continues to be fit for purpose.

18.2 Purpose of schedule review

Schedule review is undertaken to ensure that the schedule is fit, and remains fit for purpose.

18.3 Checking the schedule

Fundamental checks of the schedule should confirm that the full project scope has been included; that the schedule describes a practical methodology for delivering the work; and that all contract deliverables, constraints, key dates and milestones are included. The following sections detail further checks that may be made to test a schedule's integrity and relevance. There are two categories of checks:

- planning checks;
- scheduling checks.

Planning, Scheduling, Monitoring and Control

Planning checks deal with the practicality of the plans to direct the completion of the project. Scheduling checks check the integrity of the time model, to ensure that it flows correctly and can be used to forecast accurate dates.

The primary consideration must be the practical content of the schedule, but some useful integrity checks are also discussed in this section.

In order to review a schedule, it is important to be able to read and interpret it.

18.3.1 Understanding the project schedule

It is important to be aware that a schedule submitted in a software format will not necessarily display in the way intended, or as it was viewed on the sender's screen. Some software will default to the user's display settings. It is important to select the correct layouts and filters before viewing the schedule. It is, therefore, normal practice when submitting a schedule to include a copy in a file format that will display the schedule without the need for particular planning software to be installed on the viewer's screen.

18.3.2 Components of the schedule display

As stated, a schedule may be presented in many and various ways. Figure 18.1 features some of the elements that are typically available.

18.3.2.1 Data table

The data table contains information about each activity. There is almost a limitless amount of information that can be displayed. The example below shows a fairly standard display for the contents of the adjacent Gantt chart.

- Act ID = activity identifying number.
- Act Name = description of the activity.
- OD = original duration of the activity.
- Start/Finish = start and finish dates of the activity (usually early start and early finish).
- Total Float is self-explanatory.
- B/L Start = baseline start date.
- B/L Finish = baseline finish date.

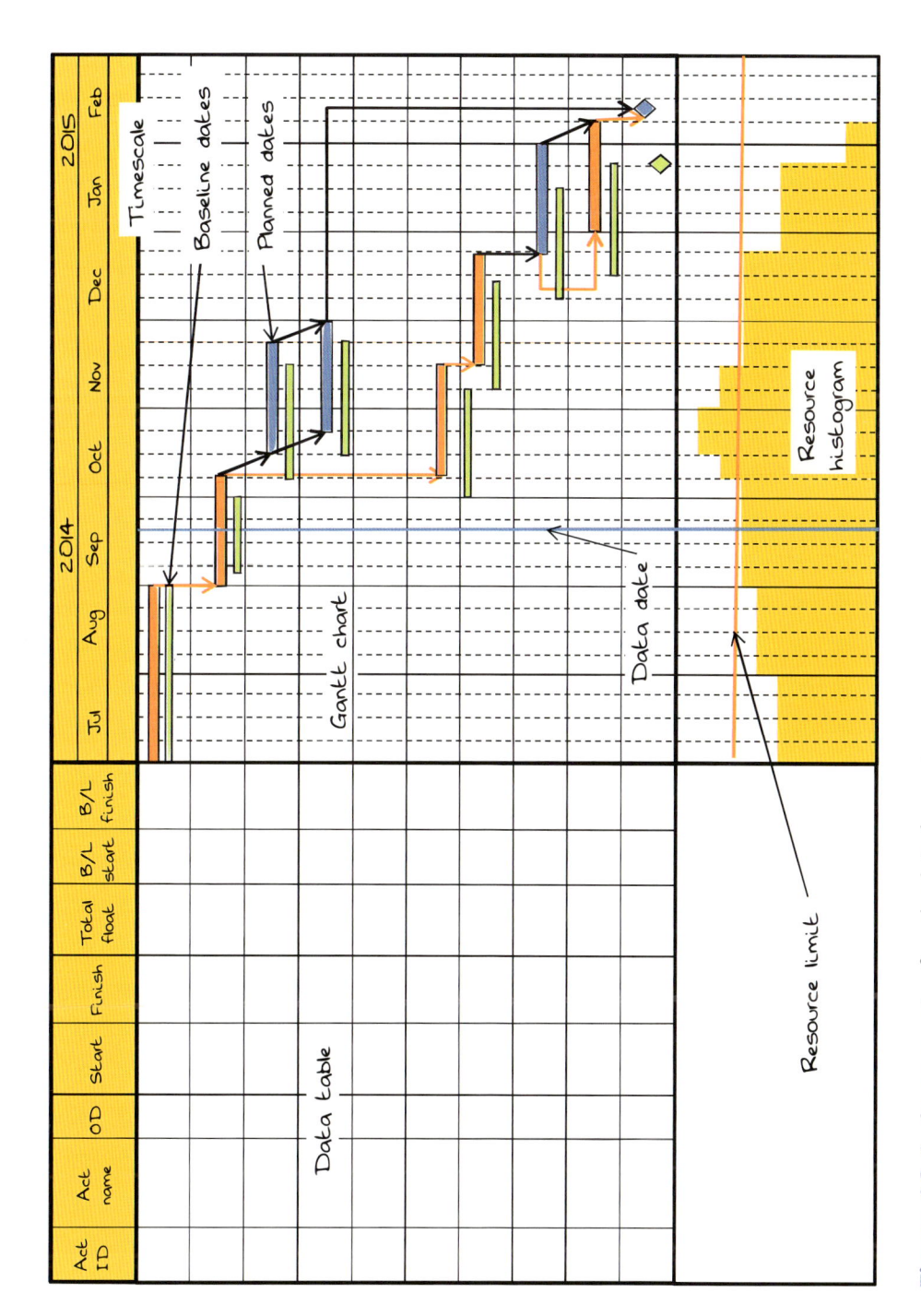

Figure 18.1 Components of a schedule for review

Planning, Scheduling, Monitoring and Control

Additional items that could be displayed may include:

- cost and budget data for each activity;
- predecessors and successors of each activity (although this may be difficult to display and read);
- progress data such as actual dates, percentage complete and remaining duration.

18.3.2.2 Timescale

The timescale can be used to display calendar dates in various levels of detail, and/or ordinal dates. The timescale can usually be expanded to aid visibility of a particular timeframe, or contracted to give an overview of a wider portion of time.

The schedule should also display the data date. The data date is the point up to which project progress is updated. It is also the point from which any network analysis would be calculated when 're-scheduling' the project.

18.3.2.3 Gantt chart

Typically called the bar chart, this displays bars between pairs of dates (start and finish dates). A number of bars may be shown, for example based on early dates, late dates or baseline dates (to visualise progress slippage or recovery). Whilst the options are many, for clarity the number of bars displayed should be kept to a minimum.

18.3.2.4 Resource histogram

The resource histogram will graphically display the resource usage that the schedule calculates to be required to complete the work. It may represent all the resources, or be filtered to display a particular type of resource, or resources, for a particular section of works.

A resource limit may be displayed (red line in Figure 18.1). If such a limit has been set, then any resource requirement over that limit may be highlighted in a different colour (not shown in Figure 18.1).

18.3.3 Critical matters not included in the display

18.3.3.1 Understanding the critical path

In reality, tracing the critical path and other network logic in a complex schedule is difficult on paper (unless specific extracts have been produced, which by their nature will give limited information), and therefore an electronic review is necessary.

18.3.3.2 Calendars

It is important to understand what calendars and work patterns have been used when building the schedule. (This can be displayed in the data table.) The calendars used will influence overall duration of activities (and hence the project), the ability to accelerate the project, and the understanding of the critical path.

18.3.3.3 Schedule drivers

Similarly to the issue of calendars, schedule duration is also driven by the availability and quantity of resources used, assumed output rates and productivity rates. It is, therefore, crucial to know this information when checking the schedule.

When reviewing the schedule, it is also vital to be aware of any constraints that have been used.

18.3.3.4 Filters and layouts

Filters are used to display a specific selection of the schedule at any one time. Filters may be used to extract a particular area of responsibility, criticality, activity coding and many others. When reading a filtered schedule, it is important to understand what element of it is being viewed (and, conversely, what is NOT being viewed).

Layouts determine how the schedule will be viewed by determining the contents of the data table, the Gantt chart, the presentation of the timescale, etc.

18.3.3.5 Risk

When reviewing the schedule, it is important to understand the associated risks. These should be found in or added to the project risk register.

18.4 Planning checks

18.4.1 Administration

- Check that all headers and footers are correct, with current date and revision number.
- It is good practice for the header or footer to also include fields for layout, filter, project ID, project name, username, version number, etc. applied to the printed version.
- Check that the schedule has been checked and approved for issue.
- Presentation: Is the schedule laid out logically and easy to read? (For example, are contract and key dates shown clearly, perhaps in their own section at the start of the schedule?)

18.4.2 Management issues

- Achieving formal buy in from relevant managers.
- Does the logical sequence of tasks make sense?
- Are adequate lead-in times allowed for material supply, manufacture of components, etc.?
- What are the main risks to the schedule?
- Are there any onerous requirements placed on the contract?
- Ensure all assumptions regarding durations and sequence are adequately recorded.
- Does the schedule at high level compare with similar projects?
- Do the activity durations compare favourably on key trades?
- Are any corporate governance/sign-off points included?

18.4.3 Contract requirements

- Does the schedule comply with contract obligations?
- Are the key client milestones included in the schedule?
- Have constraints such as working hours been accounted for?
- Are there multiple handovers? If so, does level of detail reflect this, particularly regarding trade continuity?
- Missing data required by the contract, such as missing activity coding.

Schedule review

- If the schedule includes progress, perhaps the most important check of all is that key or contract dates have not moved, or, if they have, the reasons for such movement are fully explained in the narrative.
- If required, has time risk allowance been identified against activities?

18.4.4 Scope

- Is the entire scope represented in the schedule, including latest change (up to a suitable cut-off point)? (This should include references to all works by the client, contractors and third parties.)
- Are all temporary works and other preliminaries covered? The former may be on the critical path or require critical resources.
- Are intermediate milestones identified and meaningful?
- Check that all interface milestones are paired.
- Check that the key/interface milestones for the next 12 months have signed-off milestone definition sheets and that all have SMART measures (specific, measureable, achievable, relevant and time-bound).
- Check all activities and milestones for any constrained dates.
- Check for out-of-sequence or missing logic leading to activities on data date.

18.4.5 Associated documents

Associated documents that may be required for issue at the same time as the schedule:

- information required register;
- procurement schedule;
- assumptions register;
- logistics plans (traffic management; hoist and tower crane location plans; materials storage in various phases);
- additional communication plans, e.g. time-phased layouts.

18.4.6 Planning issues

Consideration should be given to the existence of negative float or excessive positive float and the implications this has for the management of the project.

Planning, Scheduling, Monitoring and Control

If schedules with negative float are presented without showing the negative float, they can give a false impression that the schedule dates can be met.

Where positive float exists in a network, it means that the work can be delayed by the associated time and still be completed by the desired date. However, it is worth checking that 'excessive' float does not exist in the project schedule. This will be because of missing successor logic. It is always worth checking the logic through activity networks that seem to have proportionally more float than seems reasonable.

Check for an excessive number of activities starting early in the programme. Although the logic may allow this, it may not be a cost-effective approach for the project.

18.4.7 Progress update

- Have any key dates or other important milestones moved?
- Has physical % been updated (where options exist)?
- Has the correct data date been set?
- Are actual dates recorded correctly?
- Does the remaining duration of the activities roughly align with the progress achieved within the time elapsed?
- How much float has been used, particularly on the critical and near-critical paths?
- Are there any future activities marked as started or complete?
- Are there any activities in the past that are not complete?

18.4.8 Communication of the schedule

- Has a summary plan and explanation been included?
- Are activity descriptions clear and has relevant coding been applied?
- Is the critical path clearly shown?
- Are the associated tracker schedules included in the communication?
- The narrative should highlight key particulars of the schedule and key changes since the previous issue.

18.5 Scheduling checks

This process looks specifically at schedule logic and content that may distort the natural flow of the schedule, making accurate forecasting more difficult. Similarly, it reviews over-complexity in the schedule, which may increase the possibility of

Schedule review

failure. It is important to note that the review of technical quality is purely a mathematical and statistical check and does not take into consideration the project schedule as a whole. To check for scope inclusion, 'buildability' and other practical concerns, the schedule should be reviewed by suitably experienced individuals rather than by mathematical checks.

If formal checks are to be undertaken, it should be noted that these checks would not usefully be applied to summary tasks, LOE-type tasks, milestones, or activities that are 100% complete. Making changes to the latter should not generally be encouraged.

A good starting point is to see whether the schedule can be re-scheduled with no subsequent changes to the start and finish dates. It is also worth reviewing what changes have been made to the schedule since its previous iteration. Then consider the following factors.

18.5.1 Activity checks

18.5.1.1 Activity types

Scheduling software offers a variety of activities for use in schedules, and these should be used with caution; for example, WBS summary activities (activities driven by the start and end dates of other activities):

- should not contain resources, except during the development of schedules;
- should never form a part of the critical path;
- should be used very sparingly, and then only with a particular use in mind.

18.5.1.2 Activity durations

Activity durations should be achievable under normal conditions, not optimal or 'stretch' targets. In order to verify this, the schedule narrative should clearly state which output rates have been used. Assumptions related to calculated durations should also be documented.

Durations should be short enough to facilitate easy assessment of progress. It is very difficult to be specific regarding a maximum duration for an activity, but, as a guide, no activity should exceed the duration of two reporting periods. (Do not consider summary activities in this check.)

A schedule broken into very short durations (around a day or so) is generally in too much detail (the exception being short-term 'look ahead schedules').

Planning, Scheduling, Monitoring and Control

Schedules with great detail will demand more frequent updates and more management effort.

18.5.1.3 Review of deleted activities

In general, activities should never be deleted from a schedule, in order to preserve the unique numbering system for each activity and thus maintain the history of the project.

Activities should, instead, be retired and placed in a unique and specific part of the WBS. They will likely be filtered out of any print or display of the schedule. All budgets must be removed and re-allocated if appropriate. Coding and logic should also be removed. However, the logic could be replaced with links to a dummy start and finish milestone to limit the number of open ends.

In practice, leaving all redundant activities in the schedule may increase the size of the database to unmanageable proportions. In this instance, it may be decided to delete activities and introduce checks between successive versions of the schedule for deletions.

However, where practical, it is good practice to preserve activities, for the reasons stated above. A compromise might apply in a situation where large sections of the schedule are to be replaced, when activity deletion may be accompanied by a change in the structure of activity IDs, so that there is no possibility of duplication/recycling of the activity ID numbers.

18.5.1.4 Insufficient detail

Is the schedule broken down into sufficient detail? This could be defined in terms of the maximum duration of an activity in relation to the overall project duration. On a project lasting 2 years it may be appropriate to specify a maximum duration of 4–6 weeks; on a plant shut-down the appropriate duration may be 1–2 hours. This should always be a guide rather than a rule, and will not apply to summary tasks or level of effort activities.

18.5.1.5 Review of calendars used

Calendars used should be kept to a minimum, and only those authorised for use on the project should be used; they must be attributed to appropriate activities. Calendars should represent valid working times for the activities and associated resources.

Schedule review

Calendars should be named clearly, should account for holiday periods, and account for any other restraint on working; factory shut downs in manufacturing or weather in construction, for example.

18.5.1.6 Review for invalid dates

Invalid forecast dates are those that logically should have already happened, and are shown in the past, but are not shown as complete.

Invalid actual dates are those that are noted as started or finished, but are in the future (i.e. later than the current data date). This is clearly incorrect, and thus an invalid date.

The examples above can be the result of poor functionality in various types of scheduling software, or just poor practice by an individual. Either way, both need to be checked for.

18.5.1.7 Review of WBS

A good work breakdown structure (in line with the advice within this guide) is an indicator of a good schedule, and vice versa. All activities in the schedule must be attributed to a part of the WBS.

18.5.2 Logic checks

18.5.2.1 Relationship types

18.5.2.1.1 Finish to start (FS)

The vast majority of activities in the schedule should be finish to start activities.

18.5.2.1.2 Finish to finish (FF)

There may be a limited number of finish to finish relationships in the schedule, but remember that these require parallel working and the additional resources that this implies.

18.5.2.1.3 Start to start (SS)

There may be a limited number of start to start relationships in the schedule, but remember that these require parallel working and the additional resources that this implies.

Planning, Scheduling, Monitoring and Control

18.5.2.1.4 Start to finish (SF)

These relationships must be avoided; they are sometimes used as a convenience to fix activities in a particular moment in time. However, they are illogical and can distort the flow of the schedule. (Very occasionally there may be exceptions to this rule.)

18.5.2.2 Number of lags

Whilst the use of lags is common practice within scheduling, they should be used sparingly, as they can undermine the overall accuracy of the schedule. This is because they are difficult to progress accurately, and have an inherent lack of visibility. It is, therefore, good practice to use a dummy task rather than a lag. This has the added advantage that an appropriate calendar can be applied to the dummy task.

18.5.2.3 Number of leads

A lead is a negative lag, which should be avoided as much as possible. They should never be used in high-density scheduling, because they are illogical.

18.5.2.4 Missing or redundant logic

Missing logic refers to activities that have either missing predecessors, missing successors or both. A high percentage of missing logic will lead to artificially inflated float within the schedule, and will also affect the validity and reliability of the critical path and subsequent forecasts.

Redundant logic can artificially increase the complexity of the schedule without adding any value.

18.5.2.5 Out-of-sequence activities

Work that is started or completed on an activity before it is logically scheduled (before all its predecessors are complete) to occur is known as out of sequence. This may show:

- A lack of discipline in the project, as work is being progressed in the wrong sequence.

Schedule review

- Facilities or machinery not being available, so work is jumping to the next activity instead of being idle.
- A fault in the logic.
- It may also indicate a lack of detail in the schedule.

This check should be used with caution, as schedules should be pragmatic rather than infinitely precise, and some instances of this occurring will be acceptable. In short, don't panic if out-of-sequence activities are found in the schedule, but be careful.

18.5.2.6 Logic density

The average number of logic links per activity across the schedule. In general, the minimum number of links per activity is two (one predecessor and one successor); anything below this shows that the schedule is lacking the logic needed to provide a robust critical path, and anything excessively above this may lead to either redundant logic, which may complicate the ongoing maintenance of the schedule, or an increased level of risk to timely delivery.

18.5.2.7 Logic bottlenecks

Activities with a high number of predecessors (i.e. more than two). This means that there is an increased threat to delivery of this activity due to its dependence on the successful completion of many other activities. In Figure 18.2, there is a high chance that activity D will be delayed, as there are more things that can delay it; if it does start on time, it has a significant effect on the schedule if it runs late, as a number of follow-on activities would be affected by its running late.

18.5.2.8 Multiple ends

A network should have one start milestone and one finish milestone. All other activities are connected, directly or via preceding or successor activities, respectively, to the start and finish activity by logic.

Each activity or sequence of activities should, in practice, impact on the completion date of the project at some stage. For example, the supply of technical publications is generally an unrelated activity that would not impact the physical completion of an aircraft. However, any delay in the delivery of the technical publications may well impact on the handover to the customer; for example, if

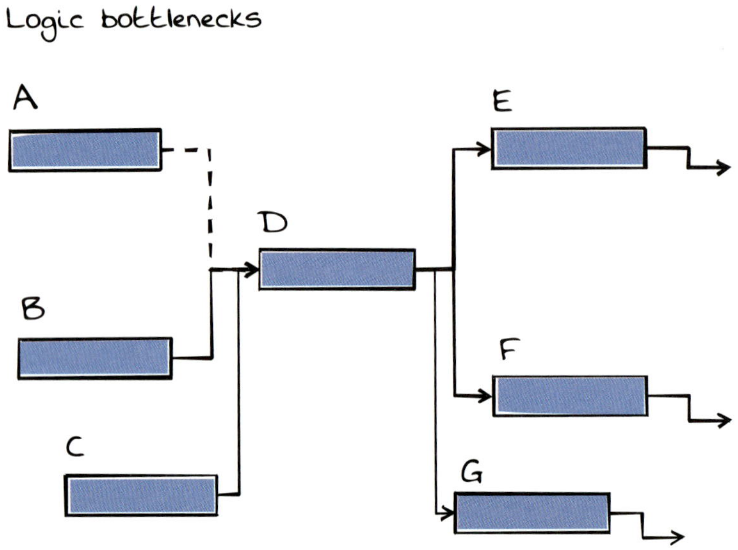

Planning, Scheduling, Monitoring and Control

Logic bottlenecks

Figure 18.2 Logic bottleneck

the contract requirements specify that a full suite of technical documentation and/or spares (sometimes referred to as initial provisioning) is required for satisfactory fulfilment of the contract.

In reality, there may be several end events/milestones which are required to be delivered by a given date. For detailed project control, each deliverable is managed in its own right, and therefore float is to be calculated for each delivery, and not calculated to the last milestone of the overall network.

18.5.3 Float and critical path checks

18.5.3.1 Review of schedule float

Whilst high levels of float can be a sign of poor schedule logic, low levels of float can mean that the project is unlikely to succeed before it has even started. Ensuring that the project has enough float to accommodate unknowns is fundamental to its success.

18.5.3.2 Negative float

Activities within the schedule that have a total float value of less than 0 are said to have negative float. Logically, the schedule cannot be completed by the required

Schedule review

target date. It is not, therefore, acceptable to have negative float in the first schedule, but it may exist in subsequent schedules if progress has been unsatisfactory. It is then a sign of a threat to the achievability of the schedule.

18.5.3.3 Review activities with high float

This may be an indicator of missing or inappropriate logic (but note that it may also indicate an activity that can be undertaken at any time!). It may also suggest missing activities, or improper sequencing within the schedule.

18.5.3.4 Review of time risk allowance

Durations are uncertain, and therefore time contingency should be allowed for. This is sometimes referred to as a time risk allowance. It may be expressly shown on the schedule, or it may be deemed to be included within each task. Therefore, the best way to verify there is adequate contingency is in discussion with the schedule owner.

18.5.3.5 Hard constraints

This refers specifically to the use of constraints that can artificially distort the CPM (critical path method) process and undermine the critical path. A hard constraint is one which constrains the critical path in both directions; constraints such as 'start on', 'mandatory start', 'finish on' and 'mandatory finish' are examples.

Constraints that only affect the critical path in one direction are known as soft constraints and are more acceptable; however, they should still be used sparingly, and never in combination to create a hard constraint.

For example, a constraint that means an activity could start on or before a certain date would be a soft constraint, as would a date that means an activity can start on or after a certain date. But, if used in combination, they effectively become a hard constraint – a mandatory start date.

18.5.3.6 Critical activities

Does the longest path represent a reasonable critical path for the project? (Pay attention to the critical path and near-critical paths in reviewing the schedule.) Review activities and milestones with a total float value of 0 days or less. (For longer and more complex schedules, the review might need to be total float of less than 1 day or 5 days or more.) High levels of overall criticality in the

Planning, Scheduling, Monitoring and Control

schedule can be the result of insufficient progress or potentially poor use of hard constraints.

The critical path should not include LOE or summary activities, leads or lags unless justified. It should also not include activities scheduled to take place as late as possible, even if they have zero float by virtue of coming before a critical activity.

18.5.4 Resources checks

18.5.4.1 Review of resourcing

The schedule should be checked to confirm that all true activities are resourced and/or budgeted. The checker should look out for budget and resourcing of summary tasks (or level of effort bars), as this may indicate a lack of detail in the budgeting and resourcing elsewhere.

It is also worth checking that only appropriate and approved resources are assigned to activities.

If there are available norms, it is useful to check the ratio of cost:resource, i.e. benchmarking.

Resource levels that the schedule requires should be measured against available resources.

18.5.4.2 Analysis of resource histogram

Resource histograms should be reviewed for practicality. Some of the checks could include:

- Are there any sudden peaks and troughs?
- Does it look balanced, i.e. are there realistic increases and decreases of labour and/or staff?
- Does each resource have continuity (unless multiple 'visits' are allowed for)?
- What is the peak staff/labour level, and is it practical for this type of project?

18.5.5 Review of schedule risk

Key risks in the project will have been identified as part of the risk management process. Some risks will have a potential impact on the timing of the project, and these should be included in the network in order to give a more realistic project schedule. The allowances for risk should be reviewed as part of the risk analysis process.

19.1 Definition of BIM

BIM is a new approach to dealing with the design, procurement and installation of an asset as well as its testing and commissioning, its handover, and its operation and maintenance. It provides information to facilitate each of these life cycle stages and can be applied to any type of asset.

Enhancements to modelling software have given the ability to directly link the project schedule to the model (3D), to visualise the construction process in real time (4D), and also to estimate the cost profile (5D).

In essence, BIM consists of a computer aided design (CAD) model of the asset. This may exist in 2D or 3D format. The model has the ability to contain information to build, operate and maintain the asset. In more mature solutions, this can extend to incorporating the project schedule and cost model. This could mean a 3D model that can visually demonstrate the build sequence (or, indeed, the progress of the works.) The BIM database will also contain metadata around each individual component of the build, such as type, cost, load-bearing capacity, supplier, etc.

The term is being used worldwide, although in the UK its adoption is mandated on government-funded projects by the end of 2016, giving it special relevance. BIM maturity has been defined as different levels, as illustrated schematically in Figure 19.1.

Although the visualisation elements of BIM remain the most recognisable aspect, it is the integration of scope using a common and consistent language in order to understand the impact of change that is the key advantage of this approach.

Planning, Scheduling, Monitoring and Control

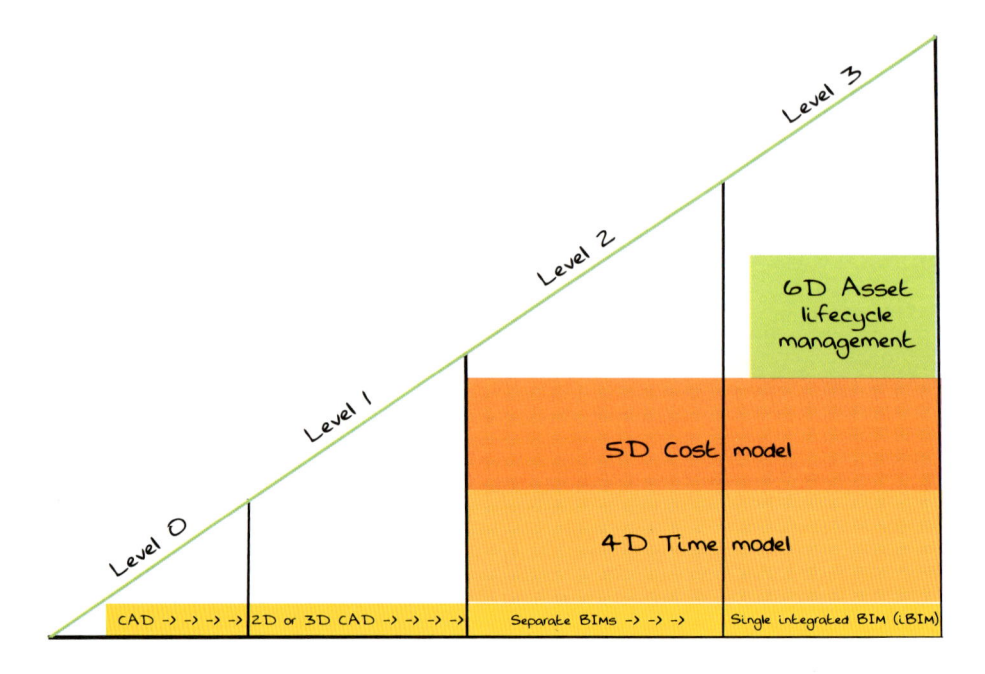

Figure 19.1 BIM level maturity map

19.2 Purpose of BIM

The BIM approach adds value to all stages of the assets life cycle because it provides access to all the elements of information associated with the assets being designed, engineered and, finally, operated and maintained. In delivering this, BIM has a great potential to promote collaboration between the various parties and remove some traditional industry barriers.

The use of 3D visualisation software is used to de-risk the delivery phase of a project by modelling the time phasing of construction in three dimensions. This process shows potential design issues and clashes within the scheduling of a project, which can then be re-phased accordingly (e.g. running electrical services before providing cable management systems).

A computer model conceived with this approach in mind will constitute a repository of the so-called 'single version of the truth', thus minimising misunderstandings deriving from working on different versions of the model. Multidisciplinary coordination and alignment are facilitated by the existence of a single model, whereby each specialist adds the specific information on an iterative basis as the design matures.

The involvement of different expert representatives of different organisations (asset owner, investor, designers, builders, operators and maintainers) at the very beginning of the project definition provides an opportunity of taking into account all the requirements that will accompany the assets to be built throughout their whole life cycle.

All the functions that use the data and information that will make the model richer and richer as the design develops will work together in a much more efficient manner (i.e. an integrated approach to cost and time is a natural result of BIM).

The transition of all the records from the construction team to the Operator and Maintainer (O&M) will occur in an electronic manner, sometimes referred to as 'digital handover', without the need for an expensive and time-consuming period of translation of asset data into a format suitable for O&M use.

19.3 BIM technology

The BIM technology has evolved very rapidly in recent times. Some mature solutions exist, especially in relation to BIM level 2. Software houses are collaborating more and more in order to offer solutions that facilitate integration in an increasing manner.

19.4 The BIM culture

Any type of change, in particular one of the magnitude of BIM, will have to deal with the human factor, by increasing awareness and knowledge of how project disciplines interact with each other. Spreading the BIM culture both internally and within interfacing organisations is a challenging task. New skills and professions will be required, currently not part of formal educational and business careers.

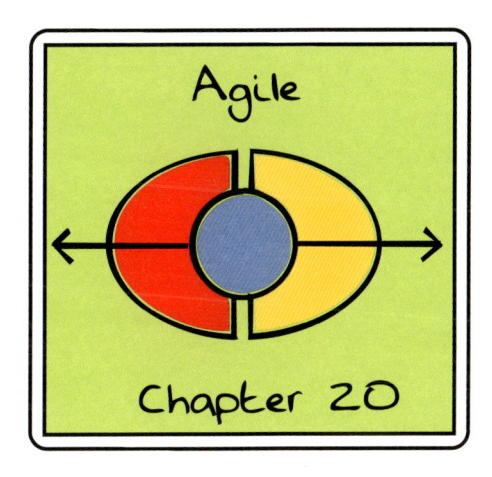

20.1 Definition of agile

Agile is a framework which describes a collection of tools, structure, culture and discipline to enable a project or programme to embrace changes in requirements. Agile methods integrate planning with execution, allowing an organisation to 'search' for an optimal ordering of work tasks and to adjust to changing requirements.

Agile is not a methodology, and does not prescribe a way of working. It seeks to provide a framework and a working mindset that helps a team respond effectively to changing requirements.

20.2 Purpose of agile

Agile frameworks are typically used in software development to help develop software which may have uncertain or poorly defined and changing user requirements. As functionality is iteratively developed in short timescales, it must be tested with the customer, and the requirements refined and agreed as appropriate. Further development is then undertaken to enhance the functionality of the end product.

Agile development is not the same as agile project management. Commonly, and often disastrously, agile thinking is not applied to the management of agile development projects; for example, when business users are not embedded in the team, and change decisions are not delegated to the agile team, but need to be escalated for approval. This slows down development, hence removing one of the key advantages.

Planning, Scheduling, Monitoring and Control

There are agile methods specific to software development, such as Scrum or XP (eXtreme Programming). However, some agile approaches are starting to be adopted in more industries outside the software development industry.

20.3 Methods

There are many distinct agile processes, which are summarised in Figure 20.1.

Irrespective of which agile process a project chooses to adopt, or if they wish to adopt more agile thinking, the following principles apply:

- The project breaks a requirement into smaller pieces, which are then prioritised by the team in terms of importance.
- The agile project promotes collaborative working, especially with the customer. This involves the customer being embedded in the team, providing the team with constant and regular feedback on deliverables and functionality of the end product.
- The agile project reflects, learns and adjusts at regular intervals to ensure that the customer is always satisfied and is provided with outcomes that result in benefits.

Scrum is the most popular agile process used in software development. It is based on delivering software features in time-boxed iterations called 'sprints'

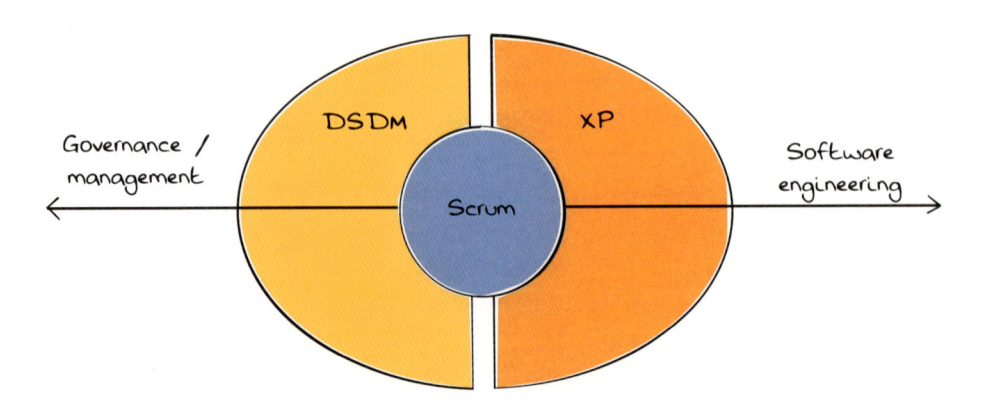

Figure 20.1 Agile processes

Software industry: the agile approach

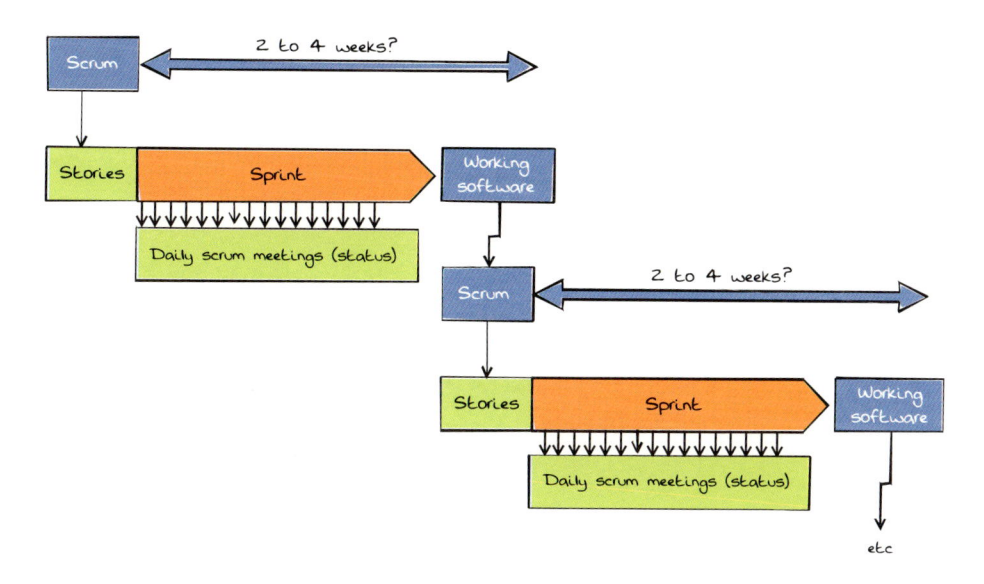

Figure 20.2 Illustration of an agile methodology using 'scrums' and 'sprints'

(Figure 20.2). The requirements are written as 'stories' that are collated into a prioritised list called the 'backlog'. Each story in the backlog is awarded points based on the level of definition of the requirements. Progress is monitored using 'burn down' charts of points; this enables the 'velocity' to be calculated, which can be used to predict the out-turn duration. Points are earned either 0% or 100%, depending on the acceptance by the client/sponsor at the end of the 'sprint review meeting'. The process is overseen by the 'scrum master', who makes sure everyone adheres to the rules. Meetings are referred to as 'ceremonies', the most frequent of which is the daily planning meeting, which identifies what has been done, what is to be done and barriers to success. Continued improvement is embedded by holding a 'sprint retrospective' at the end of each sprint to access performance and learn from experience.

20.3.1 Advantages

- Agile planning focuses on delivering what is most beneficial to the business first, identifying quick wins and earlier benefits realisation.
- Agile continuously looks for process improvements as part of the 'retrospective' review. As the team become more efficient, they can plan to achieve more in each sprint. Thus the velocity of delivery increases.

Planning, Scheduling, Monitoring and Control

- Agile assumes that changes are normal events; therefore they are managed to enable greater flexibility.
- Agile scheduling allows a greater level of flexibility in achieving the end result.

20.3.2 Limitations

- The organisation needs to be able to operate in an agile way and be willing to have a fully empowered team, typically with a full-time customer representative.
- A non-agile culture within an organisation will be a blocker on a project implementing an agile framework.
- Attendance at 'daily scrum' meetings is essential to keep abreast of the project tasks.
- Agile is not appropriate for all types of projects. Where there are significant resource constraints, securing suitably qualified teams for the full duration of each time box may not be possible in the organisation.
- Agile approaches struggle on larger-scale projects due to the degree of collaborative working required by the approach. If team sizes become too big, then development rates can slow.

Part Four

Monitoring and control

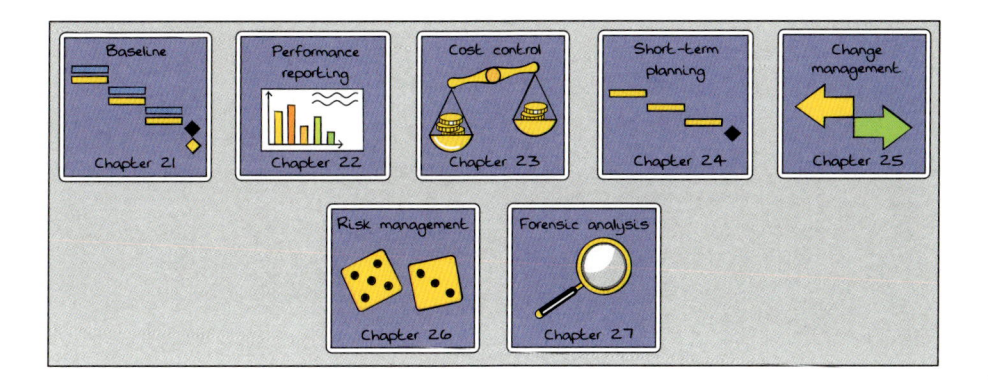

'You may not control all the events that happen to you, but you can decide not to be reduced by them.'

Maya Angelou

21.1 Definition of the project baseline

The project baseline (often referred to as the performance measurement baseline, or PMB) is an approved plan for the project, against which project performance is measured to facilitate management decision making and action. The setting of the baseline cannot be achieved until scope is defined and agreed, as the baseline must encompass the entire project scope, schedule and cost.

In practice, a baseline is a stored set of values encompassing

- planned start and finish dates
- planned resources
- planned costs.

At the point of establishing a baseline, each activity in the schedule has a duplicate set of dates ascribed to it. The duplicate dates are called the 'Baseline' dates and are illustrated in yellow in the diagrams below. Once set, these dates are not changed through the normal progress of the project, unless there is a requirement to re-set the baseline. As the project progresses, the plan will be updated and the current dates, illustrated in green in Figures 21.1–21.6, may well vary as a result of project performance, revised sequencing and detail development.

The illustration shows the effect on a project schedule of a delayed start and completion of the first activity, which has a knock-on effect on subsequent activities.

The same principle applies to management of resources and costs. A set of values is recorded as the baseline, and as the work progresses and actual usage

Planning, Scheduling, Monitoring and Control

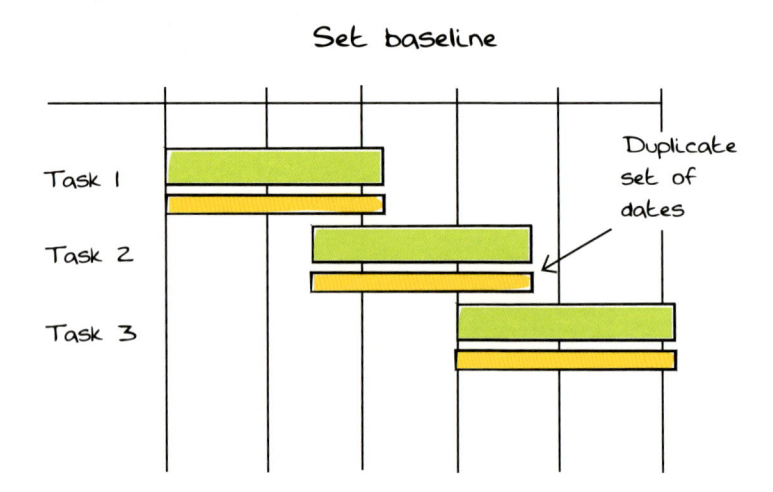

Figure 21.1 Establishment of baseline

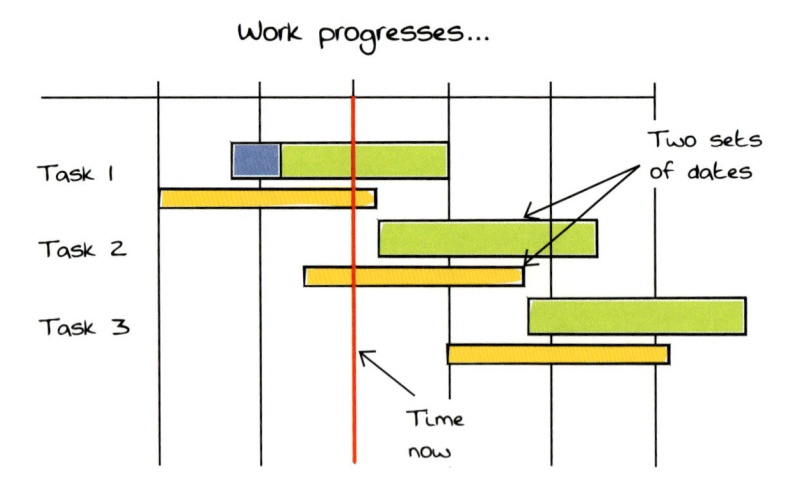

Figure 21.2 Baseline after work starts

of resource or actual costs are incurred, these are recorded for comparison with the baseline data.

A baseline to measure against is the key requirement for any form of project control. Without a baseline, there is nothing to compare the working schedule with, and therefore there is no way of measuring performance, meaning that projects will end up out of control.

21.2 Purpose of a project baseline

A project baseline is established to enable the performance of the project to be understood and controlled. This is achieved by:

- Clear identification of the schedule of the deliverables, activities, milestone dates, resources and costs.
- Measurement of project performance: progress and performance are compared against the baseline, allowing appropriate action to be discussed, agreed and taken. Thus, it is essential to apply appropriate project control techniques.

In addition, the baseline serves other purposes:

- It can motivate the project team to deliver to plan, or to mitigate delays.
- It is the contractual or other reference point from which to measure and assess the effect of change.
- It can be used in improving future estimating.

In order to achieve all of the above, the baseline must be robust, credible and pragmatic, and must therefore be maintained as changes are made to the working schedule.

The baseline will often be referred to as the performance measurement baseline, or PMB. Usually the PMB is the S-curve (or curves – early and late) derived from the baseline schedule. The elements of the total project that are included in the PMB for purposes of measurement must be defined. For example, risk and contingency may be excluded.

Following the principles below will ensure that the PMB is aligned with the master schedule objectives and contract milestones. This PMB forms the basis for measuring all future progress and performance.

21.3 Principles of project baselining

- The baseline covers the entire scope of the project and includes all project breakdown structures (by activity coding or other means).
- The baseline schedule should comply with the principles outlined in this book.
- The baseline covers all stages of the project life cycle.

Planning, Scheduling, Monitoring and Control

- The project delivery team creates controls and executes the baseline. An appropriate level of authority, as identified in the project's governance document(s), approves the project baseline.
- The baselines should be established at (or before) the commencement of each phase.
- The baseline is only changed in accordance with a robust change control process. Changes to the baseline must be controlled and recorded.
- In addition, the baseline is 'maintained' as discussed below.
- The baseline may be 're-planned', as discussed below. A 're-plan' should only be considered with the relevant level of authority (e.g. client, project manager or project sponsor, depending on circumstances).
- The baseline may be 're-baselined', as discussed below. A re-baseline is only considered with the agreement from an appropriate level of authority (e.g. client, project manager or project sponsor, depending on circumstances).

21.4 When to set the baseline

- A baseline should be reviewed, updated where necessary, and formally agreed before the project enters into the execution of the next phase.
- If a gateway approach to the project life cycle is adopted, a baseline may be set at each gateway phase.
- The level of detail in the baseline for later phases becomes greater as each phase becomes more imminent.
- The project baseline should only be set when the schedule, budget, resources, risks and other components of it are robust, i.e. it is agreed that it is possible to deliver the project to cost, time and quality.
- If a budget is significantly inaccurate it will not be useful as a measure of time and cost performance. An appropriate degree of rigour in setting the budgets is thus required.

21.5 Establishing the baseline schedule

Baselines should normally be established against early start dates, assuming that resource levelling has been undertaken to calculate these dates.

In short, a baseline is created from the first agreed plans, and should have the buy-in of the whole project team, senior management and supply chain.

21.6 Definition and purpose of baseline maintenance

21.6.1 Definition of baseline maintenance

Baseline maintenance is the routine maintenance of the baseline to ensure that any new detail in the working schedule is also captured in the baseline. This would typically include work that has been added to the scope through a proper change control process. It would also cover the addition of new activities; for example, adding granularity to the schedule.

21.6.2 Purpose of baseline maintenance

- To maintain a credible schedule to measure against.
- To revise dates, budgets or any other data where they are affected by agreed change. Only authorised change (following appropriate governance) may be substituted into the baseline. Unauthorised change must never be added into the baseline.

21.6.3 Baseline maintenance as a result of schedule changes

Some changes will require baseline maintenance. The principles of this are described below. Some scheduling software will facilitate this process with ease; others will require a number of steps to establish stored values for new or changed work. Baseline maintenance consists of changes to the baseline that enhance rather than detract from the integrity of the baseline. This includes:

- Change of planning packages into work packages (this may include the addition of detail to the medium/long term).
- Changes in contractual conditions or work scope. Where change is identified, it is managed through a change control process, ultimately leading to an update of the baseline. This will take the form of an appropriate addition, omission or revision, and will include the effects of the change on future activities. Records of baseline change should be maintained to provide traceability.
- Changes to descriptive information – e.g. activity or coding titles. Typically, this may be the correction of errors. Note, however, that changes in numbering of activity IDs should never be permitted.

Planning, Scheduling, Monitoring and Control

One example of baseline maintenance would be the addition of more detail. Figures 21.3–21.6 show how the baseline would be maintained as a result of doing this, in this instance where concurrent delays have happened on the schedule. The overriding principle here is that of rolling wave planning, and the update of the baseline should not be able to compromise the baseline by masking delays or other changes that have affected the schedule.

Baseline maintenance for schedule revisions is intended to preserve the integrity of the baseline, and should have no effect on measurement of schedule performance or cost performance reporting. Baseline maintenance never masks poor or good project performance. Project-specific rules for authorising any changes to budget should be drawn up in the project-specific change control and/or project control procedures.

21.6.4 Illustration of the principle of baseline maintenance

21.6.4.1 Project planned

The original project plan is shown in green. Once reviewed, verified and agreed, the baseline can be set. The baseline is shown here in yellow. Each activity has a minimum of four dates, albeit currently the start dates match, as do the finish dates.

Work on the activities then commences . . .

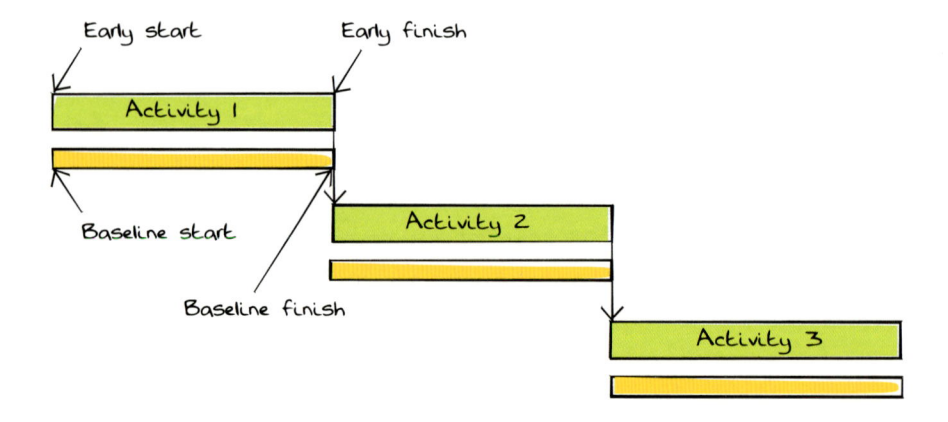

Figure 21.3 Baseline maintenance step 1

Baseline

21.6.4.2 Project progress and delays ensue

... and, as progress is not as expected, delays to the schedule occur. Each activity now has a duplicate set of dates that differ, except for the start of activity 1, which is shown with an actual start date matching the baseline start date.

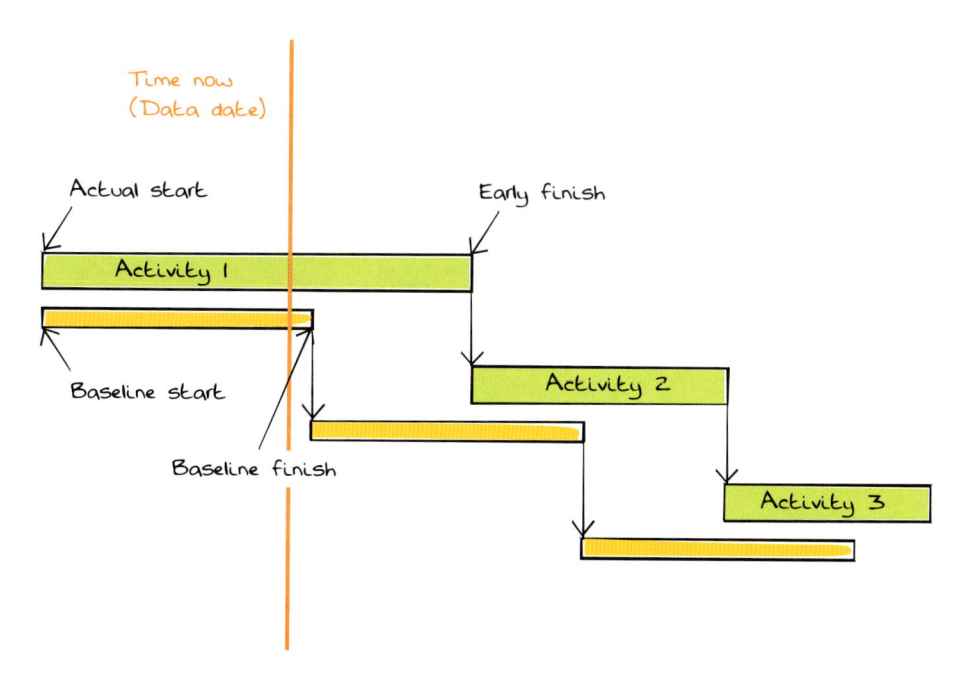

Figure 21.4 Baseline maintenance step 2

21.6.4.3 Detail is now developed on activity 2; activity 3 is re-assessed and reduced

At this stage, activity 3 is examined in more detail and re-planned. It is decided that it can be executed faster than originally intended. This is entered in the current schedule, showing the completion of this fragnet on time. There is no need to do any baseline maintenance as a result of this re-assessment: the baseline remains valid and is retained.

At the same time, activity 2 is broken down into more detail, as shown in the pink bars. Since the budgets will also be broken down to this level of detail, it is necessary to maintain the baseline – i.e. add bars into the baseline to reflect the new detail.

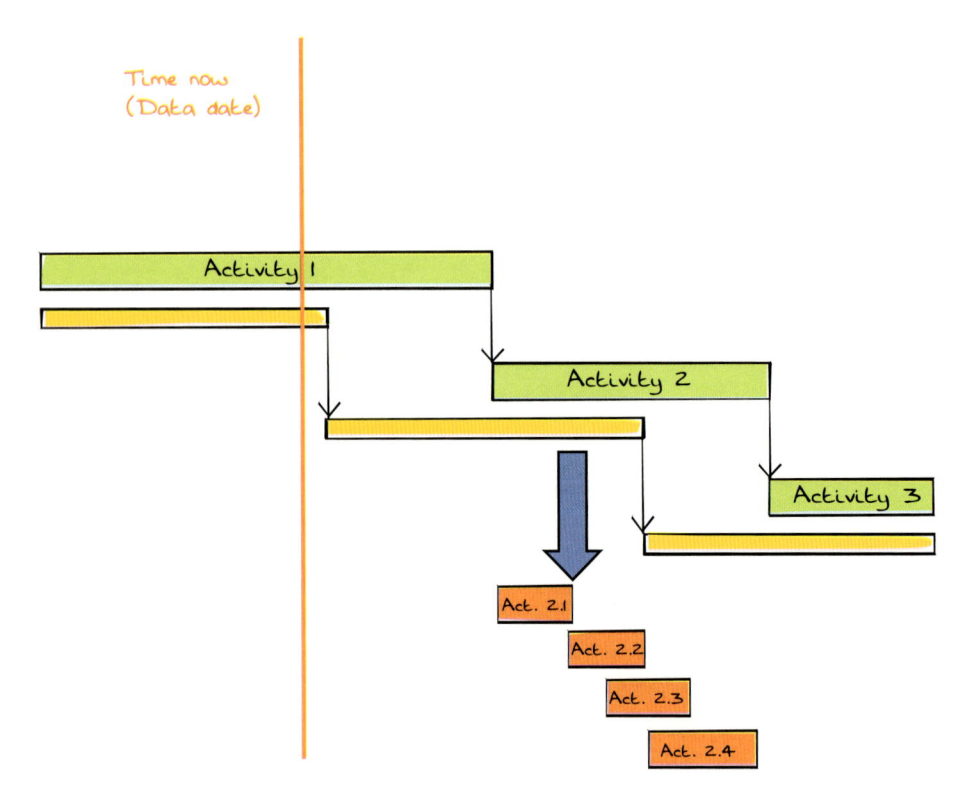

Figure 21.5 Baseline maintenance step 3

26.6.4.4 The baseline is now updated with new detail

The baseline is set by adding the new detail into the baseline and linking it with logic and/or constraints, in the same way that the original activity 2 was linked.

The final working schedule and baseline schedule will appear as shown: the original higher-level bars may be retained or deleted, but cannot be used to measure schedule variances.

21.7 Re-baselining: re-planning

Re-planning is undertaken within the scope, schedule and budget constraints of the project. This is done by maintaining the current cost variance and typically

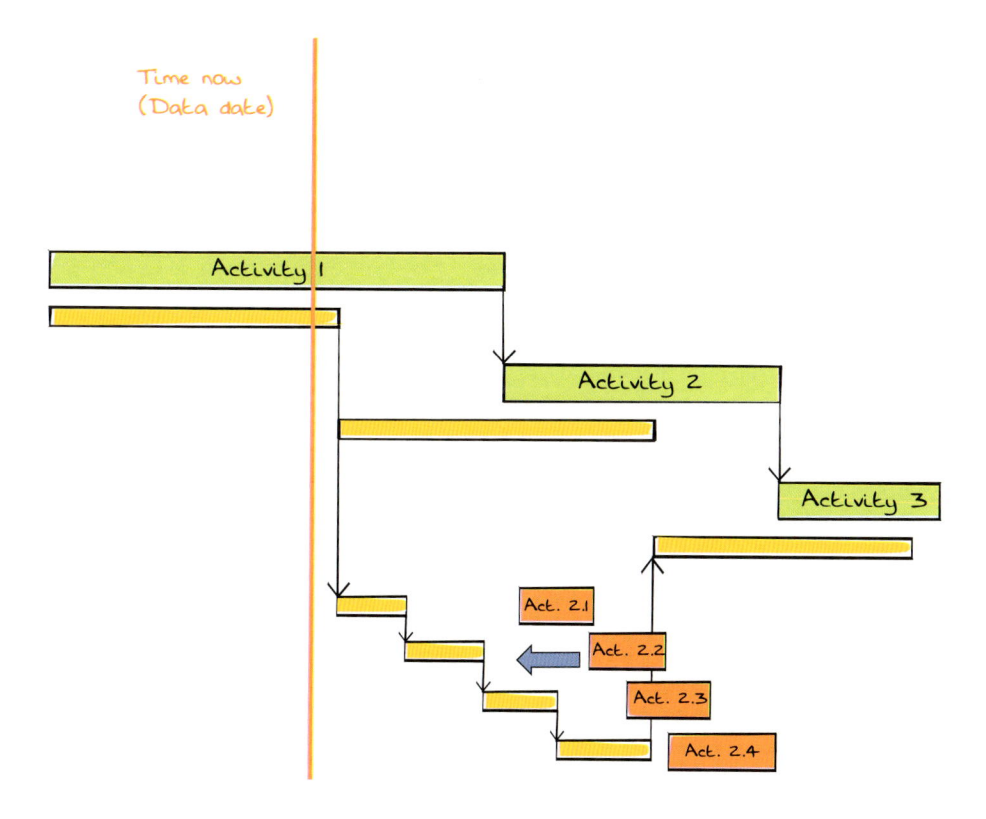

Figure 21.6 Baseline maintenance step 4

eliminating the schedule variance, i.e. the remaining work is re-scheduled with the current actual cost and earned value retained. The customer should be advised prior to (and may need to approve) re-planning.

Re-planning should only be considered in two instances:

21.7.1 When to consider re-planning

21.7.1.1 When the client requests it

This may be because of loss of credibility, the client's own reporting requirements or other events under which the client wishes to draw a line. The implications of re-planning should be discussed and the selection of this option be mutually agreed, if possible.

Planning, Scheduling, Monitoring and Control

21.7.1.2 When the credibility of the original baseline is lost

In practice, project teams are expected to know the current working schedule in detail. They are measured against a baseline that perhaps moves further from reality, and from the forefront of the project team's thoughts.

Therefore, on a project of long duration, the credibility of measuring against the original schedule may be lost on the project team. In these circumstances it may be prudent to diverge from best practice (to maintain the baseline only) and consider setting a new set of baseline dates. Since this is a divergence from best practice, it is recommended that this should not be a regular occurrence, certainly not more than an annual event, and preferably no more than half a dozen times in any project.

It is possible to measure against two baselines (the original and the latest, perhaps). However, careful consideration should be given to this and to how widely different measurements should be shared. Indeed, the use of dual baselines would be likely to be of use only to satisfy differing requirements for performance measurement. On the principle of keeping project controls as simple as possible, measurement against two baselines is to be avoided.

In conclusion, re-planning as described herein is intended to re-set the baseline with regard to the timing of operations, and will therefore re-set all schedule variance reporting. it should, however, have no effect on cost performance reporting (i.e. cost variance will remain as it was before the re-plan).

21.8 Re-baselining: re-programming

Re-programming means setting a completely new baseline for the project, including both time and budget benchmarks. Basically, this means wiping the slate clean. Both schedule variance and cost variance are returned to zero.

Re-baselining should only be considered in two instances:

21.8.1 When to consider re-programming

21.8.1.1 When the client insists upon it

This may be triggered by loss of credibility (see below), the client's own reporting requirements or other events under which the client wishes to draw a line. The implications of re-baselining should be discussed and the selection of this option be mutually agreed, if possible.

21.8.1.2 When the credibility of the original baseline is lost

In practice, project teams are expected to know, in detail and background, the current working schedule. At the same time, they are measured against a baseline that, with the passage of time and changes in the current schedule, will move further from reality, and, more pertinently, from the forefront of the project team's minds.

On a project of long duration, therefore, the credibility of measuring against the original schedule may be lost on the project team. In these circumstances it may be prudent to diverge from best practice (to maintain the baseline only) and consider setting a new baseline. Since this is a divergence from best practice, it is recommended that this should not be a regular occurrence, certainly not more than an annual event, and preferably no more than half a dozen times in any project.

In conclusion, re-baselining is intended to re-set the baseline with regard to the timing of activities, and will therefore re-set all schedule variance reporting. It will also re-set the baseline with regard to cost performance reporting. It is therefore likely that this option can only sensibly be considered in a cost plus type contract, or at a point in the contract where a significant re-negotiation has taken place.

Table 21.1 *Baseline maintenance, re-planning, re-baselining matrix*

*Authorised change only	Additional detail	Budget movements*	Additional work*	Re-set intermediate dates	Re-set contract dates	Re-set budgets
Baseline maintenance	√	√	√	x	x	x
Re-planning	√	√	√	√	x	x
Re-baselining	√	√	√	√	√	√

21.9 Notes and rules for schedule maintenance, re-planning and re-baselining

- Work transfer should be accompanied by an associated budget and be agreed by all stakeholders.
- Do not transfer unused budget from closed work packages to other work packages or planning packages.
- Do not add additional budget to work packages that are in work unless otherwise approved by the project manager.
- Transfer of budgets should not be used to cover legitimate variances, and the change control process should check for this.

21.10 The link between change management and the project baseline

Only authorised change (following appropriate governance) should be included in the baseline.

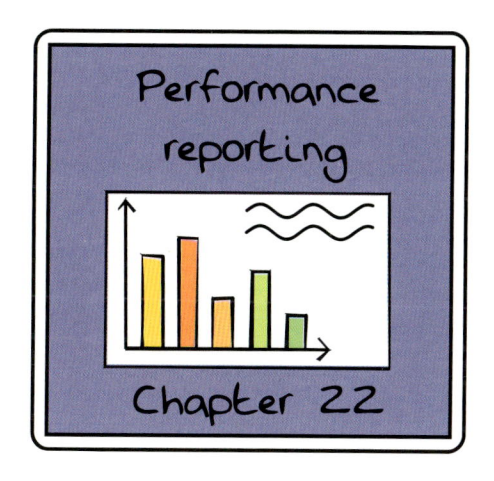

22.1 Definition of performance reporting

Performance reporting is the measurement of progress and spending made to date compared with the plan. It should inform management decision making about steps required to mitigate poor performance or maximise better than planned performance. Thus, it must:

- Measure what has happened:
    - Is the project on schedule, ahead or behind?
    - Is the project getting value for money?

- Forecast what is likely to happen:
    - Is the project going to complete on time, ahead, or late?
    - What is the forecast final cost?
    - Is the rate of work sufficient, is it decelerating or accelerating?

Performance reports may take a number of formats, from marked-up schedules through to formal written reports, though it is increasingly common for dashboard reports to be produced that combine reporting on all aspects of projects; health and safety statistics, environmental, commercial, time and cost performance, supply chain performance, and details of key risks and mitigations.

Reporting may include analyses based on a variety of methods. These may range from very simple reporting through to critical path analysis and earned value management. The latter two are considered the best methods of monitoring and controlling a project, and would be the expectation for any complex projects.

Planning, Scheduling, Monitoring and Control

There are fundamentally two types of performance reporting: variance analysis (which measures what has happened) and performance analysis (which also forecasts what is likely to happen).

Variance analysis includes the following methods, which will be discussed in this chapter:

- drop line method;
- activity weeks method;
- milestone monitoring;
- line of balance;
- cash-flow monitoring;
- resource monitoring
- cost value analysis
- quantity tracking.

Performance analysis includes the following methods, which will be discussed in this chapter:

- network analysis and measurement of float usage;
- earned value analysis.

In general, the variance analysis techniques are simple to do and understand, but they are backward-looking, often with no way of enabling projections and forecasts. Performance analysis techniques are harder to set up and run, but do have these forward-looking qualities. Most sophisticated projects will run both forms of performance analysis, as even these are complementary and measure different things. Variance analysis techniques are used to complement and help communicate where necessary or useful.

22.2 Purpose of performance reporting

Performance reporting is undertaken to check whether satisfactory progress is being made and to identify any corrective actions that may be required. Reporting is undertaken to communicate the status of the project to those who need to know. Part of the performance monitoring regime should ensure that records are made at the time, and retained in a form that allows retrieval and analysis in the future for contractual or knowledge management purposes.

Performance reporting

Consideration should be given to the various methods of performance reporting available, and deploying them as appropriate. It is worth noting that rarely, except in the simplest of projects, will one method provide a picture of project status that is accurate and understandable to all stakeholders. Most advanced projects will use a combination of network analysis and float usage with an earned value analysis, but even then additional tools such as quantity tracking (good for communication) or resource tracking (good for future resource planning) may be deployed.

A good control system:

- rapidly brings performance issues to management attention;
- motivates the correct behaviours to improve performance – on the positive side by showing what needs to be done and on the negative side by showing what will happen if nothing is changed;
- integrates time, cost and risk;
- promotes awareness of time, cost and risk;
- summarises data at an appropriate and digestible level of detail;
- enables accurate forecasting and trending;
- is easy to use and understand.

22.3 Evaluating and recording progress

22.3.1 Progress assessment

There are three elements required for any performance measurement: a baseline to measure against; actual data (cost, for example); and an assessment of what has been achieved (a physical percentage complete against an activity). Progress is best evaluated by those responsible for the work. Progress will be entered into the schedule – often by the planner. The planner's role also includes the challenge, validation and verification of the progress information. The client or his representative may also wish to verify the progress reported within the schedule.

22.3.2 What needs to be recorded in the schedule?

- The date to which the progress is being reported.
- Percentage complete (this measure should be based on the physical completion of the activity) in order to enable assessment of progress.

Planning, Scheduling, Monitoring and Control

- Remaining duration (this is based on the outstanding work on the activity) in order to facilitate re-calculation of the network (critical path analysis).
- Actual start and actual finish dates, in order to build up the history of the project.

22.3.3 What else needs to be recorded in a report?

- Reasons for any delays;
- Trend curves to display progress.

22.3.4 How often is progress recorded?

Frequency of progress update will depend on the circumstances. Hourly progress updating may be used in cases of critical plant shut-downs, but weekly updating of progress is more appropriate on most projects. On some larger-scale projects, monthly updating of progress may be considered appropriate. If this is the case, it is necessary to ensure that the mechanism for recording actual start and actual finish dates is suitably robust. In addition, any type of trend analysis will take longer to produce any meaningful results or corrective action.

Critical path analysis and trend analysis should be carried out on each progress update. It is also useful at this stage to ensure that any emerging trends are picked up as early as possible. For example, on weekly progress updating a trend will be available after 3 weeks, whereas monthly updating will take a minimum of 12 weeks.

Formal progress reporting is generally conducted on a monthly or 4-weekly basis.

22.4 Variance analysis methods of progress monitoring

22.4.1 Drop line method

A vertical line is drawn at the point of the progress assessment date (sometimes referred to as 'time-now' or data date) across the bars on the schedule. At each intersection with an activity, the line is 'diverted' to a point on the bar considered to represent its progress: for example, if a bar represents work that is scheduled to be complete, but is only 30% complete, the vertical bar is diverted to cross the bar at the 30% point. This process is repeated to produce what is sometimes referred to as a drop line or jagged line (Figure 22.1).

Performance reporting

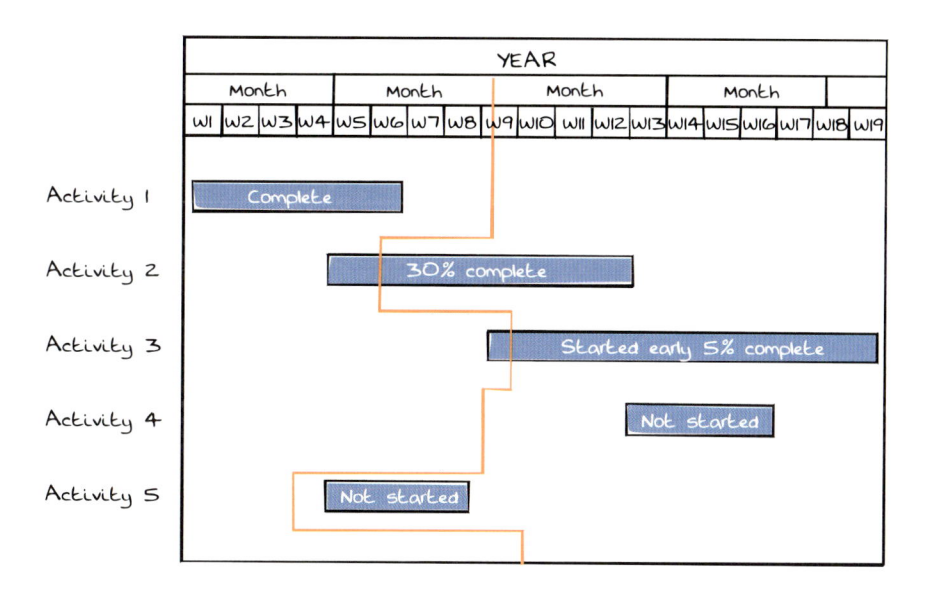

Figure 22.1 Illustration of the drop line method

If a project is perfectly on schedule, then the drop line remains vertical. Thus the deviations clearly indicate which activities are ahead and which are behind. Whilst this is a good way of looking at the detail, it is not adequate for complex logic-linked schedules.

22.4.1.1 Advantages of this method

- Provides a detailed record of each activity's progress.
- Identifies all activities that are behind and may require attention.
- A quick visual interpretation.

22.4.1.2 Limitations of this method

- Static: no re-scheduling of the schedule means effects of delay cannot be easily assessed, thus ignoring float and the possibility of avoiding unnecessarily remedial action to get the project back on time.
- Not a very meaningful description of where the project is in overall terms (or even on a sectional basis).
- Actual start and finish dates are not recorded.
- Will not be of much use in demonstrating delay.

Planning, Scheduling, Monitoring and Control

- It is difficult to change the schedule, add data etc. Adding a new activity may not be shown in a logical position if this is not done in scheduling software.
- Ultimately the schedule will not be a tool for proactively managing time, as it will have become unrepresentative of a realistic approach to the work.
- Becomes even more unrealistic if re-sequencing takes place.
- Activity-based method that does not measure 'work'.
- It measures time, but has no measure of cost versus value.

22.4.1.3 When can this be used?

Large or complex projects should have a detailed logic-linked schedule. However, this method could sometimes be used alongside other more sophisticated techniques such as critical path analysis and earned value analysis.

22.4.2 Activity weeks method

In order to monitor overall performance on a project, one simple way is to measure the number of activities each week (Figures 22.2 and 22.3). This does, of course, take into account all the activities but does not allow 'weighting' of the tasks.

This method has been proven to be not only grossly inaccurate, but also very misleading, sometimes critically so. Consequently it is not recommended as good, or even acceptable, practice in this guide and is included for completeness only.

For example, there may be 20 pipe fitters performing one activity and two painters on the next. Typically, in construction, the mechanical and electrical activities can comprise 30–40% of the value of the project, so a large part of the project could be described very briefly on the schedule and would not represent a fair proportion of the work.

It is not untypical for projects, particularly larger ones, to commence with fairly detailed schedules for the earlier stages and less detail for the later stages. This is known as rolling wave planning. In this instance, activity weeks could grossly distort the position, as the schedule would be heavily weighted in favour of the front end and the project would appear to be far more complete than it is.

22.4.2.1 Advantages of this method

- A simple one-page picture of project position, but . . .

Performance reporting

Weeks	1	2	3	4	5	6	7	8	9	10	11	12	13	14	15
Task one															
Task two															
Task three															
Task four															
Task five															
Task six															
Task seven															
Task eight															
Activity count															
Planned	1	2	2	2	3	4	3	3	3	3	5	5	6	6	4
Actual	1	2	2	2	3	4	2	3	2	0	2				

■ Planned activity
■ Actual progress

Figure 22.2 Simple 'activity weeks' monitoring chart

22.4.2.2 Limitations of this method

- This method gives no certainty about schedule position, and there is no credible or intellectually supportable approach for projecting the trend forwards.
- It measures time, but has no measure of cost versus value.

22.4.3 Milestone monitoring

Key interim milestones are set by attributing activities to them. Achievement or slippage of the milestones is then monitored. Milestones may be used to determine payment. When used in conjunction with more sophisticated methods, milestone monitoring can be a complementary means of visualising the achievements of the project and the future forecast.

Planning, Scheduling, Monitoring and Control

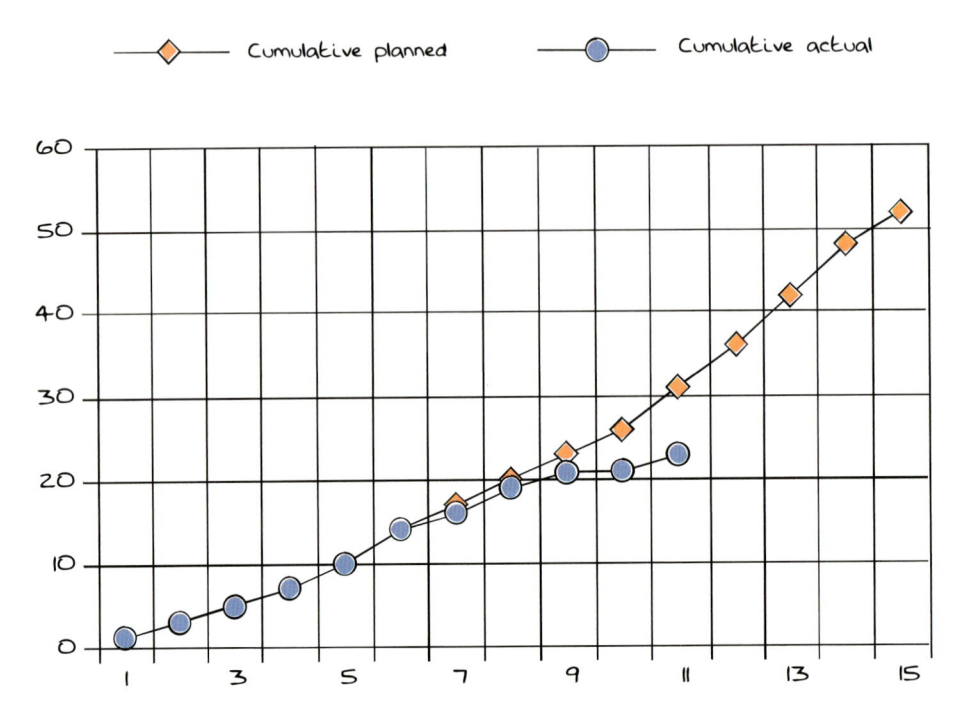

Figure 22.3 Cumulative results from the 'activity weeks' chart

22.4.3.1 Advantages of this method

- A useful way of summarising the project, and attributing responsibility and personal targets accordingly.
- Focus on key objectives.
- Simple, clear reporting.
- Easy to do and understand.

22.4.3.2 Limitations of this method

- There is a danger of this method being very misleading if milestones are not clearly defined.
- The milestones do not necessarily cover all the scope.
- It can adversely influence priorities, particularly when associated with payment milestones, as undue effort is associated with achieving these milestones as opposed to the full critical path.
- It measures time, but has no measure of cost versus value.
- There is a danger of only realising that a milestone has been missed after the event, when it is too late to take corrective action.

Performance reporting

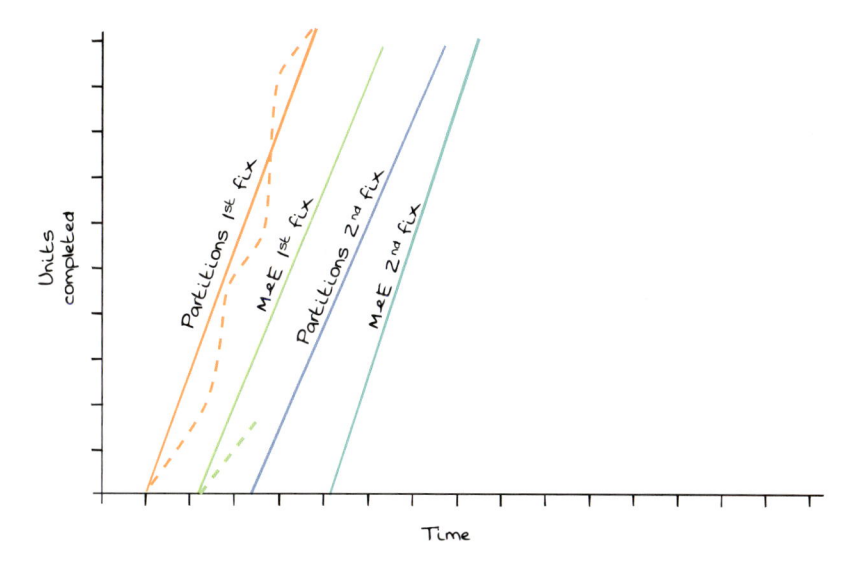

Figure 22.4 Recording actual progress in line of balance

- It tends to focus on activity completion dates to the detriment of activity start dates.

22.4.4 Progress on a line of balance chart

A line of balance chart with progress to date is shown in Figure 22.4.

Progress is monitored on these charts against the scheduled lines, and action can then be taken as appropriate. In Figure 22.4 the solid lines represent the scheduled production of units against time, and the dotted lines represent the progress recorded against each trade. It clearly demonstrates the required production rates and that which was achieved.

In this example, the first activity is shown starting on time but at a slower rate than scheduled. Eventually it accelerates until it is nearly back on schedule. It then slows before accelerating until becoming ahead of schedule. It finally finishes on time.

22.4.4.1 Advantages of this method

- Clear graphical display of progress.
- Productivity is measured, and presented graphically.
- Particularly useful for repetitive work at macro level (e.g. fit out of residential units) or micro level (e.g. monitoring number of pieces of steelwork erected).

22.4.4.2 Limitations of this method

- It is not available in mainstream software, although add-on/specialist software is available.
- It measures time, but has no measure of cost versus value.

22.4.5 Cash-flow monitoring

This focuses only on the financial spend of a project. Spreadsheets are usually prepared with planned budgets per week/month. The actual spend is then monitored against the planned budget figures.

22.4.5.1 Advantages of this method

- Project financing: if funds are finite, it gives advance warning of impending shortages.

22.4.5.2 Limitations of this method

- Does not relate spend to physical progress: it tells you nothing about project performance (i.e. it cannot be determined whether actual spending above the planned level means the project is over-spending, or that progress is ahead of schedule).
- Can be misleading if the early part of the project has a lot of expensive costs, e.g. purchase of plant or materials. Spending alone cannot be used to determine the status of the project.
- For these reasons, cash-flow monitoring should not be used in isolation.

22.4.6 Resource monitoring

A simple measure based on scheduled resource usage across a schedule. Actual resource usage is plotted against planned to give a measure of 'progress'.

22.4.6.1 Advantages of this method

- If particular resources are critical, then this can be an important measure.
- Can be used to forecast when resources are becoming available for other works.

- May be used where environmental concerns limit usage (for example, lorry movements in built-up areas).

22.4.6.2 Limitations of this method

- Can be misleading, with a lot of man-hours being expended but little actual progress on the works.
- Provides a measure of effort rather than progress.
- For these reasons, it should not be used in isolation.

22.4.7 Cost value analysis

This process compares cost against value. Cost here means the actual costs incurred or accrued, while value means the value of the work done ('earned value' or similar). The analysis is undertaken against the agreed cost breakdown structure (Figure 22.5).

This clearly highlights areas of over- or under-spend, and will provide the basis for estimates of the final cost of the project.

22.4.7.1 Advantages of this method

- Ensures project cost information is structured, analysed and interpreted.
- Relatively simple to do and understand.
- Highlights areas of poor or good performance to prompt management action.

22.4.7.2 Limitations of this method

- Does not provide trend data in the way that earned value analysis does.
- Does not require the integration of cost and time.
- Cannot be used as a time-phased financial forecasting method.

22.4.8 Quantity tracking

The monitoring of key quantities (also known as production curves) is a useful method for key tasks that are heavily dependent on the quantity of material deployed, moved or altered, or for tasks that are very numerous and broadly repetitive. An example of the former would be earthmoving in construction; an example of the latter would be the production of design deliverables (such

(Project Name)

CVR report

VALUE – CURRENT CONTRACT POSITION

Package	Contractor/Direct	Original contract budget A	Budget transfers B	Baseline budget C=A+B	Implemented compensation events D	Risk draw down E	Current budget at completion F=C+D+E
TOTAL		363,000	10,000	383,000	115,000	814,000	1,312,000
Piling	AB Ltd	100,000		100,000		10,000	110,000
Substructure	CD Ltd	195,000	5,000	200,000	50,000		250,000
Superstructure	EF SA	305,000	(5,000)	300,000			300,000
Steelwork	Direct	475,000		475,000	25,000		500,000
Risk	n/a	100,000		100,000		(10,000)	90,000

VALUE – FORECAST

Notified change events G	Forecast budget H=F+G	Early warning notices J	Anticipated final value (AFV) K=H+J
97,000	2,745,000	2,438,000	2,436,000
15,000	125,000		125,000
	250,000	2,000	252,000
	300,000		300,000
	500,000		500,000
	90,000		90,000

(shown split for illustration/clarity)

COST (Date)

		Cost to date (from accounts)			Accruals	Actual cost to date	Forecast cost to go (tbc)	Anticipated final cost (AFC)	P/L Anticipated profit/loss
		Labour L	Plant M	Material N	Sub contract O	P	Q=L+M+N+O+P	R	S=Q+R	T=K-R
TOTAL		5,000	15,000	20,000	407,000	31,000	478,000	740,000	1,218,000	–
Piling	AB Ltd				125,000		125,000	–	125,000	0
Substructure	CD Ltd				240,000		240,000	15,000	255,000	(3,000)
Superstructure	EF SA				42,000	10,000	52,000	240,000	292,000	8,000
Steelwork	Direct	5,000	15,000	20,000		21,000	61,000	485,000	546,000	(46,000)
Risk	n/a					–	–	–	–	90,000

Figure 22.5 Sample cost value report

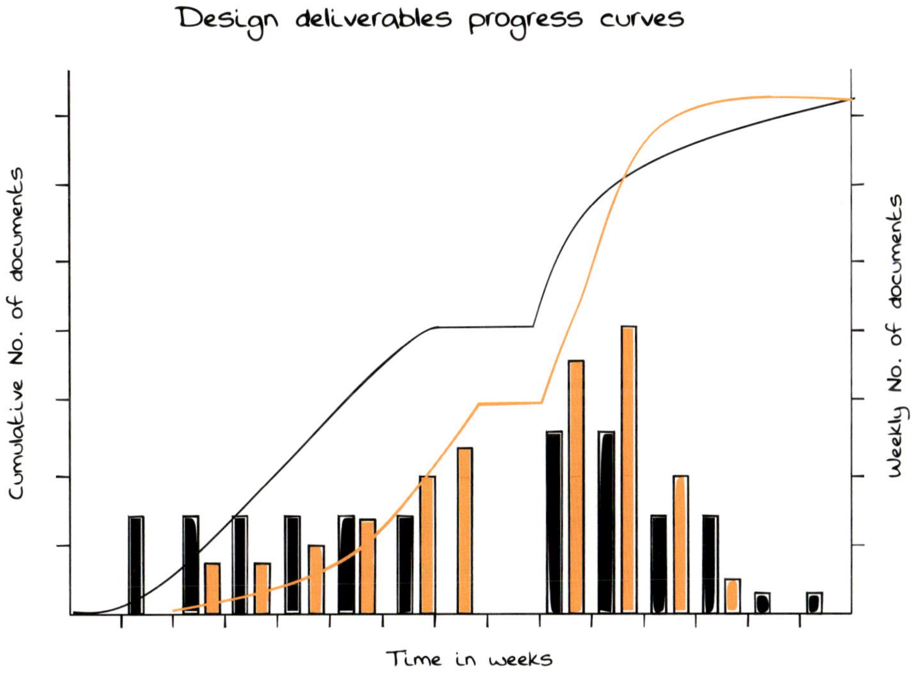

Performance reporting

Figure 22.6 Quantity tracking with production curves

as drawings) in any engineering project, or lines of code in a software development project.

Note: Although not shown in Figure 22.6, a useful additional line to show might be the assumed rate at tender or the organisation's normal output rate: this may put any peaks or troughs in the daily expected outputs into perspective.

22.4.8.1 Advantages of this method

- Easily and readily understood.
- Highly relevant if key tasks or quantities are chosen.
- Will highlight areas where corrective planning is required.

22.4.8.2 Limitations of this method

- Only really relevant to suitable items of measurement.
- Cannot be aggregated to give a holistic picture of the project.

Planning, Scheduling, Monitoring and Control

- Does not give a measure of value for money.
- May be misleading if the quantities referred to are estimated rather than accurate, or may otherwise vary when undertaking the work.

22.5 Performance analysis methods of progress monitoring

22.5.1 Network analysis and measurement of float usage

This method follows the progress update of the schedule and subsequent network and critical path analysis. This will reschedule activities to where they are now likely to take place and may therefore affect the end date, sectional completion dates or sub-contractor schedules. This, in turn, raises such potential issues as preserving continuity of work, acceleration or deceleration of activities, parallel working, or delays to activities which will need consideration and management action.

Once the critical path analysis has been run, the critical path may change, and different float paths may have been calculated. It is therefore essential to monitor the use of float where it exists. This will ensure that there is an awareness of emerging critical paths, should either under-performance or, indeed, accelerated performance create these.

Table 22.1 *Measurement of float usage*

Date	Baseline date	Forecast date	Float last report	Current float	Delta	Commentary
Key date 1	4/2/15	4/2/15	20d	18d	−2d	
Key date 2	2/4/16	4/4/16	10d	−2d	−12d	
Section date	2/4/17	4/2/17	20d	20d	—	
Contract completion	2/6/18	2/6/18	30d	28d	−2d	

22.5.1.1 Advantages of this method

- The critical path is a logical, mathematical model of the project that forces attention onto important activities.

- The critical path is always current.
- Effects of delays are more likely to be analysed.
- Actual start and actual finish dates are more likely to be recorded.

22.5.1.2 Limitations of this method

- There is a risk with just monitoring the critical path that managers only look at the critical activities rather than the near-critical paths.
- The critical path tends to be less relevant at the end of a project. The availability of resources to complete the final activities often becomes a more critical factor for project completion.
- It as an activity-based method that does not measure 'work' done.
- This is a sophisticated technique, and appropriate skills and time are required to undertake it.
- It measures time, but has no measure of cost versus value.

22.5.2 Earned value analysis

22.5.2.1 Definition of earned value analysis

Earned value analysis (EVA) is a performance analysis method that compares the scheduled amount of work (planned value) with the achieved amount of work (earned value) at a point in time. It also compares the work achieved (earned value) with the cost of achieving that work (actual cost). From these three pieces of data, performance can be trended and metrics calculated to express the status of the project.

Furthermore, it has been demonstrated that simple predictive calculations can be highly indicative of likely project outcome in terms of both time and final cost, provided that appropriate care and experience are used in creating the baseline, gathering data and interpreting the calculations.

A detail exploration of earned value can be found in the APM's *Earned Value Handbook* (APM, 2013).

22.5.2.2 Purpose of earned value analysis

Earned value analysis (EVA) is a performance analysis method that, when used properly, improves the delivery of projects. It does this by shining a light on performance issues. Using the data properly means that discussions are

Planning, Scheduling, Monitoring and Control

prompted by those who can make a difference, effecting changes necessary to improve performance. Where this is not possible, EVA provides an early warning of likely outcome in terms of cost performance and likely completion date.

EVA brings together the cost and time management of a project. It enables proactive management of a project, as it gives certainty of project status, produces metrics that aid project management by allowing visibility of performance, and permits remedial action to be understood and taken.

In addition, it reinforces best practice, as it requires a structured approach to planning. It provides a robust link between time and cost management, encouraging constructive working relationships. It forces project managers to consider and address cost and time issues at an early enough point to allow remedies to be cheaper and more effective.

EVA is a complementary method to robust techniques, in particular critical path analysis, but replaces the flawed and potentially misleading activity weeks method, which is to be avoided on all but the simplest projects.

22.5.2.3 Basic terminology

Budget at Completion (BAC): The final planned budget at completion of the project.

Planned Value (PV): The approved budget for the work scheduled to be completed by a specified date. Also known as budgeted cost of work scheduled (BCWS)

Earned Value (EV): The approved budget for the work actually completed by the specified date; also referred to as the budgeted cost of work performed (BCWP).

Actual Cost (AC): The costs actually incurred for the work completed by the specified date; also referred to as the actual cost of work performed (ACWP).

22.5.2.4 Establishing a budget-loaded schedule

The purpose of budget loading the schedule is to establish cost targets for individual elements of the work. The budget elements are shown in Figure 22.7. The performance measurement baseline (PMB) is established by allocating budget to the plan at activity level. Usually this is in terms of money and man-days/hours.

Performance reporting

It is important to allocate budget at an appropriate level of detail to facilitate accurate calculations for planned and earned values: this would normally mean activities of duration between 4 and 6 weeks, though there will be exceptions in both directions. Care should be taken with activities of longer duration than 6 weeks, and if these are used, they should be easy to assess with an appropriate, objective measure. On the other hand, the greater the granularity achieved in the schedule the more subjective the assessment can be, without compromising the essential integrity of the EVA system. (Greater granularity implies that smaller 'pieces of work' are measured, and the subjective nature of the assessment is thus reduced to an acceptable level of detail.)

Failure to allocate budgets at an appropriate level in the PMB will lead to inaccuracies in the calculation of the planned value and earned value.

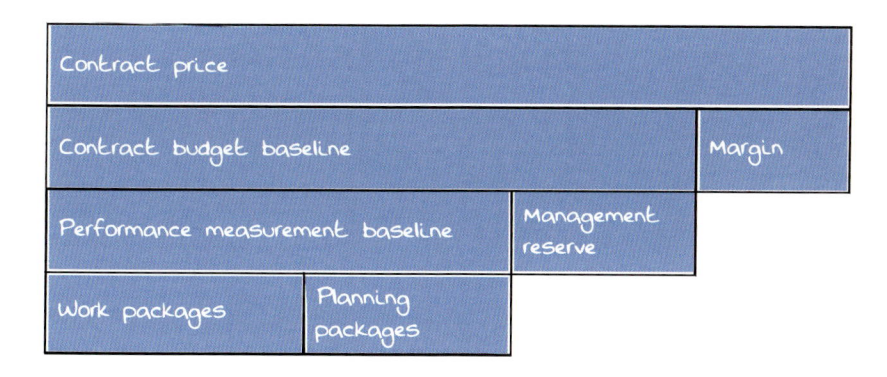

Figure 22.7 Budget allocation to the plan

22.5.2.4.1 Work packages

The work package is the lowest level at which performance data is normally analysed. It will be a node on the WBS. The work package will contain a number of activities that describe the work, and the budgets must be allocated at activity level. Attention is required to ensure that an adequate level of detail is achieved in these activities. Typically they should have a maximum of 4–6-weeks duration for projects exceeding 12 months, but there will always be exceptions. However, for longer activities it is important that progress can be easily and clearly measured.

Planning, Scheduling, Monitoring and Control

Management and support activities are included in work packages, and it is important to measure performance against budget. They are generally progressed as level of effort activities, as referred to later in this section.

22.5.2.4.2 Planning packages

Planning packages is the term used to refer to work packages where detail is not yet planned, or work is yet to be allocated. They are, by definition, some time in the longer-term future, possibly as a part of rolling wave planning.

22.5.2.4.3 Management reserve and contingency

Management reserve is budget allowed for unknown unknowns, and should not normally be included in the performance measurement baseline. EVA is not designed to give any useful measure of performance against contingency; separate measurements are appropriate for monitoring its use.

22.5.2.4.4 Risk

Risk is the budget allowed for known unknowns. As noted above, there is no practical benefit in measuring risk budget, as there is not a 100% chance of it being earned, and so it may distort performance measurement. However, it is sometimes required to be included for completeness. There are a number of ways of spreading the budget for risk. One way is across the remaining project time, but that requires adjustment at every progress update. Alternatively, it can be held in a 'risk pot' at the end of the project. In any event, risk money cannot be earned; it can only be transferred into other work packages, in line with the risk and change process.

22.5.2.4.5 Risk mitigations

Risk mitigations are agreed actions that have resulted from the risk process. These should be considered and included in the schedule where relevant – i.e. where they have an influence on time and the network of activities (as opposed to, for example, management actions such as 'additional staff brought in to mitigate risk of. . .'), although in all cases any associated budget must be reflected in the performance measurement baseline. The mitigations will be held in the relevant work or planning package.

Performance reporting

22.5.2.4.6 Contractor's fee

As noted above for management reserve, there is no practical benefit in measuring this item, though it is often required to be included for completeness. It should be treated as a level of effort activity, such that planned value always equals earned value. It should be noted that the effect of treating this as a LOE activity is to skew the overall SPI towards 1.0, as the SPI for a LOE activity is always 1.0.

22.5.2.5 How to deal with inflation

Inflation will raise the cost of labour and materials during the life of the project. If inflation needs to be taken into consideration in project budgets, for example if a project spans multiple years, then a way of dealing with it is required. It is common to use indexation tables to agree the sums involved. This is to ensure that a comparison between budgeted figures (in the form of planned value) and out-turn figures are like for like. There are two options:

- Add (or deduct!) an allowance into the value.
- Deduct (or add!) an allowance from the actual costs before calculating the actual cost in EVA.

In either case a protocol must be agreed, but the second option is likely to be the simpler.

22.5.2.6 Setting the baseline

Once the allocation of budget to the schedule is complete, a baseline is set. This baseline should not then be adjusted without the appropriate change control process approving such a change.

Once the schedule is sufficiently developed and stable, it should be set as the performance measurement baseline (PMB). This then forms the basis for measuring all future progress and performance.

22.5.2.7 Drawing S-curves with EVA

22.5.2.7.1 Planned value

Once the budget has been allocated (usually reflected in the planning software), an S-curve for the planned value over time can be created, as shown in Figure 22.8.

Planning, Scheduling, Monitoring and Control

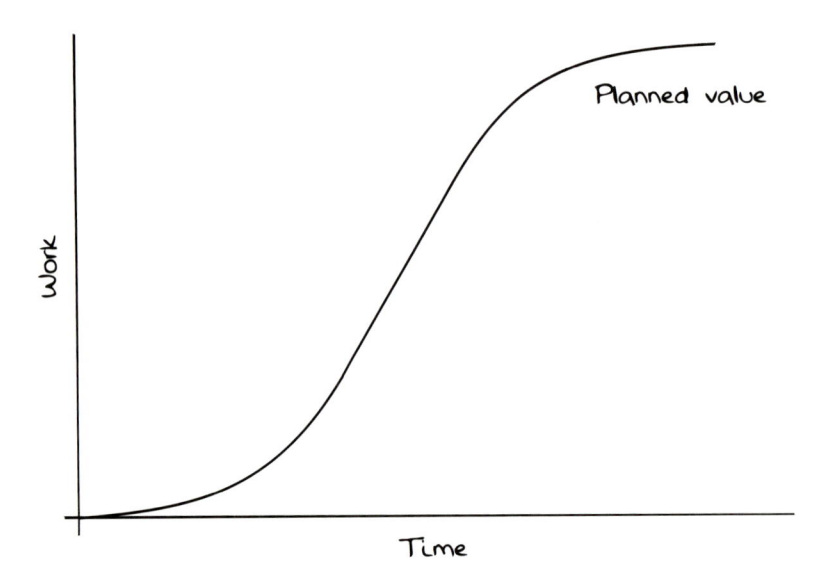

Figure 22.8 Planned value curve

22.5.2.7.2 Measuring progress to calculate earned value

Earned value is the value of the work that has been completed, and is calculated by collating the percentage completion multiplied by the total budget of each activity.

As the project is executed, progress is measured periodically, with each activity assessed for physical percentage complete. (The methods of measurement are discussed later.) Summation of all the progress recorded enables a progress curve to be plotted. This is the earned value.

Once the schedule has been updated for progress, the earned value can be plotted against the planned value, as shown in Figure 22.9. The diagram represents performance less than the planned expectation, or earned value less than the planned value line.

22.5.2.7.3 Recording actual costs

It is important to collect actual costs at the right level of detail, as increased granularity is very likely to lead to reduced data integrity. They should be collected at the appropriate level of the WBS (this may also be known as the cost breakdown structure).

Performance reporting

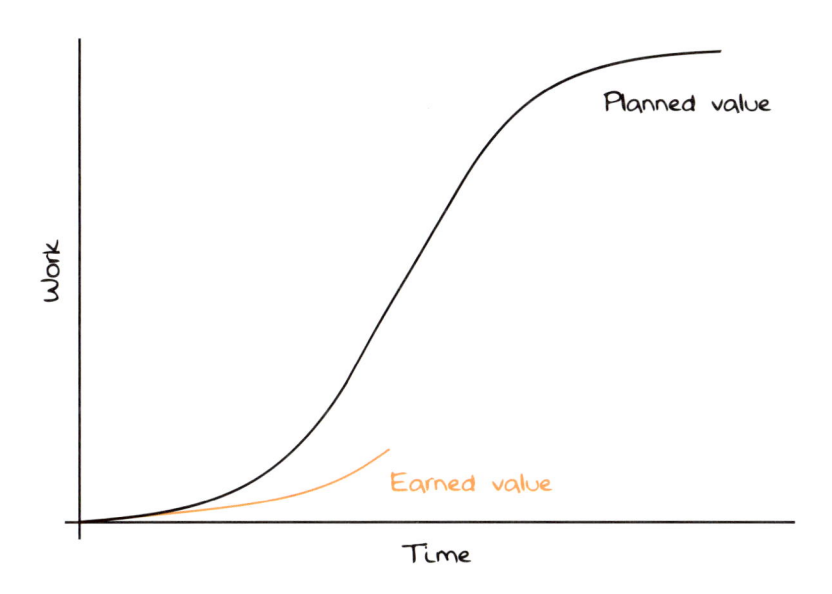

Figure 22.9 Earned value

Note: It will be necessary to allow for accruals in the cost collection system.

Once the actual costs have been added to the schedule, the cumulative actual costs can be plotted as shown in Figure 22.10. In the diagram, costs are in

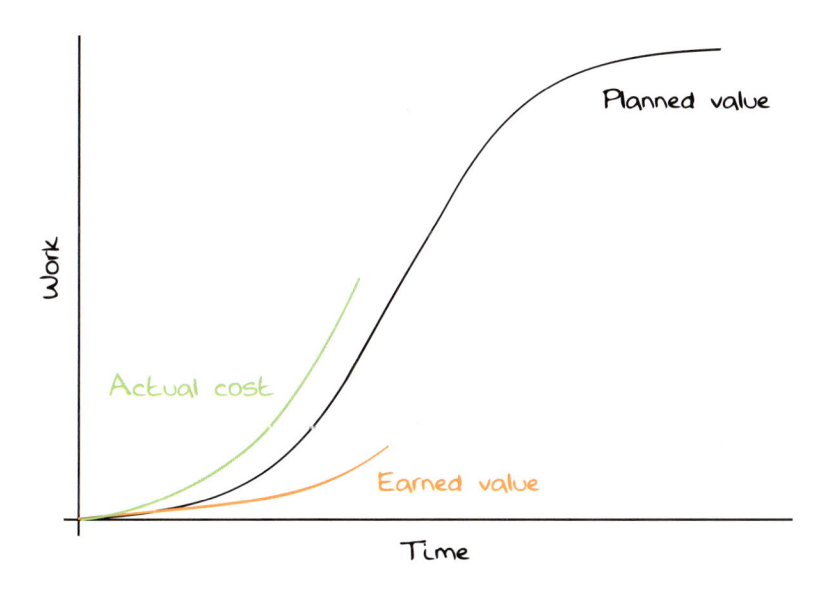

Figure 22.10 Actual costs (ACWP) added

241

Planning, Scheduling, Monitoring and Control

excess of what should be expected which would be parity with the earned value line.

22.5.2.8 Calculation of variances and key performance indicators (KPIs)

Having entered the planned value, earned value and actual cost, there are various earned value calculations that can be used to analyse this data (Figures 22.11–22.13).

22.5.2.8.1 Cost variance (CV)

Cost variance (CV) is a cost comparison between what has been earned and what has been spent ('Are we under or over budget?').

$$\text{Cost Variance} = \text{Earned Value} - \text{Actual Cost}$$

CV greater than 0 indicates a cost under-run
CV equals 0 indicates on budget
CV less than 0 indicates a cost over-run

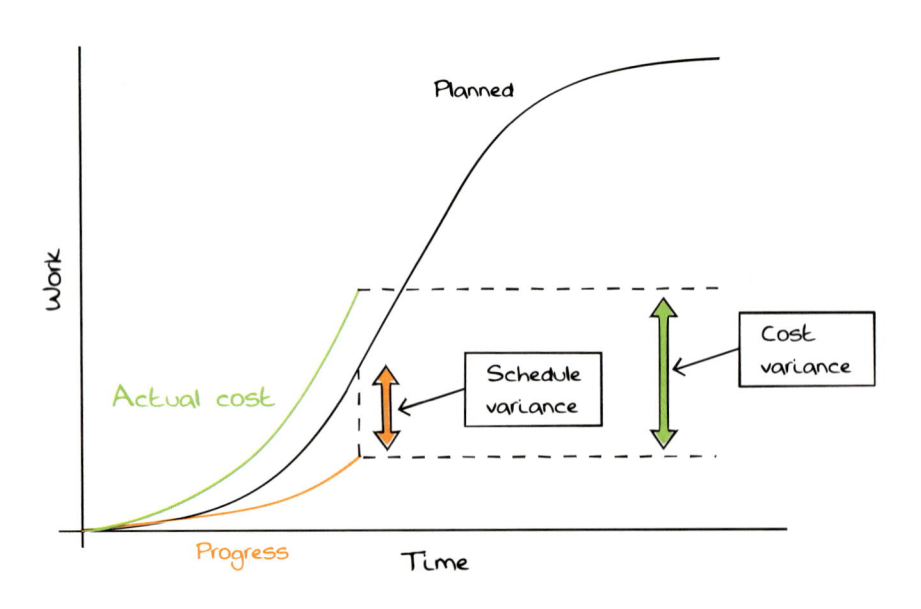

Figure 22.11 Earned value analysis: cost and schedule variance

Performance reporting

22.5.2.8.2 Schedule variance (SV)

Schedule variance (SV) is the cost comparison between what has been earned and what has been budgeted ('Are we ahead or behind schedule?').

Schedule Variance = Earned Value − Planned Value

SV greater than 0 indicates that the project is ahead of schedule
SV equals 0 indicates on schedule
SV less than 0 indicates that the project is behind schedule

Cost and schedule variance can usefully be charted, either separately or together (see Figure 22.12)

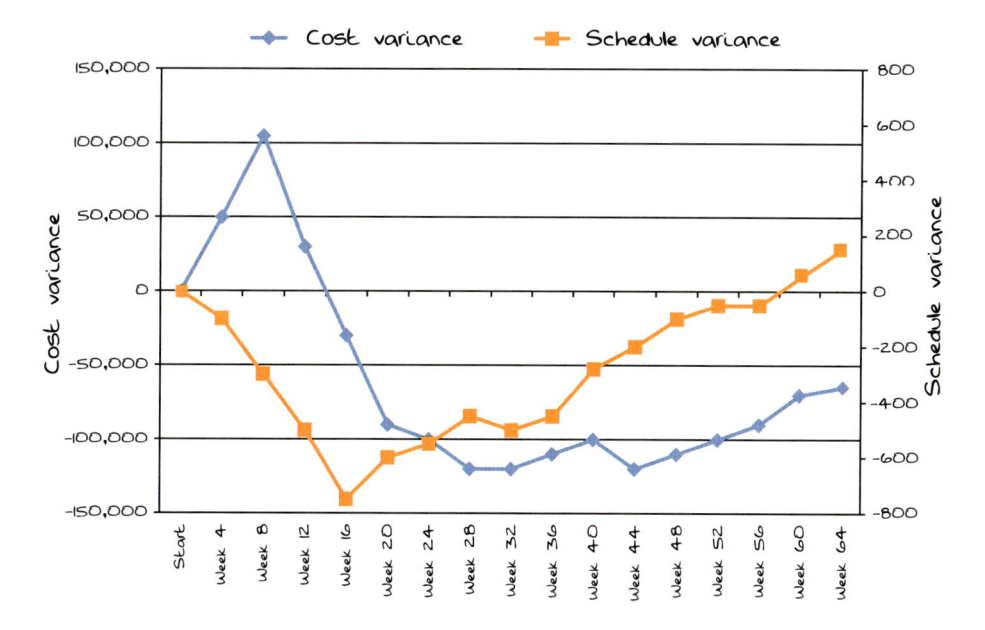

Figure 22.12 Cost and schedule variance chart

EVA measures schedule performance in terms of value as seen, but also in terms of time: time variance can be calculated or read off the graph as in Figure 22.13. This is the difference on the time axis between the quantity of work achieved to date, or earned value, and the corresponding quantity on the planned value curve.

Measuring and expressing delay in this way may help to give an alternative view of progress. It will also not suffer from the issue, already noted, that schedule performance index (SPI) and SV tend towards parity as the project nears

243

Planning, Scheduling, Monitoring and Control

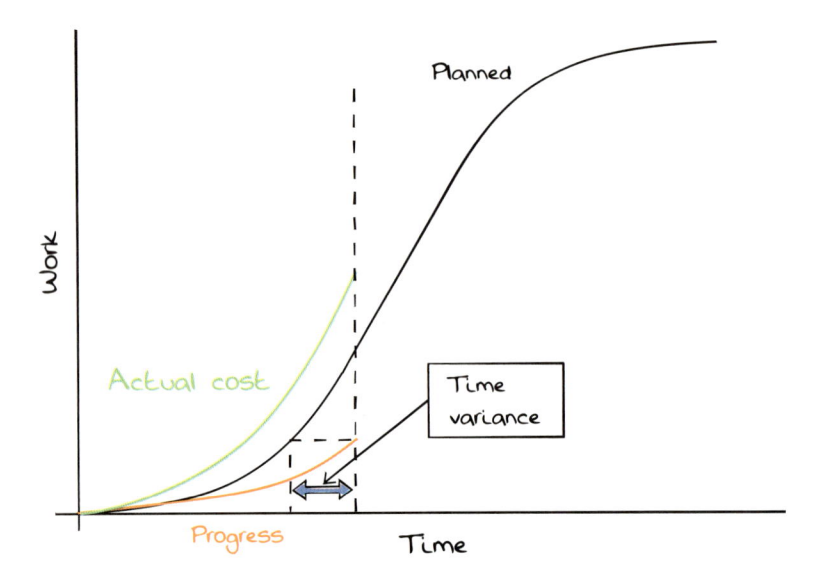

Figure 22.13 Earned value analysis with time variance

completion. (Although it has been stated that this is a flaw in earned value analysis, in reality we should expect project managers to be aware of approaching completion dates!).

22.5.2.8.3 EVA key performance indicators

A number of calculations can be made: the two most useful, and the basis for calculations of future performance, are the schedule performance index ('How are we doing against plan?') and cost performance index ('Are we efficient?'). These are calculated as follows:

$$\text{Schedule performance index (SPI)} = \frac{\text{Earned value}}{\text{Planned value}}$$

$$\text{Cost performance index (CPI)} = \frac{\text{Earned value}}{\text{Actual cost}}$$

Schedule performance index (SPI) is an indication of how far ahead or behind the planned work is compared with the actual work achieved. A result of 1.0 means that all the planned work was achieved. Its value as an indicator diminishes towards the end of a project.

SPI greater than 1 indicates that the project is ahead of schedule
SPI equals 1 indicates on schedule

Performance reporting

SPI less than 1 indicates that the project is behind schedule

Cost performance index (CPI) is the ratio of earned value over actual cost. A figure greater than 1.0 indicates that the actual cost of the work achieved cost less than planned.

CPI greater than 1 indicates a cost under-run
CPI equals 1 indicates on budget
CPI less than 1 indicates a cost over-run

SPI and CPI can usefully be plotted against each other to create a 'Bulls eye' chart, as shown in Figure 22.14.

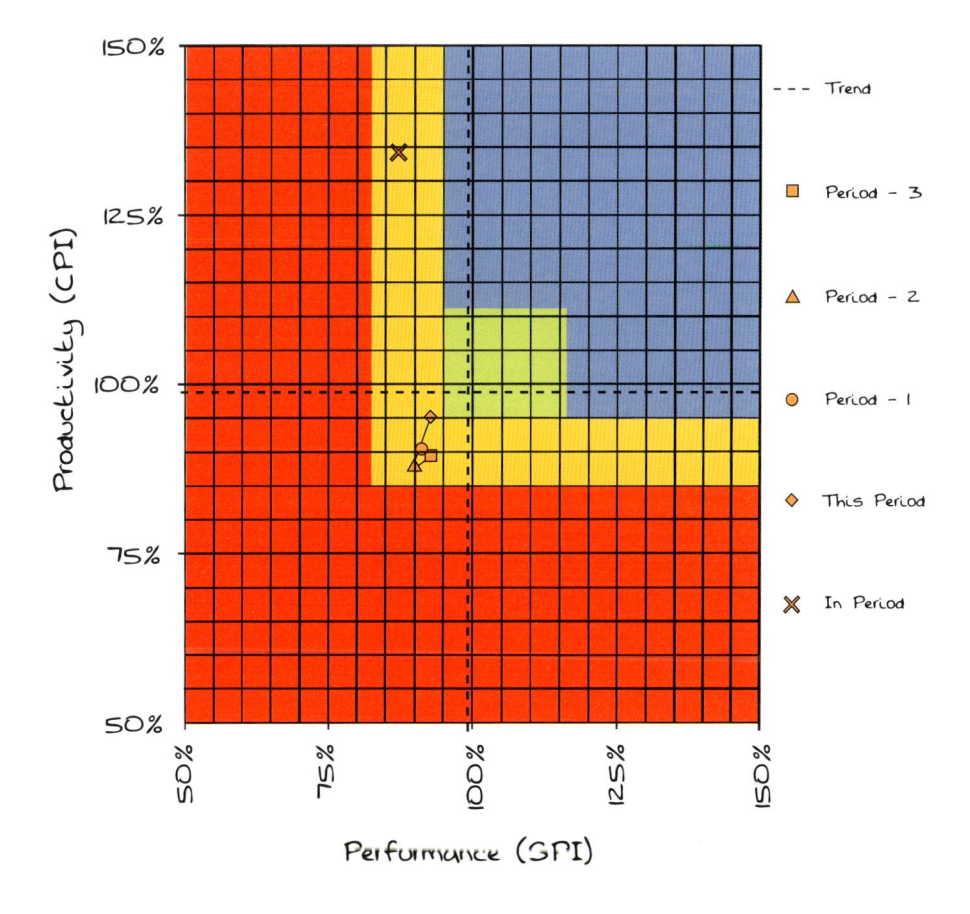

Figure 22.14 Bulls eye performance chart

Planning, Scheduling, Monitoring and Control

The shading indicates the BRAG rating that may also be allocated to the KPIs, where

B=Blue: Performance over that expected (and needs investigating)
R=Red: Performance seriously below expected (needs immediate corrective action)
A=Amber: Performance below expectation (needs planning or corrective action)
G=Green: performance within expectations (no action required)

22.5.2.9 Forecasting terminology

Estimate to complete (ETC): An estimate of the amount of funds required to complete all remaining work on the project ('What will the remaining work cost?').

$$ETC = \frac{(BAC - \text{Earned value})}{CPI}$$

Estimate at completion (EAC): The sum of the actual costs to date plus the estimate to complete (ETC) ('What is the project likely to cost?').

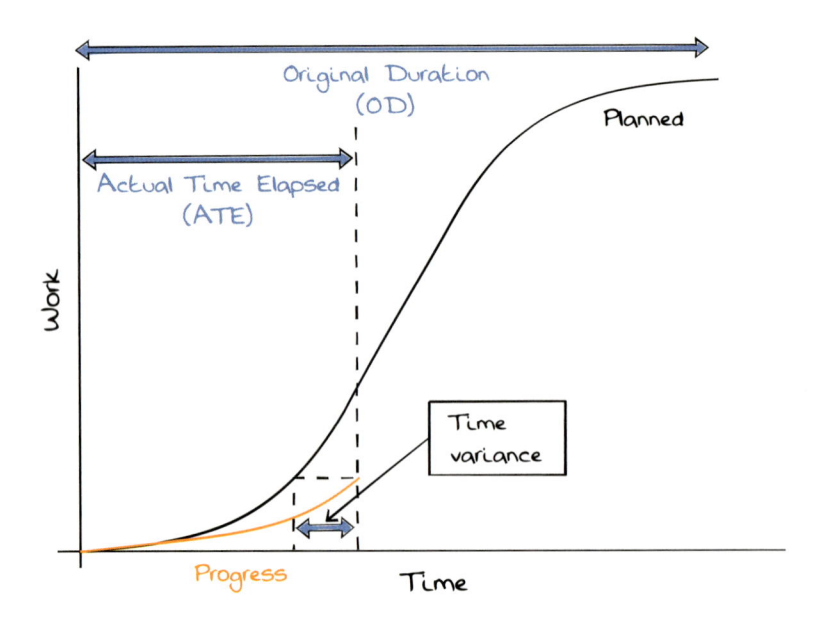

$$EAC = \text{Actual cost} + ETC$$

Figure 22.15 Calculating estimated time to completion

Performance reporting

It has been shown (Webb, Alan (2003, 26) *Using Earned Value*, Gower) that mathematically the formula for EAC can, in fact, be simplified to:

$$EAC = \frac{BAC}{CPI}$$

Estimated time to complete (ETTC) can be calculated as follows (Figure 22.15):

$$ETTC = ATE + \frac{OD-(ATE \times SPI)}{SPI}$$

Again, It has been shown (Webb, Alan (2003, 26) *Using Earned Value*, Gower) that mathematically the formula for ETTC can, in fact, be simplified to:

$$ETTC = \frac{OD}{SPI}$$

22.5.2.10 Earned value techniques (EVTs)

The different methods of measuring earned value known as earned value techniques generally vary according to the level of detail in the schedule. Short-term hourly or daily schedules would probably be progressed daily by site staff. Very often customers require different reporting techniques. Some examples are shown in Figure 22.16. It is important to bear in mind the level of reporting detail required when determining the granularity of the schedule, as detailed EV reporting is difficult from high-level summary schedules.

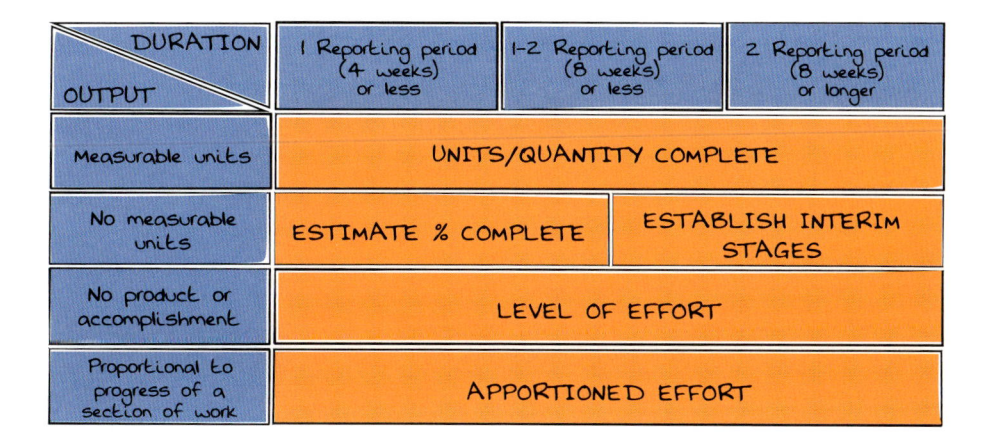

DURATION / OUTPUT	1 Reporting period (4 weeks) or less	1-2 Reporting period (8 weeks) or less	2 Reporting period (8 weeks) or longer
Measurable units	UNITS/QUANTITY COMPLETE		
No measurable units	ESTIMATE % COMPLETE		ESTABLISH INTERIM STAGES
No product or accomplishment	LEVEL OF EFFORT		
Proportional to progress of a section of work	APPORTIONED EFFORT		

Figure 22.16 Illustration of various earning techniques and appropriate uses

Planning, Scheduling, Monitoring and Control

	What is it?	Advantages	Disadvantages
Milestones	A milestone is a key event, which is based on work accomplished. Each milestone is assigned a proportion of the budget that represents the budgeted value of the work required to achieve it. When the milestone is achieved, that proportion of the budget has been earned.	Possibly the least subjective method of determining progress, if well defined.	Schedules are not built this way. Crude as work in progress (WIP) ignored, making CPI appear worse than is on labour, and on cost. Poor definition of milestones leads to inaccurate EV and possibly of manipulation. Size of schedule and purpose skewed from core purpose.
Per cent complete	Value is earned on the basis of a subjective assessment of the percentage of the total work completed. Granularity (detail in the schedule) delivers objectivity.	Easy to do and familiar. No additional work required to the schedule.	Open to abuse if granularity not achieved. Too subjective if deliverable not visible (e.g. software production; early design stages).
0/100	No value is earned until the work package is completed. Effectively a variation of using milestones.	Very easy to do objectivity achieved.	Suitable for short duration activity that falls in one period. Crude; will not recognise WIP, thus giving distorted KPI's.
50/50	50% of the value is earned at the start of the work package and 50% on completion.	Very easy to do.	Care must be taken if the duration of the task is over two periods as zero value will be earned between the start and finish. Crude; alternatively over/under credits WIP, thus giving distorted KPI's.
Equivalent units	Work packages containing a series of like units, an equal amount would be earned for each item.	Objectivity achieved and demonstrable. Useful and clearly understood production graphs can be produced.	Only appropriate when the project includes a number of repeat items or products produced at regular intervals. Potentially inaccurate if applied to complicated activity.
Level of effort	Work that is necessary for the project, but not directly related to the generation of a deliverable.	For project management and administrative effort if not covered by overhead costs. Must be kept to a minimum as it can mask variances.	Only appropriate for activity type specified.
Apportioned effort	Work that is necessary for the project that can be directly related to the generation of a deliverable.	Suitable for supervision related to a specific task, e.g. quality control.	Only appropriate for activity type specified.

Figure 22.17 Advantages and disadvantages of EVTs

Performance reporting

22.5.2.10.1 Recognised earned value techniques

Figure 22.17 summarises the advantages and disadvantages of EVTs.

22.5.2.11 Advantages of EVA

Below are some of the benefits of using earned value analysis on a project:

- Certainty of project position: what work has been achieved against plan; what it has cost to reach that level of achievement.
- Whether the work achieved represents good value for money (i.e. has been achieved efficiently).
- Gives early warning of whether the project is likely to finish on time and/or on budget.
- Improved decision making: guides attention to problem areas that need management decisions.
- Provides the basis for informed cost and/or time recovery actions.
- Ensures that a robust plan is established at the outset of the project.
- Management of scope creep through the change control system.
- Ensures cash-flow is measured properly and optimised.
- Provides corporate governance (when done across the organisation).
- Business benefits include turnover, profit and cash being achieved on time or as soon as practicable.

22.5.2.12 Limitations of EVA

The view that EVA is best practice in project management is long established, but earned value management is not the universal panacea of project management, and failure can still occur on a project monitored using earned value. One of the biggest threats is that the project team focus too much on regularly generating the data for EVA and fail to take notice of the messages it gives.

Data integrity is also key to making EVA work. With good data, the project manager has a lot of reliable information to assist in managing the project, which greatly assists in decision making.

23.1 Definition of cost control

Cost control is the process of collecting actual costs and collating them in a format to allow comparison with project budgets, identifying variances to inform decision making and allow action to be taken. In addition, it includes cost forecasting.

Cost forecasting is the process of using performance measurement, progress information and risk management to estimate how the costs will be spent going forward to the end of the project or financial year and inform the anticipated final cost (AFC).

23.2 Purpose of cost control

Cost control is necessary to keep a record of monetary (and other) expenditure, for the purposes of:

- minimising cost where possible;
- revealing areas of cost overspend;
- giving sufficient detail to allow management decision making to correct unacceptable overspending;
- providing data for lessons learned to inform future projects (or phases of the same project).

Planning, Scheduling, Monitoring and Control

23.3 The cost control process

23.3.1 Performance measurement baseline (PMB)

The initial cost model forms the basis of the cost-loaded performance measurement baseline and should be aligned with the schedule activities at an appropriate level in order to measure financial progress, forecast out-turn project costs and phasing, and facilitate earned value analysis. When updating or re-setting the baseline, it is important to ensure that the cost information is up to date, as any variances may significantly affect the project's ability to highlight and react to negative trends.

23.3.1.1 Estimates to complete

Estimates to complete (ETC) are prepared as part of the EVA process and are used to determine how project costs are trending to derive the project Estimate at completion (EAC).

23.2.1.2 Estimated final cost

The estimated final cost (EFC) is prepared as part of the project cost control process and is used to determine how project costs are performing against the authorised project budget. EAC (derived from EVA data) should be used to challenge the EFC.

23.3.2 The link between cost control and change control

It is important to ensure that any changes to project costs and/or budgets are formally managed through the project change control process. This not only facilitates quick and informed financial approvals, helping the project to move forward, but also leaves a much-needed audit trail for the lessons learned process at the end of the project. Different levels of change may require different change control processes, so ensure any change is managed in the appropriate way.

If the change results in amended scope, then the performance measurement baseline must be updated through the appropriate change control process once it is approved by the project manager or relevant authority.

23.3.3 Performance measurement

The most common method of cost performance measurement is the cost value report, in which actual costs for work undertaken are compared (usually in a spreadsheet) against the current budget for the same work. A combination of the cost value report and forecast future changes are used to inform the estimated final cost (EFC).

Forecast future changes may include:

- anticipated scope change via client or supplier formal change process;
- known or anticipated cost over- or under-spends;
- risks or opportunities;
- inflation/indexation;
- exchange rate changes.

These changes will highlight cost variance. This is the difference between the assumed costs of the project or activities in the performance measurement baseline at the point of reporting, and the actual costs that the project is committed to at that same point.

A recognised best practice around cost control is through the use of earned value management where the cost performance index (CPI) is the key indicator of project financial performance. This process is described in detail insection 22.5.2. It is ideal for identifying where a project is not progressing efficiently.

23.4 Learning lessons from cost control

Cost control information is fundamental to the lessons learned process, as it can provide a database of actual costs against activities and work packages that can be used to inform future projects at the inception phase. When dealing with suppliers, the contract administration process will reveal unforeseen changes to the project and its costs. Ensuring rigid document control around these changes can greatly increase future projects' chance of success through more accurate estimating and/or a more informed risk management process.

24.1 Definition of short-term planning

The duration of short-term planning may vary depending upon the duration of the project, but is likely to consist of a 4-week look ahead and a look back at the previous week's progress. It would normally be issued weekly. (These durations would obviously be inappropriate for a weekend shut-down schedule!)

24.2 Purpose of short-term planning

The short-term planning process takes the schedule out of the computer and puts it into the hands of the site teams supervising the work. It should also reflect current progress, with recovery of slippage if necessary.

24.3 The short-term planning process

Short-term planning should be linked to the schedules as shown in Figure 24.1. There should also be a link, or a cross-check with the schedules produced at this level back to the main project schedule(s) to ensure that the strategic requirements of the project remain achieved.

Short-term, high-density scheduling consists of four key elements:

- performance reporting against last week's planned work;
- reasons for any non-completed work;

Planning, Scheduling, Monitoring and Control

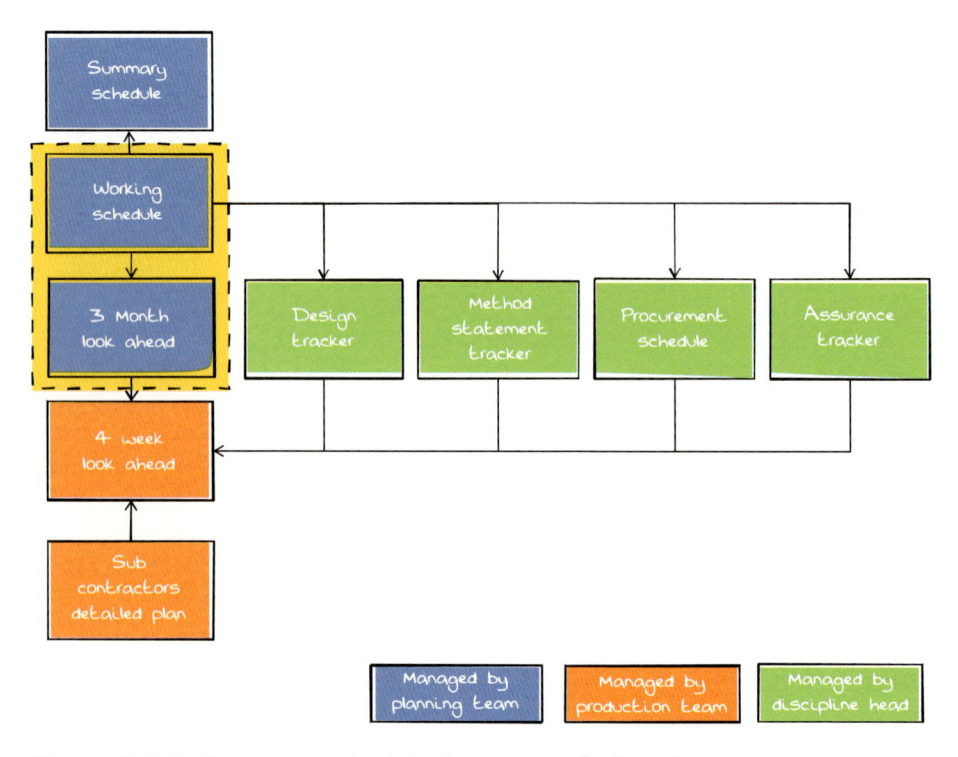

Figure 24.1 Short-term schedules in context of other plans

- the work planned over the next 3 or 4 weeks (with a strong emphasis on the next week);
- the make ready needs for these activities (these are the start criteria for each detailed task).

The short-term scheduling is undertaken weekly and is owned by the front-line staff; in order to facilitate the process an extract of the schedule is produced, typically a 3-month look ahead. This will then be used to generate the 4-week look ahead, developing detail to a day-by-day schedule.

Once produced, the schedule will be checked against the strategic requirements as defined in the current working schedule.

Having produced a 4-week 'look ahead', the following are considered:

Short-term planning

24.3.1 Make ready needs

Each activity has 'make ready needs' identified. Make ready needs are those things that must be in place to allow an activity to commence. These may include:

- safe working practices;
- material call off or availability;
- other procurement activity;
- method statement and other paperwork in place;
- offline preparation for task, e.g. in construction the building of formwork panels;
- outstanding design information or RFIs (requests for information);
- completion of works by others (which will feature elsewhere on the look ahead);
- access requirements.

24.3.2 Coordination meeting

Coordination meetings are held to review the combined schedule, to record performance against agreed objectives, and to understand and analyse issues which hinder the progress of those activities.

All schedules should be issued the day prior to the coordination meeting, allowing time for review. This is to ensure that maximum benefit is gained from the meeting. Discipline is required to ensure that schedules are delivered on time, because the process relies on a large number of people producing their part of the schedule in a timely manner. Strong chairmanship of the meeting is essential to ensure full participation and agreement of the schedule by all.

A key purpose of the meeting is to ensure that all schedules are agreed and issued at the end of the meeting; schedules can be hand amended – do not wait for electronic distribution.

24.3.3 Performance reporting

As part of the meeting, the previous week's progress should be reviewed, and any reasons for missed targets are categorised against a predetermined list. Charts will be produced for analysis outside the meeting (Figure 24.2).

Planning, Scheduling, Monitoring and Control

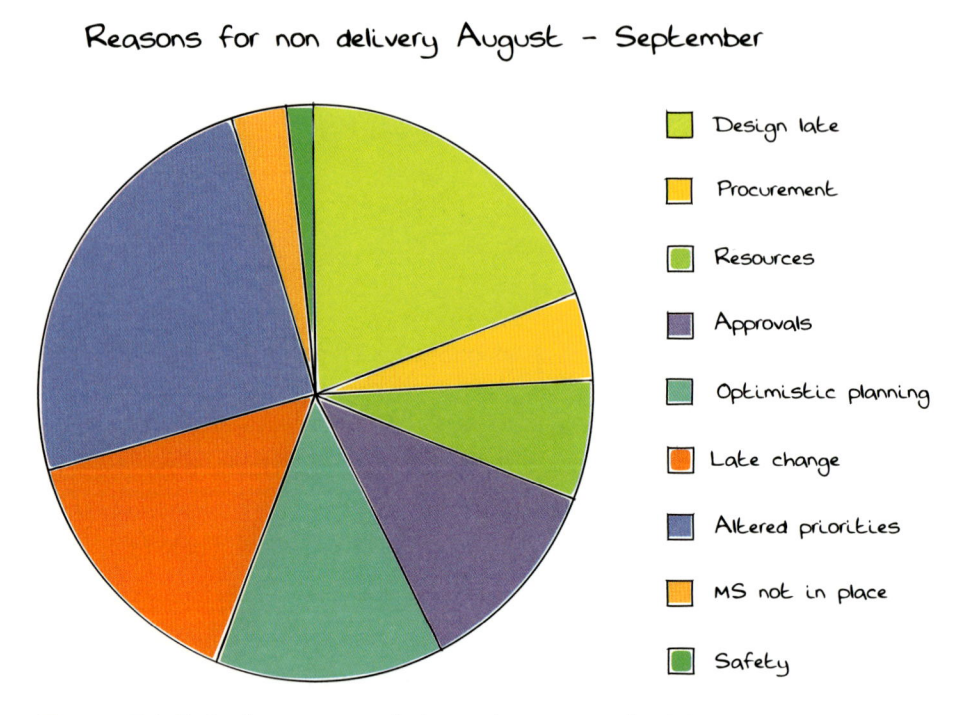

Reasons for non delivery August – September

- Design late
- Procurement
- Resources
- Approvals
- Optimistic planning
- Late change
- Altered priorities
- MS not in place
- Safety

Figure 24.2 Performance analysis on short-term schedule

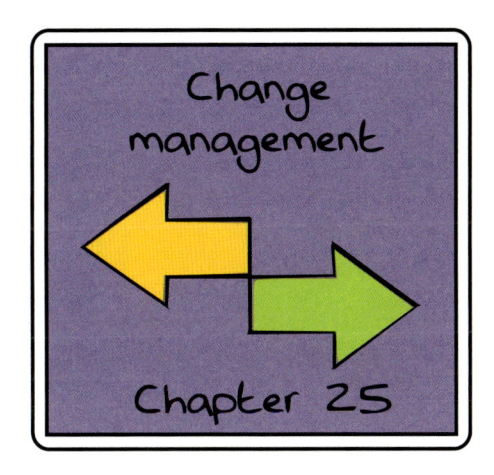

25.1 Definition of change management

Change management is the formal process through which changes to the project are raised, assessed, approved, and introduced or rejected.

'Changes' are events and issues that alter the schedule, scope or objectives. In broad terms, there are two levels of change:

- Significant additions/omissions from the schedule scope – these changes will require amendments to the control budget and related schedules.
- Amendments to the method of delivery where the fundamental scope remains the same. These amendments may be the result of clarification or development.

Significant changes may arise from:

- inside the project, such as risks impacting, adoption of wrong strategy, etc., where they will be funded from management reserve drawdown;
- outside the project, such as a new customer requirement, where they will require additional funding;
- a change in legislation.

25.2 Purpose of change management

Change management is integral to good project management because it controls and authorises:

Planning, Scheduling, Monitoring and Control

- change in scope;
- changes in budgets;
- changes in timing of the project;
- changes in risks that are managed as part of the project;
- changes in expenditure.

Thus, it ensures that costs are known and that the supply chain receive fair recompense for any additional work that they perform, whilst protecting the client from paying for works that are not performed.

25.3 Principles of change management

Any proposed change to the project must be formally controlled in order for it to be dealt with efficiently and fairly. The project team, with the support of relevant stakeholders including the sponsor, should therefore review changes fully before their approval and implementation. The impact of changes on all aspects of the project in terms of scope, budget, time, quality, safety, environment, risk and opportunity should be fully assessed, as well as their impact on business as usual and other projects.

The key points of reference when considering change are the baseline (budget/schedule plan), and the project execution plan (PEP). The baseline defines the point against which change is measured, whilst the PEP gives the detail of how the change process is managed.

All changes should be fully documented and efficiently communicated to all relevant parties.

25.4 Change control

25.4.1 Why change control is needed

- To ensure all parties are clear regarding the scope to be delivered.
- To ensure all parties are clear regarding the schedule to be delivered to.
- To ensure all parties are clear regarding the budgets to be delivered to.
- To ensure clear visibility of movements within published budgets and schedules as the project progresses.
- To enable early recognition and management of issues that could be influenced for the good, i.e. cheaper, quicker, better-quality and more efficient solutions.

Change management

- To maintain an audit trail of who authorises or rejects change: what, when, how, for what cost and why?
- To ensure potential change is identified in a proactive manner.
- To ensure appropriate levels of change review and approval are implemented.
- To ensure change is reported accurately.
- To ensure all options are considered and evaluated.
- To ensure change is implemented within appropriate time periods.
- To ensure that the project remains under control and can be delivered in an affordable, profitable, value for money manner.
- To ensure that the product delivered meets developing customer needs (i.e. is not against a requirement that is now obsolete).

25.4.2 Change control considerations

The change control process must also consider:

- Unauthorised change: If an unauthorised change is identified, it must be retrospectively put through the change control process.
- Configuration management: Change control is intrinsically linked to configuration management. Any changes need to be fed back into the project's configuration documentation. This ensures that the most current information is used to deliver the project.
- Change freezes: In certain circumstances, it is appropriate to have a change freeze on the project whereby no further changes will be considered, as to do so would jeopardise the achievement of the project objectives.
- An emergency procedure to enable certain actions (change) to be authorised, for example in the case of an emerging health and safety issue at a point in time where usual authorities are unavailable.
- Trending of change against specific areas will help to reveal underlying problems and/or provide an early warning of increasing costs and areas requiring management attention.

25.5 Project-level change: process overview

Once the project brief has been agreed, the change control procedures should commence.

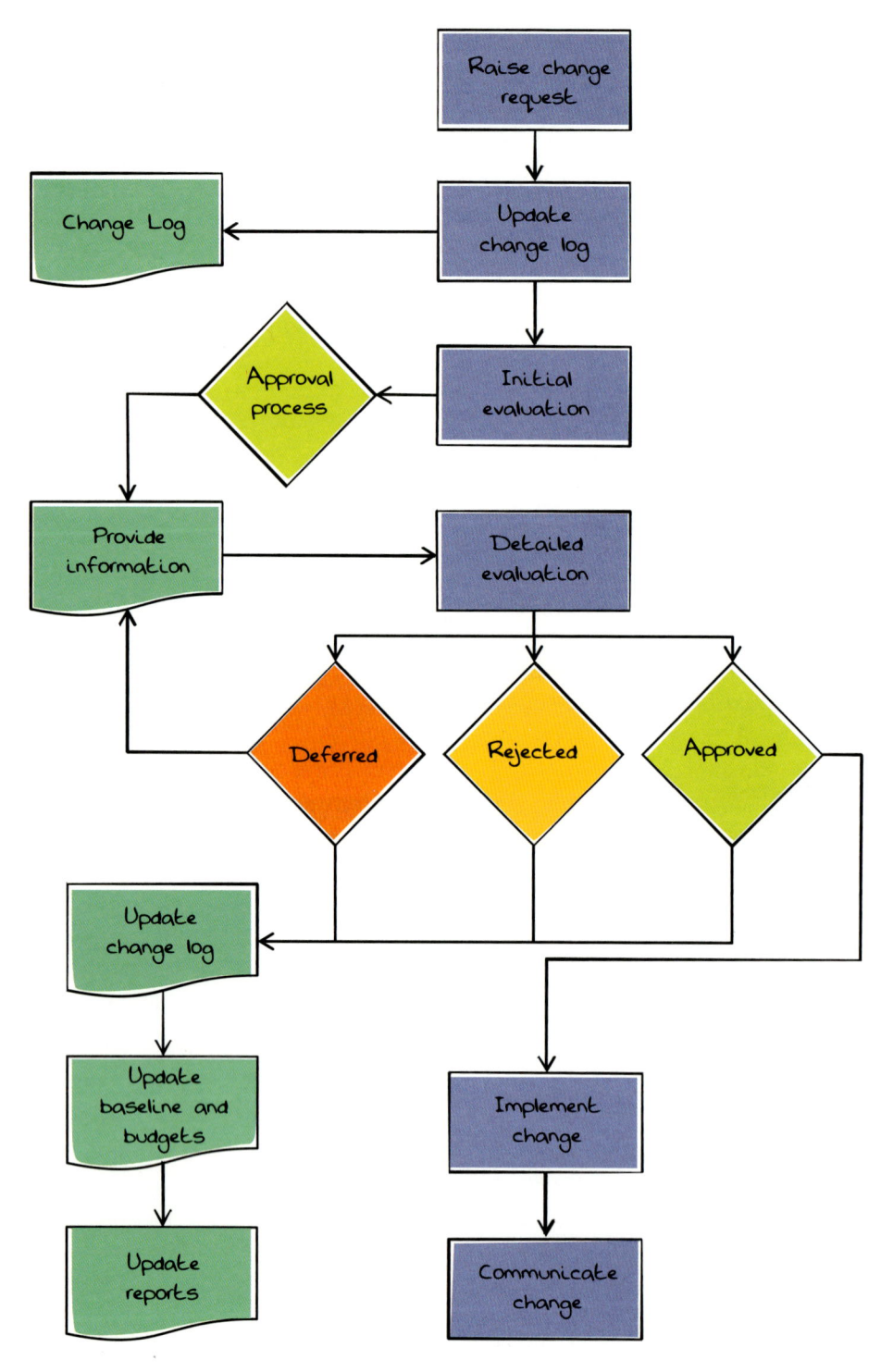

Figure 25.1 Process overview – project change control

Change management

Change on projects needs to be closely monitored to ensure that cost, time and quality are effectively controlled and reported. A change control process is likely to be different from one company to the next. Similarly, it may vary across different industries. The flow chart in Figure 25.1 gives an overview of a typical change control process.

25.6 Raising a change request

Potential change can be identified by anyone within the project team. The potential change is reviewed to determine whether a change of project brief or scope has occurred, in which case a change request needs to be raised.

A stakeholder who is requesting change provides relevant information on the nature of the proposed change. This should include a detailed description of the change (what, where, when, who and how, etc.) The positive or negative cost impact of the change and the impact on the schedule should be stated. The benefit(s) of undertaking the change should be made clear if not already evident from the foregoing.

25.6.1 Drafting a change request

All formal change requests need to be submitted using a change request form. The change request form is designed to capture the following detail:

- a description of the change;
- a classification of the change;
- the cost impact (positive or negative);
- the schedule impact (positive or negative);
- the approvals required;
- the links to the project risk and opportunity registers.

The change request should be accompanied by all relevant documentation.

25.7 The change log

The change is entered into a Change log, which is a register of all changes that have been requested, whatever their status, for example pending, approved,

Planning, Scheduling, Monitoring and Control

rejected or deferred. It contains a record of each change request and should include at least the following:

- unique ID number;
- status of the change;
- change description;
- detailed scope of the change;
- category of change;
- created by (the change originator);
- date raised;
- impact assessment – scope/budget/schedule/risk/safety, etc.;
- authority;
- funding/budget;
- decision: (approval/deferral/rejection) and date.

25.8 Initial evaluation of the change request

The change is reviewed to consider whether it is worthwhile evaluating it in detail. The evaluation of change consumes resources, which in itself is a deviation from the project baseline. The proposed change may be rejected without further evaluation.

25.9 Estimating impact of change

Impact analysis of the change and associated cost and time estimates should be prepared, reviewed and submitted for approval. The estimates should include direct cost and indirect cost such as management, and risks and opportunities should be assessed.

25.10 Detailed evaluation of change request

Upon approval of the initial estimate, the change is evaluated in detail to consider the impact on the project's baseline scope, time, cost, quality or benefits. If the request is rejected, then the relevant parties are informed and the change log updated accordingly. There may be a situation where the request is deferred as

Change management

more information is required. Once that has been supplied, then the request re-joins the process at detailed evaluation stage.

Once a change request has got through the initial evaluation, it proceeds into the detailed evaluation.

This evaluation is usually carried out in a regular change review meeting. The meetings would be attended by all the relevant parties on the project, but, importantly, they require the project sponsor or authoriser for the change request.

There are three possible outcomes for a change request:

- rejected;
- deferred;
- approved.

This section will address rejected and deferred (approved change being dealt with in the next section).

25.10.1 Rejected request

A rejected change request would be recorded in the change log stating the reason for the refusal. This is then communicated back to the requesting party.

25.10.2 Deferred request

A deferred request normally requires more information to be supplied before full consideration can be given to the request. The team will then carry out a more detailed evaluation based on the areas where further information is needed. The results of any investigation may include a revised schedule, indicating the effect of significant changes to interfaces and summary milestones. Any changes will need to be reviewed by all parties concerned.

A deferred request may also be optional change, in that the change will only be approved if the impacts are within certain parameters. Optional change may also require the consideration of alternative schedule possibilities. In these cases, 'what if' or offline schedules are used to review the different options as part of the change process. There may be more than one 'what if' schedule required to model a number of potential options. It is important that the extra information is returned within the time constraints defined in the contract and performed in parallel with the cost investigation.

Planning, Scheduling, Monitoring and Control

The extra data provided then goes back into the process for detailed evaluation.

If agreement is not achieved, the schedule effects may need to be re-visited prior to any further action.

Again, the change log would be updated and the details of the information required passed back to the requester.

25.11 Approved request

If the change request is approved by the authorised person, then the change log should be updated. The baseline and budget will also need to be revised.

25.11.1 Change orders

Change orders may also be known as change notices.

25.11.1.1 What does a change order do?

Change orders are used to authorise a change to the project, including a change of scope or agreement to accept a design solution which is outside the agreed cost and schedule parameters. Once formal approval is received for the change, the cost and schedule baselines are updated.

Change orders are also used to gain formal approval for additional funding following a change. They do not, however, change the scope of the project for the suppliers to action, and must always be supported by an appropriate instruction.

25.11.1.2 Who raises/authorises change orders?

A change order is raised by anyone with authority to do so (as defined in the project procedures). Once raised, it is endorsed by the project manager prior to being submitted to the project sponsor for authorisation.

Scope can only be instructed and authorised into or out of the project baseline by the project sponsor/client, and not the project teams.

25.11.1.3 Commercial significance

The change order only provides authorisation to change the scope. Funding approval will also be required before the formal instruction for the change can be issued.

Change management

25.11.2 Scope transfers

In circumstances where scope is being transferred between teams, a formal instruction will be issued to confirm the scope and budget transfer. Scope transfers should be mutually agreed by the original owner and the proposed owner.

25.11.3 Schedule revisions

If the change affects the scope, then it will be necessary to add the change and its effects into the baseline as well as the working schedule.

Alternatively, if the change is within the existing scope, then the working schedule should be amended. Where appropriate, the baseline will need to take into account the updated schedule.

A change request will be required for any change to the project baseline (but not the working plan).

25.11.4 Corporate governance

In order to maintain an efficient change management process, delegated authority can be granted to managers at pre-agreed levels (see Table 25.1).

Table 25.1 *Example of financial authority*

Responsible	Instruction value
Project managers	Up to and including £50k
Programme managers	Up to and including £75k
Directors	Up to and including £500k
Board	Over £500k

25.12 Implementing the change

The key part of the change process is to implement the change. The project manager will issue a formal instruction to implement the change.

Planning, Scheduling, Monitoring and Control

Once change approvals and financial authorisations are in place, the following actions should be taken:

- Update the change logs to reflect the approved status of changes.
- Issue an instruction if appropriate and record its issue.
- Update reports to reflect cost and schedule impacts.
- Update any purchase orders to reflect cost and schedule impact.
- Update project execution plans (including risk/opportunity registers) and project brief.
- Communicate within project team and any interfacing teams.
- Update the baseline with the agreed change.

25.12.1 Adjusting schedule in line with change

Change broadly comes in two categories and may be dealt with in different ways: change that is required and change that is subject to further optioneering or exploration – i.e. that might not happen. Change will be picked up in the schedule narrative.

25.12.1.1 Optional change

Optional change should be assessed in 'what if' or offline schedules as part of the change process. There may be more than one 'what if' schedule required to model a number of potential options. This type of change should only be incorporated into the schedule once it has been approved.

25.12.1.2 Required change

Once required change has been identified, it should be reflected in the schedule to ensure that it continues to reflect the intended sequence and scope of works regardless of agreement. This ensures that a realistic schedule is maintained and the critical path remains robust. Only when the change is authorised will the budgets contained in the schedule (and elsewhere) be adjusted.

25.12.1.3 Reviewing change

Where supplier's change has been approved, the supplier/contractor should submit their schedule with the agreed change incorporated. The planner should

Change management

assess the schedule to see whether the change accurately reflects the agreed change. Checks will need to be made regarding:

- key milestone dates;
- key interfaces;
- critical path.
- sub (or 'near') critical paths.

25.13 Communicating the change

Once a change request has gone through the system, and the change log has been updated accordingly, it is important to ensure that all relevant parties are informed. As change is a critical part of any project, it is important that the change information is quickly read and acknowledged by the key parties.

Sending out the latest version of the change log in an email to all the project team will not get the message across. The issue of a formal instruction does meet most contractual requirements, but it is better to also go over the approved changes at either a regular project team meeting or, better still, a specific change review meeting.

It is important to ensure that ALL parties are informed, as change often has far-reaching impacts. As a rule, it is always better to over-inform rather than risk missing people out, e.g. stakeholders or sponsors.

As well as the change log, it is important that the process also picks up the resulting changes to other key documents, such as: drawings; document control systems; specifications; procurement orders; schedules; cost plans; baselines, etc.

25.14 Monthly change reporting requirements

It is important to communicate the status of change to all interested parties on a regular basis. Figures 25.2 and 25.3 show examples from a construction project on change reporting.

Planning, Scheduling, Monitoring and Control

Monthly change report values required for inclusion within each project's monthly report

EWN/EON

Unapproved change	Unapproved change	Unapproved change	Unapproved change
Number of EWN/EONs raised in the period	Value of EWN/EONs raised in the period	Cumulative number of EWN/EONs raised to date	Cumulative value of EWN/EONs raised to date
no.	€	no.	€

To include the total value of EWN/EONs raised that are either Pending or Accepted – Pls discount rejected EWN/EONs

SIs/Architects/Engineers instruction

Approved Change	Approved Change	Approved Change	Approved Change
Number of SIs raised in the period	Value of SIs raised in the period	Cumulative number of SIs raised to date	Cumulative value of SIs raised to date
no.	€	no.	€

PMI

Approved change	Approved change	Approved change	Approved change
Number of PMIs raised in the period	Value of PMIs raised in the period	Cumulative number of PMIs raised to date	Cumulative value of PMIs raised to date
no.	€	no.	€

CO

Approved change	Approved change	Approved change	Approved change
Number of COs raised in the period	Value of COs raised in the period	Cumulative number of COs raised to date	Cumulative value of COs raised to date
no.	€	no.	€

To include the total value of both incoming & outgoing scope through change orders

BT

Approved change	Approved change	Approved change	Approved change
Number of BTs raised in the period	Value of BTs raised in the period	Cumulative number of BTs raised to date	Cumulative value of BTs raised to date
no.	€	no.	€

To include the total value of both incoming & outgoing budget transfers

Figure 25.2 Example of monthly change reporting

Top 3 outstanding EWNs to date				
Project	Description	Date raised	Value £	Action plan

Top 3 pending EWNs raised in the month				
Project	Description	Date raised	Value £	Action plan

Top 3 PMIs in the month				
Project	Description	Date raised	Value £	Action plan

Figure 25.3 Monthly change report

Change management

Definitions used in Figures 25.2 and 25.3:

NEC: New engineering contract. Now widely used in the construction industry.

EWN/EON: Early warning notices are used to contractually advise the client or customer that there could be a potential impact on cost or time (as used within the NEC contract).

SI: Site instruction. Used on construction projects where a small on-site change needs to be implemented quickly.

PMI: Project manager's instruction. The formal notification given by the project manager usually following a more detailed review of the impact of the change.

CO: Change order. These are used to authorise a change to the project, including a change of scope or agreement to accept a design solution which is outside the agreed cost and schedule parameters.

BT: Budget transfers. Budget transfers are made to formalise the movement of scope (budget and schedule) from one part of the project to another, or, indeed, to move scope into or out of the project.

The Projects shall maintain their own change logs as required according to Figure 25.3, and shall make these available for inspection or challenge from the schedule change manager at all times.

25.14.1 Managing the schedule change process

The update of the schedule should be performed (if possible) in advance of the monthly reporting cycle to ensure that logic and duration changes do not hinder the reporting cycle.

26.1 Definition of risk management

Risk management is the management of threats to the project (negative impacts) and opportunities (positive impacts). It involves the identification and management of these issues.

As part of the planning of a project, risk should be considered at all stages. Risk management techniques will be used to help define cost or budget allowances, allowances for schedule risk and, indeed, any other types of risk that a project faces. Thus, risk management is integrated with all other management processes and is part of the planning, monitoring and control of a project.

It is worth noting that there is a clear relationship between change and risk: change inevitably introduces more risk or greater opportunity. In addition, aside from identified risk and opportunity, the sheer fact of changing scope will add risk into the schedule, and the greater the amount of change, the more risk is introduced. There is, therefore, a strong relationship between the management of risk and change.

26.2 Purpose of risk management

Risk management is required in order to anticipate threats and opportunities, and manage them to ensure the best outcome of the project. This may be in the following terms:

- safe execution of the works;
- commercial outcome – the best possible value for money being achieved;

Planning, Scheduling, Monitoring and Control

- commercial outcome – no surprises;
- reputational outcome;
- delivery to time constraints;
- quality;
- avoiding events that may delay the planned progress of the work;
- incorporating opportunities to save cost or time;
- including alternative methods to better coordinate the work.

26.3 Risk management plan

A risk management plan sets out how the thorough assessment of risk associated with the project will be implemented. This process will be undertaken by working in collaboration with all relevant project stakeholders. The risk management plan aims to implement this procedure in such a way that:

- risks are minimised;
- opportunities are maximised;
- risks are owned and managed at the appropriate level;
- risk mitigation actions are appropriate and effective;
- mitigation actions are monitored and managed effectively;
- current risks to the project are communicated effectively.

26.4 The risk management process

The key stages of the risk management processes identified in this section are shown in Figure 26.1 and described more fully in the following sections.

26.4.1 Planning

26.4.1.1 Planning for risk

Before the commencement of a formal risk process, a risk management plan should be created, reviewed and accepted by all relevant parties. Regular risk workshops and review sessions will be planned and held throughout the life of the project.

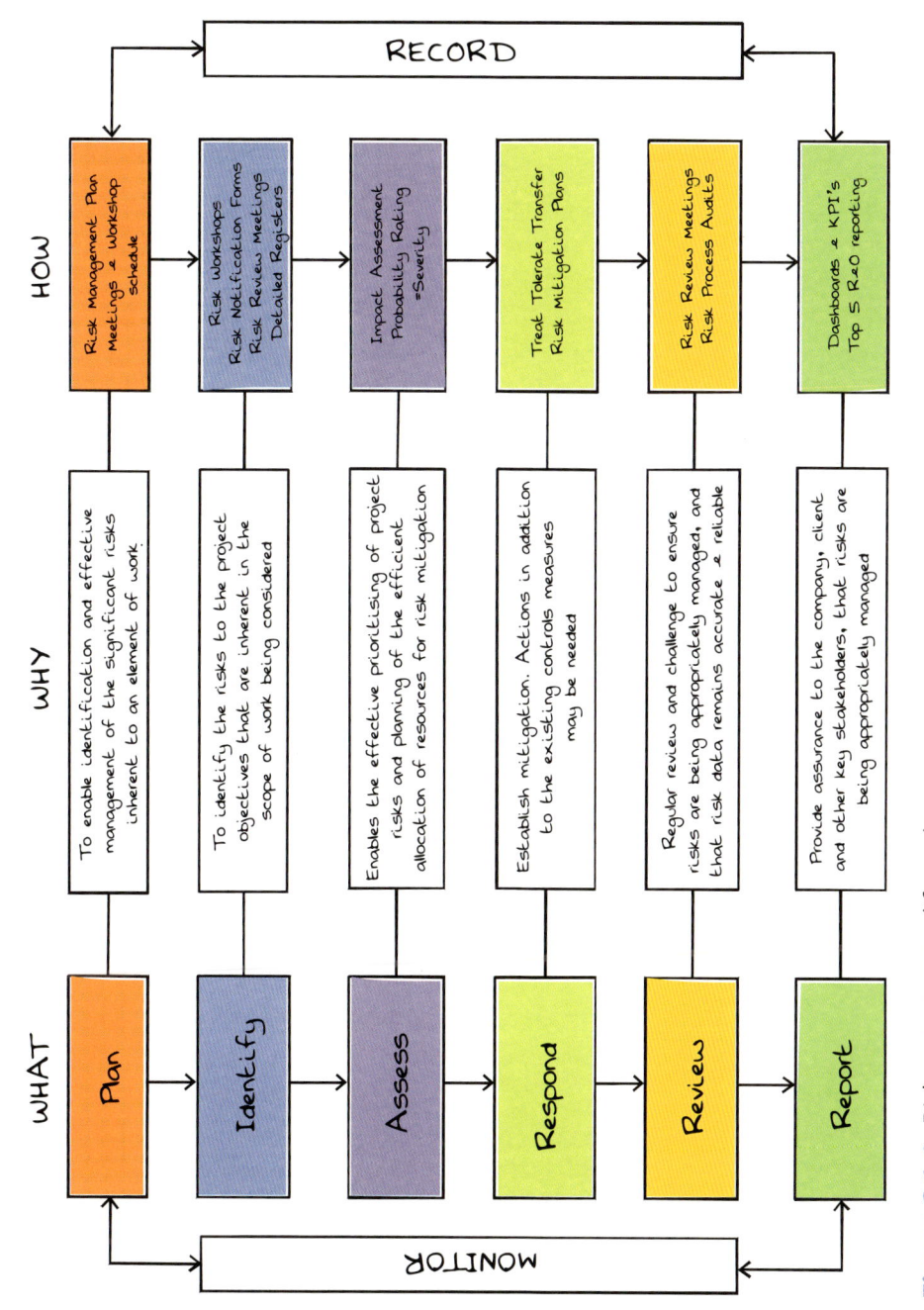

Figure 26.1 Risk management life cycle

Planning, Scheduling, Monitoring and Control

As part of the preparation for initial risk workshops, project deliverables will be clearly identified. The documents that might be consulted may include:

- contract documents;
- tender documents;
- project schedule and associated schedules;
- project execution plan and associated documents;
- risk checklists (a list of topics and regularly encountered threats and opportunities for consideration for the workshop);
- the assumptions register.

This information will be used to prompt discussion and consideration of potential threats and opportunities.

26.4.1.2 Risk management through the project life cycle

During the project, the objectives are as follows:

- identify new risks and risk mitigation actions;
- quantify and assess risks;
- establish risk owners;
- ensure management of risk mitigation actions (undertaken successfully and to schedule);
- ongoing review at all levels;
- monitor and relay the management of risk and risk mitigations.

26.4.2 Risk identification

This step concerns the capture of threats and opportunities to the project objectives. The following techniques may be used:

- risk workshops;
- interviews with relevant people to benefit from their knowledge and experience;
- risk review meetings;
- time issues that are known about or arise from progress reporting;
- investigations and surveys;
- lessons learned register/information;

Risk management

- relevant entries in interfacing risk registers;
- risks noted during development of methodology;
- assumptions and exclusions;
- sub-contractor risk registers;
- risks identified as part of the change process.

A detailed description of each key risk is recorded within the risk log, together with the cause, effect, and owners (Figure 26.2).

Where risks have been identified with owners or actions falling outside the remit of those present, the relevant stakeholders will be notified.

ID	Title	Status	Owner	Causes	Description	Effects	Existing controls
1	Brief title identifying the risk	Active, unapproved etc. categorised	Named individual	Include bullet points detailing causes of the risk	A full description of the risk – builds on the risk title	Include bullet points detailing effect of the risk if it is realised	A statement of the existing control measures to prevent identity or mitigate the risk occurence

Figure 26.2 Risk identification in a typical risk log

26.4.3 Risk assessment

To align with the project objectives, individual risks and opportunities will be considered according to project-specific impact and probability ratings. An example of what this might look like is shown in Figure 26.3.

Part of the assessment step is stating on the register what the existing control measures are (if any). These are accounted for in the current/pre-mitigation impact and probability ratings.

Each cell shown in Figures 26.3 and 26.4 may be given a numerical value; this is known as the severity rating score, and is used in creating a hierarchy of risks to highlight those needing the most attention. The criteria for making these assessments will depend on the type of risk: monetary values for commercial risks, periods of time for schedule risks, and so on. In the case of these two examples, there may be an assessment based on three-point estimates and distribution criteria, discussed later in this section. In other cases, there may be a set of qualitative statements; for example, a safety risk might be categorised by the potential for harm to individuals (reportable accidents, for example). These categories will vary between organisations based on their risk appetite.

Planning, Scheduling, Monitoring and Control

Risk assessment matrix		Negative impact or effect				
		Insignificant	Minor	Moderate	Major	Severe
Probability of occurrence	Very High	5	10	15	20	25
	High	4	8	12	16	20
	Medium	3	6	9	12	15
	Low	2	4	6	8	10
	Very Low	1	2	3	4	5

Figure 26.3 Risk assessment matrix – severity ratings score

Opportunity assessment matrix		Positive impact or effect				
		Insignificant	Minor	Moderate	Major	Severe
Probability of realising	Very High	5	10	15	20	25
	High	4	8	12	16	20
	Medium	3	6	9	12	15
	Low	2	4	6	8	10
	Very Low	1	2	3	4	5

Figure 26.4 Opportunity assessment matrix – severity ratings score

It should also be borne in mind that risks may have a time envelope within which they may occur, and another way of defining priority will be those risks likely to occur in the near-term future, whether these be threats or opportunities.

The assessments thus made may be categorised and entered in the risk log (Figure 26.5).

It is good practice to capture the justification behind the scoring (the basis of estimate) – it is often challenged, particularly where the risk mitigation actions need a cost–benefit analysis.

Risk	Current impact								Response					Sensitivity check?	
ID	Health & safety	Environment	Cost	Time	Quality	Client operations	3rd party operations	Severity	#	Mitigation actions	Mitigation owner	Status	Due date / completion date	Mitigation cost	Mitigation benefit
1									1						
									2						
									3						
									4						
									5						
									6						
									7						
									8						
									9						
									10						
									11						
									12						
									13						
									14						
									15						
									16						
									17						
									18						
									19						
									20						

Figure 26.5 Typical risk log (continued from Fig 26.2), showing current impact and response planning

Planning, Scheduling, Monitoring and Control

26.4.4 Risk response

For each risk, the risk owner must establish a level of mitigation to the satisfaction of the project manager.

Factors causing the risk must be understood to help determine the appropriate mitigation actions. These mitigations are recorded in the risk register.

If effective mitigations cannot be identified to control the risk, then mitigations need to be sought to reduce the consequences to an acceptable level. Figure 26.6 summarises risk response options.

After taking into account the anticipated effectiveness of the mitigation plan, it is usual to re-score the risk to provide a target for the reduction of risk and an assessment of residual risk (which is the element of risk that has not been mitigated). In effect, this is an assessment of the value of undertaking the mitigating actions. Mitigations that need funding (i.e. add new scope to the project's workload) need to enter the schedule through the change process.

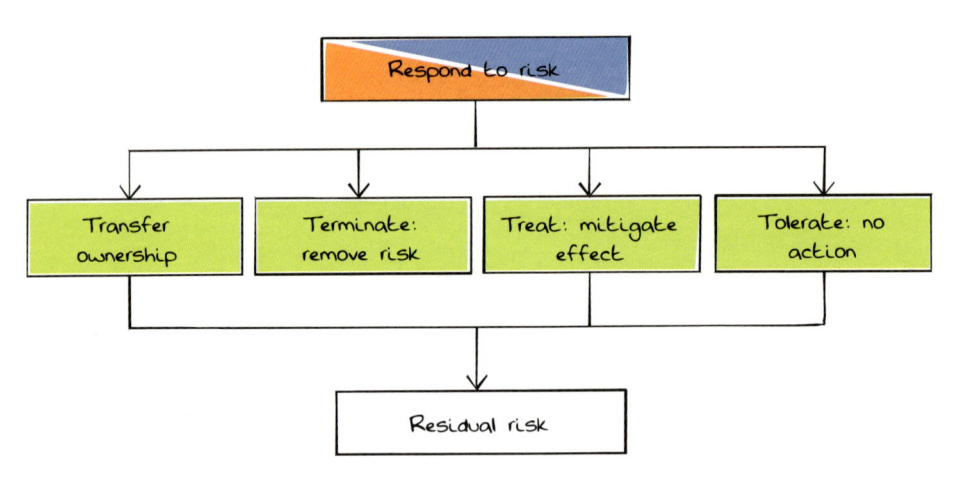

Figure 26.6 Risk response options

26.4.5 Risk review

The review process allows a final check of the key risks by the project manager. This review and validation comprises the process by which the project manager accepts accountability for the risk information.

The project manager will undertake review of the risk log regularly through the life cycle of the project. This review consists of the following:

Risk management

- Detailed review of the most critical risks and opportunities (at least, but not limited to, those risks deemed to be 'red' risks in accordance with the severity rating score).
- Have the delegated response plans been implemented, progressed or completed?
- Have existing item scores increased or decreased due to changes in likelihood or impact?
- Are additional mitigation measures required?
- Can existing risks and opportunities be closed?
- Check and agree whether any draw down of management reserve is required.
- Review the need for any focused workshops on any of the matters raised in the review.

26.4.6 Risk reporting

Reporting will be based on the data in the risk log, which will be updated and reviewed each reporting cycle. As well as the information illustrated above, additional fields may be used to capture tracking data. This will provide risk management information to support reporting requirements (see Figures 26.7 and 26.8).

26.5 Risk draw down

Risk draw down is the movement of budget in the risk pot, usually into the performance measurement baseline (PMB). The project should set guidelines for the drawdown of risk monies and the authority required to do so. It should be stressed that the contractual situation and budget ownership will dictate

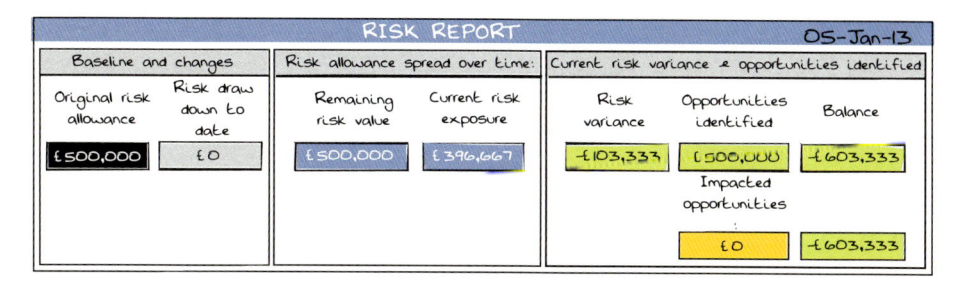

Figure 26.7 Reporting of basic risk data

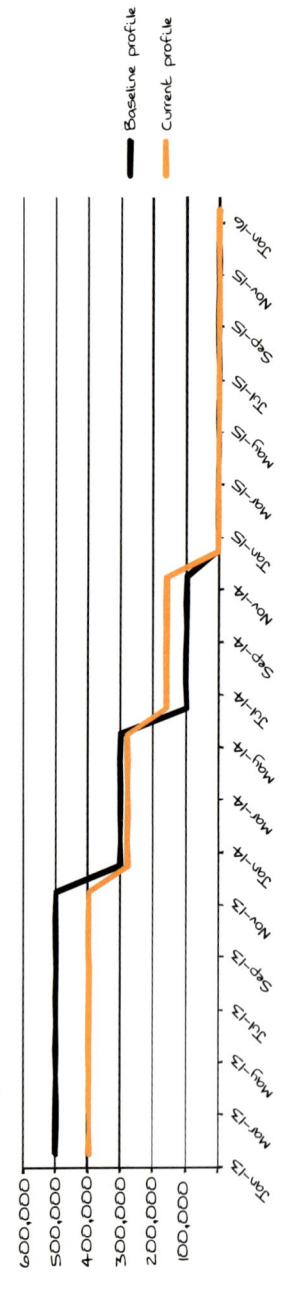

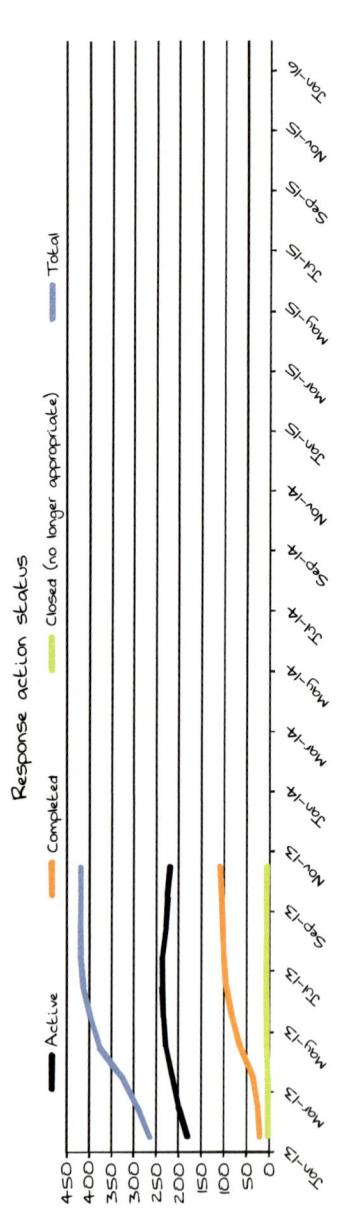

Figure 26.8 Tracking risk performance over time

Risk management

how this is dealt with; the following are suggested ways of drawing down risk budget.

26.5.1 When risks are mitigated

When mitigation plans are put in place that involve incurring cost, an appropriate sum may be drawn down from the management reserve and attributed to new or existing activities in the PMB. This is effectively an addition of scope to the activity as well as budget.

26.5.2 When risks are realised

When risks are realised that involve incurring cost, an appropriate sum may be drawn down from management reserve and attributed to appropriate activities in the PMB. This is effectively an addition of scope to the activity as well as budget.

26.5.3 When risks are closed

When risks are closed, their impact upon the risk exposure will clearly be reflected. However, depending on the contractual situation, risk allowances may be maintained. There are a number of options for dealing with this allowance:

- Where risk exposure is greater than allowance, retain the allowance in the risk register, re-allocating to new or emerging risks if appropriate.
- Where risk allowance is greater than exposure, then a portion of risk allowance may be released to 'profit'.

26.5.4 When opportunities are realised

When opportunities are realised, the budget will stay in the project. There are a number of options that may be appropriate, and the project team must consider the following:

- Move budget from relevant activities to the 'management reserve': in some cases, the realisation of an opportunity may need to be balanced by the introduction of a new risk. For example, the relaxation of strict working patterns would be an opportunity to complete work faster and more cheaply, but the risk that the relaxation in conditions may not continue in future should be captured.

Planning, Scheduling, Monitoring and Control

- Do nothing – this would result in positive variance in cost or schedule. Care should be taken that this positive value does not mask poor performance.
- If funds are used to pay for a mitigation to realise the opportunity, sufficient value to cover this expense would be allocated as appropriate, and there may also be a release of budget from the baseline to reflect the cost–benefit of the opportunity.

26.5.5 Documenting changes in the risk budget

All movements in the risk budget must be documented for control purposes. Also, records should be kept of the contingency allowances under lessons learned, for future projects.

26.6 Quantitative schedule risk analysis (QSRA)

26.6.1 Definition of QSRA

Once the schedule has been created, reviewed and verified, a quantitative schedule risk analysis (QSRA) will apply statistical techniques to test the level of confidence in meeting the completion date.

This analysis looks at the whole schedule and not just the critical path. The conclusion of this analysis may result in a completely different set of linked activities that determines a 'most likely' completion date.

A QSRA relies on Monte Carlo analysis. A Monte Carlo analysis is a set of calculations that rely on repeated random sampling to obtain a range of results – a probability distribution. The sampling is based on information provided by the user.

There are two elements to QSRA:

- duration uncertainty (a minimum, most likely and maximum spread of activity durations);
- risk impact (minimum/most likely/maximum).

In some organisations QSRA is referred to as timescale risk analysis, but this guide will use the QSRA term.

26.6.2 Purpose of QSRA

26.6.2.1 Improve the quality of the project schedule

The best mitigation strategy for risk on a project is to have a robust and logically sound schedule. It is important to ensure that the full scope and working methods are accurately modelled in the schedule. This modelling helps to drive understanding and acceptance of the project schedule, and hence commitment to delivery.

Running a deterministic schedule through a QSRA tool can derive benefit by exposing weaknesses in the original schedule which were not apparent in the static schedule. The unexpected variations (or lack of them) provoke discussions, resulting in both an improved understanding of the schedule by the project team and a better finished schedule.

A QSRA will also highlight which activities and paths are perceived by the QSRA toolset as being key drivers. These can often differ from the paths associated with the critical path analysis, where more risk is associated with (originally perceived) sub-critical paths.

26.6.2.2 Model duration uncertainty and risk

The two stages of running a QSRA are described in more detail below; a key advantage of running a QSRA is the consideration of these two facets of the schedule and risk profile. In the case of the duration uncertainty, this allows the project team to express their confidence level in the schedule, which may in itself expose certain issues.

Reviewing the risks will ensure that these are considered as part of the schedule, and the implications will be more widely understood as a result.

26.6.2.3 Assess the probabilities of completing the project on time

The fundamental purpose of QSRA is to determine the probability of finishing on or before a given point in time. It will determine the confidence level of completing the project to the required date. This can then facilitate further strategic decision making.

Planning, Scheduling, Monitoring and Control

26.6.2.4 Focus attention on areas requiring mitigation

As a result of undertaking a QSRA, it may be appropriate to consider mitigations that need to be put in place. This will particularly be the case if the exercise has identified alternative critical path(s) to the one created during the scheduling of the project.

26.6.2.5 Setting baselines

The QSRA approach may be used to establish an appropriate target to be used as a project baseline. Different organisations may have different risk appetites and establish targets based on a set probability of achievement. These are often known as, for example, 'P80' levels, where P means probability and the number refers to the percentage confidence level (80% in this case).

26.6.3 Key requirements for a QSRA

- A robust and fully logically linked schedule where only genuine constraints remain.
- If the project is in progress, the schedule must be updated to reflect current status.
- Identify duration uncertainty against all activities (three-point estimate duration for activities).
- Risks are identified, documented and their impacts assessed and allocated to schedule activity.
- A software application with which to run the Monte Carlo analysis, which produces appropriate reports.
- Terminal float or other time contingencies should be removed from the schedule prior to running the QSRA.

26.6.4 The stages of schedule risk analysis

26.6.4.1 Schedule quality check

The first step in running a QSRA is to confirm that the schedule is of the required quality. Some of the technical checks can be made by QSRA software (for example, open ends, type of logic used). Other matters may be more subjective, such as the general robustness of the schedule and the surety that all project

Risk management

scope is included. Ideally, the schedule should be checked by an independent party prior to running a QSRA.

Level of effort-type activities should be excluded from the analysis, as they do not represent true work.

26.6.4.2 Duration uncertainty

A quick risk analysis can be performed by setting a narrow uncertainty range across all activities. The purpose of this is to help highlight key activity drivers in the schedule and to ensure that the project logic is robust.

For a full assessment of duration uncertainty, the project team will need to be consulted to assess 'minimum', maximum' and 'most likely' durations for each activity to feed into the risk analysis. This could be done on an activity-by-activity basis, but this would be extremely onerous (unless the data is captured as part of the duration calculation when developing the schedule), so it is usual to categorise different types of work and apply confidence factors to each type of work.

Distribution types that can be applied are discussed below.

26.6.4.3 Monte carlo analysis – first run

After applying the duration uncertainties, it is useful to run a 'first pass', as this will assist in understanding the final results – i.e. how much of the final result is attributable to confidence in the current schedule, and how much due to the assessment of potential risk events. An understanding of this will assist in assessing and prioritising mitigation actions. For example, a disproportionally bad result at this stage may point to the requirement for more planning to further develop or mitigate the current schedule.

26.6.4.4 Adding the risks into the analysis

Once the risks have been identified and catalogued in the risk register, those that have a potential to cause a delay are added into the schedule. Durations, probabilities and distribution types are added to each risk.

The probability is the likelihood of the risk event occurring, and is expressed as a percentage.

The duration is the expression of the likely effect in terms of time (and may be a one point value, or a minimum/most likely/maximum range of effects).

Planning, Scheduling, Monitoring and Control

26.6.4.5 Monte carlo analysis – second run

This stage assesses the effect of both duration uncertainty and the risk events. An understanding of this will assist in assessing and prioritising mitigation actions. For example, an unwelcome or unexpected result at this stage may point to the requirement for more mitigating actions to be developed, which may include re-working the network.

It will be necessary to iterate through the two processes, assessing mitigation options until you have a solution that best meets the needs of the project/ programme.

26.6.5 Distribution types

The distribution type is an expression of the distribution pattern and may include the following.

26.6.5.1 Normal or bell curve distribution

Symmetrical: values in the middle are most likely to occur (Figure 26.9).

Describes many distributions, such as those around well-understood and controlled processes or tasks:

- Values in the middle near the mean are more likely to occur than in the triangular distribution.
- Use when there is moderate confidence in three-point estimates.

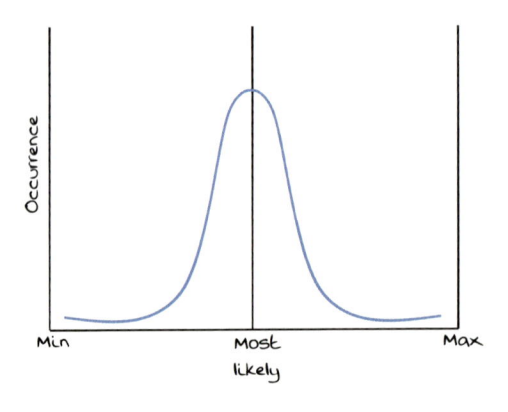

Figure 26.9 Normal distribution curve

Risk management

26.6.5.2 Log normal distribution

Values are positively skewed (Figure 26.10).

- Values are positively skewed, not symmetrical like a normal distribution.
- Used to represent values that do not go below zero but have great positive potential.

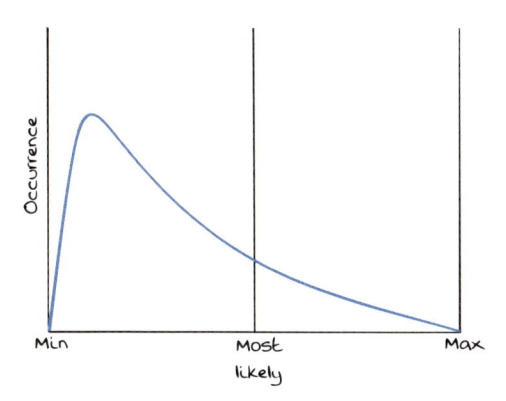

Figure 26.10 Log normal distribution curve

26.6.5.3 Uniform distribution

All values have an equal chance of occurring (Figure 26.11).

- Useful for estimates that do not appear to show any central tendency.
- Equally likely chance of occurring anywhere within a particular range.
- No 'most likely' value.

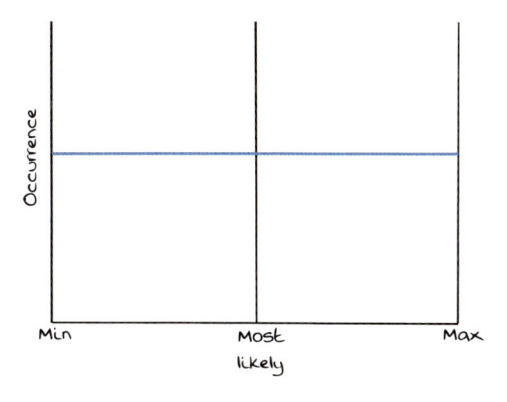

Figure 26.11 Uniform distribution

Planning, Scheduling, Monitoring and Control

26.6.5.4 Triangular distribution

User sets minimum, most likely and maximum (Figure 26.12).

- Used extensively in risk models.
- Allows skewed estimates to be modelled.
- Use when:
    - there is low to moderate confidence in three-point estimates
    - risk is high or unknown
    - global three-point estimates are applied.

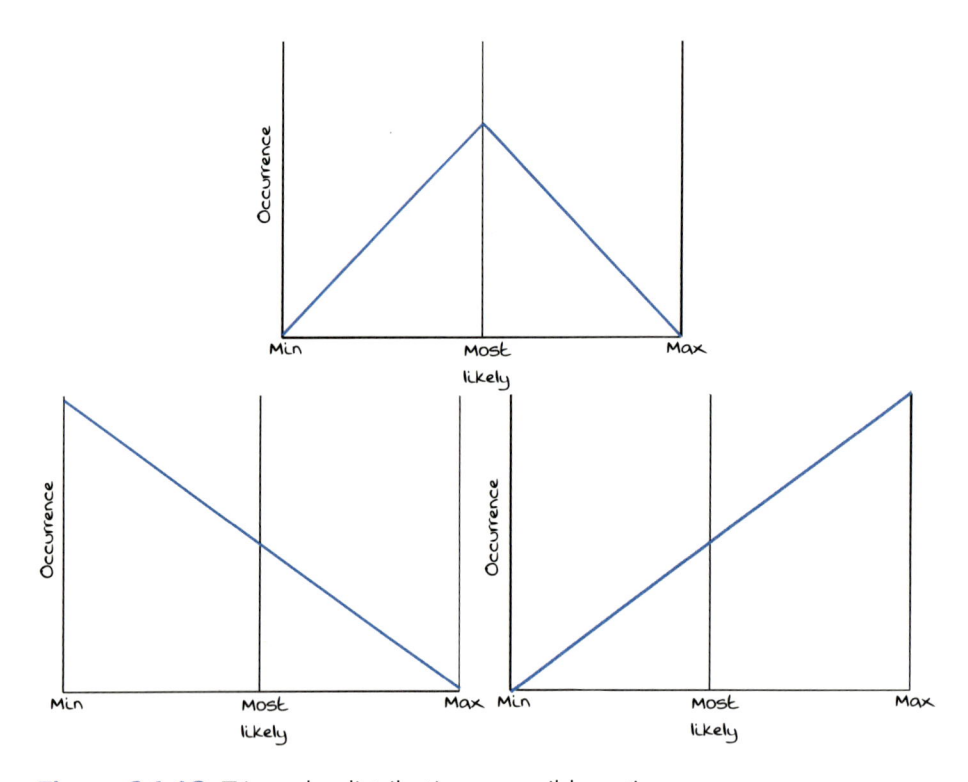

Figure 26.12 Triangular distribution – possible options

26.6.5.5 PERT distribution

Like triangular, but minimum/maximum are more likely to occur (Figure 26.13).

Risk management

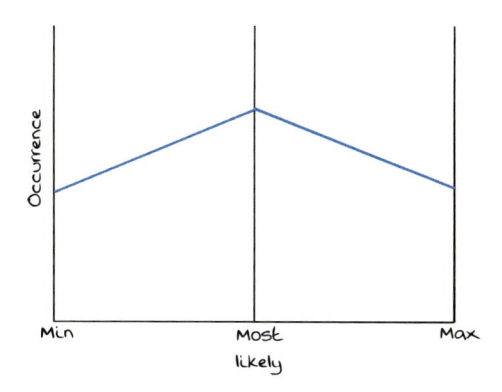

Figure 26.13 PERT distribution

- Values near the mean are more likely to occur than in the triangular or normal distributions.
- Extremes are not as emphasised.
- Use when there is high confidence in three-point estimates.

26.6.5.6 Discrete distribution

Specific values and likelihoods are specified, e.g. 'There is a 10% chance of occurrence and there will be an effect of 10 days.'

When undertaking a risk analysis, it is important to understand these distribution types and the effect they will have on results.

26.6.6 Application of risks to schedule activities

It is important to consider what effect applying risks to activities will have.

A Monte Carlo analysis works by turning the risks on and off at random based on their probability of occurrence. Each time the risk is 'on', an impact will be applied the activity(ies) that it is linked to. The effect of the risk will vary in line with the probability distributions described above.

A risk linked to many activities will, when it is 'on', affect all the activities that it is linked to. If the risk was, for example, lack of resources, is it really applicable to all the activities it is attributed to? The calculation will assume that this is the case, rather than the lack of resources affecting just one, or some, of the activities.

Planning, Scheduling, Monitoring and Control

26.6.7 QSRA output

26.6.7.1 First analysis: duration uncertainty

As previously discussed, the first analysis undertaken applies the duration uncertainty calculations. The graphics and statistics in Figure 26.14 detail the outcome of this on a specific milestone which defines the end date of this section of work. The results of this analysis can be shown in a probability chart. Charts can be viewed for the overall project or at a number of key milestones or at other points throughout the project.

Different 'risk appetites' are also (or more) dependent on the type of work; e.g. possessions or shut-downs would commonly want P90, standard construction work P80 for schedule risk and uncertainty. However, cost risk might well be P50, which would never be acceptable for the schedule.

Different organisations will have different risk appetites and choose different percentage points (P) to measure against, but the illustration in Figure 26.14 uses the P50 and P80 boundaries. P50 means a 50% chance of success; P80 means there is an 80% chance of success. In the illustration, the required completion date is 10/02/11; the results show that:

- There is a probability of achieving the current schedule date of 28% (yellow line).
- The P50 date is shown as 14/02/11 (orange line).
- In addition the P80 date is also shown as 14/02/11 (green line).

The activities that have the most influence on this outcome can be displayed in a tornado chart, as illustrated in Figure 26.15.

It is worth analysing the tornado chart prior to proceeding with the exercise to ensure that the results are meaningful and credible activities are identified as having the greatest influence on the result. The example in Figure 26.15 shows the impact in days, but sometimes this is shown in percentage terms.

Risk management

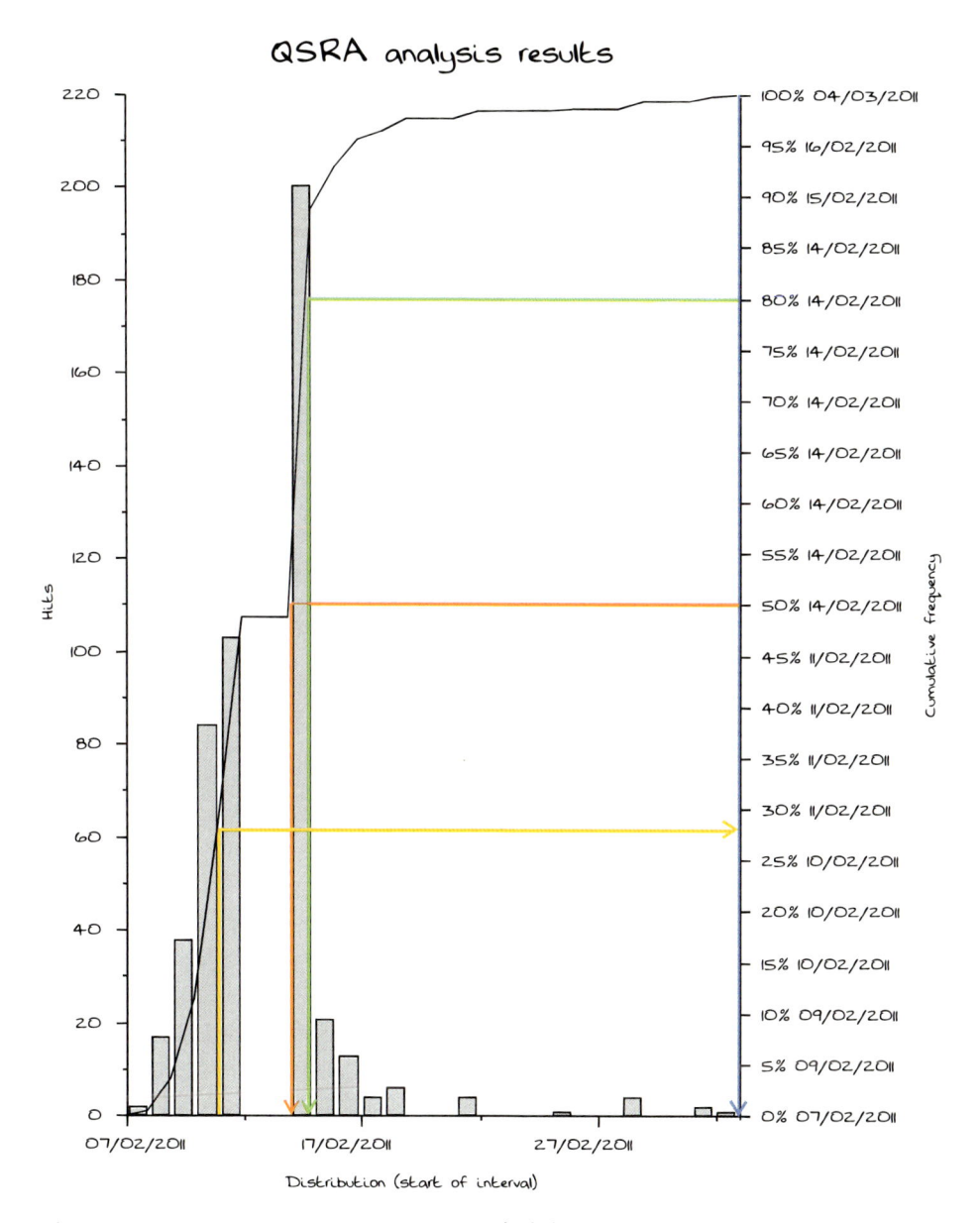

Figure 26.14 Duration uncertainty probability chart

Planning, Scheduling, Monitoring and Control

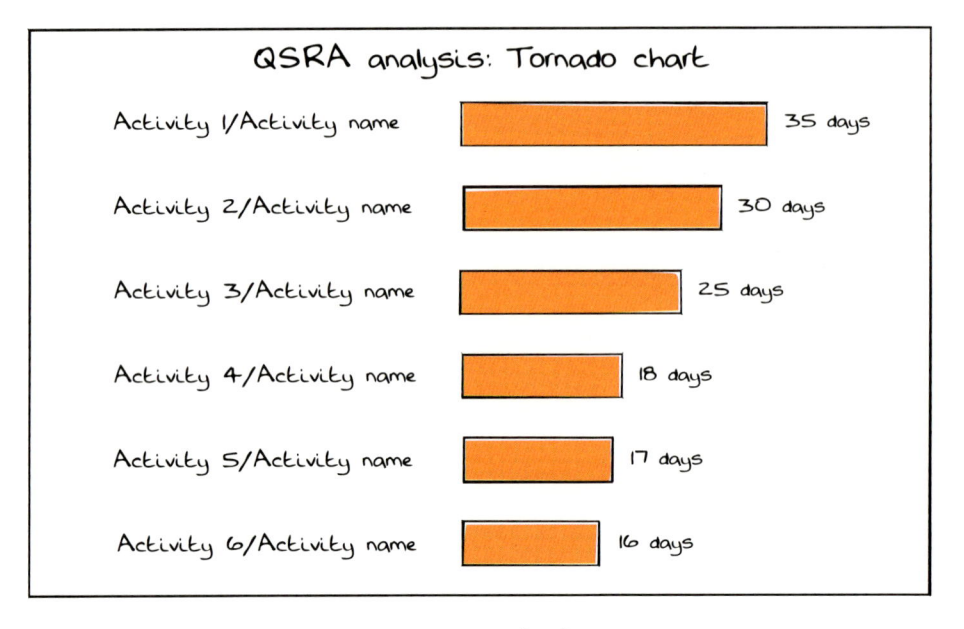

QSRA analysis: Tornado chart

Activity	Duration
Activity 1/Activity name	35 days
Activity 2/Activity name	30 days
Activity 3/Activity name	25 days
Activity 4/Activity name	18 days
Activity 5/Activity name	17 days
Activity 6/Activity name	16 days

Figure 26.15 Duration uncertainty tornado chart

26.6.7.2 Second analysis: duration uncertainty and risk

After adding in the risks the analysis is re-run (based on these risks and the duration uncertainty as before), and new output is produced (Figure 26.16).

As with the activities that have the most influence on this outcome, as seen in Figure 26.16, the risks can also be displayed in a tornado chart, as illustrated in Figure 26.17.

Again, it is worth assessing the credibility of these results prior to producing and publishing a QSRA report.

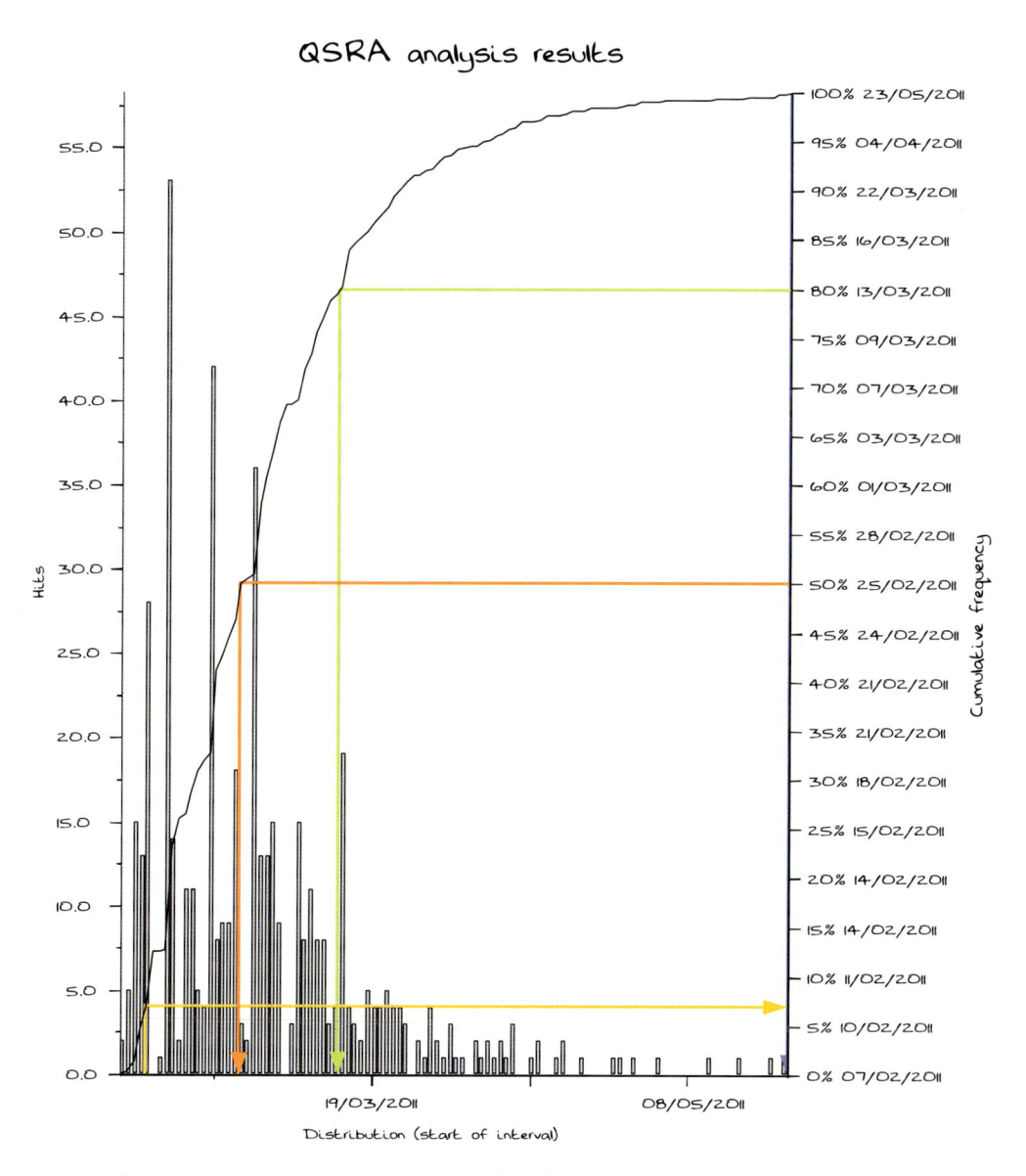

Figure 26.16 QSRA probability distribution chart

Planning, Scheduling, Monitoring and Control

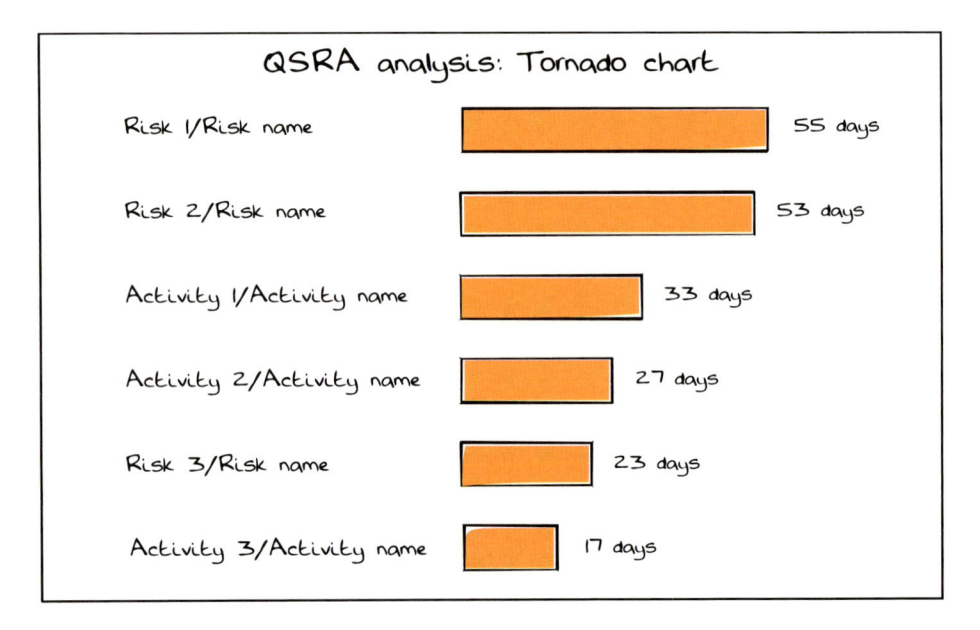

QSRA analysis: Tornado chart

Risk 1/Risk name	55 days
Risk 2/Risk name	53 days
Activity 1/Activity name	33 days
Activity 2/Activity name	27 days
Risk 3/Risk name	23 days
Activity 3/Activity name	17 days

Figure 26.17 Full QSRA tornado chart

26.6.8 Reporting

A suggested report format would include:

- commentary on the scope of the QSRA;
- notes on the method adopted so that the process and inputs are made clear;
- list of participants and their involvement;
- the results in graphical form and with written interpretation;
- recommended actions that should mitigate any concerns raised in order to deliver the most effective project possible;
- appendices of duration uncertainties and the risk register, considered with details of the risk modelling (i.e. which risks allocated to which activity(ies); distribution type; minimum, maximum and most likely values).

26.7 Quantitative cost risk analysis (QCRA)

26.7.1 Definition of QCRA

Quantitative cost risk analysis (QCRA) is often referred to as Monte Carlo simulation. (Monte Carlo is the calculation technique used, not the product.) It is a technique used to understand and quantify the impact of risk and uncertainty in cost forecasting models.

26.7.2 Purpose of QCRA

QCRA enables the project to calculate the size of its contingency, thereby increasing the accuracy of the cost aspect of the project. It can be used on an ongoing basis to review forecast risk spend against the original budget.

Organisations that consider investing in a new infrastructure or change, in its broadest meaning, need to evaluate the cost risk involved; once the quantitative assessment has been completed, the fundamental decision of who will take the risk must be made (The organisation itself? The suppliers involved?). This decision will result in different contractual arrangements.

Organisations that consider bidding for a job need to carry out a QCRA which will lead to the 'bid/no-bid' decision first. Subsequently, should the bid be successful, the contractors need to manage the cost risk in a manner that is related to the magnitude of the risk identified.

It is also useful to quantify risk to enhance 'spend to save' decision making and to show the risk retirement forecast to enable the programme to potentially re-distribute the allocated budget to other projects.

26.7.3 The QCRA process

26.7.3.1 Risk analysis

As previously discussed, risks are identified and assessed. For the QCRA, each risk is assigned a likelihood and a three-point estimate (minimum cost, most likely cost and maximum cost) should it occur.

This latter may be based on a triangular distribution, but there are other distribution methods which could be considered, such as single point (most likely cost) or a uniform distribution (minimum and maximum). These are discussed in the section above on QSRA.

Planning, Scheduling, Monitoring and Control

For the Monte Carlo simulation, a random value is selected for each risk, based on the range of these cost estimates. The result of this is recorded, and typically the model is run 5,000 times, each time using different randomly selected values. If the risk has a 50% likelihood, then the model would run half the iterations as a zero cost out-turn, as it assumes that the risk is not occurring. The remaining half of the model would pick random values dependent upon the three-point estimates.

Just as in the case of the QSRA, the results are plotted and confidence levels for various outcomes are calculated. These are often referred to as P values, e.g. P50 or P80.

This means that, for example, if the P50 is calculated at £5 million, there is only a 50% chance that the project will cost a total of £5 million or less. The more risk averse the organisation is, the higher the confidence value they may use. Therefore, they may use a P80, which means that there is an 80% chance that the project risk will cost a total of (say) £7 million or less.

26.7.3.2 Risk reporting

The above information enables an organisation to define risk budgets for projects based on a range of possible out-turns. Regular review of the risks during the project life cycle means the model can be re-run at regular intervals. This provides management information that the risk profile is remaining within an acceptable level. The information is typically collated on a pre-mitigation (current) state and a post-mitigation state. The project team can then manage the risks using mitigations.

Some typical outputs for quantitative analysis include:

- cumulated normal distributions (S-curves) for cost impacts;
- sensitivity (tornado) charts showing how much each risk influences the outcome;
- QRA percentiles (percentage rates) value for cost.

26.7.3.2.1 Cumulative normal distributions

The chart of the cumulated normal distribution (S-curve) provides an easy way to assess the level of confidence about the model outcomes. The left-hand axis of the chart (cumulative probability) is a value between 0 and 1, but can be thought

Risk management

of as a percentage of the number of times the model ran – 0 is without running the model, 1 is when 5,000 iterations of the model have been run.

Tracing a line to intersect the curve and then referring to the bottom axis of the chart (cost or time impact values) will indicate the value which, with the given level of probability, the model ran at or below.

For example, the 0.5 level of cumulative probability, traced to the curve and translated to the impact axis, will show the value that was not exceeded during half the times the model was run (5,000 times in Figure 26.18).

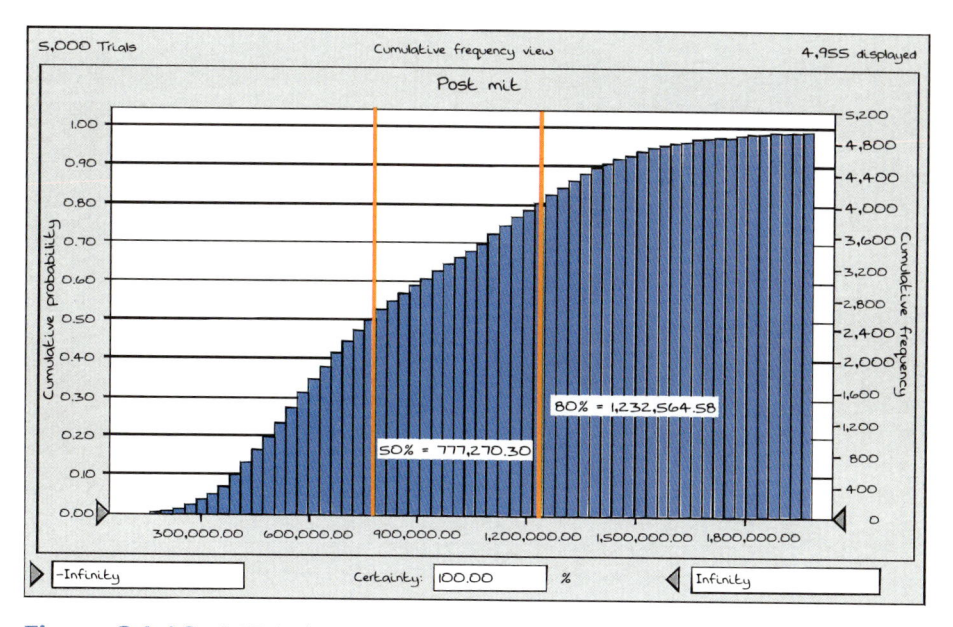

Figure 26.18 QCRA chart

26.7.3.2.2 Sensitivity analysis

Sensitivity analyses show how much a risk affects the result, with the overall sensitivity of a forecast being the combination of two factors:

- the model sensitivity of the forecast to the risk;
- the uncertainty of the risk.

The format of the sensitivity data presented here is termed the 'contribution to variance', and makes it easier to examine what percentage of the variance in the target forecast is due to a particular risk.

Planning, Scheduling, Monitoring and Control

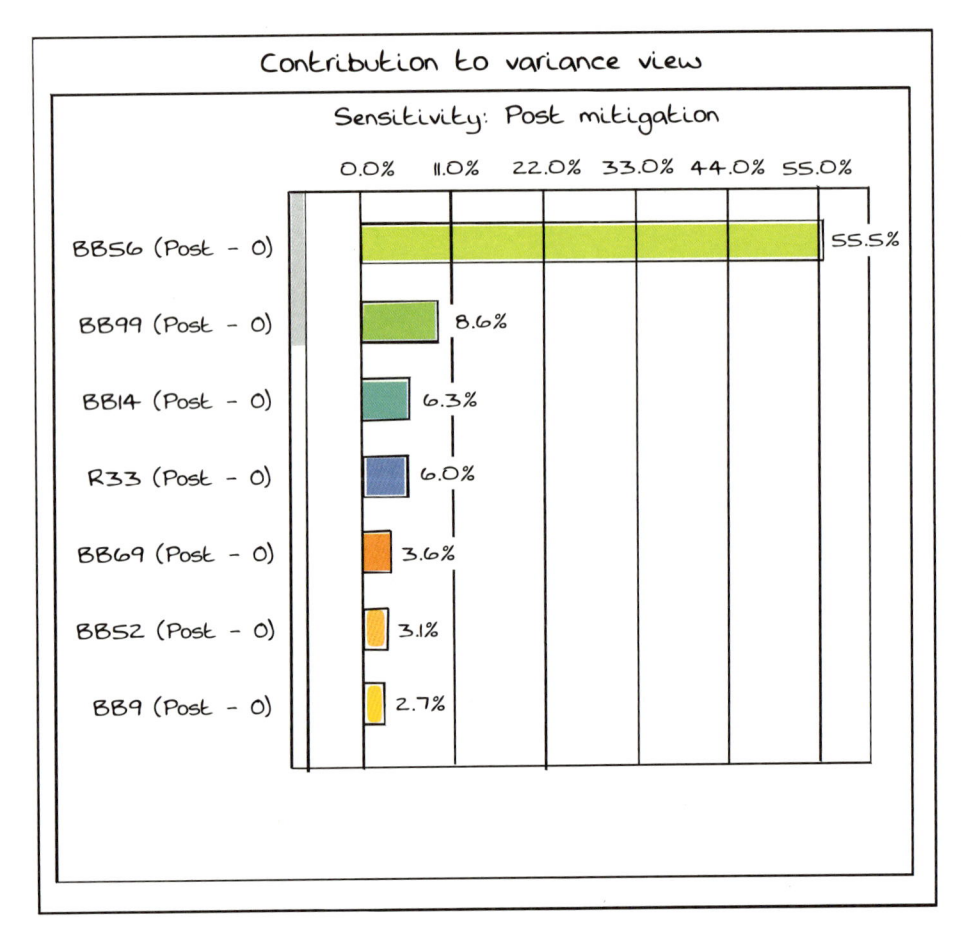

Figure 26.19 QCRA chart

26.7.3.2.3 Cost impact sensitivity (tornado charts)

The sensitivity chart shown in Figure 26.19 illustrates the risks having the greatest influence on the outcome of the analysis – the risks that change the outcome of the analysis most.

Managing these risks will have the most influence on reducing the forecast risk costs.

(Risk – O) relate to risks that influence the model due to their probability values.

(Risk – I) relate to risks that influence the model due to their cost values.

Risk management

Example:

Risks with an 'O' key on the graph indicate that those particular risks appear on the sensitivity chart mainly due to their high probability, e.g. probability of 75%.

Risks with an 'I' key on the graph indicate that those particular risks appear on the sensitivity chart mainly due to their high value, e.g. £10 million, should they occur, even if they may have a low probability of occurrence, e.g. 5% likelihood.

26.7.3.2.4 QRA percentiles summary table for cost

Table 26.1 illustrates an example of Pn confidence levels.

Table 26.1 QCRA confidence levels

Percentile	Overall total risk cost (£)
P0	100,637.71
P10	411,602.97
P20	502,275.44
P30	584,376.77
P40	673,217.44
P50	777,270.30
P60	915,880.23
P70	1,091,687.26
P80	1,232,564.58
P90	1,413,591.55
P100	2,702,304.39

26.7.3.3 Conclusions

Like any forecasting model, the analysis is only as good as the estimates made. It is important to remember that it is a simulation, and basing the estimates on current assumptions will provide greater confidence in the results.

27.1 Definition of forensic analysis

Forensic schedule analysis refers to the study and investigation of events using critical path methods or other recognised schedule calculation methods. In particular, it is the study of how actual events caused delay as measured against a defined time model.

27.2 Purpose of forensic analysis

The most usual reason for conducting forensic analysis is for the purpose of building, justifying or rebutting a contractual claim for additional monies. Indeed, given that it is likely to be an expensive undertaking, it is hard to imagine it being used for other purposes. Given that such analyses may be used in legal proceedings demonstrating delay and disruption, it is essential that experienced guidance is sought when undertaking such exercises.

27.3 Methods of forensic analysis

By implication, forensic analysis is carried out after the event. However, some contracts provide for the analysis of schedules to be carried out on a prospective basis. Events are considered at the time they occur and consequent delays are forecast, for example in the NEC suite of contracts.

A comprehensive understanding of the detailed steps to be undertaken to ensure these methods are implemented appropriately is required before using

Planning, Scheduling, Monitoring and Control

these techniques. An overview of some of the more common methods of delay analyses is provided in Table 27.1.

- as-planned versus as-built method (AP v AB);
- impacted as-planned method (IAP);
- collapsed as-built method (CAB) or as-built but for (ABBF);
- time impact analysis method (TIA).

In addition, there follows a discussion on the windows analysis approach to investigating the effect of multiple events.

27.3.1 As-planned versus as-built method (AP v AB)

Table 27.1 *As-planned vs. as-built method*

Method description	Requirements	Advantages	Disadvantages	Where can it be used?
The as-planned v as-built method compares the as-planned schedule or baseline at the outset of a project with the as-built schedule at the end of the project (or the latest schedule updated with progress). This allows the differences between the two schedules to be observed.	• Good as-planned schedule (ideally agreed or accepted at or near the outset of the project). • Good as-built data so as to be able to establish an as-built comparison with the as-planned schedule. • The works carried out need to closely reflect the logic contained within the as-planned schedule.	• Relatively simple to understand and present. • Relatively cheap to carry out. • Can be appropriate for simple situations. • Although the schedule would normally be a critical path network, this is not necessarily essential. Therefore, planning software is not an absolute requirement in some cases.	• Can only be carried out retrospectively. • Likely to be overly simplistic and not demonstrate cause and effect appropriately. • Not suited to complex projects with multiple critical paths. • Not suited to projects that have deviated from the original as-planned logic. • Does not adequately deal with concurrency, consequential delay, mitigation or acceleration.	• When as-built data is available. • Suitable for simple situations, projects and cases or where matters only need to be shown at a higher level. • Better suited to projects of a shorter duration.

(Continued)

Forensic analysis and delay and disruption analysis

Table 27.1 Continued

Method description	Requirements	Advantages	Disadvantages	Where can it be used?
The as-planned v as-built comparison can be shown either activity by activity or schedule by schedule. The overall delay is measured by the difference between the completion dates in the two schedules. This delay is attributed to the delay events that have occurred.	• Delay events need to be clearly identified. • The criticality of delay events does not need to be demonstrated if the liability for all the events is clear and rests with one party. • If there are issues with liability then the criticality of the affected activities must be clear.		• Does not necessarily recognise the order in which delays impacted a project. • Does not deal with the critical path changing as a project progresses. • Generally assumes all delay is due to one party. • As the analysis progresses through the as-planned schedule, its accuracy is likely to diminish. • It is unreliable by itself in dispute resolution.	• Where there is a single clearly defined chain or sequence of activities that were critical to the timely completion of a project throughout.

27.3.2 Impacted as-planned method (IAP)

Table 27.2 Impacted as-planned method

Method description	Requirements	Advantages	Disadvantages	Where can it be used?
The impacted as-planned method works by inserting and linking delay events into the as-planned schedule. Any change in the completion date as a consequence of the	• Good as-planned schedule (ideally agreed or accepted at or near the outset of the project). • The works carried out need to closely reflect the logic contained within the as-planned schedule.	• Can be used where the as-planned schedule has not been updated or where there is limited as-built data available. • Can be used prospectively or retrospectively.	• May only show limited cause and effect. • Does not take account of progress, resources and changes in sequence. • It is a theoretical method and therefore open to criticism. • Susceptible to manipulation (unintended or otherwise) if only one party's delays are considered.	• Can be used prospectively or retrospectively but . . . • More suited for identifying and quantifying potential delays rather than actual delays.

(Continued)

305

Planning, Scheduling, Monitoring and Control

Table 27.2 *Continued*

Method description	Requirements	Advantages	Disadvantages	Where can it be used?
insertion of the delay is attributed to the delay event. An analysis can be carried out on a step-by-step basis, inserting delay events as they arise.	• The as-planned schedule needs to be networked. • All delaying events should be identified and quantified. • If analysis is carried out retrospectively, the results should be verified by as-built data if available.	• Relatively simple to understand and present. • Relatively cheap to carry out. • Where as-built data is available, it can be used to verify the results.	• May ignore concurrency. • Sensitive to the order in which delays are impacted upon the schedule. • Less reliable in dispute resolution than other more comprehensive methods. • Relies heavily on the as-planned schedule being robust. • Tribunals generally favour factual methods of delay analysis.	• Might be appropriate for illustrating delays at high level or for negotiating purposes.

27.3.3 Collapsed as-built method or as-built but for (CAB)

Table 27.3 *Collapsed as-built method or as-built but for*

Method description	Requirements	Advantages	Disadvantages	Where can it be used?
The collapsed as-built method begins with the production of a networked as-built schedule. Then activities or parts of activities representing delay events are removed.	• Good quality, reliable and consistent as-built data produced in sufficient detail. • Requires a networked or logic-linked as-built schedule.	• Does not require an as-planned schedule. • Based on factual as-built data. • Can demonstrate cause and effect. • Can account for concurrency.	• Limited prospective use. • The networking of the as-built schedule requires a deep understanding of the schedule and its logic and normally requires access to the project team. • Expertise required to collapse out delays accurately, otherwise the collapsed schedule may not represent the true situation but for the delays.	• Where there is no as-planned schedule or it is of poor quality. • Most appropriate for retrospective delay analysis.

(Continued)

Forensic analysis and delay and disruption analysis

Table 27.3 *Continued*

Method description	Requirements	Advantages	Disadvantages	Where can it be used?
The change in the completion date as a consequence of the removal of the delay is the overall delay that is attributed to the delay event. Delay events can be removed on a step-by-step basis, usually starting with the latest delay event first.	• Detailed understanding of the logic and delay events that often requires either first-hand knowledge or access to people with first-hand knowledge. • All delaying events should be identified and quantified.	• Relatively easy to understand in principle and explain. • More reliable in dispute resolution than some simpler methods of delay analysis. • Can be carried out prospectively or retrospectively, but limited prospective use.	• Delays to be collapsed out still require knowledge about how long work should have taken, and can be subjective. • In practice, can require several iterations. • Can be perceived as a reconstruction of the facts without due consideration of the updated as-planned schedules. • Does not account for acceleration measures, as these will be implicit within the as-built schedule.	• For negotiating purposes or in tribunals.

27.3.4 Time impact analysis method (TIA)

Table 27.4 *Time impact analysis method*

Method description	Requirements	Advantages	Disadvantages	Where can it be used?
The time impact analysis method provides for the updating of a networked as-planned schedule with progress to just before the occurrence of a delay event.	• Good as-planned schedule (ideally agreed or accepted at or near the outset of the project). • The as-planned schedule and its updates are networked.	• Can be carried out prospectively or retrospectively. • Deals with delays at the time they occur or in windows providing clarity.	• More suited to quantifying potential rather than actual delays. • Requires extensive records to be kept. • Can be time intensive and slow, and therefore expensive to implement.	• Prospectively or retrospectively. • Beneficial to carry out as a project progresses. • Where the contract requires.

(Continued)

Planning, Scheduling, Monitoring and Control

Table 27.4 *Continued*

Method description	Requirements	Advantages	Disadvantages	Where can it be used?
The delay event is then inserted and linked into the schedule. Any change in the completion date as a consequence of the insertion of the delay event is attributed to that delay event. Where progress is not recorded at the specific date just before the impact of a delay event, the latest schedule updated for progress prior to occurrence of the delay event may still be appropriate to use. Each progress update may allow the schedule to be analysed at discrete intervals of time or in 'windows'.	• Reliable and consistent progress data in sufficient detail for each time period being considered, which should also be at appropriate intervals. • All delaying events should be identified and quantified. • The works carried out need to closely reflect the logic contained within the latest as-planned schedule being considered.	• Can account for progress, resources, changes in sequence and changes in the critical path. • Can identify and quantify acceleration or mitigation measures. • Can disentangle delays otherwise considered to be concurrent. • Can demonstrate cause and effect. • More reliable in dispute resolution than simpler methods of delay analysis. • Recommended method of delay analysis by the Society of Construction Law's Protocol. • Does not require a complete as-built schedule, but as-built data assists in verifying results.	• Can be complicated and difficult to communicate, with many charts. • Reliability reduced if schedule and record quality is poor. • Can produce theoretical results if not verified by as-built data, but if carried out regularly takes account of as-built data. • Susceptible to manipulation (unintended or otherwise) if only one party's delays are considered. • Accuracy can be reduced if the period between progress update and delay increases. • Sensitive to the order in which delays are impacted upon the schedule.	• For negotiating purposes or in tribunals.

27.3.5 Windows analysis

At its highest level, the windows analysis method compares the as-planned schedule with the as-built schedule during a particular period or time 'window'. The as-planned schedule at the start of the window is the schedule updated with progress at this point. Likewise, the as-built schedule at the end of the window is the schedule updated with progress at this point. The difference between the completion dates at the start and the end of the window is the overall delay that is attributed to the critical delays that occurred within the window being considered.

This method of delay analysis can be used to review delays by comparison in a similar way to the as-planned versus as-built method, but in smaller time windows; or by extracting out delays in a similar way to the collapsed as-built method; or for verifying the impacted delays as reasonable from the time impact analysis method by comparison with the as-built data.

27.3.6 Other considerations

27.3.6.1 Conditions of contract

The choice of method of delay analysis involves considering various factors, including the relevant conditions of contract dictating how delay events should be assessed. It is also quite common that the quality and quantity of schedules and records will dictate the choice of method of delay analysis. Additionally, other considerations that need to be accounted for are the values associated with any delay event or events and the time available to carry out any analysis.

27.3.6.2 Delay analysis in the courts

Theoretical calculations of delay have been found not to carry favour with the courts, and methods of delay analysis that rely on as-built data have proved more reliable in dispute resolution. However, methods of delay analysis should be considered against a background of their intended use. For example, the simpler methods of delay analysis might be appropriate for illustrating delays at high level or for negotiating purposes, whereas the more complex methods might be more appropriate for use in formal tribunals where the evidence is subject to more scrutiny.

27.3.6.3 Considering float in delay analysis

Float is the period of time by which an activity can slip without affecting other activities or the project completion date. In particular, free float is the period of time by which an activity can slip without affecting any other tasks or the completion of the project, whereas total float is the period of time by which an activity can slip without affecting the completion of the project.

Terminal float is normally the period between the planned completion date and the date for completion as stated in the contract. Who owns the float within the schedule can depend upon such factors as the type of float being considered and the provisions for float within the contract. In addition, in order to demonstrate a delay, it can be seen that the float attached to an activity will have to be used before there is an effect on a following activity. This may mean that, when there is a delay to an activity, any float in the schedule is available to whichever party uses it first.

27.3.6.4 Concurrency

Concurrency occurs when there is a delay caused by two or more events that are of approximately equal potency. Although concurrency is often claimed to exist, it is actually quite rare, and delay analysis can disentangle the causative delays and show that one cause of delay was acting before the other or that one cause of delay was far more potent than the other. Where there is true concurrency, with the customer responsible for one of the delays and the contractor responsible for the other, there has been judicial guidance from the English courts that the contractor receives an extension of time but does not necessarily receive associated prolongation costs unless they can be separated out.

Part Five

Record keeping and learning

Record keeping	Document management	Handover and closeout	Lessons learned
Chapter 28	Chapter 29	Chapter 30	Chapter 31

'A learning experience is one of those things that say, "You know that thing you just did? Don't do that."'

Douglas Adams

28.1 Definition of record keeping

Records are the physical and digital data that are required to accurately document the life of the project. Record keeping is a formal and disciplined process for capturing this information.

28.2 Purpose of record keeping

The purpose of record keeping is to provide, and preserve, a comprehensive history of what happened, when and where. In the context of planning, it is the basis of updating the schedule and of forensic planning, and provides information that will be useful in planning future projects (productivity data).

28.3 How to record

It is important to define at the outset what records are necessary and required to be kept. Since it is not possible to know in advance what records will be required, it is important to set up appropriate processes and tools to enable the capture of all relevant information.

Record keeping should be undertaken on a regular basis appropriate to the data being collected. This could be required daily (e.g. weather records), weekly (e.g. timesheets) or monthly (e.g. progress reports, safety statistics).

Effective record keeping is that which is clearly stated and understood, and is accessible in the future. Records should be kept in an appropriate electronic

Planning, Scheduling, Monitoring and Control

format. Records should be checked where appropriate and authorised where required (e.g. timesheets). Effective record keeping ensures that this is carried out on a regular basis, and ensures their authenticity.

28.4 What to record

- Actual start and actual finish dates of every activity in the schedule. This will eventually build the as-built schedule. It is appropriate to collect this information either daily or weekly, as any longer duration will probably lead to inaccuracy. Thus, this is not necessarily related to the progress reporting frequency, which may be further apart.
- Percent complete of each activity at the point of measurement.
- Remaining duration of each activity at 'time now'. This should be manually entered rather than allowing the scheduling software to automatically re-calculate.
- Time issues: it is useful to have the as-built schedule annotated with relevant details relating to progress and issues encountered. It is particularly important to build up a picture of time escalation reasons, to inform future contingency allowances.
- Cost issues: it is useful to maintain a log of relevant cost issues encountered. This will inform future contingency allowances.
- Any changes in the change log should be reflected in the schedule and clearly identified.
- If not captured in the project schedule, then the status of information (design, technical and other questions) needs to be retained in the records.
- Timesheets or labour returns that record who worked on what, when.
- Material records: a record of the source and final location of all materials used in the project.
- Plant records that confirm plant utilisation and outputs.
- Lessons learned: there is a tendency only to record lessons after a project has closed, but processes should be in place to allow collection of learning on a continual basis.
- Relevant environmental factors that may affect costs or time (e.g. weather in construction).
- Health and safety records.
- Photographic records.

Record keeping

- Delivery records.
- Quality control records.

28.5 Methods of keeping records

- Databases.
- Site diaries.
- Minuted sub-contractor meetings.
- As-built schedules.

29.1 Definition of document management

Document management is the collection, storage, dissemination and archiving of documentation in a structured manner. It is a fundamental aspect of project delivery, particularly in supporting assurance processes and the handover of a project at completion.

Document management also encompasses the process of 'document control', which involves maintaining records of document versions and an audit trail of documents exchanged with suppliers or other stakeholders. A document control process should control and be able to trace the flow of all information on the project.

The term 'document' applies to any formatted information that passes the test 'Is it in the interest of the schedule or project that this information be safeguarded?'.

An awareness of current legislation and corporate requirements is important, as some project documentation, e.g. contracts, may be required to be stored for a significant amount of time after the project has finished. Equally, some may be required to be stored in a particular manner – for example in a hard copy only, or in a soft copy only.

29.2 Purpose of document management

Document management ensures that:

- all relevant parties have all the information they require to complete their responsibilities;

Planning, Scheduling, Monitoring and Control

- all the information used in the project is up to date (i.e. latest revised information is in use);
- out-of-date information is no longer accessible for implementation purposes, but...
- all data is available for record purposes.

29.3 Document control systems

The chosen document control system must be accessible, secure and structured in a logical way that makes project information easily retrievable. This may also include metadata to be attributed to specific documents, i.e. document type, contract reference, supplier name, etc. (See also BIM in Chapter 19.)

Thought should be given to levels of sensitivity around particular documents, and user access rights aligned accordingly.

29.4 Version control

Version control is a fundamental part of document control, as it assures that all parties are working to the correct information at the correct time.

Project teams should:

- ensure that all document changes are recorded and documents marked appropriately so it is clear that a revision has taken place;
- ensure all project team members use the correct version of each document;
- maintain a tracker, e.g. an appropriate database tool, that shows the status and revision numbers of each drawing and assurance document, if required by the project team.

29.5 Handover of documentation

At an early stage, the project team should obtain detailed agreement, usually from the sponsor or asset maintainer, as to what documents need to be provided, in what format and when.

Project handover and closeout are separate processes but are often very closely related in time. Closeout cannot occur until the handover process is complete. Both processes are vital to the success of the project and often use finite resources. The handover process is very likely a part of the critical path of the project, whilst the closeout process is essential to the finalisation of commercial accounts, resolution of defects/snagging and transfer of the risk process. It will also include the final part of the lessons learned process, which is discussed in Chapter 31. Figure 30.1 outlines the context of handover and closeout.

30.1 Handover

30.1.1 Definition of handover

The handover of a project occurs when the final project deliverables are handed over from the organisation delivering the project to the user or operator of the asset.

There are many parts to this process, including scope, training and documentation, all of which need to be carefully planned and resourced.

30.1.2 Purpose of the handover process

A project does not simply end when the works have progressed to 100%. The project has to be successfully handed over to the customer or client. To allow this, appropriate time must be allocated in the schedule, and appropriate capacity must exist to effect handover and certification: an example of that capacity being

Planning, Scheduling, Monitoring and Control

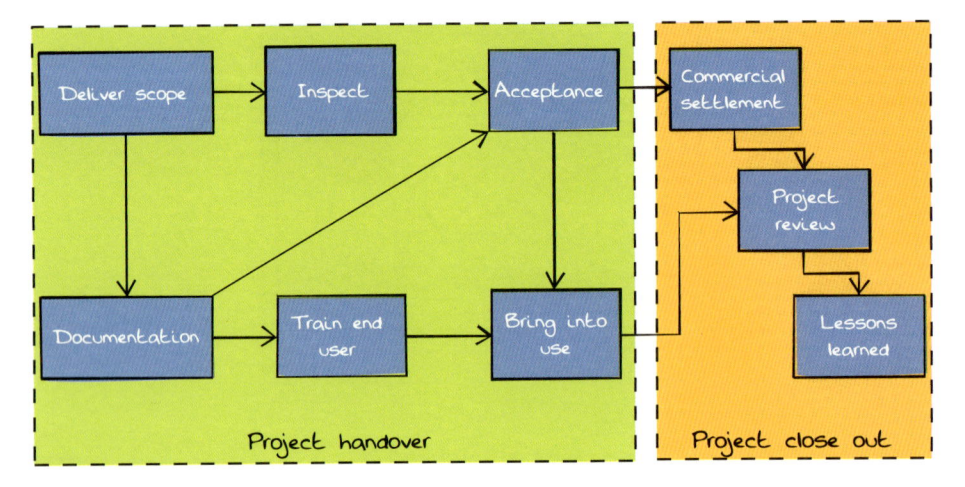

Figure 30.1 Context of handover and closeout

that there are sufficient people available, with the right skills to deliver the handover process.

The handover process ensures that:

- the project scope has been completed;
- all documentation has been completed;
- all acceptance criteria have been met, and signed off by all parties concerned;
- end-users have been trained or provided with training manuals as appropriate;
- the project (or product) has been brought into use – for example, a building can be occupied, a piece of software deployed.

30.1.3 Planning handover

The handover stage is a critical stage in the project life cycle, as an effective transition to the client's business environment will ensure that the client starts to realise the benefits of the project.

During the definition stage of the project life cycle, the project manager will need to allocate time and resource in the project schedule to ensure that the project team has sufficient time to effectively hand over the project deliverables to the client.

Handover and closeout

The nature of the project deliverables will determine how much time and resource is allocated to handing them over. The deliverable examples below will require different resources:

- delivery and installation of a new piece of equipment to the client;
- project deliverable/report;
- handing over a process.

The plan for the handover process should also include:

- acceptance of all relevant documentation (containing all specified information useful to the end-user, including guarantees, warranties, instruction or operation manuals);
- acceptance certificate(s) signed by the sponsor or delegated authority to confirm acceptance;
- transfer of responsibility for the project assets to the sponsor or users;
- formal transfer of ownership.

30.1.4 Issues in the management of handover

The handover process may vary considerably for different types of project, but, to avoid issues, the following principles should be adopted:

- all the project deliverables have been clearly defined and agreed in terms of documentation required to accompany the physical (or virtual) product of the project, training requirements and the like;
- the handover process has been clearly defined and agreed;
- the process for dealing with non-conformances or outstanding issues has been agreed;
- the handover process conforms to organisation guidelines;
- all relevant customer checklists have been used;
- all the significant stakeholders are appropriately represented at the handover event.

Poor handover can result in:

- payment delays;
- increased client retentions;

Planning, Scheduling, Monitoring and Control

- loss of or reduced profit;
- increased overhead costs (extended insurance, financing etc.);
- extended resource needs;
- extended warranty requirements;
- delays in equipment availability;
- delays in service to the final client;
- inefficient resource utilisation as work-around solutions are found;
- worsened client/customer relationship;
- potential penalty costs;
- reduced chance of future work.

30.2 Project closeout

30.2.1 Definition of project closeout

Project closeout is the financial closure of the project, including final settlement of project accounts and agreement of retentions and warranty periods.

30.2.2 Purpose of project closeout

Project closeout is the part of the project that must resolve the following:

- commercial settlement with the supply chain and all other parties;
- rectification of all defects noted at or since the completion of the handover process;
- payment of all retained monies resulting from the above.

It is also best practice to ensure that a project review takes place before the project team is disbanded, to ensure that appropriate lessons are learned from the things that went well or otherwise in the project. This is covered in the next chapter of this guide.

30.2.3 The project closeout process

The project closeout process should include:

- demobilisation of the project team, facilities and equipment;
- transfer, archive or disposal of relevant sensitive project material or assets;

Handover and closeout

- handover to a support organisation (if required);
- closedown of the project on the accounting and management systems.

These processes should be defined in the organisation procedures. Planning the closeout involves tailoring these procedures for this specific project. Provisional planning for closeout should be done early in the project life cycle. The closeout process should be controlled by maintaining appropriate trackers, for example of the various steps required to achieve commercial closeout with each supplier.

31.1 Definition of lessons learned

The lessons learned process captures two types of information from projects: objective data (facts about performance and outputs achieved) and subjective data (such as good and poor practices to be repeated or avoided in the future).

31.2 Purpose of lessons learned

Capturing lessons learned is important because it will assist in improving estimating efforts for future phases or projects. It may help avoid costly errors in the future by increasing the accuracy of planning and scheduling. It provides information for benchmarking against success criteria for task durations, costs, risks and work rate(s). Thus, it improves the quality of decision making and confidence in delivery.

From a planning perspective, there are two types of learning that should be captured.

31.3 Productivity data

First, there are the actual output rates achieved. These should include not only the man-hours expended by the resources, but also the costs incurred for these outputs (Figure 31.1). The quantity and quality of the work should also be noted, mentioning any mitigating factors affecting performance. For example, was the weather unusually cold, or very hot?

325

Planning, Scheduling, Monitoring and Control

Elem	Sub element	Contractor	Activity description	Lead in (wks)	No/units	Planned duration	Actual duration	Total mandays	Actual cost	Comments
Ground works	Site strip and excavation				m³					
	Hardcore & filling									
	Piling mat				m³					
	-ditto-				T					

Figure 31.1 Example proforma to collect output rates

Similarly, for design work, capturing the total man-hours to produce certain types of deliverables will give useful productivity data for future use.

31.4 Qualitative lessons learned

The second type of information that it is important to capture is more qualitative in nature: it is the collection of lessons learned. This will cover things that were done well and things that could have been improved. This will usually be captured in a formal review session and subsequent report.

A learning review is a simple activity which helps project team members to continually learn after the completion of a project stage or at the end of the overall project. It brings together relevant team members and stakeholders and allows them to evaluate the outcomes of their actions and to draw lessons for the future. It is usually conducted with the help of a facilitator, and is a structured method for prioritising and synthesising lessons learned across the whole project life cycle.

Lessons learned must be recorded and reviewed throughout the project life, and not just at the end of a phase (when many people have left the project to focus on other work or new projects). To achieve this, a process for recording lessons learned must be established and promoted to all members of the project team.

31.4.1 Stakeholders involved in a lessons learned review

The key stakeholders identified should be representative of the project and be able to objectively review the project performance. Below is a suggested generic list of stakeholders who could be involved in the lessons learned review:

- project sponsor;
- project manager;

Lessons learned

- responsible managers (section managers, or control account managers in defence sector);
- project controls managers;
- functional heads of departments or subject matter experts;
- client representatives;
- key supply chain representatives;
- people involved in related projects who could contribute to or benefit from the review.

31.4.2 Considerations

- Lessons should be agreed by all project team members.
- Complete individual lessons learned as soon after the task/activity/stage has completed, and try to conduct within a month.
- Focus on future improvements and re-usability.
- Categorisation of lessons learned is useful to aid future analysis of both lessons and actions.
- The document(s) where the lessons learned will reside and the relevant process (if applicable) where the lessons learned are applied.
- To update the lessons learned action plan to ensure that the lessons have been captured and the relevant documentation updated in line with the organisation's change control process.

An action plan should be created from the lessons learned exercise and will have the following headings to help complete the integration of the lessons back into the organisation:

- unique ID;
- lesson learned element description;
- lesson learned owner;
- lesson learned action;
- significance;
- relevant control document;
- change control completed.

The functional leads are responsible for verifying that appropriate personnel are aware of the learning points in the repository and that any recommendations have been implemented and any actions are closed out.

The final word

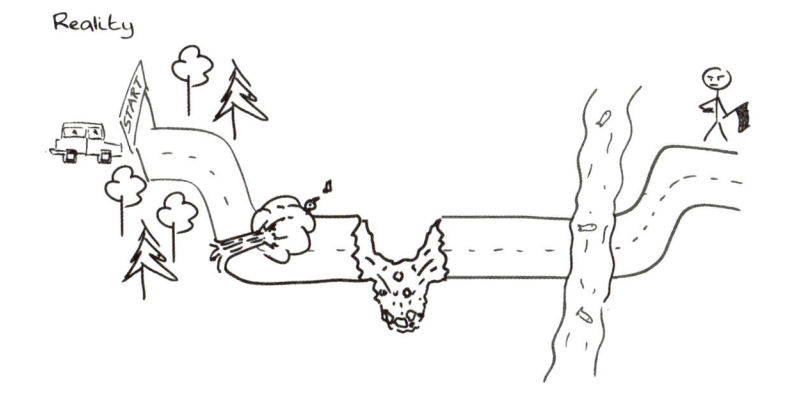

The plan

Reality

As built

The plan, the real world and how the project reacts!

Glossary

Accrual   A liability that has yet to be invoiced. The timing of payment and amount of the invoice may be uncertain.

Activity-based cost   The estimated time taken to complete the work activity, multiplied by the composite hourly rate for the personnel, together with additions for materials and equipment.

Activity weeks method   A simple method of monitoring progress by counting the number of activities in progress each week.

Actual cost   Also known as actual cost of work performed (ACWP). It is the cost of the work that has been performed. It may include costs from accounting systems with appropriate accruals.

Arrow diagram method (ADM)   A method of creating a network with activities on the 'arrows' rather than the 'nodes'.

Assurance process   The process by which one party – usually the customer – makes sure that another party – often a contractor – carries out a particular action, e.g. compliance with standards.

Bar chart   See Gantt chart.

Baseline   The reference level against which a project is monitored and controlled.

Benefit realisation review   A review of the project outcomes – the analysis of feedback from key stakeholders and the reasons for success or failure of the realisation of anticipated benefits. Actions and recommendations should result from the review.

Breakdown structure   A hierarchical structure by which project elements are broken down, or decomposed. Examples include cost breakdown structure (CBS), organisational breakdown structure (OBS), product breakdown structure (PBS) and work breakdown structure (WBS).

Budget at completion (BAC)   The total budget for the work.

Glossary

Budgeted cost of work performed (BCWP)   Earned value.

Budgeted cost of work scheduled (BCWS)   Planned value.

Capital costs   Costs that come from capital funds as opposed to funds for operational costs.

Change log   A record of all project changes, whether proposed, authorised, rejected or deferred.

Change order   Authorises a change to the brief, including a change of scope or agreement to accept a design solution which is outside the agreed cost parameters.

Configuration management   Configuration management encompasses the administrative activities concerned with the creation, maintenance, controlled change and quality control of the scope of work.

Constraint date   Used to fix the start or finish of an activity at a particular point in time.

Contingency   Funds set aside for responding to identified risks.

Cost breakdown structure   A hierarchical structure used to organise the project costs according to category, often aligning them with the organisation's budgeting system. It facilitates tracking the budget performance of the project.

Cost estimating relationships (CER)   Data analysed to find correlations between cost drivers and other system parameters such as size, design or performance.

Cost variance   Cost comparison between what has been earned and what has been spent.

Cost performance index (CPI)   The ratio of earned value over actual cost.

Critical path method (CPM)   A project modelling technique which determines the longest logical path through a network schedule.

Critical path   This is the chain of activities connecting the start of a network with the final activity in that network through those activities with zero float. There may be more than one critical path in a schedule.

Critical path analysis   An analysis of the schedule based on the critical path technique, including the examination of float usage.

Glossary

Dashboard reports　Performance metrics (normally comprising graphs and charts) to present the state of a partfolio, programme or project.

Deliverables　A product, set of products or package of work that will be delivered to, and formally accepted by, a stakeholder.

Delphi technique　A technique based upon the principle that estimates from an experienced and structured panel can provide a useful judgement-based output.

Dependencies　The relationship between activities in a network diagram. Dependencies can be internal or external. Internal dependencies are those under the control of the project manager. External dependencies are those outside the control of the project manager.

Design and build　A method to deliver a project in which the design and construction services are contracted by a single entity.

Drop line method　A progress reporting method in which a vertical line is drawn at the point of the progress assessment date, across the bars on the schedule.

'Dummy' tasks or activities　An activity added to a schedule that does not describe work. Often used in preference to adding a 'lag' to the schedule.

Early finish　The earliest possible date by which an activity can finish within the logical and imposed constraints of the network.

Early start　The earliest possible date when an activity can start within the logical and imposed constraints of the network.

Earned value (EV)　The value of completed work expressed in terms of the budget assigned to that work. A measure of progress, which may be expressed in money or labour hours.

Earned value analysis (EVA)　A technique for measuring project performance and progress.

Earned value management　A project control process, based on a structured approach to planning, cost collection and performance measurement. It facilitates the integration of project scope, time and cost objectives and the establishment of a baseline plan of performance measurement.

Glossary

Earned value technique (EVT)   A technique used to objectively assess the progress of an activity.

Estimate at completion (EAC)   A value expressed in money and/or hours to represent the projected final costs of work when completed. (Also referred to as projected out-turn cost.)

Estimate to complete (ETC)   The forecast of labour hours and costs required to complete the remaining authorised work. It is based on a bottom-up analysis of remaining work, and past and future performance, along with the availability of resources, is taken into consideration.

Float   Time by which an activity may be delayed or extended without affecting the start of any succeeding activity. Slack is an alternative term for float.

Forensic schedule analysis   The study and investigation of events using critical path methods or other recognised schedule or schedule calculation methods.

Fragnet   Template networks or schedules, usually for repetitive sections of schedules.

Gantt chart   A particular type of bar chart used in project management, showing planned activity against time. A Gantt chart is a time-phased graphic display of activity durations. Activities are listed with other tabular information on the left side, with time intervals over the bars. Activity durations are shown in the form of horizontal bars.

Hammock   A 'summary' task which can only have start to start and finish to finish logic to a group of activities. The duration of the hammock is determined by the total elapsed duration of the activities it is linked to.

Horizontal integration   This refers to the application and checking of logic through the different sections of the schedule that are running in parallel (rather than the sequential logic).

Independent cost estimate   Estimate prepared by external or third parties with the express purpose of validating, cross-checking or analysing estimates developed by project teams.

Information required register   A schedule detailing what information is required throughout a project. Usually comprising three sets of dates for each piece of information: planned/forecast/actual.

Glossary

Interface Internal interface may relate to the handover of a piece of work from one team to another. External interface may relate to deliverables to be given or received from a third party organisation.

Issues log Primarily a list of ongoing and closed issues on the project. It is used to organise the current issues by type and severity in order to prioritise.

Key performance indicator (KPI) KPIs are measures that provide managers with the most important performance information to enable them or their stakeholders to understand the performance level of the organisation.

Lag In a network diagram, the minimum necessary lapse of time between the finish of one activity and the start of another. (May also be used with finish to finish logic, etc.)

Lead A negative lag. By definition an illogical condition.

Level of effort (LOE) An ongoing activity that is carried out to support other work activities or the entire project.

Line of balance A scheduling technique for delivery of repetitive products that shows how resource teams move from product to product rather than the detail of individual activities.

Logic The links (predecessors or successors) between activities in a schedule or network diagram.

Logic density The average number of logic links per activity across the schedule.

Logistics planning The planning of the movement of physical resources such as materials, plant and equipment.

Make ready needs The things that must be in place to allow an activity to commence, e.g. designs, approvals, materials, etc.

Management reserve A sum of money held to cover the cost impact of an unexpected event.

Metadata A term used to describe data about data. Document management systems contain metadata.

Milestone definition sheet (MDS) This is a sheet to record the details of a key milestone. Includes description and date, as well as parties involved in achieving the milestone.

Glossary

MOD   Ministry of Defence (UK).

Monte Carlo analysis   A set of computational calculations that rely on repeated random sampling to obtain a range of results – a probability distribution.

Network diagram   A pictorial presentation of project data in which the project logic is the main determinant of the placements of the activities in the network. Frequently called a flowchart, PERT chart, logic drawing, activity work or logic diagram.

New engineering contract (NEC)   A suite of contracts that facilitate the implementation of many sound project management principles and practices. They also define legal relationships.

Optioneering   Optioneering estimates are prepared to establish the cost differences between two or more strategies in order to arrive at ranking to inform an economic decision.

Order of magnitude (OM)   Orders of magnitude are numbers of approximately the same size.

Ordinal dates   Where the calendar dates for a project are not yet known, the schedule can be drawn up against week or month numbers, e.g. week 1, week 2, week 3, etc.

Organisational breakdown structure (OBS)   A hierarchical way in which an organisation may be divided into management levels and groups, for planning and control purposes.

Output rate   The planning data required to enable the scheduler to work out the duration of an activity, e.g. cubic metres per hour for excavation.

Parametric estimating   This uses a methodology that is based on elements of cost extracted from historical data acquired from similar systems or sub-systems.

Performance constraints   These are usually determined by the brief or specification for a project, and may be critical to the business case, e.g. manufacturing output from a factory.

Performance measurement baseline (PMB)   The schedule of all the work to be performed, the budgeted cost for this work, and the elements that produce the deliverables.

Glossary

Planned value (PV)   The value of work expected to be completed at a point in time. This may be expressed in money or labour hours.

Planning packages   These represent work that is not defined enough to be included within a work package. Usually used to cover future work.

Possessions   These are times within a schedule when the project has to take over the work area, thus stopping normal activity. For example, a track possession stops trains running and allows work to be carried out. Can also apply to works in factories/manufacturing lines.

Precedence diagram method (PDM)   This is a network diagram method in which the node designates the activity, and the logical interface is represented by the arrow.

Predecessor   An activity that must be completed before the following activity can commence.

Prelims   'Prelims' is a short form for preliminaries: the on-cost expenses, staff costs, site overheads, etc.

Probability chart   A chart showing the likelihood of an instance occurring – for example, the likelihood of the project finishing on a specific date (usually found in QSRA).

Procurement strategy   The criteria to be considered prior to letting or purchasing services for a project. Examples are what type of contracts will be used; how the work will be packaged up; how the project will be funded.

Product breakdown structure   A hierarchy of deliverables that are required to be produced on the project. This forms the base document from which the execution strategy and product-based work breakdown structure may be derived. It provides a guide for configuration control documentation.

Programme manager   The manager responsible for a group of projects, for example a large change programme.

Project brief   This defines the customer's or client's requirements, and is key to the design. It is also a fundamental element of the business case.

Project execution plan (PEP)   The document describing how, when and by whom a project will be delivered. The targets will include the scope, timescales, costs, quality and benefits.

Glossary

Project life cycle Four major stages: 1) initiation; 2) planning; 3) execution; 4) closeout/handover.

Project management plan (PMP) Consists of the collection of key project information needed by the project board, project manager and project office to manage the project. Will comprise static elements (that are periodically reviewed but change rarely during the life of the project) and dynamic elements (that change often).

Project schedule The tool that communicates what work needs to be performed, which resources will perform the work and the timeframes in which that work will be performed.

Project sponsor This is the individual (often a manager or executive) with overall accountability for the project. They are primarily concerned with ensuring that the project delivers the agreed business benefits.

Prolongation The term used to cover the amount of time a project duration extends – usually due to a delay.

Quantitative schedule risk analysis (QSRA) A generic term for objective methods of assessing risks that cannot be identified accurately.

RACI The RACI matrix is a tool used for identifying roles and responsibilities to avoid confusion over those roles and responsibilities during the project.

Redundant logic Logic links that are duplicated through an alternative route. If 'C' cannot start until 'B' is complete, which cannot start until 'A' is complete, then a logic link from 'A' to 'C' would be said to be redundant.

Request for information (RFI) The term used – usually in a formal contract process – when a project team member requires extra information or clarification.

Requirements management The process of capturing, assessing and justifying stakeholders' wants and needs.

Resources A supply of money, materials, staff, labour, equipment or other asset that can be used to deliver a product or service.

Resource breakdown structure (RBS) The hierarchical breakdown of a project into resource requirement elements.

Glossary

Resource histogram The graphical display of resource requirement or usage on a project.

Responsibility assignment matrix (RAM) A diagram or chart showing assigned responsibilities for elements of work. It is created by combining the work breakdown structure and the organisational breakdown structure.

Risk A significant, unplanned and uncertain event or situation that, should it occur, will have an effect on at least one project or schedule activity, or business objective. A detrimental risk is often called a 'threat', and a beneficial risk is called an 'opportunity'.

Risk and opportunities register This is a central repository for all risks identified by the project. Includes information such as risk probability, impact, counter-measures, risk owner, etc. Also contains a section for opportunities, which can be time or cost-saving options.

Risk log This is a central repository for all risks identified by the project. Includes information such as risk probability, impact, counter-measures, risk owner, etc.

Risk management plan This sets out how the thorough assessment of risk associated with the project will be implemented.

Risk pot The fund where the money allocated for risk is kept. The money is 'drawn down' from the fund as required.

Rolling wave planning This describes the planning density that is achieved at different moments in time. Primarily more detailed planning in the immediate future and less detailed towards the end of the project.

Rough order of magnitude (ROM) An estimate of costs and time provided in the early stages of a project when its scope and requirements have not been fully defined.

Schedule performance index (SPI) A term used in earned value analysis. It is the ratio of work accomplished to work planned for a specified time period. The SPI is an efficiency rating for work accomplishment, comparing work achieved with what should have been achieved at any point in time.

Schedule variance A metric for the schedule performance on a project is the algebraic difference between earned value and the budget (schedule variance = earned value − budget). A positive value is a favourable condition, whilst a negative value is unfavourable.

Glossary

Schedule visibility task (SVT) Where an activity is dependent on a lead time, the schedule visibility task represents the elapsed/lead time or the customer approval time.

Scheduling Software Software used for project planning, scheduling, resource allocation and performance measurement activities. Is also used for collaboration and communication between project stakeholders.

Scope The sum of deliverables and the work content to produce a project.

S-curves Lines drawn on a graph to express a quantity planned, achieved or expended across time. Named 'S-curves', as there is a usual tendency for them to commence and complete at a slower rate.

'Scrum' Scrum is an 'agile methodology' that can be applied to nearly any project; however, it is most commonly used in software development.

Slack (or float) Slack is the term used by MS Project to describe float.

SMART Usually relates to specific, measurable, achievable, realistic, and time-bound (there are other variations).

Specific analogy estimating This method of estimating is based upon selecting a costed project that is similar or related to the project costs being estimated.

Stage plan A development of the project schedule that contains enough detail to allow the project manager to control a portion of the project (the 'stage'), usually on a daily basis.

Stakeholder Any individual, group or organisation that can affect, be affected by or perceive itself to be affected by the project.

Stakeholder management The systematic identification, analysis and planning of actions to communicate with, negotiate with and influence stakeholders.

Statement of work This explains the customer/client needs and requirements. It is often developed in line with the business case. It will then form the basis of contractor selection and contract administration.

Steps These are pre-agreed progress measures against which the project will assess the tasks, to establish per cent completion statuses in a tangible and objective (rather than subjective) way.

Glossary

Strategic schedule   The high-level schedule. Often produced early in the project life cycle to help determine the relationship with other projects.

System requirements   These define and drive the work to be completed within the system design process and subsequent subsystem and component design.

Successor   A successor is an activity whose start or finish depends on the start or finish of a predecessor activity.

Target date   The planned date to complete an activity or project. (May be earlier than the contract date.)

Three-point estimate   An estimate giving the most likely mid-range value, an optimistic value and a pessimistic worst case value.

Time analysis   The process that calculates the timeframe in which each activity can take place. It identifies the minimum time in which the network can be completed, based on the activity durations and the logical links defined.

Time chainage   Used to illustrate projects that are linear in nature (an example being road construction). When well designed and drawn, it is a very useful visualisation tool, often allowing the whole project to be displayed on a single chart.

Time contingency   An approximate duration of time assigned to an activity that takes into consideration the impact of uncertainty.

Time risk allowance (TRA)   Durations are uncertain, and therefore time contingency should be allowed for in schedules (also see QSRA).

Tornado chart   Within a quantitative schedule risk analysis, one of the outputs is a chart that resembles the shape of a tornado. The activities that have the most influence on the overall project end date are displayed in the tornado chart.

Total float   Time by which an activity may be delayed or extended without affecting the total project duration or delaying a finish date.

Validation and verification requirements matrix   This V-shaped model is useful to map the user requirements and system design, in order to facilitate the assurance process.

Vertical integration   The process that confirms that the data at different levels of detail is consistent and comprehensive throughout the whole length of the schedule – from beginning to end.

Glossary

WBS dictionary   Covers the various WBS sections and defines all the deliverables relating to the scope or statement of work.

Windows analysis   This process is used to compare the planned schedule with the as-built schedule during a particular period or 'window' of time.

Work breakdown structure (WBS)   Defines the total work to be undertaken and provides a structure for all control systems. It allows a project or programme to be divided by level into discrete groups for programming, cost planning and control purposes. The WBS is a tool for defining the hierarchical breakdown of work required to deliver the products. Major categories are broken down into smaller components. These are sub-divided until the lowest required level of detail is established. The lowest units of the WBS are generally work packages.

Work calendar   Used to define the amount of working and non-working time throughout the duration of the project. They are also used to determine when the work will be carried out, e.g. night working or weekends only.

Work package   A discrete element of project scope at the lowest level of each branch of the work breakdown structure. Collectively, the work packages specify all the work and products included in the project.

Acronyms

£RAM	Financial responsibility assignment matrix
3D	Three-dimensional
ABC	Activity-based cost estimating
AC	Actual cost
ACWP	Actual cost of work performed
ADM	Arrow diagram method
AE	Apportioned effort
AFC	Anticipated final cost
ATE	Actual time elapsed
B/L	Baseline
BAC	Budget at completion
BCWP	Budgeted cost of work performed
BCWS	Budgeted cost of work scheduled
BIM	Building information modelling
BT	Budget transfer
CAD	Computer aided design
CBS	Cost breakdown structure
CER	Cost estimating relationship
CO	Change order
CPI	Cost performance index
CPM	Critical path method
CV	Cost variance
DSDM	Dynamic systems development method
EAC	Estimate at completion
EFC	Estimated final cost
ETC	Estimate to complete
ETTC	Estimated time to complete
EV	Earned value
EVA	Earned value analysis
EVM	Earned value management
EWN	Early warning notice
FF	Finish to finish
FS	Finish to start

Acronyms

HSE	Health, safety and environmental
KPI	Key performance indicator
LOE	Level of effort
MDS	Milestone definition sheet
MOD	Ministry of Defence
MoSCoW	Must have, should have, could have, won't have
NEC	New engineering contract
OBS	Organisational breakdown structure
OD	Original duration
OM	Order of magnitude
PBS	Product breakdown structure
PDM	Precedence diagram method
PEP	Project execution plan
PMB	Performance measurement baseline
PMI	Project manager's instruction
PMP	Project management plan
PV	Planned value
QCRA	Quantitative cost risk analysis
QSRA	Quantitative schedule risk analysis
RACI	Responsibility, accountability, consulted, informed matrix
RAM	Responsibility assignment matrix
RBS	Resource breakdown structure
RFI	Request for information
ROM	Rough order of magnitude
SF	Start to finish
SI	Site instruction
SMART	Specific, measurable, achievable, relevant, time-bound
SOW	Statement of work
SPI	Schedule performance index
SRD	Systems requirement document
SS	Start to start
SV	Schedule variance
SVT	Schedule visibility task
TRA	Time risk allowance
TV	Time variance
WBS	Work breakdown structure
WBSD	Work breakdown structure dictionary
WI	Works information
XP	Extreme programming

Index

£ RAM 65, 70 *see also* **responsibility assignment matrix** (RAM)

2D BIM model 199
3D BIM model 199–202
4D BIM model 199
100% rule 61

ABBF (as-built but for method) 304, 306–7
ABC (**activity-based cost**) estimating 82
AC (**actual cost**) 236, 240–1
acceptance criteria 16–17, 26, 28
accounting systems 69–70
accruals 241
activities: activity checks 191–3; activity coding 26, 114, 120, 158–9, 192, 213; activity descriptions 114; activity durations 191–2; activity identity numbers (IDs) 113–14, 158, 192, 213; and the **baseline** 211; critical activities 197–8; deleted activities 192; and **earned value analysis** 237; out-of-sequence activities 194–5; scheduling 113–20; **steps** 116–17, 323
activity weeks method 222, 224, 226–7, 228, 236
ACWP (actual cost of work performed) see AC
AFC (anticipated final cost) 251
agile 47–9, 203–6
ALAP ('as late as possible' constraint) 138
analogy estimating 80–1
annual spend profiles 16
AOA (activity on arrow method) 123
AON (activity on node method) 122
AP v AB (as-planned versus as-built method) 304–5
apportioned effort 248
approximate estimating methods 79, 80–1
arrow diagram method (ADM) 122–3

as-built schedules 105–6, 314
assumptions: assumptions list 22, 40, 43, 150, 189, 276; assumptions register 150, 189, 276; project assumptions 27;
assurance process 29, 317
audit 30, 252, 261, 317

BAC (**budget at completion**) 236
backward passes 126–7
'banana curves' 86
bar charts 109, 147, 167–72, 186 *see also* **Gantt charts**
baseline: setting the **baseline** 209–20; and agile planning 48; **baseline** maintenance 213–16; and the business case 17; and change management 260, 264–5, 266, 267; and the contract schedule 102–3; and cost control 252; and **earned value analysis** 239; and performance reporting 223; and the planning process 39; and **quantitative schedule risk analysis** 286; re-baselining 216–20; and scheduling 93
BCWP (**budgeted cost of work performed**) 212, 236
benchmarked data 149, 198
benefit realisation review 17–19
BIM (building information modelling) 199–202
bottom-up cost estimating 82
bottom-up planning 43–7
BRAG ratings 246
brainstorming 22, 57
breakdown structures 22–4, 53–71, 211
budgeting: budget transfers 84, 87, 220, 267, 271; and cost control 251–3; and **earned value analysis** 242–3; as part of planning 83–7; and performance reporting 230, 236–7; and risk management 198, 283–4

345

Index

buffers 164–6
build method 22
'Bulls eye' chart 245
business case 11–19
business-as-usual estimating 82

CAB (collapsed as-built method) 304, 306–7
calendars 116, 118–20, 187, 192–3
capital costs 16
cash-flow: definition 49; forecasting 18, 84–6; monitoring 222, 230
change control processes 260–71; and the **baseline** 213, 214, 220; and budget transfers 87; and cost control 252; and **requirements management** 29; and scheduling 93; and scope management 22
change freezes 261
change log 263–4, 265, 266, 268, 314
change management 259–71
change orders/change notices 79, 266–7, 271
change requests 263–7
claims on the contract 106, 303
closeout/handover 14, 201, 319–22
coding **interfaces** 158–9 see also activity coding
collaborative planning 44, 204
common sense 8, 61, 181
communication 32, 167–81
comparative duration estimations 149
competitive tender, alternatives to 18
complex projects: external integration of **interfaces** 162; **organisation breakdown structure** (OBS) 64; **rolling wave planning** 45–6
compliance 26
computer aided design (CAD) 199
'conceptual'/'pre-conceptual' estimates 78–9
concurrency 310
conditions of contract 309
configuration management 261
consents 181; consents trackers 42
constraints 27, 39, 136–47, 159, 197

contingency: and the **baseline** 211; and the business case 18; **contingency** budgets 80; and **earned value analysis** 238; and **quantitative cost risk analysis** 297; and record keeping 314; record keeping 284; **time contingencies** 51, 164–5, 197, 286
contract schedule 102–3, 174
contracting strategy 18
contractor's fee 239
coordination meetings 257
cost/benefit analysis 14, 278, 284
cost breakdown structure (CBS) 23–4, 56, 69–71, 84, 231, 240
cost budgets 84–6
cost control 251–3
cost estimating 77–82
cost estimating relationships (CERs) 81
cost forecasting 251
cost management 236
cost performance index (CPI) 244–5, 253
cost value analysis 83, 222, 231, 232
cost variance (CV) 216, 218, 242, 253
critical paths: and assumptions 151; building the schedule 121–47; and change management 268; and closeout/handover 319; and constraints 138; **critical path analysis** 123–4, 152, 221, 224, 234–5, 285; **critical path method** (CPM) 49, 121–47, 197, 303–9; and **interfaces** 161; and performance reporting 234–5; planning checks (of schedule) 189–90; and **quantitative schedule risk analysis** 286; and **rolling wave planning** 47; and schedule review 187; and scheduling 41, 43, 93; scheduling checks 196–8
cumulative normal distributions see **S-curves**
customer approval 116, 179 see also closeout/handover

dashboard reports 221
data date 186, 224
data table 184–5
day zero 125, 130
deferred change requests 265

Index

definitive estimating methods 79, 80, 82
delays 74, 103, 107, 225, 243, 303–6
deleted activities 192
deliverables: and the 100% rule 61; and the **baseline** 211; and budgeting 84; and the business case 17; and closeout/handover 319, 321; and **cost estimating** 82; design deliverables tracker 109, 111; and the planning process 38, 40; as 'product' 57; **product breakdown structure** (PBS) 57; and the **RACI** matrix 68; and **requirements management** 25, 28; and the **responsibility assignment matrix** (RAM) 67; **rolling wave planning** 45–6; and scheduling 157; and scope management 21
Delphi technique 81
density of schedules 94–8
dependencies: bar charts/**Gantt charts** 170; and **breakdown structures** 55; coding 120; and **critical path** networks 125, 126; dependency management 73–4; and the planning process 38, 40; and **requirements management** 26, 27; and scheduling 157–64
design and build phase 26
design deliverable schedules 42
design deliverables tracker 109, 111
detail density, schedule 94–9
development/strategic schedule 101–2
dictionaries 30, 61–2
'digital handover' 201
discrete distributions 291
document management 317–18
drop line method 222, 224–6
dummy tasks 116, 120, 123, 136, 194
duration: duration uncertainty 285–6, 287, 292, 294; estimation of duration 147–51

early delivery 104
early finish dates 126, 127
early/late curves 50–1, 85–6, 211
early start dates 126, 212
earned value analysis (EVA) 83, 222, 231, 235–49

earned value management 221, 249, 253
earned value techniques (EVTs) 247
'easy to measure' statistics 17
'economic best fit' 50–1
emergency procedures 261
end-user benefits 17
estimating: **cost estimating** 77–82; **estimate at completion** (EAC) 83, 246–7, 252; **estimate to complete** (ETC) 246, 252; estimated final cost (EFC) 252, 253; estimated time to complete (ETCC) 247; estimating norms 40; estimation of duration 147–51; fair price estimating methods 79; impact of change 264; quantity of resources 153
'events' focused (top-down) planning 43–4
expert opinion 150
external integration 160–2

facilitated workshops 22, 44, 158
fair price estimating methods 79
feeder buffers 164
filters (on schedule views) 114, 184, 186, 187
'finish on' constraint 139, 197
'finish on or after' constraint 140
'finish on or before' constraint 141
finish to finish relationships 116, 134, 193
finish to start relationships 123, 132–3, 193
float: and budgeting 86; and constraints 137–40; and **critical path** networks 122, 124, 127–8, 130–1; and delay analysis 310; and **drop line methods** 225; free **float** 131, 155; measurement of float usage 222, 234–5; negative **float** 131, 137, 142, 189–90, 196–7; and planning checks 189–90; and **quantitative schedule risk analysis** 286; and scheduling 41, 50; scheduling checks 196–8; shared **float** 132 *see also* **total float**
'forecast schedule' 103
forensic schedule analysis 303–9

Index

forward and backward passes 93, 124, 125–7
fragnets 99, 215
free float 131, 155
'full detail' cost estimating 82
funding requirements 16, 83–4, 259, 266

Gantt charts 42–3, 66, 123, 167–72, 184–5, 186
gate reviews 45–6
gateways 16, 34, 101, 212
graphical schedules 42
group workshops 158

hammocks 115–16
handover and closeout 201, 319–22
hard constraints 197
high-density schedules 44–6, 94–9, 255
histograms for resource profiles 16, 154, 180, 186, 198
holidays and non-working days 118–19
horizontal integration 93, 156–7
HSE (health, safety and environment) 75–6, 261
human factors/soft issues 2, 40

IAP (impacted as-planned method) 304, 305–6
impact analysis 264
impact resolution 163–4
independent cost estimates 79
inflation 239
information required register 189
innovative thinking, need for 37
intellectual property 18
interfaces: coding 120; dependency management 73–4; handover/hand-back trackers as 42; **horizontal integration** 157; milestones 74; planning checks 189; and the planning process 38, 40; public interfaces and HSE 75–6; and **requirements management** 26, 27; and scheduling 157–64; **stakeholder management** 32; **WBS dictionary** 61–2

internal integration 159–60
invalid dates 193
issues log 38
iterative nature of processes: and agile planning 48, 203; and 'collaborative planning' 44; and **float** 155; and **logic** 123; and **requirements management** 26; scheduling interfaces 158; and **stakeholder management** 32; **work breakdown structure** (WBS) 60

jagged line method *see* activity weeks method

key assumptions management 22
KPI (key performance indicators) 242, 244

lags 116, 120, 123, 135–6, 194, 198
latest finish dates 127–8, 137
latest start dates 127
leads 116, 120, 135, 194, 198
learning review 326
legislative changes 259
lessons learned 253, 276, 284, 314, 325–7
level of effort (LOE) activities 82, 115, 191–2, 198, 238–9, 248, 287
levels of schedules *see* density of schedules
line of balance 43, 167, 172–4, 222, 229–30
log normal distributions 289
logic: and change management 271; **critical path method** (CPM) 121–47; displaying networks using **scheduling software** 147; **level of effort** (LOE) activities 115; logic bottlenecks 195–6; logic checks 193–6; logic density 195; **logical** networks 125; **logic**-linked scheduling 41, 43, 44, 98–9, 120; and schedule review 187; and top-down planning 43; types of logic linking 132; **work breakdown structure** (WBS) 60
logistics planning 40, 152, 153, 189
long-duration projects 45–6
'longest path' 128, 129, 197–8
look-ahead schedules 105, 191, 255–7

Index

make ready needs 256, 257
management issues: financial authority for change 267; and lessons learned 326–7; **management reserve** 238, 259, 281, 283; planning checks (of schedule) 188; and schedule density 98; senior management 98; and tracker schedules 109
'mandatory finish' constraint 142, 197
'mandatory start' constraint 143, 197
master/working schedule 42
'measured quants' cost estimating 82
medium-term schedules 105
metadata 199, 318
method statement schedules 42
'mid curves' 86
milestones: activity steps 116; as alternative schedule reporting 170–1; and the **baseline** 211; and **earned value analysis** 248; and **interfaces** 162; **interfaces** 74; **milestone definition sheets** 189; milestone monitoring 222, 227–8; and multiple ends 195; scheduling checks 191
minute-based time units 118
mission critical projects 12
modelling software 199
Monte Carlo analysis 148, 284, 286–8, 291, 297–8
MoSCoW technique 48
multiple ends 195–6

negative **float** 131, 137, 142, 189–90, 196–7
network analysis 151, 222, 234–5 *see also* **critical paths**
network diagrams 66, 93
network templates 99
New Engineering Contracts (NEC) 165, 271, 303
normal distribution curves 288

'objective criteria' (**steps**) 116–17
'one version of the truth' reporting 104, 200
opportunities *see* risk
opportunity assessment matrix 278
optioneering 79, 268

options analysis 22
order of magnitude (OM) estimates 79
ordinal dates 120, 125, 186
organisation breakdown structure (OBS) 23–4, 53, 56, 60, 64–5, 66–7
out-of-sequence activities 194–5
output rates 91, 187, 191, 325–6
output summaries 45

P values 286, 292, 298, 301–2
P0 plan 49
packages of work *see* **work packages**
parallel working 133, 134, 193
parametric estimating (estimating norms) 81
'parent'/'child' relationships in WBS 61
PDM (**precedence diagram method**) 122
per cent complete 248
performance analysis techniques 222, 234–49
performance constraints 39
performance measurement baseline (PMB) 209, 211, 236, 238–9, 252–3, 281, 283 *see also* **baseline**
performance reporting 221–49, 257–8
permits and licences 181
PERT (programme evaluation review technique) 148, 290–1
planned value (PV) 49, 236, 239–40
planning checks (of schedule) 183–4, 188–90
planning method statement (schedule narrative) 43
planning packages 93, 213, 238
planning strategies 49–51
planning vs scheduling 41–2, 91, 94
possessions 181, 292
post-build schedules 106
post-implementation survey 17
predecessor relationships 116, 123, 133, 134, 143, 159, 194, 195
preliminary estimates 79
probability charts 292, 293, 295
process step schedules 42
procurement schedules 107–9, 110, 189
procurement strategy 17–18, 84
product analysis 22

349

Index

product breakdown structure (PBS) 22–3, 26–8, 56–8, 60, 157
production curves 231, 233
productivity data 313, 325
'programme' (why book avoids use of term) 42
programme manager 22, 31
progress assessments 223
progress weightings 116
project benefits capability 151
project brief 11, 261–2, 268
project closeout *see* closeout/handover
project coding 120
project controls system 40, 41, 211
project execution plan (PEP): and the business case 11; and change management 260, 268; and the planning process 38–9; and **requirements management** 27, 29; and risk management 276
project familiarisation 33–4
project life cycle: and the **baseline** 211; and the business case 11, 13–14, 16, 19; and closeout/handover 320, 323; and **cost estimating** 77–9; and **interfaces** 158; and lessons learned 326; and project reviews 19; and **requirements management** 25; and risk management 276, 280, 298; and **stakeholder management** 32; and **time contingency** 51; and top-down planning 43–4
project management plan (PMP) 22 *see also* **project execution plan** (PEP)
project manager 31–2, 115 *see also* management issues
project procurement professional 18
project reporting system 70 *see also* record keeping
project review 19
project schedule: and **interfaces** 159; and planning 42; and the planning process 39; project buffers 164; and record keeping 314; and **requirements management** 29; resource-levelled schedules 50–1; and risk management 276, 285; and schedule review 184; **work breakdown structure** (WBS) 60

project sponsor: and the business case 11; and change management 260, 265, 266, 268; and lessons learned 326; and 're-planning' 212; and **requirements management** 25, 29; and risk 15; and scope management 22; **stakeholder management** 31
project vision 48
prolongation 310 *see also* delays
PV (**planned value**) 49, 236, 239–40

QRA percentiles 298, 301–2
qualitative lessons learned 326
quantitative cost risk analysis (QCRA) 297–301
quantitative schedule risk analysis (QSRA) 51, 93, 284–96
quantity tracking 222, 223, 231–3

RACI matrix 67–9, 157
re-baselining 216–20
record keeping 222, 313–16
recovery schedules 107
redundant activities 192
redundant logic 194, 195
relationship management 31–2
'releases' (agile planning) 47–8
repetitive schedules 99, 165, 172, 229
re-planning 216–18, 219
re-programming 218–20
requests for information (RFI) 257, 265
requirements management 25–30
requirements/needs-driven planning 43
resource breakdown structure (RBS) 23–4, 56, 70–1
resource histograms 16, 154, 180, 186, 198
'resource-based estimating' 82, 150
resource-levelled schedules 50–1, 173, 212
resources: and the **baseline** 209–10, 211; and budgeting 83; and the business case 14, 16; and calendars 118–19; and change management 264; and closeout/handover 320; **cost estimating** 77–82; 'critical

Index

resources' 152; definition 152; **organisation breakdown structure** (OBS) 65; and parallel working 134; and planning 37; and the planning process 39, 40; and **requirements management** 28; resource buffers 164; resource coding 120; **resource monitoring** 222, 230–1; resource smoothing 154–5; resources allocation 153–6; resources scheduling checks 198; resourcing the schedule 151–5; and the **responsibility assignment matrix** (RAM) 67; and scheduling 41, 92; **work breakdown structure** (WBS) 60

responsibility assignment matrix (RAM) 23–4, 56, 60, 64, 65–7

risk: and the **baseline** 211; and the business case 15, 18; and change management 273; and **earned value analysis** 238; health, safety and environment (HSE) 75–6; planning for risk 274–5; and the planning process 40; review of schedule risk 198; **risk and opportunities register** 38; risk assessment 277–8; risk draw down 281–4; risk management 273–301; **risk management plan** 274; risk mitigations 40, 238, 276, 278, 280, 283, 286; **risk pot** 281; risk register 150, 187, 268, 277, 280, 296; risk review 280–1; **rolling wave planning** 45–6; and schedule review 187; and the **statement of work** 30; **time contingency** 51, 164

risk log 277, 279, 280
rolling wave planning 45–6, 214, 226, 238
rough order of magnitude (ROM) estimates 79

safety 75–6
scenario planning ('What ifs') 107
schedule performance index (SPI) 239, 243, 244
schedule risk analysis 170
schedule variance (SV) 216, 217, 218, 219, 242–3
schedule visibility tasks (SVT) 116

scheduling: and budgeting 84–5; building the schedule 121–64; communicating the schedule 167–82; 'density' of scheduling 94–8; **forensic schedule analysis** 303–9; high-density schedules 44–6, 94–9, 255; **horizontal integration** 156–7; master/working schedule and separate trackers 42; network templates (fragnets) 99, 215; and the planning process 39, 40; planning vs scheduling 41–2, 91, 94; resourcing the schedule 151–5; and risk management 285; schedule design 113–20; schedule narrative 43, 179–81, 268; schedule review 183–98; schedule revisions 267; scheduling checks 190–8; scheduling density 94–9; scheduling process 92–3; and short-term planning 255; time-based schedules 101–7

scheduling software: and activities 191; activity coding 113, 116, 118; and **bar charts/Gantt charts** 170; **baseline** maintenance 213; and bottom-up planning 44; and budgeting 85; and **constraint dates** 137; display variations 184; displaying networks 147; and **drop line methods** 226; **line of balance** graphs 174; and planning 41, 44; **time chainage** charts 174, 175; when not to use 42–3, 103, 107, 109

scope: and the **baseline** 109; and change management 266; planning checks (of schedule) 189; 'scope creep' 21; scope development estimates 78–9; scope management 21–4; scope transfers 267

Scrum 204
S-curves 51, 85–6, 211, 239–42, 298–9
sensitivity analysis 299–300
shared float 132
short-term planning 255–7
short-term schedules 105
shut-downs 118, 119, 181, 224, 292
single point distributions 297
'single version of the truth' reporting 104, 200
'slack' *see* **float**

Index

SMART (specific, measurable, achievable, relevant, timebound) 13, 189
social media 151
soft issues 2, 40
software: 3D visualisation software 199–202; and **quantitative schedule risk analysis** 284, 286; record keeping 315, 318; spreadsheets 84, 103, 107–9 *see also* **scheduling software**
SOW (**statement of work**) 27, 30, 60
specialist products 57, 58, 152
specific analogy estimating 80–1
SPI (**schedule performance index**) 239, 243, 244
spreadsheets 84, 103, 107–9
'sprints' (agile planning) 47, 204
stage plans 57
stakeholders: and acceptance criteria 17; and agile planning 48; and the business case 12; and change management 260, 263, 268; and closeout/handover 321; and 'collaborative planning' 44; and communication of the schedule 170; and **interfaces** 158; and lessons learned 326; and performance reporting 223; and the planning process 40; and the **product breakdown structure** (PBS) 57; and the **RACI** matrix 68; and re-baselining 220; and **requirements management** 25, 27; and the **risk management plan** 274; and scope management 22; **stakeholder management** 31–2, 40
'start on' constraint 144, 197
'start on or after' constraint 145
'start on or before' constraint 146
start to finish relationships 134–5, 194
start to start relationships 116, 133–4, 193
statement of work (SOW) 27, 30, 60
steps, activity 116–17, 323
strategic fit 15
strategic schedule 16, 94, 101–2
sub-contracting 79, 165
successor relationships 116, 123, 131, 133, 134, 159, 190, 194, 195
summary schedule 103
suppliers' works information 29–30
system requirements document (SRD) 27–8

tactical planning 76
target dates 163, 197
target schedules 104
task analysis cost estimating 82
teamwork: and agile planning 204; and 'collaborative planning' 44; and planning 38; team sizes 153
technical specification 28
tender/bid schedule 102
three-point estimates 148, 286, 288, 290, 291, 297, 298
TIA (time impact analysis method) 304, 307–8
time analysis 124
time assumptions 15–16
time chainage charts 42–3, 167, 174–8
time contingencies 51, 164–5, 197, 286
time/cost/scope/quality triangle 104
time management 236
'time now' (data date) 224
time risk allowance 165, 189, 197
time units 118
time-based schedules 42–3, 101–7
timescale 186
timescale risk analysis 284 *see also* **quantitative schedule risk analysis** (QSRA)
top-down planning 43–4
tornado charts 292, 294, 296, 298
total float 124, 127–8, 131, 155, 196–7, 310
traceability 28
tracker schedules 107–9
trackers, separate 42
trend analysis 224, 235, 261
triangular distributions 290, 297

uncertainty 45–6
uniform distributions 289, 297
'unit cost' estimating 82

352

Index

V model (design and development) 28
validation and verification requirements matrix (VVRM) 29
variance analysis 222, 224–34, 242
version control 318
vertical integration 93, 157

WBS dictionary 30, 61–2
weeks, as time units 118
'what if' 107, 268
windows analysis 304, 309
work breakdown structure (WBS): as planning tool 53, 56, 57, 59–63; and budgeting 83, 84; and **interfaces** 157, 159, 161; and **requirements management** 26, 28, 30; and the **responsibility assignment matrix** (RAM) 65, 66–7; and scheduling 41; scheduling checks 193; and the scope 23–4
work calendars 92

work package scope sheet *see* **WBS dictionary**
work packages: accountability 66; and assumptions 151; and the **baseline** 213; breaking down into 18, 30, 53; and budgeting 84; and **earned value analysis** 237–8; and **interfaces** 157; **product breakdown structure** (PBS) 57; and re-baselining 220; and **requirements management** 30; and the **responsibility assignment matrix** (RAM) 65, 67; **rolling wave planning** 45–6; **work breakdown structure** (WBS) 59–60, 63
working schedule/forecast schedule 103
works information (WI) 29–30

XP (eXtreme Programming) 204

'zero free float' constraint 138